Veda as Word

~ Veda as Word ~

Edited by

Shashiprabha Kumar

Special Centre for Sanskrit Studies
Jawaharlal Nehru University
New Delhi

in association with

D. K. Printworld (P) Ltd.
New Delhi

Cataloging in Publication Data — DK
[Courtesy: D.K. Agencies (P) Ltd. <docinfo@dkagencies.com>]

National Seminar on Veda as Word (2005 : New Delhi, India)
Veda as word / edited by Shashiprabha Kumar.
xix, 289 p., 23 cm.
English, Hindi and Sanskrit.
Proceedings of the National Seminar on Veda as Word, held at New Delhi during 11-13 February 2005.
Includes bibliograhical references.
Includes index.
ISBN 8124603766

1. Vedas — Criticism, interpretation, etc. — Congresses. I. Kumar, Shashiprabha, 1951- II. Jawaharlal Nehru University. Special Centre for Sanskrit Studies. III. Title.

DDC 294.592 104 6 22

Proceedings of a National Seminar on *Veda as Word* organized by Special Centre for Sanskrit Studies, Jawaharlal Nehru University, New Delhi and Indian Council of Philosophical Research, New Delhi during Feb. 11-13, 2005.

ISBN 81-246-0376-6
First published in India in 2006

Published by:
Special Centre for Sanskrit Studies
Jawaharlal Nehru University
New Delhi - 110 067.

in association with:

D.K. Printworld (P) Ltd.
Regd. Office: 'Sri Kunj', F-52, Bali Nagar
New Delhi-110 015
Phones: (011) 2545-3975; 2546-6019; *Fax*: (011) 2546-5926
E-mail: dkprintworld@vsnl.net; *Website*: www.dkprintworld.com

Printed by: D.K. Printworld (P) Ltd., New Delhi.

देवीं वाचमजनयन्त देवास्तां विश्वरूपाः पशवो वदन्ति।
सा नो मन्द्रेषमूर्जं दुहाना धेनुर्वागस्मानुप सुष्टुतैतु॥

devīṁ vācamajanayanta devāstāṁ viśvarūpāḥ paśavo vadanti ।
sā no mandreṣamūrjaṁ duhānā dhenurvāgasmānupa suṣṭutaitu ॥

— *Ṛgveda*, 8.100.11

Divine powers created the speech divine, living creatures of all kinds speak it; may this speech, our wish-yielding cow, universally extolled as granter of gladness, bring food, strength and fame to us!

इयं या परमेष्ठिनी वाग्देवी ब्रह्मसंश्रिता।
ययैव संसृजे घोरं तयैव शान्तिरस्तु नः॥

iyaṁ yā parameṣṭhinī vāgdevī brahmasaṁśritā ।
yayaiva saṁsṛje ghoraṁ tayaiva śāntirastu naḥ ॥

— *Atharvaveda*, 19.09.03

May this divine speech, sanctified by the supreme knowledge and seated in the highest place, and with which the terrible is produced, with that only bestow peace upon us!

"Precious or durable materials — gold, silver, bronze, marble, onyx or granite — have been used by most ancient peoples in an attempt to immortalize their achievements. Not so, however, with the ancient Aryans. They turned to what may seem the most volatile and insubstantial material of all — the spoken word — and out of this bubble of air fashioned a monument which more than thirty, perhaps forty, centuries later stands untouched by time or the elements. For the pyramids have been eroded by the desert wind, the marble broken by earthquakes, and the gold stolen by robbers, while the Veda remains recited daily by an unbroken chain of generations, travelling like a great wave through the living substance of mind."

"The Veda itself is the secret of the Veda. The foundation stone that India contributed to civilization, the Veda, is said to embody the regulations, the laws of the universe as 'seen' by the gifted poets, prophets or seers, the *ṛṣis*." "Set by them in a special language to be joyfully proclaimed for future ages, it has come down to us through an elaborate oral tradition, consciously designed to prevent any distortion. Even today had we no written record available, it would still be possible to have access to the Veda as it existed when the text was fixed three or four thousand years ago! This supreme monument of an early religion which has left us with no archaeological remains, no church, no dogma, no founder, and virtually no history, forms the cannon of the Hindu scriptures, the core of which is a collection of over a thousand hymns, more than ten thousand stanzas in all, known as the *Ṛgveda*."

— Jean Le Mee

(*Hymns from the Ṛgveda*)

Prolegomena

VEDA is the fountainhead of Indian knowledge systems and has been held in the highest esteem as ultimate evidence in Indian thought. Etymologically the term Veda is derived from the root *vid*, to know, and connotes knowledge. All the branches of knowledge are supposed to be rooted in the Veda according to the Indian tradition. Most of the philosophical schools owe their allegiance to Veda in one way or the other.

Veda is transmitted orally from generation to generation and it aptly signifies the *śruti* tradition, therefore the subtle processes involved in proper recitation of Vedic verses are equally important. The seminar arranged by Special Centre for Sanskrit Studies, of the Jawaharlal Nehru University on the theme **Veda As Word** aims to highlight this very aspect of Veda which focuses upon such significant issues and finds a fully developed science for analysing various phonetic processes involved therein.

In fact, the sanctity of Veda in Indian philosophical tradition is upheld by the acceptance of verbal testimony. It is accepted by most of the *āstika* schools of Indian Philosophy that all the Vedic statements are unquestionably valid, albeit their validity may be drawn from intrinsic or extrinsic sources, as the case may be. The great Vedic commentator Sāyaṇa has rightly said that whatever can not be known through perception or inference, is known through Veda, therefore the *Vedatā* of Veda is established:

> प्रत्यक्षेणानुमित्या वा यस्तूपायो न विद्यते।
> एतं विदन्ति वेदेन तस्माद् वेदस्य वेदता॥
> *pratyakṣeṇānumityā vā yastūpāyo na vidyate* ।
> *etaṁ vidanti vedena tasmād vedasya vedatā* ॥

The Upaniṣads, the concluding portion of the Vedic *vāṅmaya*, represent the highest potency of the Vedic word. In these texts, the highest truths of existence are expressed in beautiful language. The Upaniṣads basically deal with the subtlest, infinite reality, *Brahman*, and the same cannot be contained in the limits of language or mind:

> यतो वाचो निवर्तन्ते अप्राप्य मनसा सह।
> *yato vāco nivartante aprāpya manasā saha* ।

Still, it is true that the seers of Upaniṣads had to convey their message to the seekers of truth through the device of language. Therefore, the Upaniṣadic statements like the following ones might apparently seem to be paradoxical, but essentially they are meaningful and deserve deeper study:

> यस्यामतं मतं तस्य मतं यस्य न वेद सः।
> अविज्ञातं विजानतां विज्ञातमविजानताम्॥
> *yasyāmataṁ mataṁ tasya mataṁ yasya na veda saḥ* ।
> *avijñātaṁ vijānatāṁ vijñātamavijānatām* ॥

> नाहं मन्ये सुवेदेति नो न वेदेति वेद च।
> यो नस्तद्वेद तद्वेद नो न वेदेति वेद च॥
> *nāhaṁ manye suvedeti no na vedeti veda cha* ।
> *yo nastadveda tadveda no na vedeti veda cha* ॥

I am glad to know that the proceedings of the seminar are now being brought out in the form of a book, edited by Prof. Shashiprabha Kumar. I am sure this publication will be widely read and referred by the scholars as well as students of Veda.

Śrāvaṇa Pūrṇimā **Karan Singh**
9 August, 2006

Foreword

THE Vedas have been acclaimed and accepted as a reservoir of profound knowledge both in India and abroad. This sacred literature, because of its vastness in the form of Brāhmaṇas, Āraṇyakas, Upaniṣads and Vedāṅgas, has been studied with deep faith. The oral tradition of Veda was preserved in this great country of ours for centuries together and even now this tradition is alive throughout the length and breadth of our country. It is a happy augury that scholars from India and abroad have studied, researched and debated the contents of this literature, as a result of which we cannot underrate its importance or marginalize it even today.

I, indeed, feel honoured to have been asked by Prof. Shashiprabha Kumar, Chairperson of the Special Centre for Sanskrit Studies, Jawaharlal Nehru University, New Delhi, to write a Foreword to the book ***'Veda as Word'*** which essentially is the print form of the proceedings of the national seminar held earlier. Efforts of such magnitude are always welcomed by scholars who intend to delve deep into the ocean of Vedic learning. Such publications become more meaningful when they are viewed in the context of the 1986 Education Policy of the Government of India which stated: "Efforts will be made to delve into ancient fund of knowledge and to reel it to contemporary realities. This effort will employ the development of facilities for the intensive study of Sanskrit."

In the opinion of Shri Aurobindo: "*Since our earliest ages the Veda has been, in the invincible tradition of our race, the bedrock of all our creeds; in this our goddess of veiled and ancient speech we have always persisted in seeing the fruitful mother of all our Indian spirituality. After the ingenious toils of Roth and Max Müller, as after the erudite diligence of Yāska and Sāyaṇa, the Vedic mantras remain for us what they have been for some thousands of years, a darkness of lost light and a sealed mystery.*"

It is an undisputed thought that seers of the Vedas were not infantile thinkers making uncoordinated hazes; they were rather grateful inquirers, in possession of a great system of thought, intuitional, no doubt, rather than logical, but still reposing for its variety on a method of strenuous experiment and searching observation.

Shri Aurobindo in continuation of his opinion expressed above states further that "*All human knowledge consists of three necessary elements — the thing itself which is known, the word or form in which it is expressed and the sense of the word or form which is the link between the thing and its expression. The thing itself, existing always, is always and at any given time capable of being known; the word or form can also be constantly preserved and may, then, always and at any given time.....*"

The contributors in this volume have laid due emphasis on the *guruparamparā* in maintenance of the oral tradition. This tradition forms the succession of spiritual torchbearers in preserving the knowledge system which was passed on from generation to generation in order to maintain the purity of the knowledge. It was an effort at transmitting the vast reservoir of knowledge to the dawn of another golden age of spirituality. The bond between human beings and God is brought into effect through sacrifices. The *mantras* in themselves are a collection of words strung together to create a positive effect. As such, the *mantra* is related to mind and the seer does speak to free the mind. In support of this we find that "Out of six Vedāṅgas four of them deal exclusively with the various components of words, viz. Śikṣā (phonetics), Vyākaraṇa (phonology, morphology and syntax), Nirukta (etymology) and Chandas (metrics). Vyākaraṇa is, again, considered to be the *mukham* (mouth) or spokesperson of the Vedas."

To help us in appreciating the concept of "*Śabda Brahman, eternal, imperishable and the source of all worldly appearances, here the visible or invisible pratyayas are perhaps more powerful than the original prakṛti-roots.*"

The long tradition of commentaries of Vedas has enriched our knowledge insofar as the understanding of the *mantras* as a whole is concerned. However, one has to add a word of caution while determining the importance of commentaries because our tradition implores us "*to determine the meaning of the text according to the accepted paddhati and in the shared meta-language.*"

The contributions of states like Kerala to Vedic study also draw our attention to the tradition which seems to be marginalized from the research area of other parts of our country. The great Yāskacaryas who paved the way for understanding the Vedas on the principle of etymology cannot be ignored. It is in this context that the enquiry of Nirukta Vedāṅga deserves special mention.

While browsing through all that has been incorporated in this study one feels tempted to quote the opening of Gospel where St. John says, "*In the beginning was a word, and word was with God, and the word was God. He was in the beginning with God and things were made through him....*" In the Vedas this has been called "*Śabda Brahman.*"

Last but not the least it can safely be asserted that those who wish to understand the true significance of ***'Veda as Word'*** and, unfortunately, do not have direct access to the vast treasures of Vedic literature in order to do so, will find this collection of articles by erudite scholars of an invaluable assistance. It is heartening to note that each contributor has attempted to look at the problem in a multi-dimensional way. I am sure this collection of articles will prove to be a very useful addition to the existing literature on the Veda, and all serious readers will find it of immense help. I once again take the opportunity of expressing my deep sense of appreciation for the Special Centre for Sanskrit Studies to make such a venture.

In view of Lord Bryce, "*Some books are meant to be tasted, some books meant to be chewed, finally some books are meant to be swallowed whole.*" I leave it to the discerning mind of the readers to choose its way of **enjoying** the articles **enjoined** here for wholesome results.

To conclude, in the words of Veda itself:

जानन्ति वृष्णो अरुषस्य शेवमुत ब्रध्नस्य शासने रणन्ति ।
दिवोरुचः सुरुचो रोचमाना इडा येषां गण्या माहिना गीः ॥

(ऋग्वेद 3/7/5)

Jānanti vṛṣṇo aruṣasya śevamuta bradhnasya śāsane raṇanti ।
divorucaḥ suruco rocamānā iḍā yeṣāṁ gaṇyā māhinā gīḥ ॥

(*Ṛgveda* 3/7/5)

i.e. those who comprehend the blessings of the imperishable bestower of benefits and exult in the command of the powerful fire divine, their frequent, earnest, bright and radiant **words** illuminate heaven!

Vachaspati Upadhyaya

Contents

Acknowledgement

First of all, we gratefully thank the University Grants Commission for sanctioning a special grant to the Special Centre for Sanskrit Studies for Research and Publication under Xth Plan which facilitated publication of the volume in hand.

I must acknowledge with deep sense of gratitude, the motivation for and contribution of Indian Council of Philosophical Research, New Delhi, towards organizing a National Seminar on **Veda as Word**.

My sincere thanks are due to the scholars who participated in the seminar and contributed their papers for publication. I thankfully acknowledge the helpful guidance of the members of Editorial Advisory Committee of the Special Centre for Sanskrit Studies.

I am extremely grateful to Dr. Karan Singh, Chancellor, JNU who not only inaugurated the seminar but has always been a source of inspiration for all of us at the Sanskrit Centre, JNU. He has also obliged us by writing Prolegomena to this volume.

I am highly thankful to Prof. Vachaspati Upadhyaya for his great support and encouragement; he has been kind enough to write a foreword to this publication. I must express my indebtedness to Prof. Satyavrat Shastri and Prof. Kapil Kapoor for guiding and supporting all the academic activities of the Centre.

I am sincerely grateful to the Vice Chancellor, Rector and other authorities of JNU without whose constant help, it would neither have been possible to arrange the National Seminar nor to publish proceedings of the same. I have genuine appreciation for my colleagues and students at the Centre who have always co-operated in whatever ways they could, for making the research and publication programme of the Centre a success.

Last but not the least, I thank Sri Susheel Mittal of D.K. Printworld for his personal effort and keen interest to ensure the quality of the publication.

Shashiprabha Kumar

Key to Transliteration

VOWELS

अ *a*	आ *ā*	इ *i*	ई *ī*	उ *u*	ऊ *ū*
(but)	(palm)	(it)	(beet)	(put)	(pool)
ऋ *ṛ*	ए *e*	ऐ *ai*	ओ *o*	औ *au*	
(rhythm)	(play)	(air)	(toe)	(loud)	

CONSONANTS

Guttural	क *ka*	ख* *kha*	ग *ga*	घ *gha*	ङ *ṅa*
	(skate)	(blockhead)	(gate)	(ghost)	(sing)
Palatal	च *ca*	छ* *cha*	ज *ja*	झ *jha*	ञ *ña*
	(chunk)	(catch him)	(john)	(hedgehog)	(bunch)
Lingual	ट *ṭa*	ठ* *ṭha*	ड *ḍa*	ढ* *ḍha*	ण* *ṇa*
	(start)	(anthill)	(dart)	(godhead)	(under)
Dental	त *ta*	थ *tha*	द *da*	ध* *dha*	न *na*
	(path)	(thunder)	(that)	(breathe)	(numb)
Labial	प *pa*	फ* *pha*	ब *ba*	भ *bha*	म *ma*
	(spin)	(philosophy)	(bin)	(abhor)	(much)
Others	य *ya*	र *ra*	ल *la*	व *va*	
	(young)	(drama)	(luck)	(vile)	
	श *śa*	ष *ṣa*	स *sa*	ह *ha*	
	(shove)	(bushel)	(so)	(hum)	
	क्ष *kṣa*	त्र *tra*	ज्ञ *jña*	ळ* ḷ	ॠ* *ṝ*
	(*kṣatriya*)	(*trishūl*)	(*jñāni*)	(*play*)	

अं (ˉ)*ṁ anusvāra* (nasalisation of preceding vowel) like *saṁskṛti*

अः *ḥ* (*prātaḥ*) *ḥ visarga* (aspiration of preceding vowel)

ऽ 'Avagraha' = consonant #'consonant (like:- *ime 'vasthitā*)

ꣳ (*guṁ*) = ꣳ

Anusvāra at the end of line is presented by म् = m (not ṁ)

* No exact English equivalents for these letters.

Introduction

THE present volume is a collection of papers originally presented in the first National Seminar held at the Special Centre for Sanskrit Studies, JNU, New Delhi from 11-13 February, 2005 on "**Veda As Word**." The seminar was co-sponsored by Jawaharlal Nehru University and the Indian Council of Philosophical Research, New Delhi.

It must be acknowledged at the outset that the topic of the seminar was prompted by another seminar on the theme "**Veda As Knowledge**" organized by Rashtriya Veda Vidya Pratishthan, Ujjain in collaboration with ICPR in January, 2004. It was while participating in the above programme that this idea struck my mind to organize a seminar on **Veda As Word** and I kept nurturing it till such time that an apt occasion for a full-fledged seminar was available. During this period, I not only applied to ICPR and JNU for financial assistance but also interacted with prospective participants and the idea blossomed into many aspects. Once the ICPR sanction came and the faculty as well as administration at JNU endorsed the proposal for holding the seminar, I swung into action and started executing the proposal.

II

It is worth mentioning here that the seminar on Veda was intended to focus mainly on the expressed form and features involved in the recitation of *mantra*s of the Veda. Right from the time of Yāska, the author of Nirukta, there has been a group of scholars which opines that Vedic verses are meant for recitation only, these do not have any meaning. We may agree with him or not, but this view of Kautsa highlights a point worth pondering that words of Veda are unique in the sense that mere utterance of these in the given form does have some special effect.

In the Indian philosophical tradition, the Mīmāṁsakas have been upholding this view with a firm conviction that Veda is word and every syllable of the Veda is eternal, infallible and unchangeable. On the other hand, there are the Naiyayikas who propound that all words, including the Vedic ones, are created, and hence non-eternal.

In view of the above, some significant issues which emerged during the course of discussion in the seminar on Veda as Word, may be mentioned as follows:

- Is Veda merely a word, utterance or recitation or is there some real, hidden meaning of the Vedic word?
- If there is a meaning of the Vedic word, then what is the relation between word and meaning and how to decipher it exactly, since so many varied interpretations of the same Vedic verse are available?
- How is Vedic word different from an ordinary utterance? Is *mantra* really an extraordinary, contemplated word of the *ṛṣi*s?
- Is Vedic word eternal or non-eternal?
- Is Vedic word impersonal or personal?
- What is so significant about proper accentuation of Vedic verses? Does it really have any effect?
- Do Vedic words connote history or are they simply etymological as claimed by some of the interpreters?

- Is Veda a self-validated, ultimate evidence in the process of knowledge as has been propounded by different schools of Indian Philosophy ?

These and many more aspects related to the theme were discussed in three days of the seminar wherein nineteen* papers were presented under nine academic sessions besides the inaugural and the valedictory session.

III

"Veda as Word" signifies the orality of Vedic tradition. Various appellations of Veda such as *āmnāya*, *vāk*, *śruti* or *śabda* connote "whatever is heard directly from the preceptor." In this respect, Veda considerably differs from all such literature which is characterised, classified, categorized, and elaborated on certain patterns. "From this point of view, Veda is *śruti* and not a *śāstra*. *Śāstra* is a text of systematised knowledge with a set of technical terminology. What is even more remarkable about Veda is that as *śruti*, it has the potentiality of becoming the source of a *śāstra* but by itself it is not a *śāstra*. In other words, *śruti* has the plasticity of the material of a perfect form which could, if so desired, be moulded into a *śāstra*" (Satya Prakash Saraswati in his introduction to *Ṛgveda Saṁhitā*, Veda Pratisthan, New Delhi, p. 4). This distinction of *śruti* and *śāstra* is an important point to be kept in mind before going ahead in this regard.

Further, in order to have a full conception of the Vedic prose, poetry and lyric (the *Yajus*, the *Ṛk* and the *Sāman*), one should be familiar not only with the grammar of the language and the etymology of words, but should also be conversant

---

* Two scholars, namely Prof. K.T. Pandurangi and Prof. (Ms.) S.S. Dange could not attend the seminar personally, but had been kind enough to send their papers for publication

with proper accentuations. Being the first and the earliest form of speech, words of Vedic language are in their most fluid and plasmatic state. It is not without reason then that very often even a slight change of accents brings about a considerable change in the meaning of Vedic words.

It is in the above background that for understanding the real import of *śruti*, the ancient Indian seers evolved regular systems of discipline known as Vedāṅgas (limbs of the Veda) and Upa-Vedas (sub-Vedas) as follows:

Vedāṅgas: Sikṣā, Vyākaraṇa, Nirukta, Jyotiṣa, Chanda, Kalpa

Upa-Vedas: Āyurveda, Gandharvaveda, Dhanurveda, Arthaveda

Needless to say that the words of Veda are not ordinary statements of common speakers but highly potent utterances with deep symbolic sense within them. Hence a thorough acquaintance of above subsidiaries is a basic requirement for exploring the real import of Veda. The fact has been succinctly stated in Pāṇinian Śikṣā as follows:

छन्दः पादौ तु वेदस्य हस्तौ कल्पोऽथ पठ्यते।
ज्योतिषामयनं चक्षुर्निरुक्तं श्रोत्रमुच्यते॥

शिक्षा घ्राणं तु वेदस्य मुखं व्याकरणं स्मृतम्।
तस्मात् साङ्गमधीत्यैव ब्रह्मलोके महीयते॥ (४१-४२)

i.e. *chandas* is held to be the feet of Veda while *kalpa* is its two hands. Jyotiṣa is stated to be the sight and Nirukta is said to be the hearing of Veda. *Śikṣā* is the smelling organ while Vyākaraṇa is the mouth of "*Veda-Puruṣa*." Therefore, he alone who reads Veda alongwith these subsidiaries, gets glorified in the field of knowledge.

IV

The Vedic scholars, who participated in the seminar, discussed various aspects of these Vedāṅgas and other related issues as will be clear from the following brief introduction of their papers:

In the first paper of the volume, "Veda as Word" **Dr. Kireet Joshi**, in his own inimitable style, has gone deeper into the subtle, philosophical aspect of the theme and has expounded the mystery of *Vāk* through seed-sounds. According to him, Vedic *mantra*s are the words of power born out of the secret depths of creative consciousness; Veda is the word that has been discovered by the *ṛṣi*s at the supramental level of consciousness.

In the next article, "Vedāpauruṣeyatva" **Prof. D. Prahladachar** has briefly referred to different views available in Indian philosophical tradition regarding *apauruṣeyatva* of Veda. He has discussed the arguments from both sides, namely the *apauruṣeyatvavādin*s and the *pauruṣeyatvavādins*. In this process, he has also deliberated upon the *nityātnityatva* of *śabda*, which is of two kinds — *dhvani* and *varṇa* and has established that the *apauruṣeyatva* of Veda lies in the unchanging sequencing of phonemes in Vedic sentences.

Prof. K.T. Pandurangi could not unfortunately attend the seminar in person but he had been gracious enough to send his paper on the "Pūrvamīmāṁsā Perspective on Veda As Word." In this paper, the learned scholar has clarified that both the *Jaiminī-sūtras* and the *Brahma-sūtras* enunciate *śabda* in the sense of Veda, hence the significance of the theme "Veda as Word" is well-reflected in these schools. He goes on to explain "according to Pūrvamīmāṁsā, शब्दात्मका एव देवताः ॥ The very words अग्नि, इन्द्र etc. are देवताs. This is clearly stated in शाबरभाष्य (9.1.4). The entire Veda is developed around the देवताs

— अग्नि, इन्द्र, वरुण etc. The position taken here that the words are देवता clearly indicates the importance of Veda as Word."

In the next essay, "Veda and Veda-Prāmāṇya according to Pūrvamīmāṁsā," **Prof. S.R. Bhatt** has philosophically analysed the topic from two aspects: epistemology as well as ethics. He has argued that "In the Mīmāṁsā, Veda is described as *anapekṣa śabda*. It is a mode of knowing which is unconditionally true and independent. It is this property which provides it *āptatva* (reliability and infallibility) and *nityatva* (universality)."

Prof. S.P. Singh in his paper entitled "Vāgāmbhṛṇī" has focused upon the renowned female seer of X. 125th hymn of *Ṛgveda* and has explained each verse of it in a subtle, symbolic manner. The author has contended that Vāgāmbhṛṇī happens to assume the role of power of articulation and exemplifies the established Vedic doctrine of coordination between the word and the Reality.

Prof. Usha Chaudhary in her essay "Vāg vai Saraswatī" highlights the cosmic, creative and poetic nature of *Vāk* on the basis of Saraswatī hymns of *Ṛgveda*, where the seer poets have woven her image as dynamic and moving speech representing knowledge and consciousness. Both the fierce as well as the rhythmic aspects of Saraswatī have been referred to herein.

In the next article "Vedic Mantra-Vijñāna," **Prof. Dayanand Bhargava** has examined the issue as to whether mere correct recitation of Vedic verses can yield the desired result ? He has also dwelt upon the difference in method of recitation of the four Vedas and has established that each of them represents an aspect of *adhibhūta*, *adhidaiva* or *adhyātma*, as there is nothing beyond this trinity. It is interesting to mention here that the difference in recitation of verses of the four Vedas was actually demonstrated during the seminar by a student of Prof. Bhargava.

Prof. B.B. Chaubey in his paper "वैदिक स्वर-विज्ञान" describes the various Vedic accents and related processes. Obviously, his delineation aims at highlighting the principles of Vedic accentology which is almost theoretical nowadays and the practical aspect of it is on the verge of extinction today. He has proved on the basis of textual evidences, that since Veda represents orality, hence the real sense of Vedic verses can only be grasped with the help of exact accents; he who does not have a proper knowledge of accents, cannot interpret Veda in a correct manner.

The nature of *Vāk* in ritualistic reference is the subject matter of **Prof. S.S. Dange**'s paper entitled "From Mortal To Divine Through Vāk." The learned professor has delved deep into the Brāhmaṇa texts and brought out the significance of speech in the context of sacrifice, since "Vag vai yajñaḥ": speech is verily sacrifice. As speech is said to be sacrifice, so restraint on his speech (*vāgyama*) is the essential requirement for the consecrated sacrificer. According to Prof. Dange, it is the divine aspect of speech in the *mantra* accompanying a rite or ritual which helps the sacrificer ascend to the divine plane.

Prof. Ram Karan Sharma in his paper "Vācam Artho'nudhāvati" discusses the relation of *vāc* and *artha* in the context of Sanskrit grammatical tradition. Beginning from the Pāṇinian sūtra "*Tadadhīte tadveda*" (4.2.5a), he goes on to Patañjali and his commentators, Kaiyyata and Nagesa and expounds the former as *svarūpa-mātravedana* (knowledge pertaining to the form of the object of chanting only) and the latter as *arthāvabodha* (comprehension of the import).

Prof. Kapil Kapoor in his exhaustive article has shown how over a period of time the texts: (i) grow opaque, and/or (ii) become asymmetrical with the context, and/or (iii) their connection with the tradition of knowledge in that time becomes incoherent. But it is the continuous and cumulative *ṭīkā-paramparā,* which has ensured availability, comprehensibility and contextual relevance of Sanskrit texts. He has argued that some of India's most brilliant minds have been exegets. Further, knowledge in India has not been confined to learned texts, nor has it ever been a repository of the few. While discussing three types of exegesis *śruti, smṛti* and *kāvya*, he explains that Vedic exegesis overwhelmingly faces the problem of interpretation because the language of Veda is metaphorical and symbolic.

In the essay "The Contribution of Kerala to Vedic Exegesis and Sāman Chanting," **Prof. P.C. Muraleemadhavan** has elucidated the Vedic tradition which is still very much alive in Kerala. He enunciates that the Aitareya and Kauṣītakī śākhās of *Ṛgveda* have been preserved in Kerala and the Nambutiri Brahmins of Kerala have been involved in Vedic Studies and Vedic exegesis from very early times. Besides, the valuable oral tradition of chanting the Sāman (Jaiminīya Śākhā) has been preserved in Kerala with meticulous care, which has been recorded by Sri Sankaracharya Sanskrit University, Kalady.

In the next essay "निघण्टु-निरुक्त में वाङ्नाम" **Dr. Abhaya Dev Sharma** has discussed the fifty seven synonyms of *Vāk* available in the Vedic lexicon Nighaṇṭu and has argued that all these terms should not just be taken simply at the literal level, since being Vedic words, they have an inherent potential for being the expression of subtler forms of sound and also higher powers of the spirit.

Dr. Wagish Shukla in his article "Ramblings on Nirukta" spells out the significant contribution of etymological exegesis for understanding the meaning of Vedic verses. He discusses "folk etymologies" of Nirukta *vis-á-vis* modern science of linguistics and argues that Nirukta has, in fact, inspired and informed much of modern linguistics. While explaining the "etymological technique" of Yāska, he concludes that Nirukta has provided a system of rules for interpreting the Vedic verses, which is quite comprehensive and inclusive.

In the next essay "प्रातिशाख्य ग्रन्थों में स्वरवर्ण" **Prof. Dipti Sharma Tripathi** unfolds the nature of vowels as explained in Vedic phonetics. She has discussed the etymological definitions, numbers and types of vowels on the basis of several Prātiśākhya texts and has shown how minute variations in pronunciative and auditive processes have also been described by Vedic scholars which need to be re-examined and re-interpreted in the modern context.

The subject matter of the next article "विकृतिसम्मर्शः" by **Dr. Ramesh Chandra Dash Sharma** is an elucidation of various types of recitation of Vedic verses. He describes how the Vedic seers devised several techniques for preserving the exact and accurate sequence of Vedic words. One of these techniques was eightfold recitation of Vedic verses technically termed as *vikṛti*. The paper illustrates all the eight types of *vikṛti*s with adequate details.

Dr. Satyadev Chaudhari in his essay "ऋग्वेद में वाणी की अवधारणा" has described the four types of speech on the basis of Ṛgvedic verses and other relevant references. He argues that Veda is also a *kāvya*, hence the theories are presented here in the form of poetry, this can be evidenced from the use of *śleṣa*, a figure of speech frequently available in the Vedic verses.

Dr. Umesh Chandra Dash in his article "वैदिक शब्द-श्रौत याग के सन्दर्भ में" deals with a verse of *Yajurveda* (Vājasaneyī Saṁhitā) wherein the names of three Vedic metres, namely *Gāyatrī*, *Triṣṭup* and *Jagatī* occur. He explains that when the above verse is interpreted with the help of Brahmaṇa Texts, then the three terms convey a different ritualistic perspective. Hence, Vedic words should not be interpreted only in the apparent sense, they have much deeper secrets hidden beneath them.

Prof. P. Shashirekha in her essay "Vidhivākyas — Their significance in Human Life" has discussed the nature of *dharma* in Mīmāṁsā perspective and has enunciated that the Vedavākyas should be understood as per the content. There are six *pramaṇa*s to know the procedure, namely: 1. *Śruti* — Statement, 2. *Artha* — purpose, 3. *Pāṭha* — text, 4. *Sthāna* — juxtaposition, 5. *Mukhya* — the principals, and 6. *Pravṛtti* — continual performance. It is noteworthy here that she has tried to explain the *vidhivākya*s with examples from contemporary human life.

Dr. Roopkishor Shastri in his essay "**वैदिक आख्यानों के व्यावहारिक सन्दर्भ**" has discussed the practical aspect of Vedic legends and argued on the basis of Brāhmaṇa texts that the Vedic language being derivative by nature, should not be interpreted plainly, just in the literal sense, since there is essentially some metaphorical and symbolic sense behind them. He has tried to explain two of the well-known Vedic legends, namely Viṣṇu-Vāmana and Indra-Ahalyā ones according to the above principle and proved his point.

In the last essay "Śaṅkara on Śruti as Verbal Testimony," **Dr. Ram Nath Jha** has discussed the nature of *Vāk* and verbal testimony on the basis of Śaṅkara's commentaries on the *Prasthanatraya,* i.e. Upaniṣads, Bhagavadgītā and Brahmasūtras. According to Śaṅkara, *śruti* is self-validated, eternal and impersonal. Everybody cannot, of course understand *śruti,* hence *smṛti* has to be resorted to, but in Śaṅkara's view, *smṛti* is valid only when it is in conformity with *śruti* and not otherwise.

In brief, the seminar on **Veda as Word** proved to be a fruitful exercise and raised many important points regarding various aspects of Veda, its language and interpretation. We hope that this small publication based on the proceedings of the seminar will be able to generate further quest and interest among scholars and students of Veda in future:

उप नः सूनवो गिरः शृण्वन्त्वमृतस्य ये।
सुमृडीका भवन्तु नः॥

upa naḥ sūnavo giraḥ śr̥ṇvantvamr̥tasya ye ।
sumr̥ḍīkā bhavantu naḥ ॥ — *R̥gveda*, 6.52.9

i.e. may all those who are sons of the immortal, hear our words! And be the source of happiness to us all !

Shashiprabha Kumar
Abhyudaya
295/15 - A
NOIDA (U.P.) - 201 301

1

Veda as Word

Kireet Joshi

WE are too familiar with the world. Solidity of the earth, liquidity of water, heat and cold, taste of honey, festivity of colour of the dawn and the sunset, whisper and roar of breeze and winds and wideness and emptiness of the sky and the space, and slow rapidity of ticking of time — we know them all quite well. We talk and sleep.

But as we grow quiet, the world seems to be knocking our complacency and inertia. We begin to wonder at the mind and speech, sight and sound. And, as in the *Kenopaniṣad*, we feel the pressure of the questions:

> By whom missioned falls the mind shot to its mark? By whom yoked moves the first life breath forward on its path, by whom impelled is this word that man speaks? What cosmic forces or beings set eye and ear to their workings?[1]

The mystery of the mind is perhaps the deepest. In the huge universe, which seems to be an explosion of fire in an eternal night, only a small assemblage of inexplicable organisms moving about on a small speck of what we call earth seem to be conscious or self-conscious, capable of reflection and

1. केनेषितं पतति प्रेषितं मनः । केन प्राणः प्रथमः प्रैति युक्तः ।
केनेषितां वाचमिमां वदन्ति। चक्षुः श्रोत्रं क उ देवो युनक्ति ॥ 1 ॥ *Kenopaniṣad*, 1

imposing their own ideation on the vast expanse of Matter. How has the mind managed to break in into the vast ocean of unconsciousness? And the more we reflect on this question, the more we find that mind is limited and hampered and is not able to find anything appropriate to its own formula which can conquer or sufficiently expand the limitations imposed upon its workings. Mind is obliged to call in a new principle beyond itself, freer than itself and more powerful. In our search, we may find the earliest compositions of humanity, the Vedas, which bring to us an idea or a glimpse of what we may call the mind beyond the mind, or to use the expression of the *Kenopaniṣad, "manaso manaḥ,"* mind of our mind. The Veda speaks of a faculty or principle which sees the Truth unveiled, an eternal faculty of knowledge which corresponds to the eternal faculty of the Truth. The Veda calls it *Truth-Consciousness* (*R̥ta-Cit*), which sees the Truth directly and is in possession of it continuously. That Truth-Consciousness fulfils what mind labours to effect but succeeds in accomplishing it only partially. The importance of the Veda lies in the fact that it is the only work in the history of the world which affirms and describes the nature of the Truth-Consciousness and, when we recover the algebra of its language, we find descriptions of the disciplines by which mind can surmount its limitations and attain to that supramental consciousness and further consequences of that attainment. In the Indian tradition, the Veda has come to be acknowledged as a book of knowledge, and even though ancient, holds still the attention of supreme researchers who are keen to resolve the riddle of the universe and to heal the afflictions of humanity which is ruled by the mind. And when we try to follow these researchers, one of the first things that we find is the claim that Veda is Word, and we are startled in perplexity.

To our mind that is confined to experiences of familiarity, word is only an arbitrary combination of sounds which convey a meaning because humanity in its march has erected certain practices and conventions for meeting necessities of communication and interchange. At a deeper level, however, word is a mystery and wonder. This mystery is brought to our awareness in a startling manner, when it is claimed that Veda is Word. What is sought to be conveyed is that Veda which is knowledge is itself identical with words and sounds, and this claim we are unable to understand or appreciate.

What do we mean by word? The Sanskrit word for the word or speech is *vāk*. Veda as *vāk* is, therefore, our theme of inquiry.

Word, speech, hearing, knowledge and creation are interrelated, and this interrelationship becomes clearer when we are freed from the veil of familiarity, and we begin to wonder at them with fresh eyes and begin to ask if sound is not a mystery. For, speech is only a particular application of the principle of sound. It is from sound that words are formed naturally and spontaneously to express the emotions created by an object or an occurrence. At first, the value of words and speech would seem to be only that of representation. But, as the modern science has discovered, vibration of sound has the power to create — and to destroy — forms. It may, therefore, be supposed that behind all words and even behind all forms there has been a creative vibration of sound. It is indisputable that sound, speech and music, which are all interrelated, create forms and mental images and impulses of action. Even daily and hourly, we produce by the sounds thought vibrations, thought-forms which result in corresponding vital and physical vibrations. These thought vibrations act upon ourselves, act upon others and produce actions and forms in the physical world. It is only because we do not examine the subtlety of this process that we remain ignorant of the power of the word to create.

But what about the sound itself? What about the speech itself, what about the word itself, what about its origin? How is it created?

According to the Veda, neither Mind, Life, Senses and Speech nor their objects or expressions are the Reality which we have to know or pursue. True knowledge is the knowledge of That which forms these instruments for us but It is itself independent of their utilities. Therefore, *Kenopaniṣad* speaks not only of the mind but also of the speech (*vāco ha vācam*). The *Kenopaniṣad* points out that:

> That which is unexpressed by the word, that by which the word is expressed, know That to be the *Brahman* and not this which men follow after here.[2]

The Upaniṣad also speaks of hearing of our hearing, life of our life-breath, and sight of our sight (श्रोत्रस्य श्रोत्रम्, प्राणस्य प्राणः, चक्षुषः चक्षुः). The Upaniṣad makes us aware that what we ordinarily experience as sound, speech, life, sight, and even sensations are mysterious operations behind which there are vast experiences, knowing which we can have a deeper awareness and a greater power of effectivity in life.

The world, as we ordinarily know it, is superficial; behind all that is gross, there are subtleties, and all those who surpass superficiality become aware of subtle realities. A philosopher who goes beyond words discovers behind them a creative idea, and if he goes behind the idea, he like Plato, discovers larger and larger syntheses of ideas which culminate in the

---

2. यद्वाचानभ्युदितं येन वागभ्युद्यते ।
तदेव ब्रह्म त्वं विद्धि नेदं यदिदमुपासते ॥ *Kenopaniṣad*, 4

discovery of the unity of existence. An artist goes behind the objects of ordinary sight and discovers a play of colours and mystery of the lines and proportions that reveal a form creative of forms. A poet hears sounds and words and, as he strains beyond ordinary limits, discovers sound behind sound and word behind word, and in his poetic speech, he expresses those sounds and those words which can express deeper depths of what is seen and heard. According to the Vedic theory, words are expressions of seed-sounds, and these seed-sounds are creative of the whole universe. Based on this discovery, we have in the Veda, the theory of the *mantra*, according to which the poet enters into a deeper consciousness where the seed-sounds vibrate constantly and give birth to the word of power which effects creativity, and *mantra* is the poetic expression of the Word that is heard at deeper and higher levels of consciousness.

In a rare text of occult knowledge, we find that there are three layers rising above our ordinary experiences of sight, sound and thought — three layers that connect our ordinary existence with the highest and most comprehensive state of creativity expressive of Truth-Consciousness. The lowest of these three is the layer of colours, and higher than that layer is the layer of sounds, above which is the layer of ideas. These colours, sounds, and ideas are truth-colours, truth-sounds and truth-ideas, and when a seeker passes beyond superficial existence and rises in the higher intensities of consciousness, he is able to rise into those three higher layers which can transmit their contents to the seeker's aspiring consciousness. In this process, to the extent to which the intensity of consciousness reaches its pitch, there arises the appropriate operation of the sight behind the sight, hearing behind the hearing, and mind behind the mind.

In one of the hymns of the Veda (*Ṛgveda*, I.164.39), Dirghatamas speaks of the *ṛk*s, the *mantra*s of the Veda as existing in a supreme ether, imperishable and immutable in which all the cosmic forces and beings are seated. He further alludes to four planes from where speech issues, three of them hidden in the secrecy while the fourth is human, and from there comes the ordinary word; but the word and thought of the Veda belong to the higher planes. The Vedic word is described as thought which is supreme and the topmost height of speech, the best and the most faultless. It is something that is hidden in secrecy and from there it comes out and is manifested. It enters into the truth-seers, the *ṛṣi*s, and it is found by following the track of that speech. It is also mentioned that all cannot enter into its secret meaning, and that those who do not know the inner sense are men who seeing see not, hearing hear not, only to one here and there, the Word desiring him like a beautifully robed wife to a husband lays open her body. It points out that others unable to drink steadily of the milk of the Word, the Vedic cow, move with it as with one that gives no milk; to him the Word is a tree without flowers or fruits.[3]

---

3. बृहस्पते प्रथमं वाचो अग्रं यत् प्रैरत नामधेयं दधानाः ।
यदेषां श्रेष्ठं यदरिप्रमासीत् प्रेणा तदेषां निहितं गुहाविः ॥ 1 ॥
सक्तुमिव तितउना पुनन्तो यत्र धीरा मनसा वाचमक्रत ।
अत्रा सखायः सख्यानि जानते भद्रैषां लक्ष्मीर्निहिताधि वाचि ॥ 2 ॥
यज्ञेन वाचः पदवीयमायन् तामन्वविन्दन्नृषिषु प्रविष्टाम् ।
तामाभृत्या व्यदधुः पुरुत्रा तां सप्त रेभा अभि सं नवन्ते ॥ 3 ॥
उत त्वः पश्यन् न ददर्श वाचमुत त्वः शृण्वन् न शृणोत्येनाम्।
उतो त्वस्मै तन्वं वि सस्रे जायेव पत्य उशती सुवासाः ॥ 4 ॥
उत त्वं सख्ये स्थिरपीतमाहुर्नैनं हिन्वन्त्यपि वाजिनेषु ।
अधेन्वा चरति माययैष वाचं शुश्रुवाँ अफलामपुष्पाम् ॥ 5 ॥ *Ṛ**V*, 71, 1-5.

The contention of the Vedic *ṛṣis* is that the Veda is a collection of poems which are mantric in character and according to the theory of the *mantra,* a poem can be designated as a *mantra* when it is a word of power born out of the secret depths of our being where it has been brooded upon by a deeper consciousness than the mental, framed in the heart and not constructed by the intellect, held in the mind, again concentrated on by the awakening mental consciousness, and thrown out silently or vocally — the silent word is perhaps held to be more potent than the spoken — precisely for the sake of creation. According to this theory, the Veda is the word, Veda is *vāk*, the Veda is the *mantra* that can not only create new subjective states in ourselves, alter our psychical being, revealed knowledge and faculties which we did not before possess, can not only produce similar results in others' minds than that of a user, but can also produce vibrations in the mental and vital atmosphere which result in effects, in actions, and even in the production of material forms on the physical plane.

According to the Vedic theory, the poet is the seer-will (*kavikratu*), and he sees, and he hears the word of the word, *vāco ha vācam*, and what he composes is only what he has heard, *śruti*. The Veda, that is the supreme word, is vibration of pure existence, instinct with the perceptive and originative power of the infinite omnipotent consciousness, shaped by the mind behind the mind into the inevitable word of the truth of things. Out of whatever substance of whatever plane, the form or physical expression emerges by its creative agency.

Human speech is only a secondary expression and it is at the highest a shadow of the divine Word, of the seed-sound, the satisfying rhythm, the revealing form of sounds that are the omniscient and omnipotent speech of the eternal Thinker,

Harmonist, Creator. The highest divine word has its seed-sounds, such as *AUṀ*, which carry in them the principles of things; it has its forms which stand behind the revelatory and inspired speech that comes to man's supreme faculty. As Sri Aurobindo points out, "it has its rhythms — for it is no disordered vibration, but moves out into great cosmic measures — and according to the rhythm is the law, arrangement, harmony, processes of the world it wills."[4]

The Veda as word is the word that creates, expresses, but is itself only a creation and expression. And that which stands behind the word is the Truth-Consciousness (*ṛta-cit*), and it can be said that Truth-Consciousness, which is the Supermind or the Mind behind mind using the Word is the creative Logos.

Thus, when we begin to inquire into the real nature of the word and sound and their origin, we shall be led to the awakening of the mystery of the magic of the creative power that we see in poetry, and following the track of the supreme examples of poetic expressions, we shall come to appreciate what is meant when it is said that the Vedic poetry is mantric in character and that the Veda is the Word. Veda is the Word that has been discovered by the *ṛṣi*s at the supramental level of consciousness and which is found also as the creative power of the universe expressing the truth of the ideas that move out of the unifying and underlying substance of the ultimate Reality, and which, again, when caught and expressed are capable of creating in the world vibrations of truth-ideas and truth-forms of knowledge and will and thus of a new creation enabling humanity to refashion itself in the images and forms of the supramental consciousness.

---

4. Sri Aurobindo: *The Upaniṣads*, Centenary Edition, Vol. 12, p. 171.

2

Vedāpauruṣeyatva

D. Prahladachar

THE wise ancients of this country considered knowledge as the most precious thing in the life of a human being, for if there is anything that can free a human from the cycle of births and deaths, and the endless suffering this entails, it is knowledge. The Gāyatrī Mantra which is regarded as one of the most unique found in the entire Vedic corpora, and the daily recitation of which is prescribed as the most essential part of one's religious duties, is in fact nothing but a prayer to the Lord to bless us with knowledge — *dhiyo yo naḥ pracodayāt*. Knowledge or enlightenment was thus considered the greatest asset in life, not only by the ancient Vedic seers, but also by the founders of the various schools of thought originating from this land. Statements such as *athāto brahmajijñāsā, athāto dharmajijñāsā, tattvajñānāt niḥśreyasādhigamaḥ*, found in the *sūtra* texts related with different *darśana*s, clearly indicate that knowledge has been a focal point of all the *darśana*s, including the *avaidika darśana*s such as the Bauddha and the Jaina.

It is precisely for this reason that knowledge has been given the most venerable place among the most valued goals of human life, that the Vedas have, through the ages, been held in high esteem as the most sacred literature of this land.

As a matter of fact, the very word *veda* is derived from the linguistic root $\sqrt{vid}$ meaning "to know," indicating that the name *veda* given to the text is very appropriate as it is "a [unique] means of knowledge."[1] But then the question arises: what guarantee is there that the cognition derived from the *Veda* constitutes knowledge rather than delusion? As a matter of fact, this is the allegation made by the *avaidika darśana*s — that the cognition obtained from the Vedas is liable to be in error, and hence cannot be accepted as knowledge.

However, the Vedic tradition has an answer, the likes of which are unseen in any religious discourse elsewhere in the world, to this question. The traditional argument is thus: words or sentences do not have any defects of their own. If any defect is found in them at all, it is solely due to the defect of the person who used them. If a person errs in his utterances, or else if he errs in his understanding that forms the basis of his utterances, then naturally, the words and sentences that express his views inherit his defects, and people who receive those sentences will not obtain right knowledge from them. If, on the other hand, the speaker has no defects whatsoever, either in his pronounciation or in his thinking, then he is to be considered an *āpta* — a trustworthy person — and the work he has authored or the sentences he has uttered will be considered *pramāṇa*. However, the trustworthiness of a person whom we have not seen, and who is not among us, cannot be decided easily, and doubts will certainly linger on about the validity of any work he may have written. Since the Vedas are *apauruṣeya* — not authored by any person — the tradition claims that there is no possibility of defects either in the words or in the

1. *nendriyāṇi nānumānaṁ vedā hyevainaṁ vedayanti, tasmādāhuḥ "vedāḥ"* cited in Madhva's *Viṣṇu-Tattva-Vinirṇaya*.

sentences of the Vedic texts, or in the thought content intended to be conveyed by the Vedas.

This reasoning by the adherents of the Vedic tradition has not been left unchallenged, as is well known. Apart from the Buddhists and the Jainas who proclaimed skepticism about the validity of the Vedas, even those, such as the Nyāya-Vaiśeṣika school, who regarded the Vedas as valid testimony, nonetheless saw fit to question the logicality of the concept of *apauruṣeyatva.* However, the *apauruṣeyatva-vādins* convincingly argued that if an *apauruṣeya* text were not to be envisaged, it would be impossible for there to be conclusive decisions in the matters of *dharma* and *adharma*. For *dharma* and *adharma* are supra-sensory entities, and consequently our sense-organs are of no use in knowing their characteristics. Inference based solely on sense-perception is likewise of no use, for such independent inferences can be freely applied in any manner one pleases, and might even be used by some clever persons to call as *adharma* all that is established in society as *dharma* and vice versa.

Therefore, we ultimately have to depend upon a scriptural text to know the true *dharma* and *adharma*. However, unless we are certain of the trustworthiness of the author of such a text, our faith in them will not be strong enough to persuade us to accept them without question. Then the question obtains: how is one to know that the author of some scripture, believed to have lived thousands of years ago, was an *āpta*? An *āpta* is described as a person who has perfect knowledge (including of facts concerning supra-sensory entities such as *dharma* and *adharma*), is not a deceiver, is not given to passions or hatred, and finally, who is endowed with the great virtue of kindness towards people who suffer due to ignorance.

The Vedic tradition argues that it is a great tax on one's credulity to imagine so many rare virtues in a person from so long ago who is not available for scrutiny, and was not so scrutinised even by one's forefathers. There also being many claimants to *āptatva* with conflicting claims, it also cannot be granted that asssuming such virtue in an unseen author provides any definite conclusion regarding *dharma*.[2] Therefore, it argues that there is parsimony of assumption in envisaging that the Vedas are *apauruṣeya*, and holds that this view is also supported by internal evidences, for we find several Vedic statements that describe the Vedas as eternal, such as *yāvad brahma viṣṭhitaṁ tāvatī vāk*.[3] It is therefore also held that the

2. There are many inherent logical conundrums in any one prophet claiming validity for his version of the supra-sensory entities such as merit, sin, *dharma*, etc. whose existence is dimly recognized by all of us. Apart from the inevitable conflicts with other such claimants, the facts that his statements are clearly circumscribed by the limited knowledge available to him, and are distorted by personal and parochial considerations at the time, cannot be disputed by any impartial seeker. Thus, major modifications or clarifications to the theology propounded by the supposed flawless *āpta* are sought to be introduced subsequently by successors, many times leading to the formation of different sects, all claiming allegiance to the same prophet. Such problems are nothing but clear indications of defects in the original formulations, and verily even of shortcomings in the prophet-centric approach to spiritual understanding.While the Vedānta is also subject to the problems of interpretation of texts, it should be noted that the interpretational support-base such as the Nirukta,Vyākaraṇa, etc., are also already prescribed and universally accepted, and debates are within the scope defined by them. The discourses of Vedānta are thus scholarly and of a different character than those of prophet-based ideologies, which are mainly propagated by violence or petty inducements.

3. *Aitareya Āraṇyaka* 1.3.8; also see *'vācā virūpanityayā.'* — *Ṛgveda* 8.75.6.

Vedas are the foundational authorities in respect of supra-sensory entities such as *dharma*.[4] The very term *sanātana dharma* used for the Vedic religion connotes a beginningless existence and indestructibility till eternity. Such a religion can never be based on a prophet-inspired theology.

The above are some of arguments that the *apauruṣeyatva-vādin*s put forth in support of their position. These arguments may not be convincing to all; some hold that the doctrine of *apauruṣeyatva* is just a matter of faith and that the arguments are unsatisfactory.[5]

However, within the framework of certain concepts and theories accepted by him, the *apauruṣeyatva-vādin* has to address certain pertinent questions, else the theory of *apauruṣeyatva* would lose all credibility. The point being made here is the following:

Any advocate of the theory of *apauruṣeyatva* of the Vedas, whether he be a Mīmāṁsaka, a Vedāntin, or an adherent of Sāṅkhya or Yoga, accepts that a *śabda* is of two kinds — *dhvani* (sound/utterance), and *varṇa* (phoneme). Of the two, a *śabda* that is in the form of *dhvani* has both origination and destruction. However, the *apauruṣeyatva-vādin* holds that the

---

4. See for example authorities such as *'Vedo 'khilo dharmamūlaṁ smṛtiśīle ca tadvidām'* — *Manu-Smṛti* 2.6; *'Vedo dharmamūlam, tadvidāṁ ca smṛtiśīle'* — *Gautama-Dharmasūtra* 1.1; *Vedapraṇihito dharmo hyadharmastadviparyayaḥ.'* — *Bhāgavata Purāṇa* 6.1.40.

5. It should be noted in this regard that this doctrine was evidently known to, and accepted by, the tradition of the grammarian Pāṇini who is accepted to have lived prior to the 5th century BCE, cf. his statements *'tena proktam'* — *Aṣṭādhyāyī* 4.3.101; and *'kṛte granthe'* — Ibid., 4.3.116; and his commentators' explications of the same. Thus the claim of some modern scholars that the *apauruṣeyatva* concept is an invention of relatively late theologians cannot be sustained.

other form of *śabda*, namely the phoneme, is eternal and has no origin or destruction. Further, it is all-pervasive in space also. Thus, although all the *varṇas* are eternal and everywhere in space, they can be heard by a person only when they are manifested by *dhvani.* Each *varṇa* has a different *dhvani* that manifests it, and when a speaker uses his faculties to produce the particular *dhvani,* then the corresponding *varṇa* is manifested and grasped by a listener. Likewise, a word or a sentence is a group of phonemes arranged in a particular order. For example, when the *varṇa*s given by *jakāra, akāra, lakāra, akāra,* and *makāra* are arranged in such an order and manifested so, then only a listener can grasp the word *jalam.*

Now the problem that the *varṇa-nityatva-vādin* faces is that he cannot arrange the *varṇa*s in an arbitrary manner. For ordering may be of two kinds, spatial and temporal. If one phoneme can be placed beside another phoneme in space, or if a phoneme can be associated with a moment or interval of time so that a series of phonemes is associated with a series of time, then the *varṇa*s can have spatial or temporal order. However, as per the *varṇa-nityatva-vādin* the *varṇas* are all-pervasive in space and eternal in time, and hence cannot have any kind of order, either spatial or temporal. The problem of explaining the arrangement of phonemes in a particular order as a word or sentence, it may be noted, is not specific to just Vedic sentences, but also occurs with linguistic usage in everyday life.[6]

---

6. The linguistic ordering of phonemes in everyday life is, unlike the orderings of most things in the world, neither spatial nor temporal, for it cannot be said that some phonemes exist in some areas of space and not in others, and it likewise cannot be said that some phonemes exist at some times but not at others. The speaker produces an utterance that orders the sounds

With regard to the sentences of our daily usage, the *varṇa-nityatva-vādin* has an answer. He readily grants that the *varṇa*s, being eternal and all-pervasive, cannot have any sequence. However, the cognition of the phonemes that the hearer gets following the utterance of sounds and the manifestation of the phonemes, can and does have an order associated with it. This order, as is evident upon reflection, belongs to the cognition of the phonemes, but not to the phonemes themselves. Being subject to such a cognition, the phonemes themselves may be said to have an indirect or a conditional order, one that is neither spatial nor temporal. Though the phonemes are eternal, words or sentences in common use are considered as *pauruṣeya* or the products of some person, for the underlying order of cognition of the phonemes, being dependent on the will and utterance of the speaker, is to be considered as his product, and the phonemes that are thus indirectly qualified with such an order are themselves treated as *pauruṣeya*.

For this reason, the explanation of the ordering of phonemes, given in the instance of the sentences in our daily usage, is unsatisfactory in respect of Vedic statements. For if the order of the phonemes being dependent on the will of a speaker is the criterion for being *pauruṣeya*, then even Vedic sentences would also have to be considered as *pauruṣeya* only because they have speakers who utter them, and the theory of *apauruṣeyatva* would collapse.

However, *apauruṣeyatva-vādin* has an answer here. He accepts the notion that the *varṇa*s, being eternal and all-

---

corresponding to phonemes in a temporal order, but the associated phonemes are not ordered temporally — indeed, a word or a sentence makes sense to a listener precisely because all its parts exist and are understood together.

pervasive, do not have an order of their own. He also concedes that the only possible explanation for their perceived order is to hold that the perceived order of the phonemes is really none other than the order that belongs to the manifestation of the phonemes. Then, the question of the difference between a *laukika* sentence of everyday life, and a Vedic sentence, persists. The *apauruṣeyatva-vādin* answers that the sequence of phonemes in a *laukika* sentence did not exist prior to its creation by an author. It is the will of a speaker or an author that created the sequence of phonemes initially, and the corresponding word or sentence is then considered to have been authored by whoever created the sequence. For instance, it was the will of Kālidāsa that the first stanza of his *Raghuvaṁśa* — "*vāgarthāviva sampṛktau . . .*" should have phonemes arranged in that sequence, that caused such an arrangement of phonemes that is associated with the great poet. But in case of a Vedic sentence such as "*agnimīḷe purohitam,*" it is not so. The Vedic seer who realized this sentence with the phonemes in such a sequence, did not will that such should be their sequence. In other words, he did not have any freedom to create the order of the phonemes or words, unlike Kālidāsa. While realizing the hymn, he just followed the sequence that had existed in previous Creations also. Even in the previous Creation, the seer who had then realized the hymn with the phonemes in the same order, did not then create it — he too just realized it without making any change in the order of the phonemes. But when he recited the hymn, since the phonemes became manifested by his efforts, to that extent it is his product and is *pauruṣeya* only. At the same time it is *apauruṣeya* also, in the sense that nobody ever, in the infinite, beginningless sequence of Creations until now, has had the freedom to create the sequence, other than what previously existed. Even the Brahman whose "breathing" is described as the Vedas — *niḥśvasitaṁ etad*[7] — does not change the sequence of the Vedic phonemes. He just follows the sequence of phonemes as they were in the previous Creation, and teaches the same in the next Creation also. This, i.e. the unchanging sequencing of the phonemes of the Vedic sentences is, according to the *apauruṣeyatva-vādin*, the *apauruṣeyatva* of the Vedas.

The Vedas are a unique asset of our ancient civilization, whose votaries make a bold claim of infallibility based on *apauruṣeyatva*. It is noteworthy that there is no other instance of its kind elsewhere in the world, even among ancient civilizations. The Vedas have an unbroken oral tradition of continuity for thousands of years, as has been noted by all serious students of philosophy. While those who did not have the advantage of serious study under qualified teachers tended to downgrade them as being just the poetry of an ancient pastoral/agricultural society extolling some local events, serious study has revealed nuggets of profound philosophical thought which are timeless, awe-inspiring, and contain remedies for life's problems.

---

7. *evaṁ vā are 'asya mahato bhūtasya niḥśvasitametad yadṛgvedo yajurvedaḥ sāmavedo atharvāṅgirasa itihāsaḥ purāṇaṁ vidyā upaniṣadaḥ ślokāḥ sūtrāṇi anuvyākhyānāni vyākhyānāni*. — *Bṛhadāraṇyaka Upaniṣad* 2.4.10.

3

Pūrvamīmāṁsā Perspective on Veda as Word

K.T. Pandurangi

I

IN the very *Jaiminī Sūtras* the word *śabda* is used in the sense of Veda. In the *Vedāṅtasūtras* also the Veda is referred to by the word *śabda*. This indicates that the importance of the *śabda* aspect of Veda is recognized both by Jaiminī and Bādarāyaṇa who are mainly concerned with the interpretation of Veda.

The purpose of Pūrvamīmāṁsā is to assist to comprehend *dharma* conveyed by the Veda.

धर्मे प्रमीयमाणे हि वेदेन करणात्मना।
इतिकर्तव्यताभागं मीमांसा पूरयिष्यति॥

Therefore Mīmāṁsā is primarily interested in describing *dharma*, by interpreting injunctive statements of Veda. However in the very first *adhikaraṇa* the question is raised whether there is any need to comprehend the meaning of Veda for which Mīmāṁsā has to be undertaken.

II

In this connection the statement स्वाध्यायो अध्येतव्यः is examined. The expression स्वाध्याय means Veda. The nature of Veda is explained क्रमविशेषविशिष्टवर्णराशिः। The expression अध्ययन means गुरूच्चारण

अनूच्चारण. Here the question is raised whether comprehending the meaning of Veda is the result of the *vedādhyayana* or mere *adhyayana* i.e., recitation itself leads to *svarga*.

स्वाध्यायगोचराध्ययनेन स्वर्गं भावयेत् उत अर्थज्ञानं भावयेत्॥

Pūrvapakṣin claims that there is no need to extend the scope of *adhyayana* to *arthajñāna*. Hence *svarga* has to be taken as a result of the study. This stand is based on the concept that the very recitation of Vedic hymns is a sacred act and leads to अदृष्टफल. This अदृष्टफल is taken as *svarga* (स्वर्ग) by Mīmāṁsakas as per the विश्वजिन्नाय. Pūrvamīmāṁsā does not make it clear whether the expression स्वर्ग refers to the other world or a kind of happiness. In any case मन्त्र being sacred, the mere recitation of them leads to some अदृष्टफल. Siddhantin, though, argues for the extension of the scope of अध्ययनविधि, up to the अर्थज्ञान, of स्वाध्याय i.e. Veda. He does not deny the sacredness of the recitations of the hymns, since he makes अध्ययनविधि a नियमविधि that is to say the अर्थज्ञान i.e. धर्मस्वरूपज्ञान is to be obtained only from the Veda, but not by any other means. From this it is clear that the importance of *śabda* i.e. Vedic words is recognized by Pūrvamīmāṁsā, even though its job is to provide धर्मस्वरूपज्ञान by assisting to interpret the Veda.

III

In *Mantra Lingādhikaraṇa* (1-2-4) again, the question is raised whether the recitation of मन्त्र is दृष्टार्थ or अदृष्टार्थ. *Pūrvapakṣin* argues that the very recitation of मन्त्र leads to some अदृष्टफल. There is no need to comprehend the meaning. The *siddhāntin* points out that these मन्त्रs remind द्रव्य or devatā, and therefore they are to be associated with the injunction. He does not deny the sacredness of the recitation of मन्त्र as he takes the stand that द्रव्य and देवता have to be reminded by मन्त्र only but not by any other means. This again is the recognition of the importance of Veda as word.

IV

For Pūrvamīmāṁsa explaining the implementation of Vedic injunction is the central theme. In view of this they discuss the import of the injunction in detail. In this connection they have evolved the concept of *bhāvanā*. The main task of the injunction is to prompt the person concerned to undertake the initiative to perform the sacrificial act, this prompting is designated as *śabdībhāvanā*. Ordinarily the statement that prompts to undertake initiative for performing an act conveys that the speaker desires that the initiative to perform the act concerned be undertaken by the person to whom the statement is addressed. However in the case of Vedic statements there is no person behind it. Therefore, it is the very injunctive suffix that prompts to undertake initiative to perform the sacrificial act. Therefore, the prompting or *preraṇā* conveyed by the injunctive suffix is designated as *śabdībhāvanā*. This *śabdībhāvanā* is more a function or व्यापार of injunctive suffix than its meaning. The initiative i.e. प्रवृत्ति undertaken as a result of this प्रेरणा is designated as आर्थीभावना. आर्थीभावना is only a consequential function on the part of the person addressed. There are a large number of injunctive statements in connection with the performance of sacrifice, for all these शाब्दीभावनाs that are conveyed by these injunctions, the statement स्वाध्यायो अध्येतव्यः is mother injunction. This clearly shows the importance of Veda as word.

१. लोके गवानयनादिप्रवृत्त्यनुकूलप्रेरणाख्यो व्यापारः प्रयोक्तृपुरुषगताभि-प्रायविशेषः। वेदे तु प्रयोक्तृपुरुषाभावात् लिङ्गादिशब्दनिष्ठ एव स इत्यङ्गीक्रियते। अत एव शब्दनिष्ठव्यापारत्वात् शाब्दीभावना इत्युच्यते। यागहोमादिविषय-प्रवृत्तिहेतुत्वात् प्रवर्तना, प्रेरणा इति च उच्यते।

२. इयं च शब्दभावना ज्योतिष्टोमादिप्रातिस्विक वाक्येषु स्वरूपेण प्रतीयमाना कर्तव्यत्वेन न प्रतीयते। अर्थभावनायाः एव तेषु कर्तव्यत्वावगमात्। किन्तु स्वाध्यायोऽध्येतव्यः इति वाक्य एव कर्तव्यत्वेन प्रतीयते। स्वाध्यायोऽध्येतव्य इति वाक्यस्थार्थभावनाया एव सकलविधिवाक्यस्थशब्दभावनारूपत्वात्, (मीमांसा परिभाषा, p. 17)

V

The most important concept of Pūrvamīmāṁsā is अपौरुषेयत्व of Veda. To sustain this concept Pūrvamīmāṁsā has accepted the concepts of (i) नित्यत्व of शब्द and (ii) अपौरुषेयत्व of शब्दार्थसम्बन्ध. The expression औत्पत्तिक means नित्य, which is explained as सहज. When a word is expressed its meaning is also expressed. These two arise together. However the meaning so expressed is not automatically comprehended. It is comprehended by वृद्धव्यवहार i.e. by the usage of the elders. The elders are going on using the words in different sentences generation after generation the beginning of which cannot be traced.

This relation between word and meaning is neither fixed by God nor by any other human agency. This is the foundation of the concept of अपौरुषेयत्व of Veda. At the sentence level also words are not arranged by any human agency in the case of Vedic statements. It is already stated that Veda is क्रमविशेषविशिष्टवर्णराशि. A detailed discussion of अपौरुषेयत्व of Veda is found in the first chapter of Jaiminī sūtras. The formation of the sentence without involving any human agency in the case of Vedic statements is also explained under the *sūtra*.

तद्भूतानां क्रियार्थेन समाम्नायः अर्थस्य तन्निमित्तत्वात्।

From this it is clear that the importance of Veda as word is recognised by the concept of शब्दनित्यत्व, शब्दार्थनित्यत्व and वाक्यस्यापि अपौरुषेयत्व.

VI

According to Pūrvamīmāṁsā शब्दात्मका एव देवताः। The very words अग्नि, इन्द्र etc. are देवताs. They do not have the body etc. विग्रह-हविःस्वीकार-तद्भोजन-तृप्ति-प्रसादरूपपञ्चकविशिष्टाः नैव सन्ति i.e. they are not embodied, do not receive the हवि, do not eat it. They are not pleased by it and do not bestow any grace on the sacrificer.

This is clearly stated in शबरभाष्य (9.1.4.) The entire Veda is developed around the देवताs — अग्नि, इन्द्र, वरुण etc. The position taken here that the words are देवताs clearly indicates the importance of Veda as word.

It is not clear whether this view of शबर was acceptable to Kumārila or not. He formulates the *pūrvapakṣa* and *siddhānta* of this *adhikaraṇa* without referring to it. He only puts the *pūrvapakṣa* as it is the grace of the देवता that bestows the result of the sacrifice. In *Siddhānta,* he rejects this view of *pūrvapakṣa* and states that it is the sacrifice that leads to the result without making it clear whether this देवता is mere शब्दात्मक or has विग्रह etc.

Later writers of Pūrvamīmāṁsā accept विग्रह etc. under the influence of इतिहास-पुराण view and the theistic Vedānta view. This is clear from the following remark in the अध्वरमीमांसाकुतूहलवृत्तिः

यत्तु नवमे देवता वा प्रयोजयेत् (9-1-4-6) इत्यधिकरणे देवतानां विग्रहादि-पञ्चकं निराक्रियते। तत् प्रौढिवादमात्रम् ! अतएव वार्तिके, देवताविग्रहादिपञ्चकं अनाघ्राय एव तदधिकरणं प्रवर्तयिष्यते। शब्द एव देवता न तु अर्थः इति तु बौद्धप्रलपितमेव। विग्रहादिपञ्चकरहितो अर्थो देवता इत्यपि प्रच्छन्नबौद्धप्रलपितमेव।

In any case the sacredness of the names of the देवताs is recognised in Indian tradition and the recitation of it is faithfully followed.

4

Meaning of Veda and Veda-Prāmāṇya According to Pūrvamīmāṁsā

S.R. Bhatt

HUMAN being as a rational, free and goal-oriented agent (*puruṣa*) undertakes voluntary action after acquiring knowledge of the reality which surrounds him. His purposive agency stems from free will which is guided by rational considerations. Dharmakīrti, a Buddhist thinker, rightly maintains that "All successful human endeavour is preceded by knowledge."[1] Human being is potentially gifted with the capacity to know the goal (*sādhya*), the means (*sādhana*) and the modalities (*itikartavyatā*). In the Indian tradition acquisition of knowledge is not purposeless (*niṣprayojana*) nor is it of nothingness (*nirviṣayaka*). It has an object to be known (*prameya*). It attempts to know an object as it is (*yathārtha*), through appropriate means (*pramāsādhana = pramāṇa*) and all this is done in order to derive some useful purpose (*phala*). *Prameyanirṇaya* and *pramā-sādhana phala vicāra* are thus the primary objectives of a philosophical enterprise.

Though our aim is to acquire knowledge, it is not always the case that we succeed in this endeavour. Knowledge is not the necessary acquisition of a cognitive activity. Quite often we

---

1. *Samyajjñānapūrvikāsarvapuruṣārthasiddhiḥ* (*Nyāyabindu*, p. 1)

end up in error or doubt or indecisiveness. If all cognitions were necessarily true, there would not have been any need for our epistemological enquiry about the nature of knowledge, the appropriate means of knowing, the criteria of truth and validation, and our eagerness to get away from error and doubt. All issues regarding *pramāṇa* and *prāmāṇya* arise because we quite often go astray in our cognitive endeavour. Following the Indian epistemological tradition the Mīmāṁsā school discusses these issues very succinctly which merits due consideration.

The relation between knowledge and reality is reciprocal. The two are mutually dependent. Knowledge depends upon its object, i.e., reality, for its rise and existence. If there were no object, there would be no knowledge. The real alone becomes the object of knowledge and provides content to knowledge. If the traditional Indian theory of *Meyādhīnā mānasiddhi* is understood this way, there is an element of truth and acceptability in it. Likewise, reality also depends upon knowledge for being known. Knowledge is the only gateway to reality. Only through knowledge one can establish what is real and what is not real. So the other traditional Indian theory of *Mānādhīnā meyasiddhi* also contains an element of truth and acceptability. Taken in two different contexts, there is no contradiction or inconsistency or circularity in accepting both these theories. The term *siddhi* may mean here (a) dependence in respect of *existence* and (b) dependence in respect of *awareness*. The former is *ontic* dependence and the latter is *epistemic* dependence. The dependence of knowledge on reality is ontic whereas the dependence of reality on knowledge is epistemic. In the Mīmāṁsā there is explicit approval of *Mānādhīnā meyasiddhi* but there is tacit acceptance of *Meyādhīnā mānasiddhi* as well in so far as it talks of two types of knowledge (*pramā-dvaividhya*) which is possible only on the ground of accepting two types of objects to be known.[2] It maintains a dichotomy of objects, a dichotomy of knowledge and on this basis a dichotomy of means of knowing.[3]

As our experience vouchsafes, there are two types of objects to be known, the existent (*bhūta*) and the prospective (*bhavya*). The existent object is actual, having existence in the past or in the present. We have its descriptive awareness. The prospective object is virtual, potential to be actualized. The one is already existent and the other is yet to be made existent. In human context *dharma* is *bhavya vastu* as it is to be accomplished through proper human effort (*puruṣānusṭhā-nādhīna*) and that is why it is *puruṣārtha* (*puruṣena arthyate prārthyate*).

Both the actual and the prospective are knowable but they are not of the same category and therefore not knowable in the same mode of knowing. The existent is known through sense-comprehension. Its knowledge is through empirical acquaintance and linguistic description. Its descriptive awareness is through external and/or internal senses. It is sense-dependent and contingent upon human capabilities and other causal factors. About this knowledge, which can be named as *puruṣa-tantra,* borrowing Śaṅkara's terminology, we have a very apt evaluation by Śabara when he writes that it cannot be decisive and that it can be true or false.[4] It is therfore subject to empirical verification and there is always a possibility of its falsifiability. When we refer to the devil of doubt, it is only in the context of this type of descriptive awareness. It is invariably vitiated by human fallibility.

---

2. *Mānam dvividham meyadvaividhyāt,* as Diṅnāga argues in his *Prāmāṇa-Samuccaya,* Ibid., p. 1.

3. *Ataḥ pramādvaividhyāttatkāraṇasyāpi dvaividhyam.* Ibid., 1.

4. *Yathā yat kiñcana laukika vacanam - Nadyāstīre phalāni santi - iti. Tad tathyamapi bhavati vitathamapi bhavatīti* (*Śābarabhāṣya* on *Mīmāṁsā-Sūtra* 1.1.2, p.11).

The other type of knowledge is of an object which is yet to be realized or actualized. It is an ideal which is realizable and which ought to be realized. In the human context it is a value (*sādhya*) to be realized through proper endeavour (*puruṣārtha*). It is not utopian (*asādhya*) but something which is capable of being realized (*bhavanānukūla*) and which must therefore be realized. There is an *optativeness* or oughtness associated with it. It is injunctive in nature. *Dharma* is one such object.

Dharma cannot be known through empirical means. There cannot be descriptive awareness of it, as firstly it does not exist and needs to be accomplished, and secondly, it must have universal and infallible prescriptivity. *Dharmic* prescriptions cannot be subjective and contingent. They must be adhered to unconditionally by all under a given circumstance. In a changed circumstance they may no longer be unconditional but their acceptance or non-acceptance is not arbitrary. They may be situational and perspectival but this relativism has also to be rule-based and rule-governed. There may be exceptions but they are also to be regulated.

The knowledge of *dharma* has to come from a trans-empirical source. That source is named as *codanā* in the Mīmāṁsā system. It is a qualitatively different type of source which is not human because every human claim to knowledge is a suspect which cannot guarantee universality and finality.[5] The trans-empirical source, on the contrary, must be infallible and its reliability must be absolute. Then only it can claim unwavering acceptability. To invoke universal command of adherence it must be free from all sorts of contingencies and

5. As Śabara puts it, *Aśakyam hi tat, puruṣena jñātum ṛte vacanāt. Aparasmāt pauruṣeyād vacanāt tadavagatamiti, cet tadapi tenaiva tulyam. Naivañjātīyakeṣvartheṣu puruṣavacanam prāmāṇyamupaiti, jātyandhānāmiva vacanam rūpaviśeṣeṣu.* (Ibid., 1.1.2, p. 12).

infirmities which human cognitive faculties suffer from. Śabara, therefore, insists that *codanā* is only such a mode of knowing which alone can know an object which is past or present or future and which is subtle, covered up or far removed.[6] It is free from all contingencies of time, space, circumstances and persons.[7] This source is named as *śabda* (or *śāstra*) of which Veda is a synonym.[8]

In the Mīmāṁsā we find a *vyavasthā* in the form of *prameya-dvaividhya, pramā-dvaividhya* and *pramāṇa-dvaividhya*. There is also a dichotomous distinction between the actual and the potential, the descriptive and the prescriptive. There cannot be any mixing up or *samplava* between the two types which are qualitatively different. The strict dichotomy between the two types of object entails the same dichotomy between two types of knowledge and modes of knowing. So far as the knowledge of *dharma* is concerned a *mānāntara* has to be admitted.[9] This is the Mīmāṁsā position.

This philosophical analysis takes us outside for a while from the field of epistemology to the related field of ethics. The moral norms in the form of *dharma* are universal and they must be strictly adhered to as their violation in any form is bad or wrong and leads to sin and suffering. In the *Artha-Saṁgraha* (p. 4) *dharma* is defined as *Vedapratipādyaprayojanavadarthaḥ dharmaḥ*. It is *artha*

---

6. *Codanā hi bhūtam bhavantam bhaviṣyantam sūkṣmam vyavahitam viprakṛṣṭamityevañjātīyakamartham śaknotyavagamayitum, nānyat kiñcanendriyam.* (Ibid., 1.1.2, p. 10).

7. *Na caiṣa kālāntare puruṣāntare avasthāntare deśāntare vā viparyeti. Tasmādavitathaḥ.* (Ibid., 1.1.2, p. 12).

8. Śabara writes, *"na tu vedavacanasya mithyātve kiñcana pramāṇamasti."*

9. Laugākṣī Bhāskara writes, *"apauruṣeyam vākyam vedaḥ."* (*Artha-saṁgraha*).

and not *anartha*.[10] It is conducive to well-being — both material and spiritual.[11] Its violation is detrimental to well-being. *Dharma* is thus *prayojanavat*, having an instrumental value which is cosmic or universal and not pertaining or confined to any one single individual. It is *Veda-pratipādya* in the sense that it is supra-human in origin. Its source is *Veda* which is *nirapekṣarava*,[12] i.e., a linguistic expression which is absolutely and unconditionally true.

In order to ensure the property of *nirapekṣatva*, the Mīmāṁsā system regards Veda as *apauruṣeya*, meaning thereby that it has no author — human or divine. It is eternal and authorless. It is utterly objective and it is envisioned by the seers in their intuitive realizations in subliminal consciousness. In the Nyāya-Vaiśeṣika system *nirapekṣatva* is understood as only supra-human because human knowledge is conditionally true. God is omniscient and therefore possesses knowledge which is infallible. Veda is of divine origin in Nyāya-Vaiśeṣika. In the Mīmāṁsā, it is regarded as supra-human but not divine. It is supra-human only in origin. It is meant for human being and is directed to human being only. It is not dependent upon perception etc. (*pratyakṣādi upajīvya*)[13] which are fallible and stand in need of verification which in fact is never conclusive.

---

10. (1) *ya eva śreyaskaraḥ sa eva dharmaśabdenocyate.*

    (2) *arthaśca dharmaḥ na anartha iti.*

    (3) *tatra anartho dharma ukto mā bhūditi arthagrahaṇam. Śābarabhāṣya,* 1.1.2, p. 17.

11. *yato 'bhyudayaniḥśreyasasiddhiḥ sa dharmaḥ.* Kaṇāda *Vaiśeṣika-Sūtra* 1.1.2.

12. (1) *apauruṣeyam vākyam vedaḥ.*

    (*Arthasaṁgraha,* p. 25, edited by Sukthankar)

    (2) *tatra nirapekṣo ravaḥ śrutih.* Ibid., p. 15.

13. *Laukikavyavahārasādhakasyaiva śabdasya pratyakṣopajīvakatvam na vedasyeti.* p. 53 (*Prāsthana-Ratnākara*, edited by Shyam Manohar Goswami)

→

In the Mīmāṁsā, Veda is described as *anapekṣa śabda*. It is a mode of knowing which is unconditionally true and independent. It is this property which provides it *āptatva* (reliability and infallibility) and *nityatva* (universality). *Veda* is *āpta* because it is not contingent upon human origin. The *śabdārtha-sambandha* (word-meaning relation) is *nitya* as it is naturally established. We may have a very interesting propagation of degrees of *āptatva*.[14] Of course, this should not be mistaken as degrees of *pramāṇatva*. In *pramāṇatva* there can be no degrees because it is totally and absolutely objective. But in *āpatatva* there can be degrees amenable to statistical measurement also. But this quantitative measurement is confined to human sphere only and here we do witness degrees of reliability or assuredness. In the Prasthāna-Ratnākara of the Śuddhādvaita School of Uttara Mīmāṁsā, not only a distinction is drawn between *laukika* and *alaukika āptatva*, it also advocates gradual increase in the reliability culminating in God. So divine *āptatva* is perfect and infallible. But then it can be asked, is there a difference of degrees only or of kind also between the two?

It should be pointed out that the *jyeṣṭha pramāṇatva* of *pratyakṣa* is not denied so far as the empirical sphere is concerned, but it is sharply differentiated from the Veda. It is also to be noted that there is non-reducibility of Veda to perception, inference etc. This provides for its absolute non-falsifiability. Then only Veda can stimulate *niṣkampa pravṛtti*

→ *Svarūpalābhe śrotasāpekṣatve 'pi prāmāṇyāṁśe tadanapekṣātvat 'śruta-mātreṇa śabdena cakṣurādikam anapekṣyaiva padārthopasthānāt nāpi pratyakṣopajīvakatvaṁ Vede tadabhāvāt.* p. 14.

14. *Tatrāsmadādirlaukikaḥ. Alaukikāstu ṛṣīnārabhyeśvaraparyantah uttarottaram caiṣāmāptatvādhikyāt paramāptatvamiśvare paryavasyatīti tadupadeśarupo Vedaevānapekṣyam prāmāṇyam.* p. 49.

(unwavering activity) in respect of *dharma*. A doubtful awareness can generate wavering activity only. Perhaps this is how we can understand the expressions: *Vedamukhyatva, tanmūrdhanyo Veda eva hi* etc. In fact if *prāmāṇya* is understood as *tadvati tatprakārakatva* as the Naiyāyikas do, and this includes the property of *abādhitatva,* then Vedā alone can legitimately claim absolute *prāmāṇya.*

5

Vāgāmbhṛṇī

S.P. Singh

VĀGĀMBHṚṆĪ is one of the most renowned seers of the Vedic age. She has seen only one hymn of just eight mantras compiled in the *Ṛgveda* and yet she occupies a very prestigious place in the galaxy of seers. Unfortunately, nothing is known about her personal life except for the fact that she was the daughter of one Ambhṛṇa. Regarding Ambhṛṇa also nothing is known except that he was the father of Āmbhṛṇī. Whether he himself was a seer or not cannot be said with any certainty, since not a single mantra in any of the Saṃhitās is associated with his seerhood. Thus, here is a case of a seer and at that too a female, having been born of an ordinary man. This fact enhances further the achievement of the daughter inasmuch as she rose to seerhood without any family background. As a matter of fact, most of the Vedic seers had long traditions behind them as they were sons and daughters of eminent seers. In their case, it was therefore relatively easier to attain seerhood since they had already inherited much in the form of the legacy. But to rise out of shreds of intellectual and spiritual background must have been a rare event. It, however, did happen in the case of Āmbhṛṇī, and in a most notable way as is evident from the *mantra*s seen by her. Leaving apart the spiritual height, even from the elegance of her expressions as also perfection in her metrical composition, it is evident that she must have been taught rigorously and intensively before she went for her metrical utterance. It bears out the fact that female education up to the highest standard was in vogue at that time. If the parents were not so learned and enlightened as to impart their learning and enlightenment to their progeny themselves, they were free and courageous enough to send even their daughters to suitable institutions away from their homes.

In this respect Āmbhṛṇī's case is similar to, and at that much more appreciable than that of, the Upaniṣadic Śvetaketu who for higher learning was sent by his learned and enlightened father to some distantly placed institution and yet required to be initiated by his father himself, after his return from there, in mysteries of higher order, while Āmbhṛṇī, on the other hand, got enlightened without having required any such feedback from her father.

Institutions were meant for teaching equally to all the students attending them. But, as a matter of fact, the level of learning in all the cases was always not the same. Some of the students excelled in it while the rest stopped either half-way or even as starters. The Vedic age was not an exception to it, as is evident from one of the Ṛgvedic *mantras* seen by Bṛhaspati Āṅgirasa, which states that out of a number of students gifted equally with the powers of seeing, hearing etc., some remained at the bottom and some went to the middle, a few exceptional ones excelled beyond the estimation of the teacher himself.[1]

Vāgāmbhṛṇī seems to have been such an exceptionally brilliant student. This is very much reflected in the *mantras*

1. अक्षण्वन्तः कर्णवन्तः सखायो मनोजवेष्वसमा बभूवुः ।
आदघ्नास उपकक्षास उ त्वे ह्रदा इव स्नात्वा उ त्वे ददृश्रे ॥ *Ṛ*V. X. 71.7

seen by her. In these *mantras* she speaks of her movement in the company of gods, such as the Vasus, Rudras and Ādityas. These three are the most prominent groups of Vedic gods. Out of them, Vasus are terrestrial, Rudras are atmospheric and the Ādityas are celestial. Even such an eminent seer as Vasiṣṭha once claims to have sailed in a boat in the company of god Varuṇa and to have enjoyed the voyage as one of his most memorable experiences. As such, how blessed Vāgāmbhṛṇī might have felt by having access to all the gods forming at least these three groups and to have moved freely in their company! This movement, however, cannot be anyway physical, nor might have been so that of Vasiṣṭha. It must, indeed, be an out-and-out spiritual experience as such on account of the realisation of one's inherence in everything and everything's inherence in oneself on the level of consciousness. This gets confirmed directly by one of her statements that while on the one hand she is all-comprehending, on the other she has been placed by gods differently in things.[2] This statement of her has the same spiritual bearing as the famous Upaniṣadic one contending that he who sees all the beings as inhering in himself and himself as inherent in everything, does not need to feel shy of anything.[3] Not feeling shy of anything or anyone amounts to active participation in the activities of one and all. This is stated in the next *mantra* of the hymn where she claims to provide food to all, no matter they be simply breathing, as are the vegetations, or be provided with senses and mind also. Moreover, she warns at the same time in the same

---

2. तां मा देवा व्यदधुः पुरुत्रा भूरिस्थात्रां भूयविशयन्तीम् । Ibid., X. 125.3.

3. यस्तु सर्वाणि भूतान्यात्मन्येवानुपश्यति ।
सर्वभूतेषु चात्मानं ततो न विजुगुप्सते ॥ *Īśa Up*. 6.

continuation that those who do not have any faith in her being, cannot but perish.[4]

This *mantra* tells us several significant things about Vāgāmbhṛṇī. In the first place, it makes it clear to us that in this capacity she does not remain an individual human being. She could have spoken like this only when she would have already established her complete identity with the Provident of life force, power of seeing and understanding of the world. It shows that she was a visionary not only in the theoretical sense of the term but also for all practical purposes on account of having realised her complete oneness with the Provident of the world. In the second place, having risen to that height in her experience she now sees the actual role of the Provident in running the affairs of the world. It consists in providing existence to the inert, vitality to the vital, power of sensing to lowly creatures and that of seeing, understanding and conviction to humans. As such, any deliberate act of shirking from the admittance of that Provident has the danger of blocking the passage of providence of these powers to oneself resulting in the blighting of wisdom and understanding and thus devastation of the person concerned at least spiritually and intellectually. Thus Vāgāmbhṛṇī draws our attention to the necessity of taking cognisance of the source of the vital, intellectual and spiritual in us. But for that cognisance, one is in the danger of returning to the state of inerts amounting to inertia. Lastly, her address to the addressee as *śruta* and *śraddhiva* speaks volumes concerning the learning and conviction of her contemporaries. Use of the vocative *śruta*

4. मया सो अन्नमत्ति यो विपश्यति यः प्राणिति य ईं शृणोत्युक्तम् ।
अमन्तवो मां त उपक्षियन्ति श्रुधि श्रुत श्रद्धिवं ते वदामि ॥ *ṚV*. X. 125.4.

for the person concerned is indicative of the learning of him on the one hand and that of herself on the other. Only a highly learned person can address a learned one in this manner.

Use of the word *śraddhiva,* man of faith, on the other hand, shows that in her view learning in itself was not sufficient in making one understand the ultimate nature of things amounting to that of the Reality, which she now feels herself to represent. Besides learning, what is required in this regard has been termed here as *śraddhā,* faith. This faith, however, is not supposed to be intra-intellectual and hence blind. On the contrary, it ought to supersede learning and intellection. Presupposition of learning by *śraddhā* is evident from her address to the person concerned as *śruta,* man of learning, before having been imbued with *śraddhā.* Requirement of the element of intellection, on the other hand, is implicit in her use of the word *amantavaḥ* in the same continuation for those who are condemned by her to get ruined. Adequate learning, intellection and conviction, according to her, thus, are essential for one to rise to the state of consciousness, she, at the moment, has reached, and to be in a position to understand the secret of the process under which the one and the same agency is providing vitality and powers of sensing and thinking to beings at different planes of existence.

The significance of this statement of the seer can be appreciated better if we read it side-by-side with those made by some of the most eminent Upaniṣadic sages, including Sanatkumāra and Yājñavalkya. In his teaching to Nārada, the divine sage Sanatkumāra by way of raising his meditation gradually via *vāk, manas, saṅkalpa, citta, dhyāna, vijñāna, bala, prāṇa,* etc., comes eventually to *manana, śraddhā and niṣṭhā* culminating in the realisation of *bhūman,* the Infinite. In this gradation of states one is required to pass through so as to reach the state of final fulfilment, while learning, mentation, determination, understanding, etc. are supposed to form the basis of *śraddhā*. *Niṣṭhā* is considered as the culmination of it by virtue of indicating to the state of ultimate settlement of the individual in the supernal consciousness.

What Sanatkumāra has taught so elaborately to Nārada, a highly learned pupil, has been stated summarily by Yājñavalkya to his wife Maitreyī in the Bṛhadāraṇyaka Upaniṣad at the end of his lesson to her at the time of his taking to renunciation. In response to her query regarding the path to immortality, he told her that it rested in taking lessons in, thinking over and getting meditatively settled in Ātman, the Infinite envisioned from the viewpoint of the individual through his self-consciousness.[5]

Continuance of the tradition laid down by Vāgāmbhṛṇī, Sanatakumāra and Yajñavalkya, and indeed until now, bespeaks of the amazing soundness of it. This is so because it is all-comprehending. It has proper place in it for all the capabilities of the human mind. It is in making full use of mentation, intellection and will to rise to the supramental that one hopes to attain the state of consciousness Vāgāmbhṛṇī seems to have reached.

Vāgāmbhṛṇī's access to the Reality was so profound and complete that she happens to assume the role of the power of articulation and action of it. This is evident from the next two *mantras*. In the first one of these, she asserts that it is she, herself an embodiment of the principle of articulation, *vāk*, who is pronouncing it on behalf of all the humans. Such words can be only those which are favourable to their interests. As regards the humans, what are most favourable

---

5. आत्मा वा अरे द्रष्टव्यः श्रोतव्यो मन्तव्यो निदिध्यासितव्यो मैत्रेयि । *Brh. Up.* IV. 5.6.

and to their liking are the words of their transformation into intellectuals, seers and knowers of the Reality. She observes that it is as per her wish that people get transformed into intellectuals, seers and knowers of Brahman, the Realtiy.[6] So far as her favour to the gods is concerned, it lies in empowering them to vanquish the demons, their adversaries. It is for these twin purposes that she, as *vāk*, has come to pervade the entire space marked out by the heaven and the earth. In this statement, she may be taken to pervade the earth in the interest of the humans while the heaven in the interest of gods.[7]

Such a claim on the part of Vāgāmbhṛnī is not just an emotional outburst of a novice in some kind of spiritual experience and hence something adventitious. It, on the contrary, falls in the line of the standard ethos of the Veda. It, indeed, exemplifies the established Vedic doctrine of co-ordination between the word and the Reality. The most axiomatic statement of this doctrine is to be found in another seer's observation that *vāk* or the power of articulation is as extensive as the Reality itself.[8] The extension of *vāk*, though complete in comprehension, is punctuated by variation. This is evident from all living beings expressing themselves in idioms peculiar to them each as also in humans themselves speaking in so large a number of languages in the world. This, too, is in keeping with variation in the manifestation of the Reality differently at each step.

The co-ordination between *vāk* or power of articulation and the Reality is, indeed, owing to consciousness working as

---

6. अहमेव स्वयमिदं वदामि जुष्टं देवेभिरुत मानुषेभिः ।
यं कामये तं तमुग्रं कृणोमि तं ब्रह्माणं तमृषिं तं सुमेधाम् ॥ *ṚV*. X. 125.5.

7. अहं जनाय समदं कृणोम्यहं द्यावापृथिवी आ विवेश ॥ Ibid., X. 125.6.

8. यावद् ब्रह्म विष्ठितं तावती वाक् । Ibid., X. 114.8.

the common denominator of the two. According to this scheme of things, as envisioned by Vedic seers, it is consciousness which manifests itself in the form of the reality on the one hand and the cognisance of the reality on the other. The cognisance, in its turn, assumes the form of word through articulation. This principle is to be seen in practical application in this hymn in the form of Vāgāmbhṛṇī's assumption of the role of the seer while *Ātman* having been declared as its deity. This is the rationale of she having been considered as both the seer and the *devatā* of the hymn. By virtue of representing *vāk*, she is considered as its seer, while on account of representing the *Ātman* she is regarded as its *devatā*. The coincidence of the *ṛṣi* and *devatā* here is, thus, the result of the seer reaching the climax of understanding where the knower and the object of knowledge both become one and the same. Indeed, all knowledge has its final end in the mind or self of the knower. Any sense of difference between the knower and the object of knowledge is indicative of incompleteness in the process of knowing. Vāgāmbhṛṇī's realisation of her oneness with both *vāk* and *Ātman* bears out how deeply she was involved in her realisation with pure consciousness on one side and its manifestation on the other, unlike the later Vedantins seeking to realise their identity with *Brahman* to the exclusion of the world considered as a matter of disdain.

This creativity of consciousness represented by Vāgāmbhṛṇī by virtue of having realised her identity in it is reflected in the next mantra of the hymn where she claims to have herself given birth to the Creator at the head of the creation while having her own source in the interior of the sea.[9] It is to this polarity in her source and creativity that she

---

9. अहं सुवे पितरमस्य मूर्धन् मम योनिरप्स्वश्न्तः समुद्रे ।
ततो वि तिष्ठे भुवनानि विश्वोतामूं द्यां वर्ष्मणोप स्पृशामि ॥ Ibid., X. 125. 7.

attributes the secret of her all-pervasiveness. Location of the place of her birth in the sea suggests the insoluble mystery of the origin of consciousness. It reminds one of Gārgī's question put to sage Yājñavalkya in the assembly of the learned in the court of King Janaka as recounted in the Bṛhadāraṇyaka Upaniṣad. The question related to the source of *Akṣara*, the Imperishable. To this crucial question, what the sage answered was in terms of the danger that if she insisted upon getting an answer to it, she would have her head fall on the ground. It amounted to the impossibility of getting an answer to this question. The human mind has to stop somewhere in its query and understanding about the Reality in terms of causality. While that bedrock, according to Yājñavalkya, is the *Akṣara*, it, according to Vāgāmbhṛṇī's scheme of things, is her own self as realised in its inherence in *Ātman*. *Akṣara*, *Ātman* and Vāgāmbhṛṇī's self are one and the same Ultimate Reality viewed from different perspectives. While *Akṣara* is reached through regression on causal lines, *Ātman* is realised by Vāgāmbhṛṇī through the string of self-consciousness.

In the last mantra of the hymn, she speaks again of her two phases, namely, the immanent and the transcendent. She brings out her immanence through the symbol of air which blows around the globe imparting life and dynamism to beings and things. Similarly, consciousness, as represented by Vāgāmbhṛṇī, is immanent in the world creating the world, imparting dynamism and vitality to things and beings here. That, however, is not all what consciousness does. It at the same time remains transcendent to the creation. This is indicated in the mantra through Vāgāmbhṛṇī's claim that essentially she is transcendent to the heaven and the earth and that it is by way of her expansion that she is immanent in the world.[10] It is interesting to note that what she tells us about her transcendent phase, is reflected almost in the same terminology in the Chāndogya Upaniṣad's account of the transcendent light of consciousness. After giving an account of the role of the heart *vis-à-vis* different organs and senses of the body, the Upaniṣad talks of a light casting its lustre beyond the heaven, behind the creation, behind everything and be in essence the same as one lying in the inmost being of the individual.[11] If we cast a comparative glance over these two passages, that is, the Vedic mantra and the Upaniṣadic statement, it would be clear that the latter is just an abstraction of what Vāgāmbhṛṇī has stated as a matter of her self-experience. Her presence beyond the heaven and the earth is taken in the Upaniṣad as the presence of the transcendent consciousness beyond the heaven and behind the creation as also in the inmost being of the individual.

---

10. अहमेव वात इव प्र वाम्यारभमाणा भुवनानि विश्वा ।
परो दिवा पर एना पृथिव्यैतावती महिना सं बभूव ॥ Ibid., X. 125. 8.

11. अथ यदतः परो दिवा ज्योतिर्दीप्यते विश्वतः पृष्ठेषु सर्वतः
पृष्ठेष्वनुत्तमेषूत्तमेषु लोकेष्विदं वाव तद्यदिदमन्तः पुरुषे ज्योतिः । *Ch. Up.* III, 13.7.

6

Vāg Vai Sarasvatī

Usha Choudhuri

YEARNING for wisdom, the enlightenment, the cry of the human soul to conceive, to understand is the very essence of the Vedic poetry. The universal and eternal longing of the human mind for illumination finds expression in its mythical language and symbology. The seeric poets realized that this journey is the journey of words that merge ultimately into the one, the *akṣara* as does the cosmic multiplicity into the one Supreme.[1]

"Through those our flashing songs, do thou turn towards us like heaven's radiance." They perceived the Vedic verse as pure light, *jyoti*.[2] The word *'Brahman'* refers to a Vedic verse as well as the Supreme Reality. So in the first Maṇḍala the poet seer *Dīrghatamas* poses the question about the ultimate resort of speech.

> *pṛcchāmi tvā paramantaḥ pṛthivyāḥ pṛcchāmī yatra bhuvanasya nābhiḥ* ।
> *pṛcchāmi tvā vṛṣṇo aśvasya retaḥ pṛcchāmi vācaḥ paramaṁ vyoma* ॥[3]

---

1. *ebhirno arkairbhavā no arvāṅ svarṇa jyotiḥ,*
   — *Ṛgveda*, 4, 10, 3

2. *Jaiminīya Brāhmaṇa*, 1, 76
   Jyotistad yad ṛk

3. *Ṛgveda* , I, 164, 34

and answers in the next verse that *Brahman* is the ultimate resort of speech.

iyam vediḥ paro antaḥ pṛthivyā ayam yajño bhuvanasya nābhiḥ
ayam somo vṛṣṇo aśvasya reto brahmāyaṁ vācaḥ paraṁ vyoma ||[4]

The Vedic seer's perennial concern and vision regarding the temporal, poetic and transcendental aspects of the word have found varied and multiple expression in the entire poetry of the Vedas. Sometimes it is through the most philosophical and direct diction as in the Vāgāmbhṛṇī Sūkta (X, 125), where the *vāk* is described as immanent in the entire cosmic force and functioning as the power of the supreme and is still beyond it.[5]

At other places it is through mythical and poetic symbology as in Jñānasūkta, or the hymns of Bṛhaspati, (the lord of Bṛhatī, the *vāk*) or through the hymn of *saramā* etc. Then there are most symbolic hymns of Vāmadeva on the concept of *vāk*. Special reference could be made to the last hymn of the fourth *Maṇḍala*. We are taking in this paper the references from the *Ṛgveda* where the poets have woven the image of Sarasvatī, which means literally the dynamic, moving and creative speech representing knowledge and consciousness.

In the *Ṛgveda*, only two hymns are entirely addressed to Sarasvatī. In other three hymns we find three verses in each hymn, i.e. total nine verses addressed to Sarasvatī. In other eight verses in eight separate hymns (mostly *Āpri* hymns), Sarasvatī is delineated mostly alongwith *Iḍā* and *Bhāratī* and in one verse she pairs with Sarasvān or Sūrya. To start with,

---

4. Ibid., I, 164, 35

5. *paro divā para enā pṛthivyaitāvatī mahinā saṁ babhūva* |

— Ibid., X, 125, 8

in the first *Maṇḍala* of the *Ṛgveda,* the last three verses of the third *sūkta* present a charming image of Sarasvatī.[6]

All the epithets used here for Sarasvatī are very significant. The name Sarasvatī symbolizes the dynamic flow of knowledge or luminosity or consciousness that is purifying or Sarasvatī is *pāvakā* as she voices purity[7] — sings all that is pure.

'Vajena Vājinīvatī' symbolises the prosperous and nourishing aspect as well as the luminous and enlightening aspect of Sarasvatī as *Vāja* means both *Anna* and immortality as well as vigour, joy and even heaven.[8] Then Sarasvatī is called *dhiyāvasuḥ* and according to Sāyaṇācārya, she is the cause of the wealth achieved through *karma*. The *Aitareya Āraṇyaka* (1.1.4) says "may she desire, may she lead our *yajña*";[9] *yajña* indeed is the basic paradigm for any creative act.

The inspirer of charming and truthful words,[10] she awakens the thinking ones. Sarasvatī indeed supports and sustains the

---

6. *pāvakā naḥ sarasvatī vājebhirvājinīvatī,*
yajñaṁ vaṣṭu dhiyāvasuḥ ।
codayitrī sunṛtānāṁ cetantī sumatīnām,
yajñaṁ dadhe sarasvatī ।
maho arṇaḥ sarasvatī pra cetayati ketunā,
dhiyo viśvā vi rājati । — Ibid., I, 3, 10-12

7. *pāvaḥ śudhiḥ* । *pāvaṁ kāyatīti pāvakaḥ. 'kai, gai, rai śabde'* ।

8. *amṛto 'annaṁ vai vājaḥ* — *Jaiminīya Brāhmaṇa,* 2, 193.
vīryaṁ vai vājaḥ — *Śatapatha Brāhmaṇa,* 3, 3, 4, 7.
somo vai vājaḥ — *Maitrāyaṇi Saṁhitā,* 4, 5, 4.
vājo vai svargo lokaḥ — *Gopatha Brāhmaṇa,* 2, 5, 8.

9. *yajñaṁ vaṣṭu dhiyāvasuriti vāgvai dhiyāvasuḥ* ।

10. *sutarām ūnayati apriyamiti sūn iti priyamucyate* ।
tacca tadṛtaṁ satyaṁ ceti sunṛtam ॥

yajña. With knowledge, Sarasvatī inspires great movement or achievement. This goddess of speech is indeed the all performing seer, by her is everything accomplished.[11]

Three verses (16-18) of the 41st hymn of the 2nd Maṇḍala are addressed to Sarasvatī where she is called the best of mothers, the best of the divine ones and the best of the illuminating or revealing ones.[12]

Śaunaka says about the sixty-first hymn of the 6th Maṇḍala in the *Ṛgvidhāna* (2.295) that a person who recites this *sūkta* in the morning after purifying himself becomes expert in speech and wisdom.[13]

The main idea of this hymn is that Sarasvatī cannot stand any fraud, cheating, deceit or selfishness. What goes well with the goddess of knowledge or speech is honesty, straightforwardness, truth and austerity, i.e., *satya* and *tapas*. The *Brāhmaṇa* text defines *tapas* as *svam dadātiti tapaḥ*.[14] She makes even heaven subservient to a person who is of giving nature

---

11. *vāgvai viśvakarmmarṣi vācā hīdaṁ sarvaṁ kṛtam* ।
— *Śatapatha Brāhmaṇa* 8. 1. 2. 9.

12. The epithet 'Nadītame' derived from Nad (enumerated in *Kṣīrataraṅgiṇī* as one of the 34 roots meaning, to reveal or illuminate) would mean the 'Illuminating One' or derived from √Nad (*śabde*) would mean the best speech.

13. *iyamityetadādyaṁ tu sūktaṁ sārasvataṁ japet,*
dvijaḥ prātaḥ śucirbhūtvā vāgmī bhavati buddhimān ।

14. *etat vāva tapo yatsvaṁ dadāti* — *Kapiṣṭhalakaṭha Saṁhitā*, 37, 1.
etat khalu vāva tapa ityāhuryaḥ svaṁ dadātīti
— *Taittirīya Saṁhitā*, 6, 1, 6, 3.
tasmādu tameva tapastapyamānaṁ manyante yo dadat
— *Jaiminīya Brāhmaṇa* 1, 287.

though devoid of strength, but she completely annihilates a person who is given to self-indulgence and mercenary pursuits.[15]

With the strong waves of illumination, Sarasvatī brings down the high mountains of hindering ignorance, she indeed destroys the distances (*pārāvatāghnī*). The seer prays to Sarasvatī to kill those who talk ill of the bright ones and destroy the progeny of the deceitful sorcerer.[16] In all our battles just as we need valour, we also need intelligence, information and knowledge. This is beautifully presented:

> "In the battle where all wealth is at stake, one calls upon you, O Sarasvatī, as upon Indra. Moreover like Pūṣan you protect us in all the battles and give us wealth to enjoy."[17]

The fierce aspect of "word" is well known and in the following verse Sarasvatī is described as *Ghorā* and *Vṛtrāghnī*. Her valour is unlimited and her pure luminosity is all-pervasive and its strength is manifest in the flowing sound of words.[18]

---

15. *iyamadadād rabhasamṛṇacyutaṁ divodāsaṁ vadhryaśvāya dāśuṣe* ।
yā śaśvantamācakhādāvasaṁ paṇiṁ tā te dātrāṇi tviṣā sarasvati ।
— *Ṛgveda*, VI, 61, 1

16. *sarasvati devanido ni barhaya prajāṁ viśvasya bṛsayasya māyinaḥ* ।
— Ibid., VI, 61, 3

17. *yastvā devi sarasvatyupabrūte dhane hite* । *indraṁ na vṛtratūrye* ।
tvaṁ devi sarasvatyavā vājeṣu vājini । *radā pūṣeva naḥ sanim* ।
— Ibid., VI, 61, 5-6

18. *uta syā naḥ sarasvatī ghorā hiraṇyavartaniḥ* ।
vṛtraghnī vaṣṭi suṣṭutim ।
yasyā ananto ahrutastveṣaścariṣṇurarṇavaḥ ।
amaścarati roruvat ।
— Ibid., VI, 61, 7-8

This fierce or the cruel aspect of the word is dwelt upon in the *Brāhmaṇas* at length. Says the *Aitareya Brāhmaṇa* that the speech is a thunderbolt.[19]

The *Taittirīya Āraṇyaka* (4, 2, 1) delineates this aspect in a very interesting manner:

"These indeed are the cruel forms of speech (when one says) — *khat, phat, jahi, chindi, bhindi, handhi* and *kaṭ*," (All these mean to strike or leave or break, or cut etc).

Then the seer is giving expression to the charming, poetic and musical aspect of the word and calls Sarasvatī as the dear among the dear ones.[20]

> May we sing the glory of Sarasvatī, the dearest among the dear ones, adored by the ancient seers, endowed with seven sisters.

She has seven sisters and these are the seven metres. Rhythm indeed is the quality of thinking and thoughtful speech and specially when we talk of the poetic speech which is created at the moment of aesthetic experience of the poet who conceives lyricism in the inner feeling of consciousness and joy. Musicality lends a magic; French poet Mallarme has likened it to an incantation. The Vedic poet says at another place: *tam sapta rebhā abhi saṁ namante*. These *sapta* (seven or flowing *Saraṇaśīla*) melodies move with words impregnated with the poetic vision. The words in fact get moulded with the rhythm of music resounding in the poet's heart and are automatically fused with that music. In the later Indian poetic tradition and

---

19. *vajra eva vāk — Aitareya Brāhmaṇa*, 2, 21.
vajrastena yattriṣṭubvajrastenā yadvāk — Ibid., 2.16
vāgghi śastram — Ibid; 3, 44.

20. *uta naḥ priyā priyāsu saptasvasā sujuṣṭā* ।
sarasvatī stomyā bhūt ॥ — *Ṛgveda* 6, 61, 10

thought, the relation of various *kāvyarasas* with the different musical *rāgas* has been discussed. There are fifty-seven synonyms of speech in the *Nighaṅṭu* and among them the words *Dhārā, Gandharvī* etc., point to this aspect of words. In the next verse is described the all-pervading sārasvata light.

'She has indeed fitted the extensive regions of earth as well as the mid-sky with her lustre. May she protect us from all our enemies.'[21]

She is called *ṛtāvarī, mahimnā mahinā* and *bṛhatī*. She is of course eulogised by a person desirous of knowledge.[22] As pointed out before, the seer poet Vasiṣṭha has eulogised Sarasvatī in the 95th hymn of the seventh *Maṇḍala*. It has six verses of which one is addressed to Sarasvatī. One could read it as the delineation of a moving, pure and nourishing river with its flowing water or as an invocation of the Vāgdevī Sarasvatī with her treasures of wisdom and inspiration leading mankind on the path of creativity.[23]

Direct meaning referring to a river is very clear and the epithets can also go with the goddess of knowledge provided we understand the radical metaphor inherent in the words through the poetic tool of etymology or *Nirukti*. For instance the word *ghṛta* would mean flowing luminosity as it is derived from the root *ghṛ* (*Dīptikṣaraṇayoḥ*). The epithet *subhagā* is used

---

21. *āpapruṣī pārthivānyuru rajo antarikṣam* ।
sarasvatī nidaspātu ॥ — Ibid., 6, 61, 11

22. *pra yā mahimnā mahināsu cekite dyumnebhiranyā apasāmapastamā* ।
ratha iva bṛhatī bibhvane kṛtopastutyā cikituṣā sarasvatī ॥
— Ibid., 6 , 61, 13

23. *ekācetatsarasvatī nadīnāṁ śuciryatī giribhya ā samudrāt* ।
rāyaścetantī bhuvanasya bhūrerghṛtaṁ payo duduhe nāhuṣāya ॥
— Ibid., VII, 95, 2

twice and the poet says "we may stay under your shelter as under a tree, the dearest one."[24]

And in the end says the poet:

> O Subhage Sarasvati, here Vasiṣṭha has opened both your doors of *ṛta*, i.e. has revealed the duality aspect of all cosmic functioning, the ultimate truth of all analysis of temporal existence. O the fair one, you prosper and give to your singer wealth, dynamism and light. Protect us always with your protection.[25]

The seventeenth hymn of the tenth *Maṇḍala* addressed to different deities has three verses (seventh to ninth) dedicated to Sarasvatī, wherein the poet is suggesting that the stream of knowledge is constantly flowing which our parents and forfathers have enjoyed and we always seek that whenever any creative project is undertaken. Good people with divine inclinations call upon this Goddess of knowledge, the people engaged in good deeds or *sukṛta* invoke her. She rewards the selfless person who offers everything. She is asked to give the nourishing wealth.[26] *Vāk*, in its four forms as *Vaikhari* (spoken word), *Madhyamā* (word in the thinking process) *Paśyanti* (seeric or poetic word) and *parā* (the transcendental word or

---

24. *tava śarmanpriyatame dadhānā upa stheyāma śaraṇaṁ na vṛkṣam* ।
— Ibid., VII, 95, 5

25. *ayamu te sarasvati vasiṣṭho dvārāvṛtasya subhage vyāvaḥ* ।
vardha śubhre stuvate rāsi vājān yūyaṁ pāta svastibhiḥ sadā naḥ ॥
— Ibid., VII, 95, 6

26. *sarasvatīṁ devayanto havante sarasvatīmadhvare tāyamāne* ।
sarasvatīṁ sukṛto ahvayanta sarasvatī dāśuṣe vāryaṁ dāt ॥
sarasvati yā sarathaṁ yayātha svadhābhirdevi pitṛbhirmadantī ।
āsadyāsmin barhiṣi mādayasvānamīvā iṣa ā dhehyasme ॥
sarasvatīṁ yāṁ pitaro havante dakṣiṇā yajñamabhinakṣamāṇāḥ ।
sahasrārghamilo atra bhāgaṁ rāyaspoṣaṁ yajamāneṣu dhehi ॥
— Ibid., X, 17, 7-9

śabda brahma) represents indeed consciousness in its manifest and unmanifest forms.

Vāk has been delineated as the power (*svam* or *mahimā*) of Prajāpati or Brahmā and his only associate at the time of creation. *Vāk* indeed is the power of the creator.[27] Since power cannot be conceived as separate from the possessor of power, *vāk* has been called *Brahman* in the Vedic literature.[28] Thus *vāk* or Sarasvatī symbolises the entire creative reality in all its forms.

This very idea is beautifully presented in the well known prayer to Sarasvatī with her eightfold forms as *Lakṣmī, Medhā, Dharā, Puṣṭi, Gaurī, Tuṣṭi, Prabhā* and *Dhṛti* pointing to beauty and prosperity, co-ordinating intelligence, sustaining knowledge, nourishing ideas, the correct knowledge of words, satisfying aspect of knowledge, enlightenment and stability and suggesting its all-pervasiveness and creative dynamics.

lakṣmī medhā dharā puṣṭirgourī tuṣṭiḥ prabhā dhṛtiḥ
etābhiḥ pāhi tanubhiraṣṭābhirmāṁ sarasvatī

May that Sarasvatī protect us.

---

27. *Vāgvāsya* (*Prajāpateḥ*) *Svomahimā* — *Śatapatha Brāhamṇa* 2, 2, 4, 4; 1, 4, 2, 17

28. *Vāgbrahma* — *Gopatha Brāhmaṇa*. 1, 2, 10; *Vāgvai Brahma* — *Aitareya Brāhmaṇa* 6, 3; *Prajāpatirhivāk* — *Taittirīya Brāhmaṇa*, 1, 3, 4, 5; *Vāgvai Prajāpatiḥ* — *Śatapatha Brāhmaṇa* 5, 1, 5, 6; *yā sā vāgbrahmaiva tat* — *Jaiminīyopaniṣad Brāhmaṇa* 2, 13, 2.

7

Vedic Mantra-Vijñāna

In the Light of the Traditional Method of Vedic recitation

Dayanand Bhargava

EVEN though Yāskācārya devoted a full sub-chapter of the first chapter of *Nirukta* to refutation of the view of Kautsa that Vedic *mantra*s have no meaning *"Anarthakā hi mantrāḥ"*[1] yet as late as Sāyaṇa, the commentators had to repeatedly argue that mere recitation of the Vedic mantras is not sufficient; their meaning should also be comprehended, and that, therefore, an attempt to comment on the Vedas is justified.[2] It shows that throughout such a long period, there has been a strong lobby which holds that mere recitation of Vedic *mantra*s with proper accentuation is enough and one need not take the trouble to go into their meaning. On the face of it, it appears to be an absurd idea that Vedic *mantra*s, having such deep and beautiful meaning, should have no meaning, or even if they have any, one need not go into them. On a closer look, however, it could be seen that even if we accept, as Yāska

---

1. *Nirukta,* 1.5.15.
2. (i) *Svādhyāyo 'dhyetavyaḥ* (*Taittirīya Āraṇyaka,* 2.15) — *ityadhyayanaṁ vidhīyate, paṭhamātrsyādhyayanaśabdavācyatvenārthāvabodhsyā vihitvād vedavyākhyanamayuktamiti cet na, vidherbodhaparyavasāyitvāt.*
   — *Taittirīya Saṁhitā Bhāṣya Bhūmikā,* p. 4

asserts, that full fruit accrues to him only who knows the meaning of the Vedic *mantras*, yet the tradition holds that mere recitation of them with proper accentuation has its own justification as yielding the desired result. This view predominantly establishes the importance of traditional method of Vedic recitation.

It is a known fact that words, recited in a particular way, produce particular vibrations. These vibrations bring about effects of no mean value. It was in view of this fact, that from Kautsa down till to-day, the tradition has been insisting that irrespective of the meaning of the *mantra*, even its recitation with correct accentuation can bring about the desired result. Not only that, its reverse is also true — the incorrect accentuation leads to undesired result even if the reciter has the desired result in his mind:

Mantro duṣṭaḥ svarato varṇato vā
Mithyāprayukto na tamarthamāha
Sa vāgvajro yajamānaṁ hinasti
Yathendraśatruḥ svarato 'parādhāt.

Such is the vital importance of the correct recitation. This is why the Vedic students spend so much time in learning the correct recitation even today. They go on enjoying such recitation for hours together, without caring about the meaning of the *mantra* which they recite. The Veda as word is all important for them.

A question arises as to whether the belief that mere correct recitation of Vedic *mantra* will yield the desired result is based on some logical ground or it is merely a matter of faith. To answer this question, one has to go into the origin of the *mantras* of the four Vedas. *Śāṅkhyāyana Brāhmaṇa* says that the creator fashioned *Ṛk* from Agni, *Yajus* from Vāyu and *Sāma* from Āditya.[3] As this is repeated not only by the *Śatapatha-Brāhmaṇa*[4] but by Manu also,[5] we can safely conclude that the tradition is unanimous in this regard. As regards the *Atharvaveda*, it is declared to be associated with Soma.[6]

Again, it is asserted that from *Ṛk* are born the solid and visible subjects, from *Yajuṣ* are born all the movements and from *Sāma* is born all lusture whereas the Brahma-veda, i.e. *Atharvaveda* gives birth to all.[7] Now, as Vāyu and Āditya are also the subtler and the subtlest forms of Agni; the first three Vedas, connected with Agni, Vāyu and Āditya are *āgneya;*[8] whereas the Atharvaveda, connected as it is with Soma, forms a different category of its own. It is also clear that Agni, Vāyu and Āditya are the presiding deities of earth, atmosphere and the upper region, whereas Atharvaveda is connected with the fourth region of *āpaḥ* or Soma.[9]

---

3. *So 'gnerevarco 'srjata, vāyoryajūṁṣi, adityāt sāmāni.*
— *Śāṅkhyāyana Brāhmaṇa*, 6.10.

4. *Agnerrgvedo vāyoryajurvedāḥ suryātsāmavedaḥ.*
— *Śatapatha Brāhmaṇa*, 11.5.83.

5. *Agnivāyuravibhyastu trayam brahma sanātanam*
dudoha yajñasiddhyarthaṁ ṛgyajuḥsāmalakṣaṇam. — *Manusmṛti*, 1.23.

6. *Somamayo hyāyam Vedāḥ.* — *Gopatha Brāhmaṇa*, Pūrvaṛcikā, 2.1.

7. *Ṛgbhyo jātam sarvaśo mūrtimāhuḥ*
sarvā gatiryājuṣī haiva śaśvat
sarvaṁ tejaḥ sāmarūpyam ha śaśvat
sarvaṁ hecdaṁ brahmaṇā haiva śṛṣṭam. — *Taittirīya Brāhmaṇa*, 3.2.9.

8. *Apyete uttare jyotiṣī agnī uchyete.* — *Nirukta*, 7.4.

9. *ṛcāmagnirdaivatam, yajuṣāṁ vāyurdaivatam*
antarikṣasthānam, sāmnāmādityadaivatam
atharvaṇāñcandramā daivatamāpaḥ sthānam. — *Gopatha Brāhmaṇa* to be read in conjunction with: *asti vai caturtho loka āpoloka* and *āpaḥ somaḥ.* — *Śatapatha Brāhmaṇa*, 7.1.1.22.

These four Vedas thus represent each as an aspect of *adhibhūta, adhidaiva* and *adhyātma* as is clear from the following table:

Veda	*Adhibhūta*	*Adhidaiva*	*Adhyātma*
Ṛk	Bhūḥ	Agni	Vaiśvānara
Yajuḥ	Bhuvaḥ	Vāyu	Taijasa
Sāma	Svaḥ	Āditya	Prājña
Atharva	Āpoloka	Candramā	Turīya

As there is nothing beyond the trinity of *adhibhūta, adhidaiva* and *adhyātma,* we can safely conclude that everything is included in the Veda: *sarvam vedāt prasidhyati.*

Now, we have to examine as to whether the difference in method of recitation of the four Vedas really represents the sense which we get from the above description. We have to actually listen to the traditional reciters of the four Vedas to get the answer. It is worth mentioning here that at this point of presentation, a live recitation from the four Vedas was arranged so that the audience could actually feel the basic difference in their accents.

As we listen to Ṛgvedic *mantra,* we would find that the words are recited in a way that there is the least gap between one word and the other, suggesting that we are dealing with something solid. The voice is low as if connected with the earth. The recitation of the *Yajurveda* is done in a prolonged way so much so that even *Om* becomes *Om-a,* suggesting that we are dealing with movements, the voice becomes still louder, as if to reach the middle region. In the recitation of *Sāmaveda,* the voice becomes still louder suggesting that we are dealing with the third region which is the uppermost and hiatus between one word and the other becomes so great as if we feel the lusture or light moving at a great speed. The words are prolonged so much so that even *Agni* becomes *Ognāyī*. Naturally in such a case the meaning of the word becomes irrelevant; only the word becomes all important. The recitation of the *Atharvaveda* is so calm and cooling as if Soma is flowing. This is how the difference of method of recitation of the four Vedas has a logical or scientific basis.

A question may arise here as to what shall happen to a *mantra*, which occurs in the Veda, whose connection is said to be with one deity and the *mantra* belongs to another deity, i.e. terrestrial deities being addressed in *Yajurveda* or *Sāmaveda* or atmospheric deities being addressed in *Ṛgveda* or *Yajurveda*. The answer to this question lies in triplication (*trivṛtkaraṇa*) of *Chāndogyopaniṣad*, which says that no element is found at the mundane level without the admixture of the other element. If Agni is praised, for example in the *Ṛgveda*, both the deity and the Veda being terrestrial, *Agni* is the predominating deity in that case, but if it is invoked in the other Vedas, it assumes a subordinate position in comparison to the deity which belongs to the region to which the Veda belongs. Not only that, it assumes a different name. Similar is the case of all the three deities. This is shown in the following table:

Name in the terrestrial region	*Name in the atmospheric region*	*Name in the upper region*
Agni (in its own region)	*Pāvaka*	*Śuci*
Mātariśvā	*Vāyu* (in its own region)	*Pavitra*
Vāsava	*Marutvān*	*Āditya* (in its own region)

In the terminology of *yajña*, a deity is Agni in its own region, the other two deities are absorbed by it as oblations of Soma. Thus the deities oblige each other:

parasparaṁ bhāvayantaḥ

This also solves the problem of repetition of the same *mantra* in more than one Veda. For example, if a *mantra* is recited in the Ṛgvedic fashion, it has different effect than that created by reciting the same *mantra* in the, say, Sāmavedic fashion. The repetition of the same *mantra* in different Vedas is not something superfluous but has its own significance.

For those, who care only about the meaning, this type of repetition may be irritating or at least superfluous, but not so for one who does *svādhyāya* in the traditional way while performing *Brahmayajña*.

Giving due importance to the recitation even without knowing the meaning, Pāṇini has placed on equal footing one who knows the meaning and the other who recites: *tadadhīte tadveda* (4.2.59). Thus he has given due importance to *śabdaveda*.

This also explains why the order of words (=*ānupūrvī*) is fixed in the Vedas and cannot be changed. In fact, the answer as to why this is so, lies in the fact that the change of order of words would change the effect of the vibration created by them. Same will be the case, if a word is replaced by its synonym. This, of course, does not mean that *mantra*s have no meaning, but it does mean that even Veda as a word (=*śabdaveda*) has its importance, independent of its meaning. Whereas the interpreters of the Vedas' meaning do deserve our respect, the *Vedapāṭhī*s, who are masters of the *śabdaveda*, are no less respectable.

8

वैदिक स्वर-विज्ञान

व्रजबिहारी चौबे

सृष्टि में सर्वत्र व्यापक तत्त्वों में से वाक् तत्व अन्यतम है। यह अव्यय ब्रह्म की पांच कलाओं में से एक है। दिव्या वाक्, अमृता वाक्, सहस्राक्षरा वाक् आदि के रूप में सर्वत्र व्याप्त है। मन्त्र वाङ्मय में उदधृत वाक् के 57 नामों का उल्लेख निघण्टु में मिलता है जो वाक् के विभिन्न रूपों के द्योतक हैं। शतपथ ब्राह्मण में ऐन्द्रवायवग्रह ग्रहण के प्रसङ्ग में वाक् के अनिरुक्त और निरुक्त दो रूपों का उल्लेख आख्यान के माध्यम से किया गया है। आख्यान इस प्रकार है – इन्द्र ने वृत्र को मारने के लिए वज्र से प्रहार तो किया किन्तु डरकर कि वह कहीं जीवित न रह गया हो और अगर वह जीवित होगा तो उसे वह मार डालेगा, इसलिये उसने अपने आप को छिपा लिया। देवता भी इन्द्र के छिप जाने पर भाग खड़े हुये। देवों ने परस्पर विचार किया कि वृत्र मरा या नहीं, इसको हममें से कोई नहीं जानता। इसलिये उन्होंने वायु से कहा कि वह सर्वत्र भ्रमण करता है, इसलिये वह पता लगाये कि वृत्र जीवित है या नहीं। यदि जीवित होगा तो आप अतिशीघ्रगामी होने के कारण वापस लौट आओगे। वायु ने कहा कि इससे उसको क्या लाभ होगा? देवों ने कहा कि वषट्कारपूर्वक जो आहुति सोमयाग में दी जायेगी वह केवल आप की होगी। वायु वृत्र की मृत्यु का पता लगाने के लिये गये और पता लगाकर आकर देवताओं को बताया कि वृत्र मर गया है, आप लोगों को जो करना है, करें। देवताओं ने उस सोम का एकदेवत्य, द्विदेवत्य, बहुदेवत्य रूप में आपस में बंटवारा किया। किन्तु वह सोम चूँकि पहले वृत्र के अधिकार में था, इसलिये अपवित्र होने से दुर्गन्धयुक्त और आहुति के अयोग्य हो गया। फिर देवों ने वायु से कहा कि वह सोम को पवित्र करे। वायु ने फिर पूछा इससे उसको क्या लाभ होगा ? देवों ने कहा कि वह ग्रहपात्र, जिसमें रखकर सोम की आहुति दी जायेगी, उसके नाम से ख्यात होगा। वायु ने देवों की बात मान ली, किन्तु उनसे इस कार्य में सहयोग करने के लिए

कहा। देवों के सहयोग से वायु ने दुर्गन्धयुक्त सोम को पवित्र कर दिया। जो दुर्गन्ध था उसे पुरुष, अश्व आदि पशुओं के शरीर में स्थापित किया। सोम, जो अब शुद्ध और दुर्गन्धरहित था, देवताओं के भक्षण के योग्य हो गया। किन्तु जो सोमपात्र नानादेवत्य था अब केवल वायव्य कहलाने लगा, क्योंकि वायु ने वृत्र-विनाश की सूचना देकर तथा सोम के दूषित गन्ध को हटाकर विशिष्ट रसगन्ध युक्त बनाकर यह वर भी देवताओं से प्राप्त कर लिया था कि प्रथम वषट्कार भी वायु को मिलेगा। सम्पूर्ण यज्ञ का सम्बन्ध वायु के साथ हो जाने पर इन्द्र ने विचार किया कि यज्ञ का बहुत सा भाग वायु को प्राप्त हो गया। इसलिये उसने वायु के भाग में सम्मिलित होने की इच्छा की। उसने वायु से कहा कि वह उसे भी अपने भाग में सम्मिलित कर ले। वायु ने कहा आप को सम्मिलित करने से मुझे क्या लाभ होगा। फिर इन्द्र ने कहा कि तुम्हारे अधीन जो अनिरुक्त वाक् है वह मेरे सम्मिलित हो जाने से निरुक्त हो जायेगी। इन्द्र के ऐसा कहने पर वायु ने इन्द्र को अपने भाग में सम्मिलित करना स्वीकार कर लिया। इन्द्र के सम्मिलित होने से अब सोमग्रह जो पहले वायव्य कहलाता था ऐन्द्रवायवग्रह नाम से ख्यात हुआ। इन्द्र ने वायु से आधा भाग मांगा, किन्तु वह उसे आधा भाग देना नहीं चाहता था। दोनों में विवाद हो गया। विवाद करते हुये वे प्रजापति के पास पहुंचे। प्रजापति ने सोमग्रह के दो समान अर्धभाग कर एक अर्धभाग की ओर सङ्केत करते हुये वायु से कहा कि यह तुम्हारा है। दूसरे भाग के भी पुनः दो भाग करके प्रजापति ने कहा यह एक अर्धभाग वायु का है और दूसरा इन्द्र का है। इस प्रकार सोमग्रह का चतुर्थ भाग ही इन्द्र को प्राप्त हुआ इसलिये यह ऐन्द्रवायव्य ग्रह ऐन्द्रतुरीय कहलाने लगा। प्रजापति के इस विभाजन से रुष्ट होकर इन्द्र ने कहा कि मैंने जो वाक् को निरुक्त बनाने का वरदान दिया था, वहां भी वायव्यवाक् का चतुर्थभाग ही निरुक्त होगा, शेष तीन भाग अनिरुक्त ही रहेंगे। इसलिये वाक् का जो भाग मनुष्य में है वह निरुक्त होगा तथा वाक् का जो भाग पशुओं, पक्षियों तथा क्षुद्र सरीसृप आदि में होगा वह अनिरुक्त होगा। इस प्रकार वाक् के चार भाग में जो तीन भाग हैं वे अनिरुक्त हैं जिन्हें क्रमशः पशु, पक्षी तथा क्षुद्र कीड़े-मकोड़े बोलते हैं। वाक् का एक चतुर्थांश भाग ही निरुक्त है जिसे मनुष्य बोलते हैं। याज्ञवल्क्य इस अनिरुक्त वाक् के तीन और निरुक्त वाक् के एक भाग में स्थित होने की पुष्टि में ऋग्वेद के निम्न मन्त्र को उद्धृत करते हैं—

> **चत्वारि वाक् परिमिता पदानि तानि विदुः ब्राह्मणा ये मनीषिणः।**
> **गुहा त्रीणि निहिता नेङ्गयन्ति तुरीयं वाचो मनुष्या वदन्ति॥** (*ऋ.वे.,* 1.164.45)

इसी अनिरुक्ता तथा निरुक्ता वाक् का अव्याकृता वाक् तथा व्याकृता वाक् के रूप में उल्लेख तैत्तिरीय संहिता में मिलता है –

वाग्वै पराच्यव्याकृताऽवदत् ते देवा इन्द्रमब्रुवन्निमां नो वाचं व्याकुर्विति सोऽब्रवीद्वरं वृणै मह्यं वायवे च सह गृह्याता इति, तस्मादैन्द्रवायव सह गृह्यते, तामिन्द्रो मध्यतोऽवक्रम्य व्याकरोत् , तस्मादियं व्याकृता वागुद्यते। (*तै.सं.* 604.7.5)

इसी प्रकार के अनेक आख्यान, उपाख्यान वाक् की उत्पत्ति तथा उसके व्याकृत तथा अव्याकृत रूप के विषय में वैदिक वाङ्मय में मिलते हैं। मनुष्य भाषा के रूप में जिस वाक् का प्रयोग करता है, वह अक्षरात्मक, पदात्मक तथा वाक्यात्मक है। वर्ण, शब्द और वाक्य किसी भी भाषा के संघटक तत्त्व हैं। वर्णों के संयोग से शब्द तथा पदों के संयोग से वाक्य का गठन होता है। वर्णों का उच्चारण किस प्रकार किया जायेगा इस विषय में प्राचीन भाषाशास्त्रियों ने पर्याप्त विचार किये थे। वर्णों का उच्चारण जिसकी सहायता से होता है, उसकी स्वर संज्ञा है। '**स्वयं राजन्ते**' या '**स्वर्यन्ते उच्चार्यन्ते इति स्वराः**' इस व्युत्पत्ति के अनुसार किसी भी वर्ण को उच्चरित कराने वाला तत्त्व स्वर है। प्राचीन भारतीय भाषा वैज्ञानिकों ने प्रत्येक ध्वनि के साथ मिले हुये स्वरभाग को एक रसायनशास्त्री की भांति अलग करके उपस्थित किया। इस प्रकार अ, आ, इ, ई, उ, ऊ, ऋ, ॠ, ए, ऐ, ओ, औ ध्वनियां स्पष्ट रूप से सामने आईं। ये ही ध्वनियां हैं जिनके द्वारा कोई भी वर्ण उच्चरित होता है, इसलिये इन्हीं को स्वर कहा जाता है। सामान्य रूप से वर्णों के उच्चारण का जहां तक सम्बन्ध है, इन्हीं स्वरों की आवश्यकता पड़ती है। किन्तु इन स्वरों के भी कुछ अपने धर्म हैं जो धर्मी के नाम पर स्वर ही कहे जाते हैं। ये स्वर-धर्म हैं – **उदात्त, अनुदात्त, स्वरित** एवं **प्रचय**। जब से उदात्त, अनुदात्त स्वरधर्मों के लिये स्वर शब्द का प्रयोग शुरू हुआ तब से स्वरों के लिये अक्षर, अच् आदि शब्द व्यवहृत होने लगे, यद्यपि स्वर शब्द भी पूर्व अर्थ में चलता रहा। किन्तु यह बात उल्लेखनीय है कि अ-आ आदि अच् संज्ञक जो स्वरध्वनियां थीं उनका पदगत या वाक्यगत अर्थ के निर्धारण में कोई उपयोग नहीं था, जबकि उदात्तादि स्वरों की अर्थनिर्धारण में महत्त्वपूर्ण भूमिका थी। ऋग्वेद के एक मन्त्र में विद्वानों द्वारा बोली जाने वाली वाक् की तुलना छननी से छाने हुये सक्तु के साथ की गई है और स्पष्ट रूप से यह कहा गया है कि उस वाक् में हमेशा लक्ष्मी निवास करती है।[1] वाक् में लक्ष्मी के सदा निवास का अभिप्राय उस वाक् के अन्तर्गत निहित अर्थ से है। इस शब्दार्थ की खोज में विद्वानों द्वारा अनेक प्रयास किये गये। वैदिक परम्परा में किये गये इन प्रयासों में से स्वर एक महत्त्वपूर्ण प्रयास था। तत्कालीन आचार्यों ने प्रत्येक पद के उच्चारण में उसकी प्रकृति के अनुसार किस वर्ण का क्या स्वरधर्म होगा, इस बात का निर्धारण बड़े परिश्रम से किया था। इसी प्रयास के परिणामस्वरूप वेदाध्ययन के

1. सक्तुमिव तितउना पुनन्तो यत्र धीरा मनसा वाचमक्रत।
अत्रा सखायः सख्यानि जानते भद्रैषां लक्ष्मीर्निहिताधि वाचि।। — *ऋ.वे.* 10.71.2

क्षेत्र में एक सुनिश्चित स्वर-विज्ञान प्रतिष्ठित हुआ। साक्षात्कृतधर्मा ऋषियों के अन्तःकरण से जब मन्त्र प्रथम बार निःसृत हुये, उस समय उनमें कौन स्वर प्रयुक्त हुये थे, इसके विषय में हम कुछ भी नहीं कह सकते। भवभूति ने जो यह कहा कि लौकिक विद्वानों द्वारा अपनी वाणी में अर्थ को सम्मुख रखकर तद्बोधक शब्द का प्रयोग किया जाता है, किन्तु ऋषियों की वाणी में यह नियम नहीं। ऋषियों ने जिस किसी भी अभिप्राय से शब्द का प्रयोग किया, वहां उनका अभिप्राय ही अर्थ बन गया। उनकी वाणी में किसी पूर्व-निर्धारित अर्थ की सत्ता नहीं थी। अर्थ उनके द्वारा निःसृत वाणी का अनुगामी था, उनकी वाणी अर्थ की अनुगामी नहीं थी।[2] किन्तु जब मन्त्रों का एक निश्चित स्वरूप सत्ता में आ गया तब उनके संरक्षण की समस्या आई। इस समस्या के समाधान रूप में उन ऋषियों द्वारा दृष्ट मन्त्रों को उपदेश द्वारा आगे बढ़ाने की श्रुति-परम्परा प्रचलित हुई। इसी श्रुति-परम्परा-क्रम में मन्त्रों का उच्चारण होता रहा। मन्त्रों के व्याख्यान-रूप ब्राह्मण, आरण्यक, उपनिषद् ग्रन्थों की भी वेदवत् मान्यता होने के कारण उनके भी उच्चारण में एक निश्चित स्वर-नियम की परम्परा चली। इतना ही नहीं संहिता, ब्राह्मण, आरण्यक तथा उपनिषदों के विभिन्न प्रकार के पाठ भी उनकी अपनी-अपनी शाखाओं में प्रचलित हुये।

यह परम्परा उत्तर वैदिककाल में उपनिषदों के समय से शुरू हुई। सर्वप्रथम तैत्तिरीय उपनिषद् में शिक्षा नामक वेदाङ्ग के अन्तर्गत प्रतिपाद्य विषय के रूप में वर्ण-स्वर-मात्रा-बल-साम-सन्तान का उल्लेख किया गया। यह उल्लेखनीय है कि यहां पर स्वर पद अच् के अर्थ में नहीं, बल्कि उदात्तादि स्वरधर्मों के लिये है। ऐतरेय आरण्यक के तृतीय आरण्यक में वेदपाठ के तीन रूपों का उल्लेख '**निर्भुज**', '**प्रतृण्ण**' तथा '**उभयमन्तरेण**' के नाम से किया गया है। संहितापाठ, पदपाठ तथा क्रमपाठ की ही ये प्राचीन संज्ञायें हैं। संहितोपनिषद्-ब्राह्मण भी संहिता का विवेचन करता है। यहां तीन प्रकार की संहिताओं का उल्लेख है—देव-संहिता, असुर-संहिता तथा ऋषि-संहिता। समीपस्थ या दूरस्थ व्यक्तियों के द्वारा न सुनी जाती हुई उपांशुरूप में प्रयुज्यमान सर्वपरोक्ष संहिता, देव-संहिता तथा सबके द्वारा श्रूयमाण संहिता असुर-संहिता कहलाती है। जो संहिता कहीं परोक्ष और कहीं आवश्यकतानुसार तार स्वर में उच्चरित होती है, वह 'ऋषि-संहिता' कहलाती है। एक अन्य दृष्टि से भी तीन प्रकार के संहिता-भेद का उल्लेख संहितोपनिषद्-ब्राह्मण करता है। ये तीन संहिता प्रकार हैं – '**देवहू**', '**वाक्शबहू**' तथा '**अमित्रहू**'। देवताओं का आह्वान करने के कारण एक संहिता 'देवहू'

---

2. लौकिकानां हि साधूनामर्थं वागनुवर्तते।
ऋषीणां पुनराद्यानां वाचमर्थोऽनुधावति (*उत्तररास.* 1.10)

कहलाती है। यह मन्द्र स्वर में उच्चरित होती है। जिसमें वर्णों का स्पष्ट उच्चारण नहीं होता, वह बल्बलाकार अस्पष्ट उच्चारण वाली संहिता 'वाक्शबहू-संहिता' कहलाती है। जिस संहिता का आक्रन्दन-निक्रन्दन स्वर में उच्चारण किया जाता है, वह 'अमित्रहू-संहिता' कहलाती है। संहितोपनिषद्-ब्राह्मण सामवेद की गानविधि में प्रयुक्त स्वर का विवेचन प्रस्तुत करता है।

ब्राह्मण, आरण्यक एवं उपनिषदों के समय तक चार वेदों की कई शाखा-संहितायें सत्ता में आ चुकी थीं। इसका प्रमाण एक ही वेद के अन्तर्गत कई-कई ब्राह्मण–आरण्यक एवं उपनिषद् ग्रन्थों की सत्ता है। अपनी-अपनी शाखा में उपलब्ध ग्रन्थों के उच्चारण-विषयक, वैशिष्ट्य के अध्ययन के लिये अनेकों परिषदों की स्थापना हो चुकी थी। इन्हीं परिषदों में अपनी-अपनी प्रचलित परम्परा के स्वर-विषयक सिद्धान्त सर्वप्रथम सुनिश्चित हुये। प्रातिशाख्य ग्रन्थों का प्रणयन हुआ। प्रातिशाख्यों ने अपनी-अपनी संहिता तथा ब्राह्मणों के उच्चारण में प्रयुक्त स्वर-प्रक्रिया का पूर्णरूप से विवेचन किया। अपनी ही शाखा के आचार्यों के बीच स्वर-विषयक कोई मतान्तर था तो उसका भी उन्होंने उल्लेख किया। ऐसा प्रायः उन समान स्थलों के विषय में था जहां उनमें उच्चारण का भेद उन्हें दिखाई पड़ा। इस प्रकार ऋग्वेद के अन्तर्गत विभिन्न शाखाओं में, यजुर्वेद के अन्तर्गत विभिन्न शाखाओं में, सामवेद के अन्तर्गत विभिन्न शाखाओं में तथा अथर्ववेद के अन्तर्गत विभिन्न शाखाओं मे परस्पर उच्चारणगत जो भेद था उसका आकलन प्रातिशाख्यकारों ने बड़े सूक्ष्म रूप से किया। यह उल्लेखनीय है कि स्वर-विषयक जो भेद था वह उच्चारणगत था। प्रातिशाख्यकारों के समय में स्वरविषयक उच्चारण-भेद को प्रदर्शित करने के लिये अनेक पारिभाषिक संज्ञाओं का निर्माण हुआ। ऋग्वेद प्रातिशाख्य **उदात्त, अनुदात्त, स्वरित, प्रचय, उदात्तश्रुति, जात्य, प्रश्लिष्ट-स्वरित, क्षैप्र-स्वरित, अभिनिहित-स्वरित, नियत (अनुदात्त), वैवृत्त, तैरोव्यञ्जन, जात्यवत्, कम्प** आदि का उल्लेख करता है। वाजसनेयि-प्रातिशाख्य इनके अतिरिक्त **तैरोविराम, ताथाभाव्य** संज्ञाओं का प्रयोग करता है। वेद की तत्तत्-शाखा-संहिताओं से सम्बद्ध शिक्षाग्रन्थों में भी स्वरविषयक उच्चारण प्रक्रिया का सूक्ष्म रूप से विवेचन मिलता है। प्रातिशाख्य तथा शिक्षाग्रन्थों के स्वरविषयक विवेचन से यह बात मालूम होती है कि उस समय स्वरों के उच्चारण पर विशेष जोर दिया जाता था। स्वर, अर्थ को प्रभावित करते हैं या नहीं, उसका प्रातिशाख्यों तथा शिक्षाग्रन्थों में बहुत कम विवेचन हुआ है। श्रौतसूत्रों में भी स्वर-विषयक विवेचन मिलता है, किन्तु वह भी मन्त्रोच्चारण के प्रसंग में ही है। ये प्रातिशाख्य तथा शिक्षाग्रन्थ प्राचीन स्वर-शास्त्र के ऊपर प्रामाणिक ग्रन्थ हैं। इनमें स्वरों के उच्चारण के विषय में प्राचीन आचार्यों में जो मतभेद था, उसका भी सम्यक् रूप से उल्लेख मिलता है।

स्वरों में उदात्त, अनुदात्त, स्वरित ही प्रमुख स्वर हैं। इन्हीं को त्रैस्वर्य कहा जाता है। उनके उच्चारण के विषय में प्रातिशाख्य तथा शिक्षा-ग्रन्थों में जो विवेचन मिलता है,[3] वह संक्षेप में इस प्रकार है –

उदात्त – उदात्त को उच्च स्वर माना जाता है। *ऋ॰ प्रा॰* (3.1) के अनुसार इसका उच्चारण 'आयाम'-पूर्वक किया जाता है। आयाम का अर्थ है वायुनिमित्त गात्रों का ऊर्ध्वगमन। इसके द्वारा जो स्वर उच्चरित होता है वह उदात्त है। *तै॰ प्रा॰* (22.9) के अनुसार '**आयामो दारुण्यमणुता खस्येत्युच्चैः कराणि शब्दस्य**' अर्थात् गात्रों की दीर्घता, स्वर की कठिनता तथा कण्ठविवर की संवृत्तता ही वर्ण के उच्च अर्थात् उदात्त के उच्चारण का कारण होती है। उदात्त स्वर के उच्चारण में गात्रों को ऊपर खींचा जाता है, ध्वनि को कठोर बनाया जाता है तथा कण्ठ को अत्यधिक संवृत्त कर दिया जाता है। पाणिनि ने भी 'उच्चैरुदात्तः' के द्वारा उदात्त के उच्चारण का विधान किया है। वाजसनेयि प्रातिशाख्य भी 'उच्चैरुदात्तः' का ही विधान करता है।

अनुदात्त – अनुदात्त को नीच स्वर माना जाता है। *ऋ॰ प्रा॰* (3.1) में इसका उच्चारण 'विश्रम्भ' द्वारा किये जाने का उल्लेख है। 'विश्रम्भ' का अर्थ है वायुनिमित्त गात्रों का अधोगमन। *तै॰ प्रा॰* (22.10) के अनुसार गात्रों की शिथिलता, स्वर की स्निग्धता तथा कण्ठविवर की स्थूलता वर्ण के नीच उच्चारण के कारण होते हैं। *वा॰ प्र॰* (1.109) तथा पाणिनि *'नीचैरनुदात्तः'* (1.2.30) द्वारा अनुदात्त का नीच स्वर में उच्चारण करने का विधान करते हैं। पाणिनि ने एक सन्नतर स्वर का उल्लेख किया है, जिसे *महाभाष्य* (1.2.23) में अनुदात्त से भी निम्नतर एक अनुदात्ततर स्वर कहा गया है। भट्टोजि दीक्षित के अनुसार जिस अनुदात्त के परे उदात्त या स्वतन्त्र स्वरित हो, वह अनुदात्त अनुदात्ततर होता है।

स्वरित – उदात्त, अनुदात्त की तरह स्वरित भी एक स्वतन्त्र स्वर है, किन्तु यह उदात्त-अनुदात्त के समाहार से उत्पन्न होता है। इसके प्रारम्भ की अर्धमात्रा उदात्त तथा अन्त की शेष मात्रा अनुदात्त होती है। पाणिनि ने इसी का उल्लेख '**तस्यादित उदात्तमर्धह्रस्वम्**' सूत्र के द्वार किया है। स्वरित के स्वरूप के विषय में प्रातिशाख्यों, शिक्षाग्रन्थों तथा उनके भाष्यकारों में पर्याप्त मतभेद है।[4] स्वरित स्वर के दो रूप दिखाई पड़ते हैं। एक तो उदात्त-अनुदात्त का समाहार रूप जिसको '**समाहारः स्वरितः**' के

---

3. विशेष विवरण के लिये द्रष्टव्य, डॉ॰ व्रजबिहारी चौबे, *'वैदिक स्वरबोध'*, होशियारपुर, द्वि॰ सं॰, 2004
4. स्वरित के स्वरूप के लिये द्र॰, डॉ॰ व्रजबिहारी चौबे, *'वैदिक स्वरित मीमांसा'*, होशियारपुर, 1992

द्वारा परिभाषित किया गया है। दूसरा उदात्त के बाद आने वाला अनुदात्त भी स्वरित कहलाता है, यदि उसके आगे कोई उदात्त या उदात्त-अनुदात्त का समाहार रूप स्वरित न आवे। इन दो प्रकार के स्वरितों में उदात्त-अनुदात्त के समाहार रूप स्वरित को स्वतन्त्र स्वरित कहा जाता है। यह उदात्त-स्थानीय होता है। जिस पद में यह स्वतन्त्र स्वरित होगा उस पद में कोई उदात्त नहीं होगा। दूसरा स्वरित सामान्य स्वरित, आश्रित स्वरित या छाया स्वरित कहलाता है, क्योंकि इसमें उदात्त-अनुदात्त का समाहार रूप स्वरितत्व धर्म नहीं होता। वह वस्तुतः उदात्त का अनुगामी होता है। पद में उदात्त वर्ण के बाद आने वाला अनुदात्त ही सांहितिक धर्म के कारण स्वरित कहलाता है। इसके बाद यदि कोई उदात्त या स्वतन्त्र स्वरित आ गया तो वह अपने मूल रूप अनुदात्त में बदल जाता है। किन्तु गार्ग्य, काश्यप तथा गालव के मत में स्वतन्त्र स्वरित परे होने पर भी इसका स्वरितत्व बना रहता है।[5]

इस प्रकार स्वरित के दो मुख्य प्रकार हैं – स्वतन्त्र स्वरित तथा आश्रित स्वरित। स्वतन्त्र स्वरित के चार भेद हैं–जात्य, प्रश्लिष्ट, क्षैप्र तथा अभिनिहित। इसमें जात्य असन्धिज होता है और शेष प्रश्लिष्ट, क्षैप्र तथा अभिनिहित सन्धिज होते हैं। आश्रित स्वरित के भी तीन या चार भेद दिखाई पड़ते हैं। ऋग्वेद प्रातिशाख्य, कौहलि शिक्षा, नारदीय शिक्षा तथा शैशिरीय शिक्षा में सामान्य स्वरित के तीन भेद बताये गये हैं। इनमें किसी-किसी स्वरितभेद के नाम में अन्तर भी है। *वाजसनेयि प्रातिशाख्य* तथा *याज्ञवल्क्य* शिक्षा में स्वरित का एक चौथा भेद 'ताथाभाव्य स्वरित' के नाम से मिलता है। इस प्रकार आश्रित स्वरित के चार भेद हैं – तैरोव्यञ्जन, तैरोविराम, पादवृत्त, तथा ताथाभाव्य।

जात्य, प्रश्लिष्ट क्षैप्र तथा अभिनिहित स्वरितों के उच्चारण की एक विशेषता यह है कि इनके बाद यदि कोई उदात्त या कोई दूसरा स्वतन्त्र स्वरित आता है तो पूर्व स्वतन्त्र स्वरित के उत्तर-अनुदात्त भाग के उच्चारण में एक कम्पन होती है जिसे कम्प-स्वर कहा जाता है। किन्तु *तैत्तिरीय प्रातिशाख्य* (19.4) के अनुसार तैत्तिरीय शाखा की संहिता तथा ब्राह्मण के उच्चारण में स्वतन्त्र स्वरित के बाद स्वतन्त्र स्वरित आने पर ही कम्प होता है, उदात्त आने पर नहीं। शुक्ल यजुर्वेद की संहिताओं में कम्प नहीं होता, किन्तु कुछ आचार्य माध्यन्दिन संहिता के पदपाठ में ताथाभाव्य कम्प की सत्ता स्वीकार करते हैं।

प्रचय – वेदोच्चारण में उदात्त, अनुदात्त तथा स्वरित के अलावा एक प्रचय स्वर का भी प्रयोग होता है। इसका प्रचित, प्रच, तान, निचित, उदात्तमय, उदात्तश्रुति,

---

5. उदात्तादनुदात्तस्य स्वरितः। नोदात्तस्वरितोदयमगार्ग्यकाश्यपगालवानाम्। *पा०* 8.4.66–67

एकस्वर, एकश्रुति आदि अनेक नामों से भी उल्लेख मिलता है। पद में स्वरित के बाद आने वाले अनुदात्त की, चाहे वह एक हो या अनेक हों, प्रचय संज्ञा होती है। इसके उच्चारण के विषय में काफी मतभेद है। तैत्तिरीय प्रातिशाख्य के भाष्य वैदिकाभरण में प्रचय और स्वरित का अन्तर यह बताया गया है कि जो उदात्त और अनुदात्त के करणों से रहित हो, वह प्रचय होता है तथा जो दोनों के समावेश से उत्पन्न हो वह स्वरित होता है। काशिका के अनुसार प्रचय न तो उदात्तधर्म वाला होता है न अनुदात्तधर्म वाला और न स्वरितधर्म वाला ही। वह तीनों का अभेद रूप होता है। *आश्वलायन-श्रौतसूत्र* (1.2.9) के अनुसार उदात्त-अनुदात्त-स्वरित स्वरों का अतिशय सन्निकर्ष ही एकश्रुति है। *ऋग्वेदप्रातिशाख्य* में शौनक ने प्रचय का उदात्त के समान उच्चारण करने का विधान किया है। यही मत नारदीय शिक्षा का है। महाभाष्य के वृत्तिकार कैय्यट के अनुसार उदात्त अनुदात्त का योग स्वरित होता है किन्तु दोनों का ऐक्य प्रचय है। वाजसनेयि-प्रातिशाख्य के अनुसार प्रचय में उदात्त धर्म का आधिक्य होता है। कई प्रचय यदि लगातार हों तो उदात्त का स्वतन्त्र स्वरित परे होने पर अन्तिम प्रचय की सन्नतर संज्ञा होती है, जो अनुदात्त का ही एक नाम है।

ऊपर जिन स्वरों का हमने उल्लेख किया वे विभिन्न शाखाओं की संहिताओं, ब्राह्मणों, आरण्यकों तथा उपनिषदों के पाठ में प्रयुक्त होते हैं। सामवेद के अन्तर्गत दो प्रकार की संहितायें मिलती हैं – आर्चिक-संहिता तथा गान-संहिता। आर्चिक-संहिता के पाठ में उदात्तादि स्वरों का उच्चारण होता है, किन्तु उनके गान में इन उदात्तादि स्वरों का उपयोग न होकर गान-स्वरों का प्रयोग होता है। ये गानस्वर सात प्रकार के हैं – क्रुष्ट, प्रथम, द्वितीय, तृतीय, चतुर्थ, मन्द्र, अतिस्वार। इन्हीं की गान्धर्व सङ्गीतग्रन्थों में षड्ज, ऋषभ, गान्धार, मध्यम, पञ्चम, धैवत तथा निषाद संज्ञा है। ये सप्त स्वर भी मूलतः उदात्तादि स्वरों से ही उद्भूत होते हैं। *याज्ञवल्क्य शिक्षा*[6] में इस बात का स्पष्ट रूप से उल्लेख किया गया है कि गान्धर्ववेद में जो षड्जादि स्वर-सप्तक हैं वे वेद में उदात्तादि तीन नामों से जाने जाते हैं। *नारदीय शिक्षा*[7] तथा *याज्ञवल्क्य शिक्षा*[8] के अनुसार निषाद और गान्धार उच्च या उदात्त स्वर हैं, ऋषभ और धैवत नीच या अनुदात्त स्वर हैं तथा षड्ज, मध्यम और पञ्चम स्वरित स्वर हैं। पाणिनीय शिक्षा भी

---

6. गान्धर्ववेदे ये प्रोक्ता सप्त षड्जादयः स्वराः।
त एव वेदे विज्ञेयास्त्रय उच्चादयः स्वराः। — *या. शि.* 1.6

7. उदात्ते निषादगान्धारावनुदात्ते ऋषभधैवतौ।
स्वरितप्रभवा ह्येते षड्जमध्यमपञ्चमाः। — *ना. शि.* 1.875

8. उच्चौ निषादगान्धारो नीचावृषभधैवतौ।
शेषास्तु स्वरिता ज्ञेयाः षड्जमध्यमपञ्चमाः। — *या. शि.* 1.7

इसी मत का उल्लेख करती है। किन्तु पारिशिक्षा के अनुसार मध्यम और गान्धार को उदात्त से, षड्ज और ऋषभ को अनुदात्त से तथा निषाद, धैवत एवं पञ्चम को स्वरित से उत्पन्न माना गया है।[9]

संहिता, ब्राह्मण, आरण्यक एवं उपनिषद् रूप में विभिन्न शाखाओं में विभक्त विशाल वैदिक वाङ्मय का उच्चारण इन्हीं उपर्युक्त स्वर-प्रक्रियाओं के अनुसार होता है। कोई भी ऐसा वैदिक ग्रन्थ नहीं जो बिना स्वर के उच्चरित हो। वेद की विभिन्न शाखाओं के अन्तर्गत जो परिषदें थीं उन्होंने अपनी-अपनी शाखागत स्वरोच्चारण प्रकार को बड़े प्रयत्न से सुरक्षित रखा। प्राचीन स्वर-प्रक्रिया को निरन्तर आगे तक प्रवहमान रखने में देश-काल और व्यक्ति के कारण कई कठिनाईयां थीं। प्राचीन स्वरोच्चारण को सुरक्षित रखने तथा उनका शिष्यों को अभ्यास कराने की दृष्टि से हस्त-प्रचालन के साथ भी इन स्वरों का सम्बन्ध जोड़ा गया। वाणी और पाणी के साहचर्य की अद्भुत परम्परा वेदपाठियों में प्रचलित हुई। वाजसनेयि-प्रातिशाख्य तथा यजुर्वेद से सम्बन्धित शिक्षाओं में उदात्तादि स्वरों के उच्चारण के साथ-साथ हस्त-प्रचालन की परम्परा चली और उनके लिये तत्कालीन आचार्यों द्वारा नियम निर्धारित किये गये। याज्ञवल्क्य शिक्षा इस विषय को अधिक महत्त्व देती है। दोनों के महत्त्व का प्रतिपादन करते हुये याज्ञवल्क्य शिक्षा कहती है –

> **स्वरश्चैव तु हस्तश्च द्वावेतौ युगपत् स्थितौ।**
> **हस्ताद् भ्रष्टः स्वराद् भ्रष्टो न वेदफलमश्नुते॥** *या. शि.* 1.16
>
> **हस्तहीनं तु योऽधीते मन्त्रं मन्त्रविदो विदुः।**
> **न साधयति यजूंषि भुक्तमव्यञ्जनं यथा॥** *या. शि. 1.39*
>
> **ऋचो यजूंषि सामानि हस्तहीनानि यः पठेत्।**
> **अनृचो ब्राह्मणस्तावद्यावत्स्वारं न विन्दति॥** *या. शि.* 1.40
>
> **हस्तहीनं तु योऽधीते स्वरवर्णविवर्जितम्।**
> **ऋग्यजुःसामभिर्दग्धो वियोनिमधिगच्छति॥** *या. शि.* 1.41

जिस प्रकार शुक्ल यजुर्वेदियों में उदात्तादि स्वरों को हस्त-सञ्चालन के द्वारा प्रदर्शित करने की परम्परा चली, उसी प्रकार सामवेदियों में भी सात स्वरों के उच्चारण के साथ हाथ की अङ्गुलियों के विभिन्न स्थानों के स्पर्श के साहचर्य द्वारा दिखाने की परम्परा चली। नारदीय शिक्षा के समय में यह प्रवृत्ति प्रचलित थी इस बात की

---

9. गान्धारको मध्यम उच्चजातः षड्जर्षभौ द्वौ निहितोद्भवौ तौ।
स पञ्चमो धैवतको निषादस्त्रयः स्वराश्च स्वरितात्तु जाताः। — *पारि. शि.* 83

जानकारी 'गात्रवीणा' के उल्लेख से मिलती है। सामगान करते समय हाथ की अङ्गुलियों पर स्वरों का आरोप कर कृत्रिमभाव से सुर (स्वर) कायम रखने की पद्धति ही 'गात्रवीणा' कहलाती है।[10] नारद ने गात्रवीणा को सामगान में सहायक माना है। नारदीय शिक्षा में स्पष्ट रूप से यह कहा गया है कि सामगायकों की परम्परा में गान के समय 'दारवी' अर्थात् काष्ठनिर्मित वीणा तथा गात्रवीणा इन दोनों प्रकार की वीणाओं का प्रयोग किया जाता है।[11] गात्रवीणा में दोनों हाथों को दोनों जानुओं पर सीधा रखा जाता है तथा दोनों हाथों की अङ्गुलियां प्रसारित अवस्था में होती हैं। अङ्गुष्ठ से अङ्गुलियों के मध्यमपर्व का स्पर्श किया जाता है, क्योंकि यहीं पर सप्तस्वर-मण्डल स्थापित किया जाता है।[12] इसी प्रकार ऋग्वेदियों में भी शिर को हिलाकर उदात्तादि के उच्चारण को दर्शाने की प्रथा प्रचलित थी।

वैदिक वाङ्मय में प्रयुक्त जिन स्वरधर्मों का ऊपर उल्लेख किया गया है, उनका सम्बन्ध उच्चारण के साथ था, इसलिये गुरु-शिष्य परम्परा में उनका प्रचलन मौखिक रूप से ही बहुत दिनों तक रहा। पुनः एक समय आया जब वैदिक मन्त्रों के उच्चारण में प्रयुक्त स्वरों को हस्त-चालन के साथ जोड़ा गया। वैदिक वाङ्मय कब से लिखित रूप में आया, यह निश्चित रूप से नहीं कहा जा सकता, किन्तु यास्क के अनुसार यह लिखित रूप में उस समय आया जब उपदेश के द्वारा वेदों के अध्ययन-अध्यापन में ग्लानि महसूस होने लगी। अर्थात् उपदेश के द्वारा बताने पर भी शिष्यों को मन्त्रों का ज्ञान नहीं हुआ। इसी समय वेदों तथा वेदाङ्गों का लिखित ग्रन्थरूप में प्रणयन हुआ।[13] इसी समय से वैदिक ग्रन्थों के स्वराङ्कन की प्रवृत्ति विकसित हुई। यद्यपि प्रातिशाख्यों में ऐसा कोई प्रमाण नहीं मिलता जिससे पता चले कि किस स्वर के लिए कौन चिन्ह किस शाखा में निर्धारित था। उस समय सभी वैदिक ग्रन्थ अपनी-अपनी शाखाओं में स्वराङ्कन युक्त रहे होंगे, ऐसा हम अनुमान कर सकते हैं। पतञ्जलि के समय तक ऋग्वेद की 21 शाखायें, सामवेद की एक हजार शाखायें, यजुर्वेद की 101 शाखायें तथा अथर्ववेद की 9 शाखायें प्रचलित थीं और उनका स्वराङ्कनपूर्वक अध्ययन-अध्यापन चलता था। विक्रमपूर्व तृतीय-चतुर्थ शताब्दी से वैदिक यज्ञवाद के विरोधी सम्प्रदायों के

---

10. गात्रवीणा तु सा प्रोक्ता यस्यां गायन्ति सामगाः।
स्वरव्यञ्जनसंयुक्ता अङ्गुल्यङ्गुष्ठरंजिता। — *ना॰ शि॰* 1.6.2

11. दारवी गात्रवीणा च द्वे वीणे गानजातिषु। — *ना॰ शि॰* 1.6.1

12. विशेष विवरण के लिए द्र॰ डा॰ पंकजमाला शर्मा, '*सामगान : उद्भव, व्यवहार एवं सिद्धान्त*, कात्यायन वैदिक साहित्य प्रकाशन, होशियारपुर (1996), *पृ॰* 392

13. उपदेशाय ग्लायन्तोऽवरे बिल्मग्रहणायेमं ग्रन्थं समाम्नासिषुर्वेदं च वेदाङ्गानि च। *निरु॰* 1.27

आविर्भाव तथा विदेशियों के शृंखलाबद्ध आक्रमण के परिणामस्वरूप वैदिक परम्परा को काफी क्षति पहुंची। अनेकों वैदिक ग्रन्थ, जो भूर्जपत्रों तथा ताडपत्रों पर थे, नष्ट हो गये, जला दिये गये। आज हमारे पास जो ग्रन्थ बचे हैं वे अत्यल्प हैं जो पहले स्वराङ्कित थे, अब बिना स्वराङ्कन के मिलते हैं।

प्राचीन स्वर-विज्ञान (accentology) से सम्बन्धित प्रातिशाख्य आदि ग्रन्थ जिस प्रकार वैदिक स्वर-विज्ञान का सुव्यवस्थित विवेचन करते हैं उसी प्रकार स्वराङ्कन-विज्ञान (accentography) से सम्बन्धित ग्रन्थ भी उस समय प्रणीत हुये होंगे, जो हमें आज उपलब्ध नहीं हैं। किन्तु इस दिशा में जानकारी हमें प्रातिशाख्य तथा शिक्षा ग्रन्थों से ही मिलती हैं। प्रातिशाख्यों ने पद का मूल स्वरूप दिखाने की दिशा में भी पर्याप्त कार्य किया था। अपनी शाखागत संहिता के पदस्वरूप का विवेचन करते समय उन्होंने आद्युदात्त, मध्योदात्त, अन्तोदात्त, द्वि-उदात्त, त्रि-उदात्त, सर्वानुदात्त आदि पदों का प्रयोग किया है। *ऋग्वेदप्रातिशाख्य*, '**अप्रत्याम्नाये पदवच्च पद्यान्**' (1.61) में समस्तपद को अलग-अलग न मानकर पदवत् मानने का विधान करता है, किन्तु स्वर को छोड़कर। स्वरविधान में समस्तपद एक ही माना जायेगा। इस सूत्र की व्याख्या में उवट ने उदाहरण के रूप में 'पुरोहितम्' पद को **उदधृत** किया है। उवट लिखते हैं – '**अत्र पुरःशब्दस्यान्तोदात्तस्य हितशब्दोऽनुदात्तो मात्राकालव्यवहितः। तत्र पदवद्भावे सति पूर्वमन्तोदात्तं पद्यमनपेक्ष्यैव हितशब्दोऽनुदात्तः स्यात्**'। इसी प्रकार 'अस्मे युष्मे त्वे अमी च प्रगृह्याः' (*ऋ० प्रा०* 1.73) सूत्र में अस्मे, युष्मे, त्वे तथा अमी पदों की प्रगृह्य संज्ञा का विधान किया गया है, किन्तु '**उपोत्तमं नानुदात्तं न पद्यम्**' (*ऋ० प्रा०* 1.74) में 'त्वे' पद के विषय में कहा गया है वह प्रगृह्य तभी होगा जब वह अनुदात्त तथा समस्तपद का अङ्ग नहीं होगा। भारद्वाज शिक्षा में *तै० सं०* के समान दीखने वाले पदों के शुद्ध रूप को निर्धारित करने के लिये अकारादि-क्रम से उनका स्वर के आधार पर विवेचन किया गया है। उदाहरण के लिये 'वृजिन्' और 'वृजन' दो शब्द है। इनमें जब जकार उदात्तयुक्त होगा तब वह शब्द निश्चित रूप से 'वृजन' ही होगा। इसी प्रकार 'पर्शु' और 'परशु' शब्दों में अन्तोदात्त की स्थिति में 'परशु' शब्द ही सिद्ध होता है। पदों के भेद का यह सूक्ष्म ज्ञान इन पदों में स्वरों को बिना चिह्न के दिखाने से सम्भव नहीं हो सकता था। संहिताओं के पदपाठ में भी पदगत वर्णों पर स्वरों की स्थिति को चिह्नित किये बिना पदों का मूल स्वरूप नहीं समझा जा सकता था। इसलिये हमें मानना ही पड़ेगा कि मन्त्रों में स्वराङ्कन की प्रक्रिया भी वेदाङ्गकाल में ही प्रचलित हो चुकी थी। किन्तु यह ऐसा नहीं था कि सबकी स्वराङ्कन प्रक्रिया समान ही हो। स्वराङ्कन में शाखागत भेद भी प्रचलित था।

आज उपलब्ध वैदिक वाङ्मय में जो स्वराङ्कित हैं वे हैं – ऋग्वेद-संहिता (शाकल, आश्वलायन), यजुर्वेद-संहिता (माध्यन्दिन एवं काण्व), तैत्तिरीय-संहिता, मैत्रायणी-संहिता, सामवेद-संहिता (कौथुम) अथर्ववेद (शौनक) काठक-संहिता (आंशिक), पैप्पलाद-संहिता (आंशिक)। ब्राह्मणों में शतपथ ब्राह्मण (माध्यन्दिन एवं काण्व) तथा तैत्तिरीय ब्राह्मण (आरण्यक एवं उपनिषद् संहिता), मैत्रायणी आरण्यक। इन ग्रन्थों में स्वराङ्कन प्रकार एक जैसा नहीं है। एक में जो स्वरित का चिह्न है वहीं दूसरे में उदात्त का चिह्न है। सामवेद की संहिता में इन उदात्तादि स्वरों को वर्णों के ऊपर अङ्कों के द्वारा दर्शाया गया है।[14]

उदात्त – ऋग्वेद, यजुर्वेद, तैत्तिरीय (ब्राह्मण, आरण्यक एवं उपनिषद् सहित), मैत्रायणी आरण्यक तथा शतपथ ब्राह्मण में उदात्त को अचिह्नित छोड़ दिया जाता है। कृष्णयजुर्वेदीय काठकसंहिता (जो आंशिक रूप से स्वरांकित है), मैत्रायणी संहिता, कश्मीर में प्रचलित ऋग्वेद संहिता तथा पैप्पलाद संहिता (आंशिक रूप से स्वरांकित) में उदात्त को वर्ण के ऊपर खड़ी रेखा के चिह्न से अङ्कित किया जाता है, जैसे – अ॒ग्निः॑। सामवेद की आर्चिक संहिता में उदात्त को वर्ण के ऊपर सामान्य रूप से 1 अङ्क से चिह्नित किया जाता है, जैसे – अ॒ग्निः।

अनुदात्त – ऋग्वेद-संहिता (शाकल, आश्वलायन) शुक्लयजुर्वेद-संहिता (माध्यन्दिन, काण्व), अथर्ववेद-संहिता (शौनक), तैत्तिरीय-संहिता (ब्राह्मण, आरण्यक, उपनिषद् सहित) तथा मैत्रायणी में अनुदात्त स्वर को वर्ण के नीचे एक पड़ी रेखा के चिह्न से अङ्कित दिखाया जाता है, जैसे – **अ॒ग्निः**। पैप्पलादशाखा की अथर्ववेद-संहिता में अनुदात्त स्वर को वर्ण के नीचे एक खड़ी रेखा से दिखाया जाता है, जैसे–अ॒ग्निः। ऋग्वेद-संहिता के कश्मीर पाठ में अनुदात्त को अचिह्नित छोड़ दिया जाता है, जैसे–अग्निः। सामवेद (कौथुम) में अनुदात्त को वर्ण के ऊपर अङ्क 3 के द्वारा चिह्नित किया जाता है, जैसे–अ॒ग्निः।

स्वरित – ऋग्वेद-संहिता (शाकल, आश्वलायन) काण्वसंहिता तथा तैत्तिरीय संहिता (ब्राह्मण, आरण्यक, उपनिषद् सहित) में सभी स्वरितों को वर्ण के ऊपर खड़ी रेखा से चिह्नित किया जाता है, जैसे – **अ॒ग्निना॑**, क॒न्या॑ इत्यादि। माध्यन्दिन-संहिता में सामान्य या आश्रित स्वरों को तो वर्ण के ऊपर खड़ी रेखा से चिह्नित करते हैं, किन्तु स्वतन्त्र स्वरित को वर्ण के नीचे एक समकोण (⌊) जैसे चिह्न से चिह्नित करते हैं,

---

14. स्वराङ्कन प्रकार के लिये द्रष्टव्य, डॉ॰ व्रजबिहारी चौबे, *'वैदिक स्वरबोध*, एवं *'वैदिक स्वरित मीमांसा,'* कात्यायन वैदिक साहित्य प्रकाशन, होशियारपुर।

जैसे – यातुधान्यः। यदि स्वतन्त्र स्वरित के ठीक बाद कोई उदात्त या स्वतन्त्र स्वरित आये तो उस स्वरित को वर्ण के नीचे अंग्रेजी के (ω) जैसे चिह्न से चिह्नित करते हैं, जैसे – तन्वा शन्तमया। शतपथ ब्राह्मण में स्वरित की सत्ता नहीं इसलिए उसके लिये कोई चिह्न नहीं। वेबर ने अपने शतपथ ब्राह्मण के संस्करण में स्वतन्त्र स्वरित को स्वतन्त्रस्वरित वाले वर्ण के पूर्व वर्ण के नीचे दो पड़ी रेखाओं से चिह्नित किया है, जैसे – **वीर्यम्**। अथर्ववेद शौनक में आश्रित स्वरित को तो वर्ण के ऊपर खड़ी रेखा से चिह्नित किया जाता है, किन्तु स्वतन्त्र स्वरित को यदि वह अनुदात्त से पूर्व है या उसके परे कोई स्वर नहीं है तो वर्ण के आगे (ऽ) इस चिह्न से चिह्नित करते हैं, जैसे – **दिवीऽव, स्वःऽ** इत्यादि। पैप्पलाद अथर्ववेद संहिता में सामान्य स्वरित को वर्ण के नीचे बिन्दु लगाकर चिह्नित किया जाता है, जैसे – कामो दाता। किन्तु स्वतन्त्र स्वरित को वर्ण के नीचे समकोण (⌞) के चिह्न से अंकित किया जाता है, जैसे – **तन्वा शंन्तमया**। मैत्रायणी संहिता में सामान्य स्वरित को वर्ण के नीचे अंग्रेजी के (ω) जैसे चिह्न से चिह्नित करते हैं, जैसे – **अग्निना**। अनुदात्त से पूर्व सामान्य स्वरित को वर्ण के नीचे समकोण के चिह्न से चिह्नित करते हैं, जैसे – **वसिष्ठो**। स्वतन्त्र स्वरित को वर्ण के नीचे अर्धचन्द्र से चिह्नित करते हैं, जैसे **ह्यस्विमन्**। सामवेद में सामान्य स्वरित को वर्ण के ऊपर अङ्क 2 से चिह्नित किया जाता है, जैसे – **अ॒ग्नि॑ना॒**।

कम्प स्वर – ऋग्वेद (शाकल) में कम्प स्वर को स्वरित वर्ण के आगे 1 या 3 के द्वारा चिह्नित किया जाता है। यदि स्वतन्त्र स्वरित ह्रस्व वर्ण पर है तो उसे 1 के द्वारा तथा यदि दीर्घ वर्ण पर है तो 3 के द्वारा दिखाते हैं।[15] दोनों अवस्थाओं में अङ्क के ऊपर खड़ी रेखा से तथा नीचे पड़ी रेखा से चिह्नित करते हैं। ह्रस्व कम्प और दीर्घ कम्प के अङ्कन में एक अन्तर यह भी है कि ह्रस्व स्वतन्त्र स्वरित वाले वर्ण पर कोई चिह्न नहीं लगाते, जबकि दीर्घ स्वतन्त्र स्वरित वाले वर्ण के नीचे एक पड़ी रेखा का चिह्न लगाते हैं, जैसे अप्स्व1न्तः, पस्त्या 3 स्वा, इत्यादि। ऋग्वेद के कश्मीर-पाठ में कम्प को सर्वत्र, चाहे ह्रस्व हो या दीर्घ, 3 के द्वारा दर्शाते हैं। यहां अङ्क के ऊपर स्वरित का चिह्न नहीं होता।

अथर्ववेद (शौनक) में ह्रस्व कम्प को स्वतन्त्र स्वरित वाले वर्ण के ऊपर खड़ी रेखा तथा वर्ण के आगे 1 के अङ्क से चिह्नित किया जाता है, जैसे – अप्स्वं1न्तः। दीर्घ कम्प को ऋग्वेद जैसे ही चिह्नित करते हैं।

'तैत्तिरीय-संहिता' में स्वतन्त्र स्वरित के बाद यदि उदात्त आता है तो कम्प नहीं

15. विशेष विवरण के लिये द्र॰, डॉ॰ व्रजबिहारी चौबे, 'वैदिक स्वरित मीमांसा', होशियारपुर (1972) में "कम्पस्वर" शीर्षक अध्याय (पृ० 76-117)।

होता, अतएव वहां उदात्त पर स्वतन्त्र स्वरित को सामान्य स्वरित जैसा ही दर्शाया जाता है। किन्तु स्वतन्त्र स्वरित के बाद स्वतन्त्र स्वरित आने पर यहां कम्प होता है, जिसे स्वतन्त्र स्वरित वाले वर्ण के आगे 1 के द्वारा दर्शाया जाता है, चाहे स्वरित ह्रस्व वर्ण पर हो, चाहे दीर्घ वर्ण पर। यहां स्वतन्त्र स्वरित को भी अथर्ववेद के ह्रस्व कम्प के समान वर्ण के ऊपर खड़ी रेखा से चिह्नित किया जाता है, इसलिये अङ्क के ऊपर खड़ी रेखा का चिह्न नहीं देते, केवल अङ्क के नीचे ही पड़ी रेखा का चिह्न लगाते हैं, जैसे – **बहुदेवत्यों** 1 द्यौष।

'मैत्रायणी-संहिता' में कम्प को स्वतन्त्र स्वरित वर्ण के नीचे पड़ी रेखा तथा वर्ण से पूर्व 3 के अङ्क द्वारा दर्शाते हैं, चाहे स्वतन्त्र स्वरित ह्रस्व वर्ण पर हो, चाहे दीर्घ वर्ण पर, जैसे – अक्षित3व्यानं।

वैदिक स्वर-विज्ञान के अन्तर्गत एक महत्त्वपूर्ण प्रश्न यह उठता है कि क्या वैदिक स्वरों का प्रयोग केवल उच्चारणमात्र वैशिष्ट्य को दिखाने के लिये था या पदों या वाक्यों में उसके कारण अर्थ निर्धारण पर कोई प्रभाव पड़ता था। यास्क ने यही प्रश्न वैदिक मन्त्रों के उच्चारण के प्रसङ्ग में उठाया था और पूर्वपक्ष के रूप में कौत्स का यह मत प्रस्तुत किया था कि '**निरर्थका हि मन्त्राः**' अर्थात् मन्त्रों का कोई अर्थ नहीं, उनका मात्र प्रयोजन उच्चारण करना है। यास्क ने उसके इस मत का खण्डन किया और सिद्धान्त रूप में यह प्रतिष्ठित किया कि मन्त्रों का अपना अर्थ है, केवल उच्चारण मात्र उनका प्रयोजन नहीं (*निरु०* 1.15-16)। यही प्रश्न पूर्वपक्ष के रूप में उठाया जा सकता है कि उदात्तादि स्वरों का उच्चारणमात्र प्रयोजन है उनका अर्थबोध के साथ कोई सम्बन्ध नहीं। किन्तु वैदिक परम्परा में इस पक्ष की मान्यता नहीं। मन्त्रों में प्रयुक्त स्वर से पद तथा वाक्य के अर्थ निर्धारण में सहायता मिलती है। जैसा कि हमने प्रारम्भ में कहा था वाक् के अन्दर निहित अर्थरूप लक्ष्मी को खोजने में स्वर एक महत्त्वपूर्ण भूमिका अदा करते हैं। निरुक्त की महत्ता का प्रतिपादन करते हुये यास्क ने यह बात कही थी – '**अथापीदमन्तरेण मन्त्रेष्वर्थप्रत्ययो न विद्यते। अर्थमप्रतियतो नात्यन्तं स्वरसंस्कारोद्देशः**' अर्थात् निरुक्त के बिना मन्त्रों का अर्थबोध नहीं हो सकता और जबतक अर्थबोध नहीं होगा तबतक पदगत स्वर तथा प्रकृति-प्रत्यय का ज्ञान नहीं हो सकता। यह कथन स्वरों का अर्थ के साथ घनिष्ठ सम्बन्ध जोड़ता है। यास्क ने स्वरों के आधार पर अनेक पदों का अर्थ निर्धारण किया। उदाहरण के लिये ऋग्वेद का एक मन्त्र है '**वने न वायो न्यधायि**' (*ऋ० वे०* 10.29.1) इसमें 'वायः' पद को पदपाठकार शाकल्य ने 'वा। यः' ऐसा करके दो पद मानकर अर्थ किया। यास्क का कथन है कि यहां ये दो पद नहीं हो सकते। यदि दो पद मानेंगे तो वाक्य में प्रयुक्त 'अधायि' क्रियापद

उदात्तयुक्त होना चाहिये। किन्तु यह उदात्तयुक्त न होकर सर्वानुदात्त है इसलिये 'वायः' एक पद होगा दो पद नहीं और इसका अर्थ होगा 'वेः पुत्रां वायः' अर्थात् पक्षी का पुत्र[16]। 'इदम्' शब्द का तृतीयादि विभक्तियों में जो 'अ' आदेश होता है और उसके जो रूप बनते हैं वे प्रथम बार प्रयुक्त होने पर उदात्तयुक्त होते हैं और अन्वादेश होने पर सर्वानुदात्त होते हैं। इसका कारण यास्क यह बताते हैं कि आदेशरूप में प्रयुक्त होने पर उसमें तीव्र अर्थ अभिप्रेत होता है। जबकि अन्वादेश में अल्पीयार्थ होता है।[17] इसी प्रकार यास्क 'चित्' शब्द के विषय में कहते हैं कि यदि यह अनुदात्त है तब यह निपात होगा, यदि उदात्तयुक्त होगा तो वह पशु का द्योतक है।[18]

मन्त्रों के अर्थ-बोध के लिये स्वरों का बड़ा महत्त्व है। जब तक स्वर का ज्ञान नहीं होगा तब तक मन्त्रार्थ का भी ज्ञान नहीं हो सकता। प्राचीन आचार्यों ने वेदार्थ में स्वरज्ञान की उपयोगिता को देखकर ही शिक्षा नामक वेदाङ्ग का प्रणयन किया था, और वेदाङ्गों में इसका स्थान सर्वोपरि था। प्रातिशाख्यों तथा शिक्षाग्रन्थों में मन्त्रों में प्रयुक्त उदात्तादि स्वरों का विस्तारपूर्वक विवेचन किया गया है। पाणिनि शिक्षा का कहना है कि गलत स्वर में मन्त्र का उच्चारण करने पर वह मन्त्र अभिप्रेत अर्थ को प्रकट नहीं कर सकता। गलत-स्वर-प्रयुक्त मन्त्र से अनर्थ हो जाता है, जिस प्रकार **इन्द्रशत्रुर्वर्धस्व** इस मन्त्र में गलत स्वर का उच्चारण करने के कारण वृत्रासुर मारा गया।[19] **इन्द्रशत्रु** शब्द अन्तोदात्त होने पर तत्पुरुष समास होता है और आद्युदात्त होने पर बहुव्रीहि। **इन्द्रशत्रुर्वर्धस्व** इस मन्त्र में तत्पुरुष समास को अन्तोदात्त **इ॒न्द्र॒श॒त्रुः** पद अभिप्रेत था जिसका अर्थ था 'इन्द्र का शत्रु'। किन्तु ऋत्विजों द्वारा आद्युदात्त **इन्द्र॑शत्रुः** पद का उच्चारण हो गया जिसका अर्थ था 'इन्द्र जिसको सताने वाला' है। महर्षि पतञ्जलि ने व्याकरण-अध्ययन के प्रयोजनों का उल्लेख करते हुए लिखा है कि स्वर के द्वारा पद के अर्थ में उत्पन्न होने वाले संशय का निराकरण किया जा सकता है।[20] 'मीमांसासूत्र' के भाष्य में शबर स्वामी ने लिखा है कि मन्त्रों में उदात्तादि त्रैस्वर्य के

---

16. 'व॒ने न वा॒यो न्य॑धायि' (*ऋ० वे०* 10.29.1)। वने इव वायः वे पुत्रः। चायन् इति वा। कामयमान इति वा। वा इति च यः इति च चकार शाकल्यः। उदात्तं तु एवमाख्यातमभविष्यत्। (*निरु०* 6.28)

17. अस्या इति चास्येति चोदात्तं प्रथमादेशेऽनुदात्तमन्वादेशे। तीव्रार्थतरमुदात्तमल्पीयार्थमनुदात्तम् 'अ॒स्या ऊ॒ षु णु॒' (*ऋ० वे०* 1.138.4), अथानुदात्तम्-'दी॒र्घायु॑रस्या॒' यः पति॒ः (*ऋ० वे०* 10.85.39)

18. चिदिति निपातोऽनुदात्तः (*निरु०* 14)। अथापि पशुनामे भवति उदात्तः, 'चिं॑दसि मना॑सि' (*मै० सं०* 1.2.4) चिताः त्वयि भोगा, चेतयसे इति वा। *निरु०* 5.5

19 मन्त्रो हीनः स्वरतो वर्णतो वा मिथ्याप्रयुक्तो न तमर्थमाह।
स वाग्वज्रो यजमानं हिनस्ति यथेन्द्रशत्रुः स्वरतोऽपराधात्। *पा० शि०* 52

20. *महाभा*; पस्पशाह्निक।

उच्चारण की जो व्यवस्था है, वह मन्त्रों के अर्थ-ज्ञान के लिये है।[21] भर्तृहरि का कहना है कि सामान्य रूप से जब किसी शब्द का अर्थ-निर्धारण न हो सके, ऐसी परिस्थिति में उदात्तादि स्वर विशेष अर्थ के ज्ञापक होते हैं।[22] ऋग्वेद के भाष्यकार तथा स्वर-शास्त्र के परम वेत्ता आचार्य वेंकटमाधव ने लिखा है कि जिस प्रकार अन्धकार में मशालों की सहायता से चलता हुआ मनुष्य कभी मार्ग में ठोकर खाकर नहीं गिरता, उसी प्रकार स्वरों की सहायता से किया गया मन्त्रार्थ स्पष्ट तथा सन्देहरहित होता है।[23] वेङ्कटमाधव ने इस बात का स्पष्ट रूप से उल्लेख किया है कि जहां कहीं एक शब्द का अर्थ समान होगा उस शब्द का स्वर सर्वत्र समान होगा, जहां स्वर में भेद होगा, वहां अर्थ बदल जायेगा।[24] भरत, मम्मट, विश्वनाथ, आदि काव्यशास्त्रियों ने भी अर्थज्ञान के लिये उदात्तादि स्वरों की महत्ता स्वीकार की है।[25] स्वामी दयानन्द सरस्वती भी वेदार्थ ज्ञान के लिये स्वरों की उपयोगिता को स्वीकार करने से अपने को नहीं रोक सके।[26]

इस प्रकार सर्वत्र पद में, समास में, या वाक्य में जहां उदात्त की स्थिति है, उस अंश में काकु होता है[27], अर्थात् उस अंश पर वक्ता का बल होता है। स्वर का ज्ञान बड़ा सूक्ष्म है। किस पद में किस अंश पर काकु है, इसका पता लगाना कठिन है। जो सूक्ष्मविद् हैं वे ही इसको जान सकते हैं। वेङ्कटमाधव ने लिखा है कि किस पद पर काकु है इसका पता केवल देवताओं को है; समास में कहां काकु हैं इसको सूक्ष्मविद् ही जानते हैं, तथा तिङ् पदों में कहां काकु है, इसको प्राकृत लोग भी जानते

---

21. अथ त्रैस्वर्यादीनां कथं समाम्नानमिति? उच्यते, अर्थावबोधनार्थं भविष्यति। शबर, *जै. मी. सू. भा.* 9.2.31

22. सामर्थ्यमौचिती देशः कालो व्यक्तिः स्वरादयः।
शब्दार्थस्यानवच्छेदे विशेषस्मृतिहेतवः। — *वाक्यपदीय,* 1.318

23. अन्धकारे दीपिकाभिर्गच्छन्न स्खलति क्वचित्।
एवं स्वरैः प्रणीतानां भवन्त्यर्थाः स्फुटा इति। वेङ्कट॰ *स्वरानु॰* 1.8.12

24. अर्थाभेदे तु शब्दस्य सर्वत्र सदृशः स्वरः।
यदा न तं स्वरं पश्येदन्यथार्थं तदा नयेत्। वही॰ 1.8.2

25. (अ) तत्र हास्यशृङ्गारयोः स्वरितोदात्तवर्णैः पाठ्यमुपपाद्यम्, वीररौद्राद्भुतेषूदात्तकम्पितैः करुणबीभत्सभयानकेष्वनुदात्तस्वरितकम्पितैः। भरत, *ना॰ शा॰* 17.110

(आ) स्वरस्तु वेद एव विशेषप्रतीतिकृत्। विश्वनाथ, *सा॰ द॰* 3

26. वेदार्थोपयोगितया संक्षेपतः स्वराणां व्यवस्था लिख्यते। *ऋ॰ भा॰ भू॰* तृतीय संस्क॰ पृ॰ 374

27. एवं पदे समासे च यत्रोदात्तो व्यवस्थितः।
वर्णे पदे वा तत्रापि काकुरस्तीति निर्णयः। वही॰ 1.1.22

हैं।[28] वेङ्कटमाधव के इस कथन से मालूम होता है कि तिङ् पदों में काकु स्पष्ट दिखाई पड़ता है, समास में उससे सूक्ष्म और पद में उससे भी सूक्ष्म होता है। वेङ्कटमाधव का कहना है कि पद में, समास में तथा वाक्य में जो काकु की व्यवस्था है, वह स्वर के द्वारा ही है।[29] इसीलिये पदार्थ या वाक्यार्थ के लिये स्वर-ज्ञान अत्यावश्यक है। जिसको स्वर-ज्ञान नहीं, वह वेदार्थ नहीं कर सकता।

---

28. तत्रैकस्मिन्पदे काकुर्दैवैरेवावगम्यते।
सूक्ष्मविद्भिः समासस्थः प्राकृतैरपि तिङ्स्वरः।। वही॰ 1.1.23

29. वाक्यवृत्तिप्रकारोऽयं सदृशो लौकिकेष्वपि।।
मन्यन्ते पण्डितास्त्वन्ये यथाव्याकरणं स्वरम्।
व्यवस्थितो व्यवस्थायां हेतुस्तत्र न विद्यते।
माधवस्य त्वयं पक्षः स्वरेणैव व्यवस्थितिः। वही॰ 1.1.24–26

9

From 'Mortal' to 'Divine' Through Vāc

Sindhu S. Dange

SACRIFICE among any tribe or people has at its basis the concept of connecting the "mortal" to the "divine," with the sole aim of having harmony between the two. As the human beings desire everything from the gods, the gods also need strength for sending timely seasons, especially the rains. On the Vedic scene also this bond between the human beings and the gods is brought into effect through sacrifice, for through sacrificial offerings the human beings give strength to the gods, who in turn extend their help to the human beings. The *Bhagavadgītā* in later times has immortalized this "give-and-take" in the concept of "Yajñacakra" (III. 14-16).

Sacrifice is the patent form of *Ṛta* — the Divine Order — which works on the cosmic level and also on the terrestrial level, the latter with respect to the sacrificial sphere and the sphere of human relationships from the moral standpoint. While the cosmic order is beyond the actual control of human beings and the moral order laid down for humans in the society cannot be seen but can be experienced, the *Ṛta* (order) on the sacrificial sphere can be actually seen to be brought into effect. Hence it is that everything connected with sacrifice has to be very perfect and thus complementary to the sacrifice.

Sacrifice comprises two component parts — one, the actual ritual (*vidhi*) and the other, the *mantra* supporting this ritual. The appropriateness and the exactitude of a *mantra*[1] (chant or prayer) gives perfectness (*samṛddha*) to the form (*rūpa*) of the sacrifice. This is the doctrine of *rūpasamṛddha* stated by the *Ṛgveda*-Brāhmaṇas[2]. *Mantra* without the *vidhi* is no sacrifice[3] and the *vidhi* without the accompaniment of *mantra* or *mantra*s is regarded to be without any life, for speech, of which the *mantra* is a potent form, is an expression of human existence. Hence it is that the statement which often occurs in the Vedic ritual texts is: *vāg vai yajñaḥ* (Speech is verily Sacrifice).

The importance of speech in the life of an individual is stated by the *Kauṣītaki Brāhmaṇa*. Every single experience of an individual such as that of breathing, seeing, touching etc.

---

1. For the wellknown myth regarding the *mantra* — *indraśatrur-vardhasva* see *Taittirīya Saṁhitā* II. 4.12.1; *Śat. Br.* 1.6.3. 1-10. *Tvaṣṭṛ* used this expression with a wrong accent. The compound *indraśatruḥ* should have been accented on the last (i.e. here second) member, giving the meaning "Grow you, the destroyer of Indra." But it was accented on the first member, giving the meaning "Grow you, who has Indra as his destroyer or slayer.' The first is the case of the *Tatpuruṣa* compound, while the second that of the *Bahuvrīhi* compound. Because of the wrong accent, Indra immediately slew Vṛtra when he arose from fire. Also see *Pāṇini-śikṣā* verse no. 52.

2. *Ait. Br.* 1.13=3.2; 1. 16=3. 5; 1. 17=3. 6 etc; *Kauṣ. Br.* I. 1; III. 19; VIII. 6 etc. Here *ṛc* is mentioned as a *mantra. Nirukta* mentions both *ṛc* and *yajus* and says that ṛc or *yajus* gives a perfect form to the ritual (*Nir.* 1.16)

3. *Kātyāyana Śrautasūtra* 1.2.2. Vedic sacrifice consists of three constituents viz. (1) *dravya* — material; (2) *devatā* — deity to which offering is made, and (3) *tyāga* — ritual of offering.

is expressed by him by speech alone. A *ṛc* stated here is: "Not without Indra is any form made pure." Indra is Speech[4], for not without speech is any form made pure (*Kauṣ. Br. II. 7.*). The *Kauṣ. Br.* here clearly points out that the faculty of speech alone enables a person to give expression to all experience.

A mythical account in the form of *arthavāda* in the *Śatapatha Br.* is important for being noted in this connection, as it makes a distinction between the articulate and inarticulate speech. Vāyu and Indra quarrelling over a share in the Soma-cup approached Prajāpati for his final word. Prajāpati divided the cup into two parts, allotting one part (i.e. half cup) to Vāyu. Then he divided the other part (i.e. other half) into two, giving again one part to Vāyu and one to Indra, Vāyu thus getting in total three parts of the cup and Indra only the fourth part. Indra said that as per his share (i.e. the fourth part of the cup) Speech would speak intelligibly only one-fourth part (and that is the human speech), while the three-fourth parts of Speech spoken by beasts, birds and small vermin are unintelligible (*Śat. Br.* IV. 1.3.14-17). The *Śat. Br.* at this place quotes a verse from the *Ṛgveda* (*ṚV* I. 164.45), which we will have occasion to discuss further.

The articulate and intelligible human speech coming in the form of *mantra* used for sacrificial purpose in the sacrificial atmosphere attains the divine status, for the consecrated sacrificer while performing sacrifice is near to the gods and ceases to be a mortal being (at that time).[5]

This divine level is maintained even while reciting the

---

4. For Indra as Speech see *Śat. Br.*XI. 1.6.18.

5. *Śat. Br.* III. 2.2.10, 22; also *Pañcaviṁśa Br.* V. 5.1. The *Udgātṛ* priest seated on a throne-seat (*āsandī*) chants a specific part of the *Mahāvrata* laud on the *Mahāvrata* day. Being seated higher even he is nearer to the gods.

morning litany (*Prātar-anuvāka*) in the sacrifice before the inarticulate chirping of the birds starts. Birds and fowls are the mouth of *Nirṛti*, says the *Aitareya Br.* (II.15=7.5). The priest should begin to recite when night is far advanced before the emission of speech, but before the time when cattle, common men and birds take up to speech (*Kauṣ Br.* XI. 8.). In this hour there should not be any other sound heard, for fear of contamination, except that of the recitation of the hymns and some detached verses viz. *Gāyatrī, Anuṣṭubh, Triṣṭubh, Bṛhatī, Uṣṇih, Jagatī* and *Paṅkti*. The gods to be addressed successively are Agni, Uṣas and Aśvins (*Śat. Br.* III. 9.3.8.).

A clear-cut difference is made between the speech of the consecrated and that which is used in the daily dealings. The person who is consecrated expresses his speech falteringly (*parihvālām vācam*)[6] and not effusively like the normal ordinary speech (*na mānuṣīm prasṛtām*), says the *Śat Br.* (III 2.2.29). The speech intended here is the one used for the sacrificial purpose (*Śat Br.* XIV. 1.3. 11-14) and hence the divine one.

Restraint on his speech (*vāgyama*) is the essential requirement for the consecrated sacrificer. As Speech is said to be Sacrifice (*vāg vai yajñaḥ*), if the sacrificer utters any sound not suiting to the sacrifice, the sacrifice being set free flies away. In that case he has to mutter either a *ṛc* or a *yajus* addressed to Viṣṇu (Ibid. III 2.1.38.). As Viṣṇu is Sacrifice, (*viṣṇurvai yajñaḥ* — an oft-repeated expression in the ritual texts) the sacrificer again gets hold of the sacrifice. Thus purity of speech is to be maintained by the sacrificer by not talking to each and everybody, for as we have noted earlier, when consecrated the sacrificer goes near to the gods and

6. See Eggeling, J. (tr) *The Śatapatha Brāhmaṇa*, pt. II, SBE, Vol. 26, 1988 (1885), p. 46, footnote 1. Literally 'falteringly' (i.e. hesitatingly, cautiously), he speaks speech, not human effusive speech.

becomes one of them and the gods do not speak to all (Ibid. III. 1.1.10).

Speech in sacrificial context was always thought to be endowed with truth. Āsuri, the ritualist thinker says that there is one rule, which the gods meticulously follow and it is of truth. Hence a person (in the ritual-context a consecrated sacrificer) should speak nothing but truth (Ibid. XIV. 1.1.33). In the context of the Tānūnaptra rite, it is said that the gods do not transgress their covenant for they abide by truth (Ibid. III. 4.2.8). The *Aitareya Br.* says that the gods are established in truth, but the human beings in falsehood (i.e. are prone to falsehood). Hence the consecrated sacrificer should utter *vicakṣaṇavatī vāc*. Eye is the discerning agent (*vicakṣaṇa*) and by it he sees in correct manner (*Ait. Br.* 1.6). Sāyaṇa explains the expression *vicakṣaṇavatīm vācam vadet* by laying down that the consecrated sacrificer has to use the word *vicakṣaṇa* while uttering any sentence. Thus he should say "Devadatta *vicakṣaṇa* bring the cow," "Yajñadatta *vicakṣaṇa* tie the cow" etc. As per this explanation of Sāyaṇa the responsibility of discerning and seeing the truth is placed by the consecrated sacrificer on the person addressed (Devadatta, Yajñadatta etc.). The person who is addressed as *vicakṣaṇa* serves as the sacrificer's eye and he takes up the responsibility of bringing the correct or right things. In a way this explanation of Sāyaṇa is correct, for the consecrated sacrificer cannot leave the sacrificial chamber, it being his womb from which he is to be born again (for the second time) after the completion of sacrifice.[7] Even taking note of Sāyaṇa's explanation of the statement from the *Śat Br.* (*vicakṣaṇavatīm vācam vadet*), we have to say that the statement

7. The *yajñaśālā* is called *vimita, Ait. Br.* 1.3; for the consecrated sacrificer said to be an embryo see *Śat. Br.* III. 1.3.28; III. 2.1.16; cf. III. 3.3.12.

points out that the consecrated sacrificer should utter such speech, which is true by his self-experience and that too by his direct perception, as one's eye is the discerning factor. The quotes Sāyaṇa has cited in his commentary on this section from the *Vājasaneyi* and *Taittirīya Saṁhitās* of the *Yajurveda* support this.

We have seen that speech used in sacrifice should be pure and should conform to truth. The Brāhmaṇa-texts state that it should also be not impure. The *Śat. Br.* says in the context of Horse-sacrifice that life and deities depart from persons, who utter impure speech at sacrifice (*Śat. Br.* XIII. 5.2.10.). The *Ait. Br.* in the context of the *Kuntāpa*-hymn states that having recited the *Āhanasyā* verses, which are for getting offspring and have sexual overtone, he has to recite the *Dadhikrā* verse (*ṚV* IV. 39.6). This verse is said to be a "divine filter" (*devapavitram vai dadhikrā*) by which he purifies the divine speech (*Ait. Br.* VI. 36 = 30.10).

As against the pure and clear or intelligible speech we see the speech of the *asuras* (*asuryā vāk*) which is unintelligible. A mythical account from the *Śat. Br.* states that the gods and *asuras* both being the children of Prajāpati got by inheritance "Sacrifice" and "Speech" respectively. The gods asked Sacrifice to beckon Speech to come to him, which he did and then he could have Speech turned towards the gods. When Speech came to gods, the gods separated her from the *asuras* and offered her up as a holocaust in fire. Being deprived of Speech, in all helplessness the *asuras* cried *"he' lavaḥ he' lavaḥ."* This was the unintelligible speech they uttered. The *Śat. Br.* says that he who speaks thus is a *'mleccha'* i.e. barbarian (*Śat. Br.* III. 2.1.18-24). Sāyaṇa is convincing here when he says that *"he layo"* (i.e. *"he alayaḥ"*) stands for *"he arayaḥ"* "Oh, the spiteful enemies!!" The letter *"la"* in the word *alayaḥ* stands for *"ra"* which the *asuras* could not utter in a correct manner and hence their words were unintelligible.

Speech to be uttered in sacrifice was to be in loud voice and in a clear tone to make it audible. While enjoining the recitation of the *prātar-anuvāka* (morning litany) the *Kauṣ. Br.* says that the part of speech which comes in clear tone is the one which is not infested with evil and this clear tone is to smite away the evil from the sacrificer (*Kauṣ. Br.* XI. I). But the clear and audible speech is to be differentiated from the loud speech which a proud person or an infatuated person speaks, for the latter is the speech of the *rakṣasas* (*Ait. Br.* II. 7=6.7). It is worthy of taking note that while laying down the norms of Divine Speech the ritual texts have a clear distinction between cultured and uncultured or rustic speech.

Speech used in daily dealings as well as in sacrificial rites and rituals has to be connected with thought in order to be meaningful. Hence the Vedic ritual texts at several places dwell on the mutual relationship between Speech and Mind. In spite of saying that Mind and Speech when yoked together convey the sacrifice to the gods (*Śat. Br.* 1.4.1.1), the ritual texts point out that of the two Mind is more important than Speech. In the well-known *Ahambhadriya* dispute which comes as an *arthavāda* recorded in *Śat. Br.*, each of the two — Mind and Speech — said that he or she was more excellent than the other. When the two approached Prajāpati, he decided in favour of Mind saying that Speech was only an imitator of Mind's deeds and his follower. Speech becoming angry with Prajāpati for denying her claim of superiority over Mind, said that she would never be an oblation-bearer of Prajāpati. This *arthavāda* is clearly to explain the reason for giving low-voiced (*upāṁśu*) offerings to Prajāpati. Nevertheless it also brings out how Mind was thought to be superior to Speech. This *arthavāda* vouchsafes for the inter-relationship between the psychic and the vocal powers. Apart from the accostic value of every syllable in a word, the fact remains that Speech follows the dictates of Mind and in rituals it is not only Speech but the mental process also which takes part. In the absence of the mental process pertaining to a particular event in daily life or ritual in sacrifice, mere articulate speech will be nothing but simply a physical effort with the tongue.

It is said that the triple *veda* is the thousandfold progeny of *vāc* i.e. Speech (Ibid. V.5.5.12). In fact the scope of Speech[8] has to be extended to other forms of compositions also such as precepts (*anuśāsana*s), Sciences (*vidyā*s), dialogue (*vākovākya*), traditional myths and legends (*itihāsa-purāṇa*), *nārāśaṁsī*s and *gāthā*s.[9] All these form part of one's daily study, which is in the form of recitation, thus connected to Speech. With the help of Speech is the daily study of a person possible, and when carried out it is said to be a sacrifice to *Brahman* (Ibid. XI. 5.6.3-9). Even *śloka*s which occur in the Vedic ritual texts are to be considered here.[10] The vocal and instrumental music employed in the Vedic ritual tradition also can be regarded as the inarticulate (but certainly not unintelligible) form of Speech.[11] All these forms can be regarded as the thousandfold progeny of Speech.

We have already referred to a verse from the *R̥V* (1.164.45)

---

8. For the several aspects of Speech in Vedic ritual, see (Mrs) Dange, Sindhu S., *Aspects of Speech in Vedic Ritual*, Aryan Books International, New Delhi, 1996.

9. Ibid. "Songs from Secular Tradition", pp. 206-15.

10. Ibid. pp. 215-28.

11. Ibid. "Vocal and Instrumental Music in Vedic Ritual", pp. 247-56.

as mentioned in the *Śat. Br.* (IV 1.3.17). The verse speaks of four forms of Speech. Out of these, three forms deposited in a secret place move not i.e. do not become patent (Sāyaṇa: *na ceṣṭante na prakāśante*); men speak only the fourth division of Speech. According to Agrawala V.S. this verse inculcates the full-fledged doctrine of Vāk in twofold aspect viz. *Parā* Vāk and *Aparā Vāk, Amṛtā Vāk* and *Martyā Vāk*. The later grammatical tradition while explaining the doctrine of *sphoṭa*[12] states such kind of division, which can be seen in the following verse:

> *parā vaṅ mūlacakrasthā paśyantī nābhisaṁsthitā*
> *hṛdisthā madhyamā jñeyā vaikharī kaṇṭhadeśagā.*

The Speech beyond — *Parā Vāk* — stays in the human body at the *mūlacakra* (lower end of the spinal cord). The further stages of *Vāk* are viz. *Paśyantī* as situated at the navel; *Madhyamā* staying in the heart and *Vaikharī* as escaping the glottal region to come out of the mouth. *Mantra* accompanying any ritual in the Vedic sacrificial tradition though is an expression of this last stage of Speech i.e. *Vaikharī* — the actual speech or sound in view on the mortal plane — gets connected to Speech Beyond (*Parā Vāk*). It is this divine aspect of Speech in the *mantra* accompanying a rite or ritual which helps the sacrificer to go to the divine plane, where he comes to stay near the gods when he is perfoming a sacrifice and from the same sacrifice he is believed to be born for the second time (Ibid. XI. 2.1.1.).

---

12. The etymology of the word *sphoṭa* is suggested from the root √*sphuṭ* 'to burst, split open (with a sound), expand, blossom, bloom.' The √*sphoṭa* makes the meaning of a word patent or open, which is suggested through the letters in a word. *See* Agrawala, V.S. *The Thousand Syllabled Speech* (*Sahasrākṣarā Vāk*), Varanasi, 1963.

10

Vācam Artho 'nudhāvati

Ram Karan Sharma

VEDIC tradition has maintained its continuity through the process of *svādhyaya* represented by oral transmissions (*Gurūccaraṇā-nūccāraṇa*). It is with a view to strengthening this chain of transmissions that out of the six *vedāṅgas*, four of them deal exclusively with the various components of words, viz. *Śikṣā* (Phonetics), *Vyākaraṇa* (Phonology, Morphology and Syntax), *Nirukta* (Etymology), and *Chandas* (Metrics). *Vyākaraṇa* is, again, considered to be the mouth (*mukham*) or spokesperson of the Vedas.

Patañjali, while commenting on the Pāṇinian *sūtra; "Tadadhīte tad veda"* (4.2.59) dealing with the secondary affixes (*taddhitas*) signifying the proficiency of a person in a given discipline distinguishes between the term *adhīte* and *Veda*. As usual, he first questions the very propriety of using both the terms *adhīte* and *Veda* in the above *sūtra* saying that one who chants, also knows and one who knows, also chants. Then again he reconciles and justifies the use of both the expressions by saying that one who just chants, may not know and one who knows, may not chant. Kaiyyata explains the former as *svarūpamātravedana* (knowledge pertaining to the form of the object of chanting only) and the latter as *arthāvabodha* (comprehension of the import).

The relevant *Mahābhāṣya* text followed by Kaiyyata's and Nagesa's commentaries, as follows is very interesting:

> किमर्थमिमावुभावर्थौ निर्दिश्येते ? (किं) न योऽधीते वेत्त्यप्यसौ यस्तु वेत्त्यधीतेऽप्यसौ? न। एतयोरावश्यकः समावेशः। भवति हि कश्चित् सम्पाठं पठति न च वेत्ति, कश्चिच्च वेत्ति न सम्पाठं पठति। — महाभा.
>
> न य इति। यो हि यं ग्रन्थमधीते स तं स्वरूपतोऽवश्यं वेत्ति यश्च स्वरूपतो वेत्ति सोऽवश्यमधीत इति भावः। नैतयोरिवि। अर्थावबोधो वेदनमभिप्रेतं न तु स्वरूपमात्रवेदनं, तत्र परस्परव्यभिचारदर्शनादुभयोपादानमित्यर्थः। सम्पाठमिति। अर्थनिरपेक्षं स्वाध्यायं पठतीत्यर्थः। — कै. प्रदीपः
>
> यो हीति। वेदनम्-अधीयमानग्रन्थविषयमेवेति चोद्याभिप्राय इति भावः। भाष्ये-न य इत्यत्र नञि काकुः। यश्चेति। अध्ययनं विना स्वरूपतो वेदनासम्भ-वादिति भावः। 'सम्पाठ' शब्दः कर्मणि घञन्त इत्याशयेनाह-स्वाध्यायमिति। स्वाध्यायो वेदः। — नागे. उद्द्योतः

So, according to Patañjali, *śabda* or the word forms the central theme of what he calls *śabdānuśāsana*. Quoting extensively from the Vedas he presents his views regarding indispensibility of the knowledge of the *svarūpa* of words so essential for *svādhyāya*. He considers the world of words as infinite, so much so even Bṛhaspati could not complete his enumeration of words to Indra in one thousand divine years.

> बृहस्पतिश्च प्रवक्ता। इन्द्रश्चाध्येता। दिव्यं वर्षसहस्रमध्ययनकालो न चान्तं जगाम। — महाभा. प.

The objective of the *śabdaśāstra* is the preservation (*rakṣā*) of the 'words' of the Vedas. While Patañjali apparently distinguishes between the worldly and Vedic words (*laukikānām vaidikānāṁ ca*), Kaiyyata explains that the separate mention of Vedic words is just to give a special position to them just as Vaśiṣṭha is separately mentioned among other *brahmaṇa* guests (*vaidikānām laukikatve 'pi prādhānya-khyāpanāya pṛthag upādānaṁ yathā brāhmaṇā āyātā vasiṣṭho 'py āyāta iti vaśiṣṭhaśya*).

While explaining the famous *Asyavāmīya mantra, "Catvāri vākparimitā padāni"* (*Ṛgveda*. 1.164.45), Patañjali accepts Yāska's fourfold classification of words viz. *nāma, ākhyāta, upasarga* and *nipāta.* Nageśa gives an updated interpretation of the *mantra* by dividing each one of them into four parts, viz. *parā, paśyantī, madhyamā* and *vaikharī,* as follows:

> अन्येषां तदज्ञाने हेतुमाह-गुहेति। एकैकस्य नामादि-रूपस्य चतुर्थ भागम्। एकैकस्य चतुरंशत्वात्। परादीनां वा त्रयोंऽशा मध्यमान्ताः। गुहा अज्ञानं, हृदयादिरूपा च। वैयाकरणस्तु शास्त्रबलेन तद्बललब्धयोगेन च गुहान्धकारं विदार्य सर्व जानातीति भावः। . . . तस्मात् सकलपदज्ञानाय मनीषित्वाय चाऽध्येयं व्याकरणम् . . . हरिरप्याह
>
> वैखर्या मध्यमायाश्च पश्यन्त्याश्चैतदद्भुतम्।
> अनेकतीर्थभेदायास्त्रय्या वाचः परं पदम्॥ *वाक्यप.* 144
>
> तत्र श्रोत्रविषया वैखरी। मध्यमा हृदयदेशस्था . . .। पश्यन्ती तु लोकव्यवहारातीता। योगिनां तु तत्रापि प्रकृतिप्रत्ययविभागावगतिरस्ति। परायां तु नेति 'त्रय्या' इत्युक्तम्।
>
> स्वरूपज्योतिरेवान्तः परा वागनपायिनी।
> तस्यां दृष्टस्वरूपायामधिकारो निवर्त्तते॥
>
> -इत्युक्तेः। अनेकतीर्थभेदायाः-नामाख्यातादिवीणावेणुमृदङ्ग-इत्युक्तेः शब्दादिरूपानेकभेदायाः। . . .

The above four stages of the manifestation of words are explained in *Pāṇinīyaśikṣā* as follows:

> आत्मा बुद्ध्या समेत्यार्थान् मनो युङ्क्ते विवक्षया।
> मनः कायाग्निमाहन्ति स प्रेरयति मारुतम्। *पा. श.* 6
>
> सोदीर्णो मूर्ध्न्यभिहतो वक्त्रमापद्य मारुतः।
> वर्णान् जनयते तेषां विभागः पञ्चधा स्मृतः।
> स्वरतः कालतः स्थानात् प्रयत्नानुप्रदानतः।
> इति वर्णविदः प्राहुर्निपुणं तन्निबोधत। वही 6-10

No other *ṛṣi* of the *Ṛgveda* except *ṛṣikā* Vāk (who identifies herself with Brahman — so says Sāyaṇa) is so confident about her Supreme Power (*Aham rāṣṭrī saṁgamanī vasūnām — Ṛgveda* X. 125.3, *Yam kāmaye taṁ tam ugraṁ kṛṇomi — Ṛgveda* X.125.5.

No less forceful is *ṛṣi* Bṛhaspati (Vācaspati) about the supreme power of *vāk,* specially processed by the enlightened.

Saktum iva titaunā punanto-bhadraiṣām
lakṣmīr nihitādhi vāci.
uta tvaḥ paśyan na dadarśa vācam
uta tvaḥ śr̥ṇvan na śr̥ṇotyenām.
Uto tvasmai tanvam visasre
jāye 'va patya uśatī suvāsaḥ

— *R̥gveda* X. 71.2, 4.

The speech displays herself before the enlightened as a devout wife does before her husband.

So Pāṇinian tradition, as *śabdānuśāsana* or *śabdaśāstra,* considered as a spokesperson (*mukham*) of the Vedas recognizes the entire Vedic and worldly corpus of speech as *Śabda Brahma*, eternal, imperishable and the source of all worldly appearances. Here the visible or invisible *pratyayas* are perhaps more powerful than the original *prakr̥tī*-roots. Commenting on *Vā 'sarupo 'striyām* (3.1.94), Patañjali very clearly states that unlike *taddhitic prakr̥tis* the *dhātu prakr̥ti* devoid of *pratyayas* has no meaning at all.

प्रकृतिस्तत्र प्रकृत्यर्थे वर्त्तते अन्येन च शब्देन प्रत्ययार्थोऽभिधीयते। इह पुनर्न केवला प्रकृतिः प्रकृत्यर्थे वर्त्तते।

There are at least two words, which in Pāṇinian tradition, constitute just *pratyayas* with *prakr̥ti* entirely missing. They are *iyat* and *adhunā*. The following verse quoted in the *Bālamanormā,* taking advantage from these *Prakr̥ti*-less *pratyayas* constituting meaningful accomplished words rightly equates *śabdaśāstra* with Vedānta:

उदितवति परस्मिन् प्रत्यये शास्त्रयोनौ गतवति विलयं च प्राकृतेऽस्मिन् प्रपञ्चे।
सपदि पदमुदीते केवलः प्रत्ययो यत् तदियदिति मिमीते कोऽधुना पण्डितोऽपि॥

(*vide*, 5.2.40, 3.3, 3.17, 6.3.90, 4.148).

To sum up, the Vedic tradition as visualized by Pāṇini or *Pāṇinīya*s attaches greater importance to words rather than meanings, despite its strong semantic leanings. *Svādhyāya* representing *svarupavedana* occupies the first position; *arthāvabodha* follows.

11

Vedic Exegesis[1]

Kapil Kapoor

I

INDIA has a long, continuous and cumulative tradition of commentaries on seminal intellectual texts. Knowledge has always enjoyed a privileged status in India — the sheer amount of knowledge-literature, that is texts of knowledge available in Sanskrit, is amazing[2] but that knowledge-literature over

1. For a full discussion of the commentary tradition in India, please see Kapil Kapoor, *Text and Interpretation: The Indian Tradition*, D.K. Printworld, New Delhi, 2005.
2. We get some idea of this from the fact that despite losses due to calamities and vandalism, more than a million Sanskrit manuscripts are still in existence. They are sometimes preserved carefully, as is the case with European collections, but more often they are just stock-piled and stored in private collections and public libraries, with a large number of them not even catalogued yet. Sanskrit word for literature is *vāṅmaya*, compositions in words/language. The primary texts in this *vāṅmaya* span a large number of disciplines — philosophy, medicine, grammar, architecture, geography, literary theory, political economy, logic, astronomy and mathematics, biology, military science, sociology, metallurgy, agriculture, mining, shipbuilding, veterinary science and commerce besides the sixty-four arts and crafts that are conventionally enumerated and include, for example, sculpting, bangle-making, etc.

long stretches of time can grow opaque and be lost. There is (i) the availability of the text, (ii) the ability to understand the text, and (iii) the relevance of the text. The continuous and cumulative *ṭīkā paramparā*, the commentary tradition, ensured all the three — availability, comprehensibility and contextual relevance of the texts. Almost all the major intellectual texts have been cumulatively commented upon.[3]

These commentaries take many forms from bare annotation (*pañjikā*) to exhaustive, encyclopedic analysis (*mahābhāṣya*).[4] Rājaśekhara in *Kāvya-Mīmāṁsā* gives a complete

---

3. For example, the commentaries, *Ṭīkā*, on Jaiminī's *Mīmāṁsāsūtra: Śābarabhāṣya* (first centry CE?); Kumārila Bhaṭṭa's *Ślokavārttika* and *Tantravārttika* (sixth century/seventh century CE?); commentaries on *Śābarabhāṣya*; Prabhākara Miśra's commentary on *Śābarabhāṣya, Bṛhati* (seventh century CE?); Śālikanātha's commentary on *Bṛhati, Ṛjuvimalā* (ninth century CE); Pārthasārathy Miśra's *Śāstradīpīkā* (fourteenth century CE?); Madhavācārya's *Nyāyamālā* (fourteenth/fifteenth century CE); Appayadīkṣita's *Upakramaparākrama*, Apadeva's *Mīmāṁsānyāyaprakāśa*, Khaṇḍadeva's *Mīmāṁsākaustubha*, Gāgabhaṭa's *Bhaṭacintāmaṇi*, Nārāyaṇa Bhaṭṭa's *Mānamayodaya* (all seventeenth century); Kṛṣṇayajavana's *Mīmāṁsāparibhāṣā* (eighteenth century CE).

   The commentary literature is indeed endless; we have mentioned here only those that are most frequently cited and discussed. There are indeed commentaries on these commentaries (which is what makes the tradition "interlaced") such as the two major *Ślokavārttika* commentaries *Kāśikā* by Sucarita Miśra and *Nyāyaratnākara* by Pārthasārathy Miśra, the *Tantravārttika* commentaries *Nyāyasudhā* by Someśvara Bhaṭṭa, *Tauttātītamatatilaka* by Bhavadeva Bhaṭṭa, to mention only two. (For a complete list, please see Ganganatha Jha's Introduction in his translation, *Ślokavārttika*, 1983, reprint, Delhi: Satguru Publications.)

4. Rājaśekhara in his *Kāvyamīmāṁsā* (ninth century CE) in chapter 1, lists eight forms.

list of different kinds of commentaries. He distinguishes eight kinds — "commentary that explains the ideational content of a *sūtra* is called *vṛtti*; analysis of a *vṛtti* is *paddhati*. *Bhāṣya* is a detailed analysis that takes into account the possible objections and counter-arguments. *Samīkṣā* gives an explanation of the intended and deeper meanings and issues implicit in a *bhāṣya* analysis. A mere indication of meaning in the simplest and briefest language is *ṭīkā*. Explanation of only the difficult words is *pañjikā*. A brief statement of the meaning of a *sūtra* is *kārikā*. In the same manner, an analysis of the unexpressed or suggested meanings and implications of a *sūtra* is called *vārttika*. These are *śāstra*-divisions" Chapter 1.

What K.A. Subramania Iyer says about the purpose and value of commentaries is true of commentaries in general:

> "[These] . . . supplied the context and brought out the full implications of the main idea . . . [they also explain] the logical sequence [of topics and ideas] . . . [handing down the old tradition] was also one of the original motives of those writers . . . [they also placed the text in the context of the totality of philosophical systems]."[5]

Commentaries interpret the text in the light of later developments of thought. This on the one hand requires careful reading to separate the old from the new, and on the other, it develops the discipline. At the same time, the commentators as also the writers of primary texts are extremely careful about handing down the old tradition faithfully, and this, in fact, "was also one of the original motives of those writers" (K.A. Subramania Iyer, 1969, p. 50). The commentaries also place the given text in the context of the philosophies and compare the discipline-specific categories with the categories of other disciplines.

5. *Bhartṛhari*, Poona: Deccan College, 1969, pp. 50-51.

Thus as Vāmana-Jayāditya note in the first *kārikā* of their *Kāśikā*:

> "The purpose is to bring together and unify the . . . knowledge that lies scattered in *vṛttis*, *bhāṣyas* and all *śāstras*. . . ."

Texts over a period of time (i) grow opaque, and/or (ii) become assymetrical with the context, and/or (iii) their connection with the tradition of knowledge in that domain becomes incoherent. If the Indian intellectual texts have not become "dead" and are still studied in the learned, though now relatively esoteric, sphere, it is because the *ṭīkā paramparā* has kept them alive and pertinent. As already noted, some of India's most brilliant minds have been exegetes — Yāska (ninth century BCE), Śabaraswāmī (first century CE), Kumārila Bhaṭṭa (sixth century CE), Ādi Śaṅkara (seventh century CE), Rāmāṇuja (eleventh century CE), Madhavācārya (thirteenth century CE), Sāyaṇācārya (fourteenth century CE) Jñāneśvara (fourteenth-fifteenth century CE) right down to "The Great Moderns," Sri Aurobindo, Mahatma Gandhi, Radhakrishnan, Vinoba Bhave (who all wrote commentaries on the *Bhagavad-Gītā* in the illustrious line of Śaṅkara and Rāmānuja). As already noted, existence of this continuous, cumulative tradition of interpretation apart from attesting the society's commitment to knowledge also attests the freedom of mind that the culture allows the individual to exercise in reaching different, competing interpretation/construction. Freedom to interpret means the freedom to think. Above all, this tradition ensured continuity of the habits of mind, of what is called the culture of a community.

II

The tradition has several knowledge typologies for the large body of literature to classify and arrange the compositions in a hierarchy of their status as valid discourses of knowledge.

There is for example the fundamental division between Śāstra and Kāvya. In such typologies, the Vedas are assumed to be repositories of "non-contingent" knowledge, knowledge that is independent of time, place and person, the kind of knowledge that is coded in the laws of science, for example. We have the well-known threefold division of all *vāṅmaya*, verbal discourse, into Śruti-Smṛti-Kāvya. Śruti is directly apprehended knowledge, totally non-contingent. This covers Vedas and Upaniṣads — texts that handle metaphysical questions. Smṛti is next in degree — it is non-contingent knowledge but one that is recalled and therefore there is the intervention of a thinker. This applies to the primary texts of philosophy and the six auxiliary sciences. Kāvya is knowledge that is contingent on an individual, his particular perception and his location in time and space.

As we had noted in an earlier study,[6] contrary to the popular impression knowledge in India has not been confined to learned texts, nor has it ever been a repository of the few. Along with the learned, scholarly tradition, there has always been a parallel popular tradition of exposition of texts, the *kathā pravacana paramparā*, which has all through mediated between the learned tradition of the texts of learning and the ordinary masses. Even Ādi Śaṅkarācārya, one of the greatest minds, besides being a composer of numerous intellectual texts, was also a *pravacanakāra*, a popular expounder, who travelled through the length and breadth of India addressing village congregations and explaining to them and sharing with them his understanding of Vedānta.[7] Similarly, Śrī Rāmānujācārya

6. *Knowledge, Individual and Society in Indian Traditions*, Chandigarh: Saini Memorial Foundation Lecture, Punjab University, 2002.

7. In a personal conversation with Śrī Śaṅkarācārya of Śāradā Pīṭha, Śṛṅgeri, it was confirmed that in the seventh century apart from the fact that Sanskrit was a very widely understood language, →

expounded for twelve years in Tamil, the people's language, his Viśiṣṭādvaita philosophy in the village of Melkote near Mysore. In fact, there are strong reasons to believe that Śaṅkara's learned commentaries originated in his popular discourses. The popular expositions are marked by an abundance of illustrations and analogies, *upamā* and *dṛṣṭānta,* borrowed from activities of day-to-day ordinary life of the people — the spheres of ornaments, cooking, family relationships and obligations, activities of importance to the day-to-day life (such as digging wells). Even in logic, in the five-step syllogism, the third step is *udāharaṇam*, a real life example, the applied example ". . . characteristic of India's practical outlook and its practical conception of proof. . . ."[8] Both these attest the fact that in India, knowledge is not a privileged discourse, nor a discourse of the privileged. And what decisively attests the non-esoteric and non-elitist nature of knowledge and above all its **continuity** is the fact that what was once the learned vocabulary of Indian thought is today a part of the ordinary language of the people. Trans-disciplinary philosophical terms such as *jaḍa, cetanā, jīva, ātmā, saṁsāra, dhyāna, kṣamā, dayā, maitrī, karuṇā, aṇu, jñāna, jñānī, citta, buddhi, pratyakṣa* continue to be present in almost all Indian languages and, what is more significant, are present as ordinary words in the speech of the people. Not only the terms of philosophy, even technical terms of grammar, *saṁjñā*s, such as *vṛddhi* and *guṇa* are high frequency words in the ordinary speech of the

---

→ the Indian speech community was covered by five Prākṛts and that Śrī Ādi Śaṅkarācārya gave his discourses in Prākṛt followed later by his compositions in Sanskrit, the pan-Indian language of learning.

8. Betty Heimann, *Indian and Western Philosophy: A Study in Contrasts*, London: George Allen and Unwin, 1937, 1st Indian edn., from Delhi: Aman Publishing Company, 1994, pp. 86-87.

speakers of almost all Indian languages. Further, even the conceptual propositions,[9] as maxims, are a part of the ordinary thinking of the people. It is not just a question of words or clauses being present — it is a matter of ideas permeating and continuing to be alive. It is also an example of what may be unequivocally termed as a true democratization of thought in India. This democratization makes possession of the *right* knowledge[10] a civilizational value in India.

III

Great value thus has always attached to knowledge and that is why tremendous intellectual effort has gone into **maintaining** the texts of knowledge. As we have noted elsewhere[11] even though Hindu culture is not bibliolatrous, it has accorded a special status to certain texts, the texts of

---

9. such as "... death is certain for the born" (The *Bhagavad-Gītā*, 2.27).
10. As we have said elsewhere, "The goal of knowledge in the Indian tradition therefore is so very different — it is to promote the freedom of the individual. Of course, what constitutes "freedom of the individual" in our thought has to be clearly understood. . . . For true individual freedom, the only goal has to be *mokṣa*. So the individual seeks/pursues his *mokṣa*. But the instrument or means of *mokṣa* is Knowledge. But what Knowledge? That which promotes *dharma*, which is defined in *Mahābhārata* as that which promotes the general welfare of mankind. So the individual has to seek knowledge that promotes what the *Bhagavad-Gītā* calls *loka-saṁgraha*, the collective well-being. Knowledge informed by *dharma* binds the individual and the society." (please see, *Knowledge, Individual and Society in the Indian Tradition* an Endowment Lecture delivered at Punjab University, Chandigarh, December, 2001, to be published by Panjab University).
11. Kapil Kapoor, "Some Reflections on the Interpretation of Texts in the Indian Tradition" in *Structures of Signification*, H.S. Gill, ed., vol. I, Delhi: Wiley Eastern Limited, 1990.

knowledge, and made them perennial objects of study. The difference, however, is that there has been a complete freedom to interpret and come up with competing interpretations, a freedom that is not always present in other cultures. A distinction therefore has to be made between the conformist, undifferentiated study of a single sacred text and a freely interpretive study of an intellectually important text (such as *Ṛgveda*) that generates a multiplicity of what are often the contending interpretations.[12] Śruti and Smṛti texts as texts of knowledge have been objects of perennial study.

Tradition records in India repeated **loss and recovery** of its seminal cultural texts. Even in known/written history we can observe the operation of both loss and of various text-recovery/renewal mechanisms.

Renewal needs to be understood as a different process, one that in the course of recovery or maintenance involves extension or deepening of the thought. These processes deserve to be studied though the evidence is scarce and culture-specific. The intellectual texts with the passage of time tend to become opaque and be lost. When a text grows asymmetrical[13] with what it seeks to explain and loses its relevance and position as a primary text in a given domain of knowledge, it may finally get dropped[14] from the people's consciousness. But dynamic communities do not allow their systems of thought to die. A civilization such as India's that

12. Bhartṛhari says: "Monism, Dualism and any number of points of view (*pravādā bahudhā mata*), all equally valid, are all rooted in and argued from the *Veda*" (*Vākyapadīya*, 1.8).
13. As would be the case of a book dealing with medicinal plants which have since become extinct.
14. Particularly in the oral tradition, where texts occupy space in the mind and that space has to be economically used and according to priorities.

puts a premium on knowledge would strive and develop techniques for maintaining its texts. As we have described elsewhere,[15] oral cultures have built-in mechanisms for the recovery of texts. As it is, strong cultures resist both kinds of loss — that due to the text-internal factors and that due to the text-external, contextual factors — to preserve culturally central systems of ideas. A culture may, therefore, employ one or any of the following seven text maintenance/renewal mechanisms to keep the thought alive and re-contextualized:

(i) **commentary (*ṭīkā*)** such as Kātyāyana's *Vārttika*, 350 BCE; Patañjali's *Mahābhāṣya* second century BCE; *Kāśikā*, seventh century CE, *Mahābhāṣya* and Śaṅkara's *Bhāṣya*;

(ii) **recension** (a critical revision) such as *Cāndra Vyākaraṇa*, fourth century CE, a Buddhist recension of *Aṣṭādhyāyī* that interestingly eschews what it believes is its philosophically loaded technical vocabulary; Jainendra's *Vyākaraṇa/Śabdānuśāsana*, composed in the fifth century CE by Devanandin or Siddhanandin, and *Aṣṭāvakra Gītā*;

(iii) **redaction** (a re-arrangement) such as *Rūpamālā* of Vimala Saraswati, *Siddhāntakaumudī* of Bhaṭṭtojīdīkṣita, sixteenth century CE, and *Laghusiddhāntakaumudī*, eighteenth century CE of Varadarāja;

(iv) **adaptations**: *Hemaśabdānuśāsana* by Hemacandrācārya, eleventh century CE, an adaptation of Pāṇini's grammar to describe Prākṛt, contemporary spoken Prākṛts or

15. See, "Vyāsa Paramparā, Text renewal Mechanisms, Max Müller and European Scholarship" in *Max Müller and Contemporary European Scholarship*, Proceedings of the International Seminar Ramakrishna Mission, Kolkata, 2000, pp. 117-35. The discussion of "Recovery" process here in section II is based on this paper. But I make a distinction now in this paper between "Recovery" and "Renewal" mechanisms.

Śaṅkaradev's Assamese adaptation of Vālmikī *Rāmāyaṇa* and such other adaptations, thirteenth-fourteenth centuries onwards in almost all Indian languages;

(v) **translation**: for example, all the many translations of major literary and philosophical texts in almost all the modern Indian languages, fourteenth century or so onwards; Hindi paraphrase of *Aṣṭādhyāyī*, Nārāyaṇa Miśra and English translation of the text with incorporations from *Kāśikā* by S.C. Vasu, 1898;

(vi) **popular exposition**: the *kathā pravacana paramparā*, a hoary tradition, has been chiefly instrumental in both the maintenance and renewal of texts of thought.[16] The two parallel traditions, the learned and the popular, have been all through and are even today mutually enriching each other and contributing in equal measure to the development of thought through processes of paraphrase, explication, verification, falsification, and illustration; and

(vii) **re-creation:** Both *Mahābhārata* and *Rāmāyaṇa*, for example, are maintained by repeated creative use of its themes and episodes, by re-creations, such as those by *Bhāsa* and Bāṇabhaṭṭa who composed works on themes, characters and episodes from these two patronymic epics.

---

16. This *kathā pravacana paramparā* continues to be vigorous and alive even today with many distinguished expounders of Upaniṣads, Vedānta, *Bhagavad-Gītā* and *Rāmāyaṇa* drawing huge crowds in their live discourses and having millions of devoted followers across the country. Murāri Bāpū is one good example. Their discourses are learned but *sarasa* and in the functional mode laid down by *Nāṭya-Śāstra* make profound thought accessible to the people.

IV

Of all these mechanisms, commentary or *ṭīkā* is the primary mechanism for the renewal and maintenance of texts.

India has a long and continuous interpretive tradition.[17] Pāṇini's *Aṣṭādhyāyī* (seventh century BCE) indicates the presence of literature of commentaries, *vyākhyāna* (Act IV, 3.66), and Patañjali in his *Mahābhāṣya* lays down the broad rudiments of the mechanics of *vyākhyāna* or explanatory interpretation (I.I). Commentaries were written on almost all the major texts belonging to different types of literature, *vāṅmaya* (literally, "permeated by speech"). Pāṇini has distinguished four classes of literature from the point of view of authorship and their status as discourses of knowledge:

(1) *dṛṣṭa*: revealed (by unknown thinkers)

(2) *prokta*: (IV.3.101) composed by one different from the one who taught, viz., Chandas and Brāhmaṇas)

(3) *upajñāta*: discovered/laid down by someone (IV.3.115) viz., Pāṇini's own *Aṣṭādhyāyī*.

(4) *kṛta*: (IV.3.87, 116) or ordinary compositions, viz., *ākhyāyika*s, poetical literature, etc.

To this he adds the fifth class of literature, *vyākhyāna*, the commentary, thus attesting to the existence of this form of exposition prior to his times. The rule IV.3.66 suggests that

17. The tradition of interpretation in India is (i) hoary, (ii) continuous, and (iii) cumulative, originating as it does in the Ṛgvedic exegesis. It is hoary because, in any case, while dealing with this tradition we are dealing with the world's earliest poetry and the earliest prose. The attested tradition begins with Yāska, the eighth century BCE *nairukta*, "expositionist," who composed his *Nirukta* to explain and determine the meanings of 2041 *parokṣa*, "obscure," uses in the *Ṛgveda*.

the object of commentary, the thing to be explained "must be a book" (Vasu 1980: I.772).

The commentary tradition is a *cumulative* tradition, i.e. a number of commentaries on a given text follow each other, each succeeding commentary taking into account and building on the preceding one.

V

What motivated this enormously rich body of literature of interpretation, this *ṭīkā paramparā*? Even though a culture is not bibliolatrous, it would often accord a special status to a text or texts. A distinction may thus be proposed between a text that is repeatedly made to conform to, or "produce," one given reading, and a text that has provenly generated competing philosophies (viz., *R̥gveda*) as the source of different philosophic systems). Where the interpretive traditions originate and are built around such "sacred" texts — sacred in the sense of being the source-books for ideas, customs and practices — a rigorous system of interpretation, a science of exegesis, tends to develop, for great store is laid by the exact knowledge of the meaning of these texts. From the beginning, of the three paths laid out to guide an individual's conduct in life — *karma* (action), *upāsanā* (belief), *jñāna* (knowledge) — "knowledge" is held to be superior, though it is recognized that it is a highly complex entity and that *dharma* is the superordinate principle of life — it is *dharma* which determines the validity and value of knowledge and conduct. Thus the sanctity of properly acquired valid knowledge no doubt generated the scholarly pursuit of interpretation, and, hence, we note the growth and development of *darśana* known as Mīmāṁsā, the system of interpretation attributed to Jaimini (third century BCE).

The task of interpretation is threefold:

(i) to determine and explain the meaning of the text;

(ii) to establish the relevance and significance of, and sometimes to amend, the rules of conduct or the significance of a thesis when they grow out of tune with either the usage or the knowledge of the time; and

(iii) to re-contextualize or articulate the rationale or/and the rationality of the assertions and, that way, defend against counter-philosophies or objections.

Basically what sets the interpretive process in motion, therefore, is not just the symbolic and the seemingly irrational text alone, but also the *ambiguous*, the *contradictory*, the apparently *meaningless* and *controversial* propositions or ideas. Apart from this, the very nature of Indian intellectual discourse demands explicatory commentary.[18] Indian texts are a product of the oral tradition and as oral texts they are a disembodied storehouse. As oral texts, they are:

(i) de-contextualized statements,

(ii) composed in complex and abbreviated *sūtrāic* syntax,

(iii) made terse through devices of economy such as class-markers, meta-terms, technical terminology, understood repetition and ellipsis, etc., and more importantly,

---

18. Through several devices, the writers achieved economy-class-makers, meta-terms, technical terminology, understood repetition, ellipsis, eschewing the verb — "hardly ever use a verb and of the cases only a few are to be met. . . . The nominative and ablative singular prevail, and long compounds are constantly employed. All our ideas are thrown into the form of nouns, mostly abstract, and even the participles have become rare. This style is the style of formulas rather than of discourse. . . ." (Bhandarkar, 1883)

(iv) unlike contemporary Western texts, statements of conclusions and not descriptions of the processes "this (the author's) own mind has gone through in arriving at the doctrine,"

(v) organized in an intricate thematic (or topic) organization, and

(vi) at least in the Śruti-literature, are expressed in a symbolic language.

The commentator, the *ṭīkākāra* therefore has his threefold task cut out for him — he has to:

(i) determine the meaning through

  (a) *explication* of a clearly worded statement, focusing perhaps on particular lexical choice, if need be,

  (b) *establishment* of the meanings of a seemingly clear or of a multivalent statement, and

  (c) *determination* of the symbolical meaning of a transparent statement.

(ii) establish the relevance, and

(iii) articulate the arguments for and the sustainability of the thought-system.

There are specific text situations, which set these interpretive processes in motion. The content or meaning of a text has an internal validity and an external validity, an inner conference and an outer coherence. In itself, internally, a text may (i) conform to the visible facts, or (ii) be neutral with respect to them, or (iii) be asymmetrical, (iv) be meaningless, or (v) be ambiguous. Ambiguity may be (i) lexical or (ii) prepositional. Asymmetry, on the other hand may take any of the three forms — (i) contradiction within the proposition where one part of the text is asymmetrical with some other part; (ii) contradiction between the text, its content, and the known laws of this world (implausibility) and, (iii) between the text and the cultural context both general and of the whole composition (inappropriateness). With respect to the rest of the text, the statements may be (i) discontinuous, when for example the topic is changed suddenly or when there are a series of apparently unconnected words, (ii) superfluous or repetitive, and (iii) contradictory when it says one thing at one place and something quite the opposite in another place. The Mīmāṁsā theorists use the term *arthavāda*s for the three kinds of statements — those that are in conformity with known facts (*anuvāda*), those that are against the known facts (*guṇavāda*), and those that are neither against the known facts nor are provable by perception (*bhūtārthavāda*); viz., "Indra uplifted his thunderbolt against *Vṛtra*."

A *discontinuous* text needs "fillers" or explication, for example, Patañjali in 1.1 of *Mahābhāṣya* reads off words of current usage one by one, but cites *contextualized* words from texts. Why? Because words from texts are in the given form, while words cited from daily use may be found in any of the many forms. *Repetitiveness* often adds proportion to the idea and is to be justified on that ground. *Contradiction* may be apparent or real. Apparent contradiction appears in *Mahābhāṣya* (1.1) where it is first said that form (*ākṛti*) is changeless (*nitya*) while substance (*dravya*) is *anitya*, later it is said that substance (*dravya*) is *nitya* and *ākṛti* is *anitya* and both the thesis are justified. Real contradictions may be found in *Manusmṛti*, in matter of foods, for example, where something is proscribed at one place and then allowed at another place. Such contradictions are resolved through metarules (see below) II.2d.

The incidence of these elements or "triggers" differs from one kind of text to another and accordingly we talk of different types of exegesis. We may distinguish between:

1. Vedic (Śruti) exegesis,
2. Smṛti exegesis: (a) *darśana* (philosophy) (b) *vyākaraṇa* (grammar), and
3. *Kāvya* exegesis.

Vedic exegesis overwhelmingly faces the problem of symbolic expression and is marked by a multiplicity of schools, approaches and methods of interpretation. Modern European interpreters are divided into two schools — one regarding the *Ṛgveda* as predominantly an Indo-European document so that its interpretation demanded the basis of comparative philology and comparative mythology and consequently considering the traditional commentators in the background as of little or no help. The other School, however, preferred the orthodox Indian tradition, represented by Yāska and Sāyaṇa, to the modern philological methods.

Smṛti exegesis wrestles more with conceptual and categorical problems and depends heavily on reasoning as a mode of exposition. It banks heavily on Mīmāṁsā principles and methods. It accepts the epistemological role of language and secondly borrows from and extends the concept of Nyāya, meta-rules, both learned and of common life (*loka-nyāya*). Thirdly they adopt and refine the mode of disputation: the *tarka-vidhi*. Ādi Śaṅkara's various commentaries on diverse Smṛti-texts are supreme examples of Darśana-Smṛti exegesis.

The *kāvya* exegesis employs the analytical models of the long line of poeticians from Bhāmaha (first century CE) to Jagannātha (seventeenth century CE), models that are built on the two sources of grammar and the theory of word-meaning relationship. The theory of symbolic meaning articulated by Ānandavardhana must be recognized as the characteristic instrument of interpretation in *kāvya* exegesis as *kāvya* is chiefly constructed with suggestion (figurative meaning) and therefore its interpretation leans heavily on theories of verbal symbolism in its exposition.

The whole exercise of *vyākhyāna*, in this manner, resolves itself into *arthanirdhāraṇa* — the determination of meaning.

VI

Vedic exegesis overwhelmingly faces the problem of interpretation because of the nature of its discourse.

Vedas are composed in what is called *saṁdhyābhāṣā* (संध्याभाषा), a "twilight" language fluctuating between concrete and abstract, mundane and divine, terrestrial and extra-terrestrial, ordinary and extraordinary. The *Mīmāṁsā-Sūtra* says that *śabda* (in Veda) is the root/origin of *dharma*[19] and in Veda, language (*śabda*) is metaphorical[20] and its intended meaning (*bhāvārtha*) is to be grasped,[21] not its referential meaning, and that reasoning (*anumāna*) is only one of the means of grasping its meaning.[22] The text on account of its mode of constitution is polysemous. Bhartṛhari shows how the same Śruti text is variously grasped to support different competing systems.[23] The following statements have been adduced as support for different doctrines noted in the parenthesis:

— *ātmaiva dehamaya*: (अद्वैत, द्वैत)

— *tat tvamasi* (जीव-ब्रह्म)

— *dva suparṇā. . .* (भोक्ता-साक्षी)

The Vedic statements are classified into four sets by Mīmāṁsā:

---

19. *Mīmāṁsā-Sūtra, "dharmasya śabdamūlatvāt . . .,"* 1.3.1.
20. *Mīmāṁsā-Sūtra, "rūpāt prāyāt,"* 1.2. 11
21. *Mīmāṁsā-Sūtra,* 2.1.1.
22. *Mīmāṁsā-Sūtra,* 2.1.1.
23. *Vākyapadīya,* I.8.

— *bhūtārthavāda,*

— *guṇavāda,*

— *aṇuvāda,* and

— *arthavāda,*

and they have to be understood as such. Of these, only *anuvāda* has truth of correspondence. Yāska (ninth century BCE) also gives a classification of Vedic hymns — prayer, praise, description, and says praise and blame are modes of *dharma* and *adharma*. In these hymns, the object/addressee may be addressed in all the three persons and described in all the cases creating interpretive situations. Again both the narrative and the dialogic modes are used. Upaniṣads explain what is stated, touched upon in the Veda. In the Upaniṣadic discourse it is noted that the path of realization, *mokṣa*, is described through:

— *dr̥ṣṭānta,* example (*Muṇḍaka,* 3.2.8),

— *udāharaṇa* (*Māṇḍūkya,* p. 648),

— *rūpaka,*

— *saṅketa,*

— *vidhi-niṣedha,* prescription and proscription, and

— *yuktis* (cf. *Arthaśāstra,* chapter XV).

All the moods are employed in the Veda, therefore injunctive is not the only mood for *dharma*. But some commentators suggest that all moods are paraphrasable into the indicative eternal.

Further, meaning is often expressed through symbolism or in an allegory.

All these factors make the Vedic discourse polysemous and indeterminate and invited the drastic critique of the kind proffered by Kautsa (noted above).

VII

The learned tradition, which forms the core of this popular tradition, seeks to determine the meaning of the text according to the accepted *paddhati* and in the shared meta-language. This imposes certain conditions on the interpreter. There is in the tradition the concept of *adhikāra*, the problem of competence to interpret. A process of saturation, resulting in participation mystique, must set in before the eyes are ready to see and the mind to grasp (*Anirvan* 1937: 326). This "process of saturation" involves mastering all the pertinent knowledge. The boundaries of this universe of knowledge have been described by Rājaśekhara — the four Vedas; the five sub-Vedas — *Itihāsa* (history), *Dhanurveda* (military science), *Gandharvaveda* (dancing), *Āyurveda* (medicine and surgey), *Gānaveda* (music); the seven auxiliary sciences — *Śikṣā* (phonetics and phonology), *Kalpa* (ritual) or conduct, individual and social, *Vyākaraṇa* (grammar), *Nirukta* (etymology), *Chanda* (metrics and prosody), *Jyotiṣa* (astronomy), *Kāvya* (literary compositions); and six *vidyās* (disciplines) — *Varta* (commerce, agriculture, animal husbandry), *Kāma-sūtra* (sex and sexual life), *Śilpa-śāstra* (sculpture, painting and architecture), *Arthaśāstra* (economics) *Sāhitya-vidyā* (poetics), and *Āṇvikṣīki* (philosophical disputation). Besides, says Rājaśekhara, each Śāstra, the seminal scholastic work of discipline, is like a river, small (*alpa*) in the beginning and grows vast (*vipul*) and more vast with the passage of time. It is the exegetical scholarship and exegetical literature (*bhāṣya, vr̥tti, ṭīkā, samikṣā, pañjikā, kārikā* and *vārttika*) which is responsible for the refinement, extension and increasing precision and profundity of knowledge. A learned man who takes upon himself the task of interpreting a Śāstra has to have mastered all this knowledge — twenty-two sciences and the commentary literature — if he is to make an enduring contribution to knowledge. Great exegetes of the Indian tradition — Yāska, Patañjali, Śabara, Kumārila Bhaṭṭa, Ādi Śaṅkara, Rāmānuja and Madhvācārya — were such men.

The interpreter conducts his inquiry following a given pattern, *vyākhyāna-prakriyā*, that is a part of the *śāstra-paddhati*. A self-contained total act of interpretation includes (i) what the earlier thinkers of the same school, *sampradāya*, have said, (ii) the differing opinion, *matāntara*, and (iii) the context, *prasaṅga*. It consists of paraphrase, explanation example, and counter-example. Since an interpretation can be arrived at only through controversy, the *śāstra-paddhati* permits only one kind of *kathā* (controversy) — the *vāda*. Thus *vādakathā*, which is the best of *kathā*s will continue until truth is arrived at. Almost all the philosophical treatises we know of have adopted *vādakathā*.

The exegesis tradition, *ṭīkā-paramparā*, produced the *śāstra-paddhati*, a method of reading texts, and its existence defined India as an interpretive community. The *śāstra-paddhati* (i) imposes certain conditions on the interpreter through the twin concepts of *adhikāra* and *adhikārī*; (ii) requires the *vyākhyāna-prakriyā*, a total act of interpretation involving (a) what has been said earlier, (b) the opposite point of view, *matāṅ*, (c) the original and the changed context, *prasaṅga*, and (d) the linguistic paraphrase and explanation; (iii) allows only one kind of argument structure or *kathā* which is *vādakathā* (*Nyāyasūtra* 1.2.1.); and (iv) accepts broadly, with school-specific variations, four *pramāṇa*s in this left-to-right strength hierarchy: *pratyakṣa* (perception); *anumāna* (inference); *upamāna* (analogy); *abhyāsa* (experience) and *śāstra vacana* or *śabda* (verbal testimony). Finally, the *śāstra-paddhati* dominantly employs ten instruments of exegesis which may be classed as those pertaining to:

A. The Interpreter's belief system

1. *sārvabhaumasiddhānta* (the principle to be upheld)

B. Verbal testimony

2. *śruti*
3. *darśana-smṛti*
4. *itihāsa-purāṇa dṛṣṭānta*

C. General Rules of Interpretation

5. *saṅgati* (coherence)
6. *paribhāṣā nyāya* (rules of interpretation)
7. *loka nyāya* (rules of interpretation) (judgement from common experience)

D. Language

8. *nirvacana* (etymology)
9. *vyākaraṇa* (grammar)
10. *śabda-śakti* (lexical and propositional meaning including verbal symbolism).

In the polyvalent philosophical texts, the interpreters search for *mūla-siddhānta*, the core meaning of the text in accordance with the assumptions of the *sampradāya* to which they subscribe. Thus in his *Gītā Bhāṣya*, Ādi Śaṅkara as an exponent of the *nivṛtti-mārga*, seeks to establish the principle that liberation from sorrow is attained only through a particular knowledge (*Vivekacuḍāmaṇi* 58).

The use of verbal testimony in philosophical exegesis is generally ancillary — to support a position, and it is rare for an interpreter to argue a position purely on verbal testimony. In grammatical exegesis, verbal testimony is infrequent. In *kāvya* exegesis also, other texts are cited only as examples of parallel use. Its extensive use in philosophical exegesis argues the strong intertextuality of the philosophical texts as well as a continuity of thought. For instance, a recent commentator of the *Gītā*, Swami Ramsukhdas, cites fifty-one sources as evidence apart from major commentaries and *ṭīkā*.

Saṅgati, a text-internal strategy is used (i) to eliminate contradictions, and (ii) to reinforce a thesis in one part of the text with the help of other parts of the text. The exercise is philosophical/linguistic while the governing principle is a reconciliation of thought also achieved through application of meta-rules (see Śrī Rāmānuja, *Gītā Bhāṣya*, 11.20, 24).

Meta-rules, *paribhāṣā*s, a signal achievement of the Indian logico-grammatical-philosophical system,[24] of two kinds — *śāstric* and *laukika* — have an important place in grammar, philosophy, poetics and literature. They are used widely in *śāstra* — exegesis in grammar to interpret and determine the domain or order of application of, for example, Pāṇini's rules; in Mīmāṁsā they are employed to resolve contradictions (*Mīmāṁsāsūtra* 3.3, 4.3), to fill in gaps (*MS* 6.4) and to ascertain the right meaning — for determining the meaning of ambiguous or polyvalent text — between propositional and contextual, for example (*MS* 1.11, 3.1, 4.1, 6.1). In poetics, meta-rules are chiefly employed to ascertain the meaning of a rich text, to decide between possible meanings, lexical, lexical versus propositional, direct versus indirect.[25] Nyāyas are also employed in literature as analogies to reinforce or substantiate

24. Pāṇini's *Aṣṭādhyāyī* expressly includes some *paribhāṣā*s (viz. 1.1.66, 1.3.10, 1.4.2, 3.1.2., etc.) while others are inferrable (cf. Kielhorn 1887). Patañjali enunciated the latter. Jaiminī's *Mīmāṁsāsūtra* has both *Sūtrāmaka* and *jñāpaka sidhamsta* rules. In the *Nyāyasūtra*, the *paribhāṣā*s are given a logical foundation and explanation. Nāgeṣa Bhaṭṭa's eighteenth-century *Paribhāsandu-Śekhara* is an authoritative study of 134 meta-rules.

25. See Vāmana 2.15-18, Viṣwanātha 4.2 ff, 4.4 ff and Mammaṭa 10.457 ff.

a proposition.[26] In *Vivekacuḍāmaṇi*, Ādi Śaṅkara employs various *nyāyas* (repeatedly) also as part of his analogical reasoning.[27]

The instruments of interpretation described so far are decision-procedures to decide between available meanings — but the establishment of meaning in the first instance is a matter of establishing a correlation between the form and its referent, and this is a philological/linguistic exercise that depends on *nirvacana* (etymology) and *śabda-śakti* (theory of meaning), and the categories and structure of language (*vyākaraṇa*). Thus grammatical categories are available as exegetical devices in all textual situations to interpret, to disambiguate or to exclude meaning.[28]

---

26. See Bhartṛhari, *Nītiśataka* 28, 9-10, 6, 68; *Kumārsambhava* 4.31-36; *Raghuvaṁśa* 8.38-56, *Abhijñānaśākuntalam* 2.3 ff; *Rāmacaritamānasa* 5.57; Pañcatantra 5.3.

27. Of the serpent in the rope (verses 138, 198, 235, 388, 405, 570; of water in a mirage (verse 27), of the tree's indifference to the falling leaf (verse 556), of indestructible space in the destructible jar (verse 134), of wave and water (verse 204), of gold and the transient form of the ornament made out of it (verse 26.2), of dream-reality (verses 170-72). Sometimes to establish one idea, he uses a series of analogies — to establish the need of self-knowledge he uses three different analogies in verses 170-72, 252, 448, 458.

28. See, for example Swami Ramsukhdas (1987:201) on the significance of pronouns in the *Bhagavadagītā* (1.21-23; 1.32-33, 36, 37, 39; 3.2; 11.4 etc); on gender and agreement (*BG* 18.5; 2.38, 5.11); on person and agreement (*BG* 2.12; 3.11); on the shift from *kartṛ-vācya* (agentive construction) to *karmakartṛ* (impersonal construction) (*BG* 2.68); on demonstrative pronouns (*BG* 13.1; 6.39; 11.19-21, 26, 28, 33, 45, 51), and on the domain of qualifiers (*BG* 17.9; 4.20; 12.17, 19).

Major exegetes employ these devices to interpret the texts and differ from each other in using one instrument more than the other. Thus, for example, compared to Śrī Rāmānuja, Śaṅkara employs verbal testimony only as *antima pramāṇa* (as the Śruti also says) after perception and inference, his dominant epistemology being *anumāna* — logical inference; with Rāmānuja's textual coherence, what is said elsewhere in the text is very important. Exegetes also differ in the sources cited — thus with Śaṅkara, the *Bṛhadāraṇyaka Upaniṣad* is a great favourite, while Śrī Rāmānuja cites the Vedas more often than does Śaṅkara.

VIII

The Vedic exegesis overwhelmingly faces the problem of symbolic expression and is marked by a multiplicity of schools, approaches and methods of interpretation. Modern European interpreters are divided into two schools — one regarding the *Ṛgveda* as a predominantly Indo-European document, so that its interpretation demanded the basis of comparative philology and comparative mythology and consequently keeping the traditional commentators in the background as of little or no help. The other school, however, preferred the orthodox Indian tradition, represented by Yāska and Sāyaṇa, to the modern philological methods. At present, due importance is attached to traditions of ritual, and internal evidence serves as a powerful tool in Vedic interpretation in several ways, e.g. in ascertaining the meanings of words, supplying lacunae, etc. (Suniti Kumar Chatterji 1937, 1958 rpt. ii, iii).

In modern India also several attempts at Vedic exegesis have been made. Some of them, such as the one by the Ārya Samāj thinkers represented a reaction to uncritical and unjust attacks on the Vedas by ill-informed foreigners of the early nineteenth century (Chatterji 1937, 1958 rpt iii). In any case, in the process the symbolic nature of the Vedic texts was commented upon and explained as requiring different approaches separately or simultaneously. "According to Sri Aurobindo the Veda is mystic and symbolic poetry. . . . Coomaraswamy finds the Veda as mystic and symbolic physical tradition." (Chatterji 1937, 1958 rpt: ii). These two schools, the Ārya Samaj and of Pondicherry, seek to build both on reason and mystic faith. No doubt, the Western ideologists inducted the rational spirit into the task of Vedic exegesis — and often wrote in despair when the text would not yield to modern logic — but it is important to remember that reasoned interpretation had in fact, originated with Yāska himself: "Concerning the *mantras*, none can claim to have perceived their truths if one is not a seer. . . . When seers passed beyond, man asked the gods, "who are going to be seers for us?" To them the gods gave reason as the seer. And hence, whatever one speaks with reason, *following* the track of the work, becomes as good as the utterances of a seer . . ." (*Nirukta*, XIII.12, 13)

Shrimat Anirvan in his essay "Vedic Exegesis" talks of the mist that veils the Śruti texts and hopes that "the mist can be cleared if we approach the problem of interpretation with a penetrative insight and a sound historical sense that can discover the motive of a great thought-movement covering immense stretches in space and time and arrays its events in accordance with the rhythm inherent in it." (Anirvan 1962: 311). What is needed, he says, is a proper interpretive technique, a technique founded on correct assumptions about the nature of experience embodied in these texts. Anirvan has strongly argued that the evolutionary hypotheses, "which can arrange forms in time but cannot explain the timeless spirit that inspires the forces" (p. 312) "a stumbling block to a correct appreciation"

(323) of the content of these texts. The *mantras* portions of these texts are an exposition of an inner reality, of reality experienced as consciousness, of the images that the external reality projects on our consciousness. The essence of that reality as experienced in our consciousness is seen as an ocean of reality (*Ṛgveda*, 1.164-41) a non-segmented and a non-segmentable, a non-discrete and a non-sequential while its external manifestation in the objective world is of course segmented, discrete and sequential. What is essentially *abheda* becomes characterized by *bheda*. India's intellectual effort has been directed towards characterizing the two levels of reality and explaining the relationship between the two. Consciousness (or awareness or comprehension) of the essential reality constitutes the religious experience. This religious experience has a psychological reality, and the forms that appear and are cognized in this reality are projected as gods. The Vedic theory of gods as names of the same one indivisible reality is not therefore an expression of the primitive mind, as the Western Evolutionists have assumed, but an explanation of "a supernormal fact" of a reality that can be experienced only in a heightened state of consciousness in which the mind becomes an acutely sensitive instrument. This content is not amenable to the evolutionary or the historical method and needs to be studied on the basis of other postulates as Anirvan explains (Anirvan, 1962: 328). "It is the epistemological assumption: of the Vedanta, laying stress on the concretely realizable identity of the subject, the object, and the transcendent subsuming both, which supplies the motive of the Vedic religion. Its real nature like that of *vāc* will be revealed only when, with a clear grasp of this identity, one moves up . . . to its source in simple intuition . . . of an integral whole, symbolically described by the seers as the flash of lightning (*Kenopaniṣad*, iv.4).

The Vedic understanding is thus the subjective experience of an objective unified non-discrete and non-sequential reality. It is an intuitive awareness of an order of reality that in its essence and dimensions differs radically from the reality perceived through the spatio-temporal coordinates of our wakeful consciousness. As such it is not possible to capture it or to express it in the ordinary language, which is intrinsically discrete, sequential and "concrete." The Vedic poets, therefore, like all poets, took recourse to symbolism to embody this reality. Symbolism is the inverse of rationalism — a symbol is the sensuous expression of mystical experience . . . suggestive of something elusively transcendent. It requires atmosphere quite different from rationalism which seeks to translate the concrete into abstract symbolism, as an art tries to transform the abstract of the intuition into concrete images. (Anirvan, 1962: 312). Everything in the Vedic literature, particularly the *mantra-Saṁhitā*, is couched in images and one has to "paraphrase" or decode them, but interpretation of the ancient symbols that embody mystical and often occult experience is an extremely difficult if not an impossible task. But the *mantra-Saṁhitā*s, the Vedas, are on the surface virtually opaque making little or no sense.

And this was in fact the objection of the early rationalist thinkers of ancient India. Kautsa, mentioned by Yāska, is a known pre-eminent representative of this early anti-Vedic scepticism, founded essentially in the apparent meaninglessness and irrationality of the Vedas.

For a brief revise of the history of this movement, we may turn to Lakshman Sarup's introduction to his translation of Yāska's *The Nighaṇṭu and the Nirukta* (1926; 1967 rpt., 71). "Kautsa was the leader of a movement, which may be described as materialistic rationalism, and which was the result of a remarkable literary activity, a characteristic of the epoch of Yāska . . . (and) the beginning of which can be traced to an earlier period" (L. Sarup, 1926: 72). Its beginning is to be traced to the sectarian efforts of the followers of the *Atharvaveda* who demonstrated the superiority of the *AV* by allegorically describing the ineffectual character of the three other Vedas. The method of *Atharvans* gave rise to a movement of inquiry and scepticism — a movement the traces of which can be discovered even in the Āraṇyakas and the Upaniṣads (L. Sarup 1926: 74) a fact that leads one to adduce that this rationalist movement was so strong and widespread that even the orthodox thinkers here and there expressed heterodox belief. Sarup cites the belief system: *Bṛhadāraṇyakopaniṣad*, 1.5.23; *Kauśītaki Upaniṣad*, II.5; *Chāndogyopaniṣad*, V.11-24; *Taittirīyopaniṣad*, II.5, *Vivekacudāmaṇī* (Śaṅkara) 2. *The Jain Uttarādhyāyana Sūtras*, IV.12, XIV.12; *Gītā*, II.42, 45; IX.21, XI.48, 53. (1926 : 75) Both in *Kenopaniṣad* (1.2.23) and *Muṇḍakopaniṣad* (III.2.3), the knowledge in Vedas is regarded as *avidyā* (*aparā*), as lower knowledge.

The Buddhists, the Cārvākas and the Jaina *arhat*s continued this line of materialist scepticism. The Buddha carried out "vehement denunciation of Vedic rites and practices. He held them (Vedas) up to ridicule, and discarded them as an obstacle to final emancipation" (L. Sarup 1926: 75). The *arhat*s and the Cārvākas were obviously influenced by, and carried forward, the Buddhist arguments against the existence of an omniscient being and the need and validity of the consequent rituals. This line of thought "created in course of time a considerable amount of opposition to the teachings of the Vedas. It was therefore necessary for the followers of the Vedas to answer to the objections of their opponents and to re-establish their position. (L. Sarup, 1926: 78). The first thinker at the head of this line of materialist sceptics is Kautsa and the first Vedic thinker to counter his arguments is Yāska, the *Nairukta* (etymologist?). However, it is Jaiminī who develops a whole system of thought — *Pūrva-Mīmāṁsā* to examine and refute the position held by the diverse non-Vedic philosophers.

The basic objection of the non-Vedic philosophers and most of their arguments emanate from the symbolic mode of expression in the Vedas, a mode that generates transparent statements making no sense on the surface. That this intrinsically provoked reasoned objections is evident from the explicit statements of the Cārvākas on this point — the Veda is tainted by the three vices of untruth, *self-contradiction*, and *tautology* . . . the three Vedas themselves are only the incoherent rhapsodies of knaves . . . (quoted by Madhvācārya, 5). It is however Kautsa who formulated the critique that remained the bedrock of all later non-Vedic thinkers. His criticism is reported and countered by Yāska (Yāska 1.15, 16) and the Kautsa. Yāska controversy is critically reported by Jaiminī in the first chapter of his *Mīmāṁsā-Sūtras*. Kautsa's objections are reported briefly but essentially contradicted by Yāska (I.15).

Kautsa says that the Vedic statements are open to any or all of the following objections:

(1) they are *meaningless*,

(2) they are *implausible*, and

(3) they are *self-contradictory*.

All the objections pertain to the nature of relations that obtain between the expression (*lakṣaṇa*) and the expressed (*lakṣya*). Hence they all include among others, the relationship of symmetry with the known facts, statements, and accordingly are classified by Mīmāṁsakas into *anuvāda*s, *bhūtārthavāda*s and *guṇavāda*s for which we are employing the more familiar English terms above (which, however are neither translations of nor correspond to the Sanskrit terms). The first illegality is identified as "meaninglessness." Now there are no "meaningless" statements as such — this is the credo of Indian linguistic philosophy, for, the moment we verbally predicate, we create what we predicate. The only question is the relationship of that predication to the available knowledge of facts. "Meaningless" statements are those that relate to known facts in such ways that they fail to make sense, or we fail to see the reason why such statements should at all have been made in the first instance.

Thus a statement like "The mind is a thief" makes a proposition the truth or falsehood of which cannot be verified by the scripture and the sensuous perception. (Mohan Lal Sandal, 1923-25 xx viii). Again, Kautsa argued that Vedic statements are incomprehensible and one has to employ highly esoteric and technical system of orthography, grammar and rules to understand their meaning, and so in themselves they do not mean anything. Thirdly, in any case, in the traditionally handed-down system of using the Vedas, meaning is subordinated — thus it is laid down that the sequence of words in a Vedic statement is sacrosanct. Now in orderly language, one has only to bother about grammaticality and meaningfulness, but here it is the sequence (*krama*) which is superordinate. Meaning thus is of no consequence. Again, the meaning is shut off in opaque words. There are word-uses in the Vedas — such as *amyak, yadrsamir, zarayaci, kanuka* whose meanings are completely lost on the readers. Finally, many Vedic utterances are tautological — they repeat known facts and are therefore redundant or irrelevant. These four arguments are forwarded by Kautsa to show that Vedic *mantra*s are *anarthaka* (devoid of meaning).

The second textual illegality is that of *implausibility*, which may also be realized in one of several ways. Thus Vedic passages often refer to non-existing things — a celebrated often-cited example is the *Ṛk* about the four horned bull (*catvāriṣṛṅga* . . . *ṚV*, 4.5.8.3.). Prohibition of the impossible also belongs here. Sandal cites the example from *Taittirīya Saṁhitā* . . . the fire should not be piled on the earth, in the sky or in the heavens (25.2.7.1.). Piling of fire in the sky is an impossible performance. Then why the prohibition? Again there are passages which in addition contain an address to some inanimate object. Thus in the same Saṁhitā, at one place (*TS*, 1.2.1.1) the branch being cut with a sickle is invoked to protect the tree, and then the sickle-blade which is cutting the branch is addressed and invoked to protect the branch! Finally, Kautsa draws attention to the difficulty of reconciling contradictory statements. Several examples are cited from the Saṁhitās. Thus, in the *Taittrīya Saṁhitā* (*TS*) at one place it is asserted that "only one Rudra exists — no second" (*TS*, 1.8.6) while at another place it is said that thousand, innumerable Rudras have been on this earth (*TS*, 4.5.13).

Kautsa stimulated a whole tradition of Vedic exegesis. As already noted, faced with the sensory rationality of the materialist thinkers, the Vedic philosophers and linguists respond by "interpreting" separately the portions of the Vedas that appeared irrational, implausible or contradictory, achieving in the process increasingly finer understanding of the nature of language, and of the relationship between language and reality. This, no doubt, in turn made possible the development of both linguistic and non-linguistic principles and devices of interpretation. For at the heart of these problems lay the twin imperatives of logical and literal expectation. Once the learned *paṇḍit*s had mastered the principles of judgement (*nyāya*) and the essential symbolic mode of language, the foundation was laid for the organized rejoinder of the *Pūrva-Mīmāṁsā*. Even in the much more ancient Yāska (eighth-ninth century BC) we have evidence of a thorough understanding of the issues involved (*Nirukta* I.15, 16). His *Nirukta* is in fact the first text devoted to the task of interpretation. The rejoinder formulates the concept of "suggested meaning" of what the words mean as against what they state, and this was a remarkable advance in the philosophy of meaning. This takes care of most of the objections. This construct takes care directly of the objections based on *unverifiability, implausibility* and *contradiction*. "The four-horned bull" (unverifiability) stands for *yajña* (sacrifice) according to Śabara, and/or language according to Patañjali (*MB*, I.I) and in each interpretation the *Ṛk* is given a consistent explanation that has the merit of illuminating the nature and structure of *yajña* in one case, and of language in the other. The implausibility of addressing inanimate objects and of requiring or prohibiting impossible performance are similarly interpreted. Thus when the knife-blade cuts the branch it is beseeched to protect the branch — a seemingly *violent* agent and act is explained as protective and protector, very much after the surgeon who amputates a gangrenous limb. The contradiction between one Rudra and a million Rudras disappears when we are told that we are talking of quality and not of a being, very much as we say — "you are my father, you are my mother." The interpretation of opaque words is taken care of by the rules *nirvacana*, "etymology," and of complex and multivalent linguistic expressions by *vyākaraṇa*, the science of linguistic analysis. The question of the status of sequence in *mantra*s which is used by Kautsa to set up a rupture between the literary language of the Saṁhitās and the ordinary language is settled by Śabara by explicating Jaiminī's theory of language, which subsumes both and whose principal claim is that words in the Saṁhitās have the same meaning as in ordinary language and usage. The rest of the objections are taken care of by rules of interpretation (*nyāya*). The sciences of etymology, grammar, rules of interpretation (*nyāya*) and the principles of judgement prevalent in common life (*lokanyāya*) and the philosophy of word-meaning relationship — each, except the last, became a specialized branch of knowledge and was developed and refined as such to a degree where each of them became an independent "science" in its own right, complete with a theoretical framework and tools of analysis.

However, it is the Mīmāṁsā thinkers who explicitly formulated the theory and practice of interpretation. They made *three* great contributions:

1. They systematically analysed word-meaning relationship and set-up typologies of lexical, prepositional and discourse meaning.
2. They discussed the pros and cons of the role of grammar (and meter) and sharply defined and delimited their role in interpretation.
3. They formalized the concept of meta-rules, i.e. rules of interpretation which operate over the whole text and are the overriding conditions of or constraints on meaning.

These intellectual attainments were the product of a uniquely continuous and dedicated scholarship. Beginning before Yāska (eighth century BCE) by the time of Kumārila Bhaṭṭa (sixth century CE) it had made available finished theories and methods of interpretation. Besides in the prolonged contention between the Vedic and the materialist thinkers, the rules of dialectics had been laid down and an essential acknowledged system of disputation had also developed.

IX

Vedic exegesis proved seminal: it generated methods that were possible of application and were extended to other fields of inquiry as well — Smṛtis and Kāvya — and in turn motivated new constructs, besides generally refining the tools and techniques of interpretation. Smṛti exegesis may be subdivided into the exegesis of (i) philosopher (*darśana*) texts, such as the *Bhagvad-Gītā*, and (ii) of grammatical (*vyākarṇik*) texts such as *Aṣṭādhyāyī*. The two differ a little. The *darśana-smṛti* texts are built on theories that may be characterized as metaphysical, in that they assume the existence of extra-sensuous entities — of course, the ground of the assumption of an entity such as *ātman*, "self," for example its rationality, is logically demonstrated and this demonstration is the primary task of exegesis. The grammatical texts emanate from theories that are grounded in the material facts of language use, and its assumptions, such as the grammatical categories of *kāraka*, *sup*, *tiṅ*, etc. — though abstract, are empirically inferred constructs. Therefore, the grammatical exegesis seeks to establish the validity of the theoretical constructs by testing and demonstrating their sufficiency in describing the linguistic phenomena, their explanatory adequacy. For the rest, *contradiction*, *tautology*, *discontinuity* and *implausibility* may be identified as the major specific textual problems of *darśana-smṛti*. In *vyākaraṇa-smṛti-contradiction*, *implausibility*, *discontinuity*, *ambiguity* and, specially in the case of Pāṇini, *incomprehensibility* are the major islands of reflection.

Kāvya-exegesis is literary criticism in our parlance. *Kāvya* resembles grammatical exegesis in the nature of its theoretical constructs — *rūpaka*, *upamā*, *prabandha* are also realities from empirical phenomena (though the reality of this phenomena, the literary fact is a second-order reality). Although the *kāvya* construct such as "metaphor" (*kāvya*) differs from a construct such as "noun" (grammar) it is not sharing the latter's capacity to enter into duality of patterning to yield next higher order constructs. The task of *kāvya*-exegesis is not to show the integration and interaction of different constructs in the explanatory process but to identify the constitutive devices of expression, to measure and explicate their effect by determining their meaning. Since suggestion is the essence of poetry according to Ānandvardhana (ninth century CE) the *kāvya* interpreters wrestle with the problems of symbolic language and try to give poetic statements as "this generally boils down to analysing how the suggested meaning is as such textually impertinent" as *ambiguity, transparency, repetition, redundancy* and *proposition-internal-asymmetry.*

The Smṛti exegesis banked heavily on Mīmāṁsā principles and methods. They accepted the epistemological role of language as detailed and exemplified by Jaimini and Śabara and Kumārila Bhaṭṭa. Secondly they borrowed and extended the concept of *nyāya*s, meta-rules, both logical and of common life (*loka-nyāya*). Thirdly they adopted and refined the mode of disputation, the *tarka-vidhi*. Ādi Śaṅkara's various commentaries on diverse Smṛti-texts, are supreme examples of *darśana-smṛti* exegesis.

The *kāvya* exegesis employs the analytical models of the long line of poeticians from Bhāmaha (first century CE) to Jagannātha (seventeenth century CE), models that are built on the two sources of grammar and the Mīmāṁsā theory of word-meaning relationship. Grammar figures in a major way in Kuntaka's *vakrokti* (deviation) theory, while Mīmāṁsā theory of symbolic-use — owing a debt both to Yāska and Pāṇini — led in successive stages to Ānandavardhana's final and authoritative *dhvani*-theory of literary meaning, besides influencing and making possible the *Riti* and the *Alaṅkāra*-schools. Theory of symbolic meaning, inspired by Mīmāṁsā but fully formulated by the poeticians, must be recognized as the characteristic method of interpretation in *kāvya* exegesis.

In this manner, the principles and methods of interpretation conceived and sharpened by the Vedic exegetes became the foundation of all kinds of exegesis, so that there is a common core of methodology to interpret texts of different disciplines. The term for this common core is *śāstra-paddhati*, the method of interpreting intellectual texts.

12

The Contribution of Kerala to Vedic Exegesis and Saman Chanting

P.C. Muraleemadhavan

THE contribution of Kerala to Vedic exegesis is immense in volume and importance. Scholars from Kerala have written several exegetical works on Vedic texts. They have also preserved intact the oral tradition for thousands of years. Here the tradition is authentic and alive, and is not the result of recent revivals. In the apparently isolated corner of South-West India, a few orthodox Nambūtiri brāhmaṇa families have maintained their Vedic tradition with meticulous care, preserving it from generation to generation. Two of the ancient Vedic rituals, the Agniṣṭoma lasts five days and the Agnicayana or Atirātra lasts twelve days. During the last one hundred years Atirātra has been performed 20 times and the Agniṣṭoma nearly 100 times. One who has performed an Agniṣṭoma is called Somayājī or Comātiri, and one who has performed an Atirātra is called Akkittiri. The Agnicayana performed at Pañjāḷ in 1975 with international co-operation, and the two volumes of its proceedings and studies, edited by Professor Frits Staal,[1]

1. Frits staal, *Agni: The Vedic Ritual of the Fire Altar*, Motilal Banarsidass, Delhi 1981.

have brought to light much information about Kerala tradition regarding Vedic Studies. Last year another Atirātra was performed at Kuṇḍūr with much publicity and attracted Vedic scholars from different parts of India and abroad. Leading newspapers in Kerala wrote long articles on the daily procedure, and there were discussions. It may be hoped that the tradition has been saved from extinction.

The Aitareya and Kauṣītakī Śākhās of the *Ṛgveda* have been preserved and kept alive in Kerala. The Kauṣītakins are in a minority and are now available only in Kerala, Gujarat and to a limited extent in Mahārāṣtra. The Aitareyins follow the Śrautasūtra of Āśvalāyana and the Kauṣītakins there of Sāṅkhāyana. The Kauṣītakins are called Sāṅkhāyanas in Gujarat and Mahārāṣtra, but solely by the name of Kauṣītakī in Kerala. The Jaiminīya Śākhā of Sāmaveda is preserved only in a few families in Kerala and Tamil Nadu. The Jaiminīya Brāhmaṇa is probably the earliest Brāhmaṇa. One complete manuscript was discovered by E.R. Sreekrishna Sarma in Kotuntirappaḷḷi near Pālghāt and was the source of Raghuvīra Lokeshchandra edition in 1954.

Three or four manuscripts were later discovered by Asko Parpola and E.R. Sreekrishna Sarma from Nellikkāt Akkittirippād at Pañjāl, and Sarma has prepared a critical edition with translation of the Brāhmaṇa for Indira Gandhi National Centre for Arts. The Nambūtiri brāhmaṇas of Kerala began to specialize in Vedic studies and Vedic exegesis from very early times. In the seventh century CE, Daṇḍin refers in his *Avantisundarīkathā*, to two scholars from Kerala as his friends: Mātṛdatta, a poet who also wrote some commentaries, and his father Bhavatrāta, commentator on Kalpasūtras. This Bhavatrāta is probably identical with the author of the commentary on *Jaiminīya śrautasūtra*. Ṣadgururśiṣya,[2] who flourished in Kerala during the twelfth century, has written several commentaries on Vedic texts — Sukhapradā on the *Aitareya Brāhmaṇa*, Mokṣapradā on the *Aitareyāraṇyaka*, Abhayapradā on the *Āśvalāyana-śrautasūtra* and Vedārthadīpikā on the *Sarvānukramaṇī* of Śaunaka. He refers to some Malayalam *tadbhava*s of Sanskrit words — 'caṅṅata' for *saṁhitā*, 'kirihyam' for *gṛhyam*, 'takkaṇā' for *dakṣiṇā* etc. We are not concerned with the correctness of all these so-called *tadbhava*s, but the reference suggests his acquaintance with Malayalam words. (*Aitareyāraṇyaka*, TSS 167, p. 265)

This scholar calls himself Ṣadguruśiṣya, since he considers six deities as his preceptors: his real name is not known. This commentary is published by Ramlal Kapur Trust, Sonepat, Haryana, 1985.

Another scholar commentator of Vedic texts is Udaya of Muriyamaṅgalam family of Brahmakkaḷam,[3] not far from Guruvayur. He was the son of Nārāyaṇa Yajvan and Sāvitrī. He wrote the Sukhadā commentary on the *Kauṣītakī Brāhmaṇa* of the *Ṛgveda*, which is not only an excellent piece of textual exegesis, but also a lucid exposition of the ritual application. It shows Udaya's intimate knowledge of the rituals dealt with in the Brāhmaṇa. His father had performed a *jyotiṣṭoma yāga*, as the epithet *yajvan* suggests. Prof. E.R. Sreekrishna Sarma edited and published from Germany, the Kerala recension of the *Kauṣītakī Brāhmaṇa*[4] and the Sukhadā commentary of Udaya.

---

2. K.K. Raja, *Contribution of Kerala to Sanskrit literature*, Appendix p. iii, Univesity of Madras 1980. (See also, Travancore Sanskrit Series No. 172, 13-14).

3. Venkita Subramania Iyer, *Kerala Sanskrit Literature — A Bibliography*, p. 9, Kerala University, Trivandrum, 1979.

4. E.R. Sree Krishna Sharma, *Kauṣītakī Brāhmaṇa*, I Text, Franz Stainer Verlag GMBH, Wiesbaden, 1969.

He used all available manuscripts including the one in the Adyar Library which has been noticed by Prof. C. Kunhan Raja. He also got a manuscript from the Late Erkara Rāman Nambūtiri.[5] He also got advice and help from Erkara. According to Sarma, there is a tradition making Udaya a nephew of *Ṛṣi*, probably of the Payyūr Bhaṭṭa family flourished in the fifteenth century.

Kātyāyana's *Ṛgveda Sarvānukramaṇī*, well-known general index, has been very popular in Kerala. Ṣadguruśiṣya's commentary was partly published from Oxford by Macdonell. Nārāyaṇa of Akkittam family of Veṅṅanād near Trippūṇithura has written the Dīpaprabhā commentary on it. Nārāyaṇa was the son of Ārya, and belonged to Āṅgirasa *kula*. He wrote Dīpaprabhā commentaries on Kaiyata's *Bhāṣyapradīpa* and on the *Vararuca saṅgraha* which is an anthology of Ṛgvedic stanzas generally used in daily rituals like *Sandhyāvandana*. His family name Akkittam shows that there were many ancestors in that family who performed *Agnicayana*.

Kerala has produced another elaborate commentary on *Sarvānukramaṇika*: it is called *Sarvānukramaṇipadyavivṛti*, the author is from Kerala, but his name is not known. As the title indicates, it is written in verse form. A rare copy of this manuscript belonging to C. Kunhan Raja is with Dr. K.K. Raja, and Dr. Parameswara Aithal has edited it at Heidelberg University in Germany. Another manuscript originally belonging to Erkara Raman Nambutiri was with Dr. E.R. Sreekrishna Sarma. Nīlakanṭhayogiar of Taikkāt Vaidika family who was alive during the sixteenth century wrote the *Śrautaprāyaścittasaṁgraha* on Śrauta expiatory rites.

Another very important Kerala work on Vedic exegesis is *Nirukta-vārttika*, an elaborate metrical commentary on Yāska's

5. Ibid., Preface, p. vi.

Nirukta. Its author became a sanyāsin taking the name Padmapādācārya;[6] before taking to saṁnyāsa, he was Nīlakaṇṭha belonging to a brāhmaṇa family at Koṇṭayūr on the banks of the Bhāratappuḻa (Niḷā). He belonged to the Yajurveda and the Gārgyagotra. His father was Kīraśarma who was well versed in yajña performance; and his mother was Nīlī of Bhāradvāja gotra. His grandfather was a Vedic scholar named Rudra Śarma. Nīlakanṭha had brothers like Rudra and sisters like Datta. Kubera was his younger brother. All these details are given by the author himself thus:-

जामदग्न्येन रामेण गार्ग्याय प्रतिपादिते।
कोष्टयूरिति विख्याते ग्रामे केरलपूजिते॥
ब्राह्मणानां सहस्रेण जुष्टे शिष्टजनार्चिते।
याज्ञिकैर्वेदविद्भिश्च सर्वे देवोपशोभिते॥
अव्यवछिन्नयज्ञानां यजुर्वेदविदां कुले।
कुले महति गार्ग्यानां नीलकण्ठोप्यजायत॥
कीरशर्मा पिता यस्य यज्वा यज्ञविशारदः।
बहुयज्वी चतुर्वेदो रुद्रशर्मा पितामहः।
भारद्वाजी च कौबेरी नीली माता बहुप्रजा॥
रुद्राद्याः भ्रातरो यस्य दत्ताद्याः ज्यामयस्तथा॥
किञ्चित् सोधीत्य वेदस्य मस्करी समपद्यत।
पद्म इत्यपरां संज्ञां लब्धवान् स गुरोः पुनः॥
श्रुत्वा किञ्चित् स शास्त्राणां वेदान्तेषु कृतश्रमः।
अकरोत् श्रद्धया युक्तो निरुक्तश्लोकवार्तिकम्॥

Jāmadagnyena rāmeṇa gārgyāya pratipādite ।
koṣṭayūriti vikhyāte grāme keralapūjite ॥
brāhmaṇānām sahasreṇa juṣṭe śiṣṭajanārcite ।
yājñikairvedavidbhiśca sarve devopaśobhite ॥
avyavacchinnayajñānām yajurvedavidām kule । *kule mahati gārgyānām nīlakanṭhopyajāyata* ॥ *kīraśarmā pitā yasya yajvā yajñaviśāradaḥ* । *bahuyajvī caturvedo rudraśarmā*

6. *Contribution of Kerala to Sanskrit Literature,* Appendix, p. iv.

pitāmahaḥ ॥ *bhāradvājī ca kauberi nīlī mātā bahuprajā* ॥ *rudrādyāḥ bhrātaro yasya dattādyāḥ jyāmayastathā* । *kiñcitsodhītya vedasya maskarī samapadyata* । *padma ityaparām saṁjñāṁ labdhavān sa guroḥ punaḥ* । *śrutvā kiñcitsa śāstrāṇam vedānteṣu kr̥taśramaḥ* । *akarot śraddhayā yukto niruktaślokavārtikam* ॥[7]

On the basis of the copy of a manuscript got from Kerala, probably from the Govt. Sanskrit College, Tripūnithura by Prof. C. Kunhan Raja, he published a paper on *Niruktavārtika* in the *Adyar Library Bulletin*. Later, the work had been published by Ramlal Kapur Trust, edited by Dr. Vijayapal in 1982 on the basis of this paper manuscript. Recently I found the exemplar of this manuscript in Tripūnithura Sanskrit College.

The six verses quoted by Payyūr Parameśvara in Gopalikā commentary on Maṇḍanamiśra's *Sphoṭasiddhi*, are actually found in Nīlakanṭha's work — *Niruktavārtika*. While explaining the Nirukta passage:-

साक्षात्कृतधर्माण ऋषयो बभूवुः — यथोक्तं
निरुक्तवार्तिके एव।
असाक्षात्कृतधर्मस्य ते परेभ्यो यथाविधिः
उपदेशेन सम्प्रादुर्मन्त्रान् ब्राह्मणमेव च॥
उपदेशश्च वेदव्याख्यायां यथोक्तम्
अथोऽयमस्य मन्त्रस्य ब्राह्मणस्यायमित्यपि
व्याख्यैवात्रोपदेशस्स्यात् वेदार्थस्य विवक्षितः इति।
वेदार्थं चोपदेशेन ग्रहीतुमशक्तः अङ्गानि च
समाम्नासिषुरिति यथोक्तम् ॥
अशक्तसूपदेशेन ग्रहीतुमपरे यथा।
वेदमभ्यस्तवन्तस्ते वेदाङ्गानि च यत्नतः इति॥
बिम्मशब्दो ह्यानान्तरमेव तत्रनिरुक्तः

7. *Niruktavārtika*, (ed.) C. Kunhan Raja, p. 162, Adayar Library, 1948.

बिम्ममभिम्मामिति वाह विभर्तयार्तविवक्षया
उपायो हि विभर्तयर्थामुपेयम वेदगोचरम
अथवा भाषण् भिम्मन भासते दीप्तिकर्मणाः
अभ्यासेन हि वेदार्थो भासते दिप्यते स्फुटम् इति ॥

Śākṣātkṛtadharmāṇo ṛṣayo babhūvuḥ — yathoktam nirukta vārtike eva
Asākṣātkṛtadharmasya te parebhyo yathāvidhiḥ
upadeśena samprādur mantrān brāhmaṇameva ca ॥
upadeśaśca vedavyākhyāyāṁ yathoktam
atho 'yamasya mantrasya brāhmaṇasyāyamityapi
vyākhyaivātropadeśassyāt vedārthasya vivakṣiṭaḥ iti ।
vedārthaṁ copadeśena grahītumaśaktaḥ aṅgāni ca
samāmnāsiṣuriti yathoktam ॥
aśaktasūpadeśena grahītumapare yathā ।
vedamabhyastavantaste vedāṅgāni ca yatnataḥ iti ॥
bimmaśabdo hyānāntarameva tatraniruktaḥ ।
bimmam bhimmāmitivāha bibhartyārtavīvakṣayā ॥
upāyo hi vibhaktyārthāmupeyam vedagocaram
athavā bhāṣaṇam bhimmam bhāsate dīptikarmaṇāḥ
abhyāsena hi vedārtho bhāsate dipyate sphuṭam iti[8]

Since Payyūr Parameśvara, commentator on the *Sphoṭasiddhi* quotes *Niruktavārttikā* as an authority, its author cannot be later than the fourteenth century. Keḷallūr Nīlakanṭha Soṁayājī has also quoted from the *Niruktavārttika* in his Bhāṣya on *Āryabhaṭīya.*[9] It is also referred to in the anonymous *Sarvānukramanīpadyavivṛtī*. *Niruktavārttika* is an excellent commentary which is sure to help in furthering Vedic exegesis. Melputtūr Nārāyaṇa Bhaṭṭa wrote a short poem in nine verses, the *sukha śloka* which is apparently a *stotra* in praise of the goddess, but which gives statistical details relating to the *aṣṭaka-*

8. Ibid., p.176.
9. *Contribution of Kerala to Sanskrit Literature*, Appendix, p. iv.

adhyāya-varga classification of the *Ṛgveda* using the *katapayādi* notation. This has been edited by C. Kunhan Raja. Godavarma, Yuvarāja of Koṭuṅṅallūr (1800-1850) wrote a *Garuḍacayana pramāṇa*[10] on the construction of the Vedi of the *Garuḍacayana*.

Besides these there are several Malayalam works which deal with ritual exegesis, for example the *Cerumukkil pacca* by Cerumukku Parameśvaran Nambūtirī. The procedures for the various rituals are described in Malayalam works called *Caṭaṅṅu*; these were the popular texts used by the Nambūtirīs as handbooks to keep them in performing the rituals.

Coming to the modern period we have to mention a few scholars. Erkkara Rāman Nambūtirī who was an embodiment of the Kauṣītakī tradition; his articles collected in *Āmnāyamathanam*[11] were also translated into Sanskrit. He edited the Malayalam monthly journal *Anādi*,[12] to popularize Vedic rituals. He took an active and decisive role in the Pañjāḷ Atirātram. Nellikkāṭ Iṭṭiravi[13] who was an authority on the Jaiminīya chanting was also responsible for the preservation of the tradition of this Vedic Śākhā; he was also a leading figure at the Pañjāḷ Atirātram. V.K. Narayana Bhattathiri[14] tried to stress the importance of studying the meaning of Vedic texts profusely on Vedic interpretation using Yāska and also Aurobindo. Mahākavi Vallathol Narayana Menon's[15]

---

10. V. Rajarajavarma Raja. *Keraliya Samskrita Sāhitya Caritram* — Vol. 5, Sree Sankaracharya University of Sanskrit, Kerala, 1998.
11. *Samskṛta Sāhitya Caritram*, (ed) K.K. Raja & M.S. Menon Vol. I, p. 261, Kerala Sahitya Akademi, Trissur, Kerala.
12. Edited by Erkkara Raman Namboothiri.
13. See '*Vedārṇavavandanam*,' p. 65, Felicitation volume presented to Asko-Parpola, (ed.) Petteri Koshi kkallio, University of Helsinki, Finland.
14. A Vedic Scholar and Social reformer of Kerala, 20th century.
15. Great Malayalam Poet of 20th century.

translation of the *Ṛgveda*, prepared in his seventies, brought this ancient text to the ordinary people. O.M.C. Nambūtirippad published the *Ṛgveda*[16] with his Malayalam translation and notes based on Sāyaṇa which was a boon to the generally-educated Malayalees to enter the heart of the *Ṛgveda*.

The name of C. Kunhan Raja deserves special mention in modern Vedic exegesis. He studied under Macdonnell at Oxford, and had discussion with Goldner in Germany and Louis Renou in France. Though he was taught that Sāyaṇa was explaining the Vedas without any traditional basis, and modern research methodology using comparative and historical approaches is found to help more than Sāyaṇa, Kuñhan Rāja on his return from Europe was able to get many pre-Sāyaṇa commentaries[17] on Vedic texts, and published them for the first time. He was convinced that Sāyaṇa was using a continuous tradition, though a ritualistic tradition. Besides editing commentaries, he wrote several expository volumes — *Vedas, a Cultural Study,*[18] *Poet-philosophers of the Ṛgveda, Quintessence of the Veda,* etc. His edition of *Asyavāmīya sūkta* with Ātmārāma's Advaitic interpretation, together with translation and notes explaining the riddles is specially praiseworthy. As a successor in the field, the name of E.R. Sreekrishna Sarma has already been mentioned. K. Kunjunni Raja also contributed several research articles on Vedic exegesis.

Sāma Chanting

Chanting of Sāman is the most attractive among Vedic recitals, since it is musical in character. The Nambūtiri families of Kerala

---

16. Translated *Ṛgveda* into Malayalam.
17. C. Kunhan Raja, *The Quintessence of the Veda,* p. 138.
18. Andhra University, Waltair, 1957.

preserved this valuable oral tradition intact for several centuries. Jaiminīya Śākhā is being preserved in Kerala with meticulous care.

In Kerala, even though there were more than 25 families altogether belonging to this Śākhā, only five remain at present. 5 Nambūtiris — all of them above 70 years — are only capable of chanting the entire text with all its *vikṛtīs*. Since the number of scholars in the field of Jaiminīya is fast dwindling; Sree Sankaracharya University of Sanskrit, Kalady, Kerala decided to document the entire chanting of *Sāmaveda* with all its *vikṛtīs*, on war footing. The Audio/Video recording of the entire *sāma* took 70 hours.

The following scholars participated in *Sāman* chant.

1. Neelakaṇṭhan Namboodiri of Nellikkaṭṭu Mana
2. Vasudevan Namboodiri of Nellikkaṭṭu Mana
3. Āryan Namboodiri of Thoṭṭam Mana
4. Nārāyaṇan Namboodiri of Thoṭṭam Mana, and
5. Vāsudevan Namboodiri of Perumaṅgād Mana.

The most illustrious scholar on the subject was late Iṭṭiravi Māmuṇṇu of Muṭṭatukaṭṭil family.[19] Even scholars like Prof. Asko Parpola and Prof. J. Frits Staal used to approach him for scholarly advices.

The earlier attempts for recording *Sāma* chanting were not complete and fruitful. Even though Prof. Staal recorded the *Ārcika* portion completely in 1971, it is in a dilapidated condition and no reproduction from the master cassettee is possible.

Prof. E.R. Sreekrishna Sarma recorded the chanting except *Ūha* and *Ūṣāṇi* portions in 1980. Tirupati Devasthanam also

19. *Introduction to Kauṣītakī Brāhmaṇa* (ed.) E.R. Sreekrishna Sharma.

recorded the *Ārcika* through audio system. All India Radio Calicut recorded some portion of *Sāman* Chant. But it is only a little portion. (The efforts of Prof Guni from Denmark and Dr. K.V. Krishna Das from Trivandrum are also incomplete since it covers only Audio System). The other *Vikṛtī*s were also not recorded in the earlier attempts. In the light of the above-said facts it is clear that the step taken by Sree Sankaracharya University is the first one of its kind since it covers all *Vikṛtī*s in both audio and video. Even though some agency from Nasik has recorded the chanting, it is only 18 hrs. duration and that too the *Ārcika* portion only.

Chanting of Sāma is divided into:-

1. *Ārcika* or *Ṛk* (*Saṁhitā* text chanted in musical accent. There are 112 sections called *Ott*s (like *Sūkta*s in *Ṛgveda*). Each one contains 15 to 20 hymns).
2. *Grāmageya* or *Sāma*
3. *Āraṇyaka* or *Chandasāma*. The second and third items are more sophisticated methods of chanting *Ārcika* in various musical accents.

Apart from these two systems, there are two other types of chanting *Sāman* which is highly technical and complicated. They are *Ūha* and *Ūṣāṇī*.

The first one — Ūha is the *vikṛti* of *Grāmageya* and the second one — *Ūṣāṇī* is the *vikṛti* of *Āraṇyaka* or *Candasāma*. It is also known as *Rahasyagāna*.

After a detailed study of all types of *Sāma* chant, we could decide that a duration of 70 hours would be required for documenting the *Sāman* chant with all its *vikṛti*s. Under the leadership of Śree Sankaracharya University of Sanskrit, the documentation was completed in the year 1999.

Before starting the actual documentation work, we have referred to mostly all the literature connected with *Sāman* Chant. I have also gone through the book *Sāmavedic Chant*[20] of Prof. Wayne Horward. The auther of the book took meticulous care to cover mostly all information available in the field.

The brāhmaṇas of Kotuntharappilly Grāmam belong to *Jaiminīya Śākhā* of *Sāmaveda*. But their style is different from that of Nambūtiris. This style has close resemblance with *Makara Pāṭha* of Makara Bhūṣaṇam of Śrīraṅga.

In a trip to Palakkat to gather more information about *Sāman* chant, I could come across a *Sāman* scholar namely Gopāla Vādhyār. To my surprise I could hear a new style of *Sāman* chant called 'Putukkoṭṭu Style' belonging to *Kauthuma Śākhā* perhaps older than that of the existing one called 'Rāmaṇṇa Style'. By hearing the style I came to know that it has a close resemblance with the Nambūtirī recitation of *Grāmageya* belonging to *Jaiminīya Śākhā*. More than that, 'Ja', 'Ṇa' and 'Ṇa' are clearly pronounced in this style which are not audible in the other style called 'Rāmaṇṇa *Pāṭha*'. Hence it is known as 'Jā ṅa ṇa pāṭham' (Putukoṭṭu pāṭham).

I could refer to the *Vedārṇava-vandanam*[21] the 'Felicitation Volume dedicated to Prof. Asko Parpola' edited by Sri Petteri Koskikallio and read the statement of Prof. Wayne Howard in his article, that he could not get any information about this *Prācīna* style, during his studies and that Sri. L. S. Rajagopal from Kerala gave this precious information about Putukkoṭṭu Style of *Sāman* chant through a series of letters and tapes, and that only one scholar lives at present in Kerala, i.e. Gopala

---

20. Wayne Howard, *Sāmvedic Chant*, New Heven and London, Yale University Press, 1977.

21. University of Helsinki.

Vadhyar of Putukkoṭṭu Grāmam[22] who can recite the *Sāma*, that too the *Gṛhya portion* only. The existing style *'Rāmaṇṇa Pāṭha'* is generally studied mostly by all Tamil brāhmaṇas, at present, which was prepared by Rāmanātha Śrauti some 250 years back, at the time of Maharashtra rule. Rāmanātha Śrauti with the help of some Maharashtra scholars edited the text and modified the style of chanting. Later it came to be called *'Rāmaṇṇa Pāṭha'*.[23] The main feature of this *pāṭham* is that, it has omitted the letters 'Jā' 'Ṅa' and 'Ṇa' since it is difficult to pronounce for Tamil speaking people. At the advent of the new style which is more easier and attractive, the old style slowly vanished from the scene. The Maharashtra rulers patronised the new style in all *Pāṭhaśālā*s throughout the state. In Tañjāvūr, the brāhmaṇas were isolated from the outside world and the Maharashtra rulers occupied Tanjur. With the help of these rulers the brāhmaṇas of Tanjur got acquaintance with Puna scholars and with the help of them, they made Vedic chanting more easier by omitting difficult letters like 'Jā, Ṅa and Ṇa,'.[24] This is called *'Rāmaṇṇa Pāṭham'* because Rāmanātha Śrauti a veteran scholar in *Sāmaveda* is the patron of this style. Scholars have gone to the extent of rendering *Sāmaveda* on harmonium. In the book *Sāmagāna*s published in 1880 in Kumbhakonam a picture showing the keys of harmonium and the so-called corresponding *Svara* of the *sāman* scale was given.[25] But Sundara Iyer of Putukkoṭṭu, the retired judge of Madras High Court was not happy with the mentioned *pāṭham* and he started a *pāṭhaśālā* separately for teaching and preserving this

---

22. Ibid., p. 18.
23. Ibid., p. 29.
24. "A Report on the Prācīna Kauthuma Sāmaveda of Pālghāṭ," L.S. Rajagopal and Wayne Howard, *The Journal of Indian Musicological Society*. Jan.-Dec. 1989, Vol. 20 Nos. 1&2 p. 5-16.
25. Ibid.

ancient prestigious Putukkoṭṭu style known as 'Jā' 'Ṅa' 'Ṇa' *pāṭham'*. The brāhmaṇas got annoyed with the king Śekhara Varman of Palghat due to his immoral life and they left Palghat. Thunchattu Ezhuttachan, the famous poet of Kerala helped the king to bring some brāhmaṇas to Palghat to perform Vedic rituals, from Thañjāvūr and Kumbhakonam.[26] The king built houses and temples for them at different places like Śekharipuram, Kalpatti and Puttukkoṭṭu village. The *sāman* scholars brought from Tañjāvūr started living in these villages. The Tamil immigrants came to Kerala some 400 years back and they belonged to the old *pāṭham* of *sāman* namely 'Jā, Ṅa, Ṇa *pāṭham'*. The present *pāṭham* popularly available is known after Rāmanāthaśrauti and it had originated some 250 years back. The montif of Naṭuvil *maṭham* (the followers of Śrī Śaṅkarācārya) extended all facilities to Vedic brāhmaṇas to build houses and temples at Putukkoṭṭu. The Vedeśvara *Pūjā* conducted even now in Putukkoṭṭu by household brāhmaṇs is the continuation of their practice at Thañjāvūr. The name Vedeśvara is common both at Tañjāvūr and Putukkoṭṭu.

A sample of the *sāman* Chant of *Jaiminīya* Recension of Nambūtirīs recorded by the Sree Sankaracharya University along with Potukkoṭṭu Style of *sāman* Chant will be displayed at the end of my presentation.

Among Vedas *sāma* is significant due to its character of music. The word *sāma* is interpreted in different ways. It means music, since music plays a vital role in it. Other interpretations are *Sammitamvca yā sā sāma* means the one which is measured by Ṛk. is *sāma, samayati santoṣayati* or *ramāyati.* (*sā sāma*) *sā - vāk - amah - prāṇah ṭayoḥ ekatrāvasthitiḥ - sāma, syati khaṇḍayati dukhāni yena tat sāma* etc. In Vedic studies *sāma* is all the more important since it is used throughout the rituals in sacrifices.

---

26. Ibid.

Even though *sāmaveda* is known as *Sahasra vartmā*, only 3 *śākhā*s are available at present: they are *Kauthuma, Rāṇāyaṇīya* and *Jaiminīya*. I am of the opinion that the expression *sahasravartmā sāmavedaḥ* doesn't mean 1000 *śākhā*s but of 1000 styles (many styles). In other Vedas also we come across several styles of chanting in each śākhās. Hence this is applicable to other Vedas also. The *Kauthuma* and *Rāṇāyaṇīya* are still preserved in Karnataka, Tamil Nadu, Maharashtra and Bengal. Nearly 2000 phrases are common to both *Kauthuma* and *Rāṇāyaṇīya* styles of chanting. But these phrases are kept intight only by the scholars now living at Koṇavār the place between N. Kanera and Goa.

In Kerala mostly *Jaiminīya Śākhā* is prevalent among Nambūtirīs. *Kauthuma* and *Jaiminīya* are also known as *Chāndoga* and *Talavakāra* respectively. Even though the differences in both the texts are very little, the recitals are entirely different. Some textual evidences are available in support of the fact that *Kauthuma Śākhā* was also popular among Nambūtirīs in Kerala. In the *Āṭṭaprakāra* (stage manual) of Bhagavadajjuka, a Sanskrit drama written some four centuries back, we can trace out this fact from the long statement of Śāṇdilya a Sāmavedic brāhmaṇa.[27] Among 1000 branches of the *Ṛk, Yaju*s and *sāma*, six branches were popular in Kerala namely *Āśvalāyana* and *Kauṣītaki* of *Ṛgveda, Bodhāyana* and *Bādhūlaka* of *Yajurveda* and *Talavakara* (*Jaiminīya*) and *Chāndoga* (*Kauthuma*) of *Sāmaveda*. The Mantredath Mana, the famous Nambūtirī family at Lakkiti, Kerala, belonged to *Kauthuma* recension and this family later changed the *caraṇa* during the Upanayana of the children. Changing from one *Veda* to another is called *Caraṇam Māral*. The family temple of this "mana", known as "Kutiraśśeri", and Śrauta text found of the same name from

27. Ed. by N.P. Unni, Nag Publishers, New Delhi.

that family are not accidental, since the word Kutira means horse and the Hayagrīva is the deity of *Sāmaveda*. Incidentaly it is interesting to note that Śāndilya of Bhagavadajjuka belongs to one of the gotras of *Sāmaveda*.

The argument of L.S. Rajagopal in his article "Studies in Samaveda — some problems encountered," that among Nambūtirīs, only *Jaiminīya*s were found, will not stand to test in the light of the above said facts. It is true that now in Kerala mostly all Sāmavedins belong to *Jaiminīya* recension. But it is very difficult to say that no Nambūtirī brāhmaṇa is available who belongs to *Kauthuma Śākhā*. In this context it is to be noted that those who claim to be *Jaiminīya*s are all actually not belonging to *Jaiminīya Śākhā* since they chant similar to that of *Kauthuma* recension. This happens in the branches of other Vedas also. The change of *Caraṇa* is also prevalent in several parts of Kerala not only among Sāmavedins but also among Ṛgvedins and Yajurvedins. The characteristics of the chanting of previous Vedic recension influences the succeeding one.

At the time of the invasion of Tippu Sultan many brāhmaṇas left Palghat and when British rule came they gave pension to Rājas and practically there was nobody to patronise the Vedic scholars.[28]

Vedic rituals vanished day by day and the *sāman* chant also lost its importance, since *sāman* is mainly to be used in rituals.

L.S.R. and Wayne Horward in their article 'A report on the *Kauthuma Sāmaveda* of Palghat' mentioned the names of some scholars who still preserve the *prācīna* style: (1) Parameśwara Iyer of Thrissur (2) V.N. Narayana Vadhyar (now staying at Bombay) and Sri Gopala Vadhyar of

28. *J.I.M.S.* June-Dec. 1989, Vol. 20 Nos. 8.1 & 2.

Putukkoṭṭu village. Among them the first one is no more. The second one is staying at Bombay and due to the absence of practice, he lost the field. Now there is only one scholar namely Gopala Vadhyar who can recite *Prācīna* style that too only *Gṛhya* portion. I could find out recently two scholars - Narāyaṇa Śāstri and Rāmanātha lyer who are experts in the old style and can chant the entire *Śrauta* portion. At present they live in Kumbhakonam. Now the Sanskrit University has taken steps to document this style. The so-called *purohitā*s in the villages of Tanjur are familiar only with the *Gṛhya pāṭha*. Now-a-days the traditional styles of chanting are modified musically, mostly in all the regions.

I am not aware of the progress of the project proposd by L.S.R. and Wayne Howard for documenting the *Prācīna* style. I have gone through their study on notations and perfectly agree with their statement that the notational numbers represent *mudrā*s and not the tones of the scales.[29] This is true in the case of all styles of chanting *sāman* belonging to *Kauthuma*.

It is obvious that, in this *prācīna* chant and all other types of *Kauthuma* chants, the music connected with the notational numbers (that is the *mudrā*s) depends on such factors as vowel length and types of numbers that precede and succeed.

Wayne Howard cautioned the readers of Nārada Śikṣā, against the literal interpretation of the passage (1-5-12-*Narada* 1964) that states a correspondence between the numbers and tones of a secular scale.

> *Yaḥ sāmagānām prathamaḥ sa veṇormadhyamaswaraḥ*
> *Yo dvitīyaḥ sa gāndharvaḥ tṛtīyo ṛṣabhaḥ smṛtaḥ*
> *Caturthaḥ ṣaḍjā ityāhuḥ pañcamo dhaivato bhavet*
> *Ṣaṣtho niṣādo vijñeyaḥ saptamaḥ pañcamaḥ smṛtaḥ*

29. Ibid., p. 10.

It is true that the *prācīna sāman* chant encompasses seven tones. But these tones can't be related to the notational numbers, which represent *mudras*. Not a single style of chanting of *sāman* all over India, is sung in the manner described by the *Naradīyaśikṣā*.

Wayne Howard published his work *Sāma Vedic Chant* at Howard in 1977. He discussed one *prācīna* style of *sāman* chant existing in Mullantiram village of North Arcot district, Tamil Nadu.[30] He recorded this in tape with the help of T.K. Gopala lyer of Madras in 1975. But L.S.R. mentioned one older style of *sāman* chant extant in Palghat — exactly at Putukkoṭṭu village which has escaped the attention of Wayne Howard. Dr. V. Raghavan acknowledged that the style mentioned by Wayne Howard belongs to Tanjur and is different from the style prevailing at Putukkoṭṭu. It is much older. Prof. Wayne Howard admitted that he is not aware of such a *prācīna* style. He was under the impression that Kauthuma *sāman* chanted at Tañjāvūr and Pothukkoṭṭu are the same.

In Palghat the identical chant to that of Tañjūr can be seen, but apart from that a more older style prevails still at Putukkoṭṭu.

Wayne Howard is under the impression that the Uduppi Sāmavedic Chant of *Kauthuma Śākhā* also belongs to *prācīna* style. But he has stated that they claim it as *Jaiminīya*. Actually the Tuḷu Sāmavedins chant somewhat differently from the other style. If we go through carefully we can see that it is actually *Jaiminīya* branch strongly influenced by *Rāmaṇṇa pāṭha* the new style which is more musical. I have heard the chant and also recorded some portion, of a Tuḷu brāhmaṇa scholar named Narāyaṇam Embrāntirī from Trichur, Kerala. Rather

30. Wayne Howard, *Sāmavedic Chant*, p. 69.

the Tulu style is a mixture of *Prācīna Jaiminīya* style and *Naveena Kauthuma* style. It is very clear from the recitation that some efforts were taken to make the *prācīna* style of *Jaiminīya* more attractive and musical. I have gone there and recorded some portions to prove this fact.

It has some resemblance to *Grāmageya* recitation of Nambūtirīs in Kerala. L.S.R. would have changed his several views on *Sāma* chant if he gets a chance to hear the Uduppi style of *Jaiminīya sāman*.

The *Jaiminīya Śākhā* of Nambūtiris contains clear-cut differences from other styles in respect of readings, style of chanting, order of application of Ṛks, internal structure and classification. Even the hand gestures are entirely different.

Kauthumaśākhā

The Saṁhitā portion of *Kauthuma Śākhā* is divided into two namely *Pūrvārcika* and *Uttarārcika*. *Pūrvārcika* contains Ṛks. of Agni, Soma, Varuṇa etc. Uttarārcika is mainly concerned with rituals. The Ṛks are arranged as *tṛcā*s (3 Ṛks combined together) These *tṛca*s are classified into two i.e. *Grāmageyā*s and *Āranyakā*s. *Grāmageya* is later known as *sāma* and *Āraṇyaka*s *Chandasāma*. Ūha and Ūṣāṇī are the two vikṛtīs of the above mentioned divisions respectively.

The *Pūrvārcika* contains four *kāṇḍa*s namely *Āgneya, Aindra, Pavamāna* and *Araṇya*. Each *kāṇda* is again divided into *adhyāya*s and *daśati*s (group of ten Ṛks) The total number of Ṛks in *pūrvārcika* is 650. *Utharārcikạ* is also divided like *Pūrvārcika* and contains 1225 Ṛks. Hence the total number of Ṛks are 1875. Among the eight Brāhmaṇās of *Kauthuma Śākhā*, *Pañcavimśa* plays a significant role. The *Chāndogyopaniṣad* belongs to Chandoga Brāhmaṇa of this recension. The famous *Mahāvākya Tat-tvam-asi* belongs to this Upaniṣad.

Jaiminīya Śākhā

Jaiminīya Śakhā is found mainly in Kerala, especially among Kerala Nambūtiri brāhmaṇas. There are 1698 *Ṛk*s altogether in this text. Different from the *Kauthuma Śākhā*, *Jaiminīya* contains five *kāṇḍa*s which are further divided in to *adhyāya*s namely *otts*. The *kāṇḍas*, *otts* and number of *Ṛk*s are as follows.

Kāṇḍa	Otts (Chapter)	No. of Ṛks
1. Āgneya	1-12 (12 Nos.)	1-116 (116 Nos.)
2. Aindra	13-48 (36 Nos.)	117-468 (352 Nos.)
3. Pavamāna	49-59 (11 Nos.)	469-587 (119 Nos.)
4. Dvādaśāha	60-106 (47 Nos.)	588-1344 (757 Nos.)
5. Uttara	107-112 (6 Nos.)	1345-1698 (354 Nos.)
Total	112	1698

The division of *Prapāṭhakā*s and *Daśatī*s cannot be found in the *Jaiminīya* text. There were 21 families of Nambūtirīs in Kerala belonging to *Jaiminīya Śākhā* of *Sāmaveda*. At present we have only five namely Muṭṭattukāṭ, Nellikkāṭ, Toṭṭam, Perummaṅgād and Koraṭṭikkara. The scholars available in these families are all above the age of 70 years and after them this unique style will become extinct. Hence Sree Sankaracharya University of Sanskrit, Kalady, Kerala took up the responsibility of documenting the *sāman* chant of Nambūtirīs belonging to *Jaiminīya* recension, on war footing. We could record (audio/video) the entire text of *Jaiminīya* with all its *vikṛtī*s with in a duration of 70 hours.

Sāmaveda is considered to be the main source of Indian music. There are references like

> *Sāmabhyo gītameva ca,*
> *Sāmavedāt svaro jātaḥ*
> *Svarebhyo gānasambhavaḥ* (*Bṛhaddeśi - Mātaṅgaḥ*)

Sāmavedādidam gītam sañjagrāha pitāmahaḥ (*Saṅgīta-ratnākaraḥ*)

saptasvarastu gīyante sāmabhis sāmagaiḥ budhaiḥ (*Māṇḍūkya śikṣā*) prove that *sāma* is the source of our ancient music. The *sāman* recited in rituals connected with sacrifices are known as *stotriyas*. These are actually collection of *Ṛk*s presented with different *svarasthānas*. *Tṛcā*s are used for chanting in various contexts.

Each *stotriya* is divided into *vibhakti*s namely *prastāna, udgīta, pratihāra* and there are three types of musicians called Prastāva, Udgāta and Pratihārta. Each *sāman* is being started with a particular *svara* and changes to another. There are some guiding rules for it.

We come across the use of *svarabheda* in *sāman* chant as *gamaka*s in classical music. There are different types of *svarabheda*s called *pratyutkrama, atikrama, karṣaṇa* and *namaṇa*. The place and change of *svara* are indicated by hand gestures. These are known as *gātravīṇā*s — Nambūtirīs use the complete hand for a gesture. They shake the hand in different angles and they are known in Kerala as 'Kaikāṭṭal'.

When a *Ṛk* is presented as a *sāman*, various changes are being effected. They are called *vikāra, viśleṣaṇa, vikarṣaṇa, abhyāsa, virāma, stobha, lopa* and *āgama*. Each *gāna* is split into *parvans* and when it is split the meaning of the *Ṛk* is not counted.

It is very interesting to examine the recital of a *Ṛk* according to the eight types mentioned above.

Example: *agna āyāhi vītaye*

gṛṇāno havyadātaye

nihota śatsi barhiṣi

The musical presentation of this according to the above mentioned *vikṛtī*s are as follows:

1. *Vikāra: agne ognāyi* (akāra becomes okara)
2. *Viśleṣaṇa: vītaye voyi toyāyi* (splitting the joint svaras)
3. *Vikarṣaṇa:* (*ye yāyi*) (lengthening of *hṛsva*)
4. *Abhyāsa: taye to yāyi* (Repetition)
5. *Virāma: gṛṇāno havyadātaye gṛnānoha vyādā toyāyi* (break in the middle of word)
6. *Stobhā*: the letters like '*O*', '*Ho*', '*Va*' are added to the *Ṛks*, they are called *stobha* and are very helpful for musical presentations.
7. *Lopa:* is dropping a letter in recitation *pracodayāt* is musically presented as *prācohum-a-da-yo-a*. The letter 't' is dropped here.
8. *Āgama:* is the arrival of a new letter in the word recited *vareṇyām* is presented as *vareṇiyam*. The letter 'ya' arrived here.

The *Ṛks* are recited in various *svaras*, *ārcika* in a single *svara*, *gāthika* in two, *sāmika* in three etc. *Svarāntaram* of four *svaras*, *audava* and *ṣādava* of five and six *svaras* respectively. In *sāma* chant of Kerala Nambūtirīs we can trace *svarasthanas* upto five.

Based on *Nāradīyaśikṣā* some scholars identify the *svarasthānas* of *sāman* chant with that of classical music *Yaḥ sāmagānām pradhamaḥ* etc.

Grāmageyas are divided into seven. They are *gāyatram, āgneyam, aindram, pavamānam, ārkadvandvavṛta, sukriyā* and *mahānāmnya*.

The *Ūha* portion is also divided into seven thus: *daśarātra, saṁvatsara, ekāha, ahīna, satra, prāyaścitta* and *kṣudra*.

The seven *svarasthānas* could not be fully traced as identical, since the *sāman* chant doesn't have the frequency to the extent as we experience in classical music. The trouble is further brought in, by confusing the position in fingering techṇiques with the *svaras* in music.[31]

Very rarely, we come across in *sāman* chant all these *svarasthānas* mentioned above.

Sāman chant is in the reverse order *avarohakrama* of *sārīgāmā Padhani* since *kruṣtasvara* the first is in highest pitch and the succeeding *svarasthānas* are comparatively lower to the preceding one and finally comes to *atisvaryam* in the lowest pitch.

---

31. "Studies in Sāmaveda — some problems encountered," L.S. Rajagopal. *Pūrṇatrayī*, Vol. XVI No. 1, Govt. Sanskrit College, Trippunithura, Jan. 89.

13

निघण्टु-निरुक्त में वाङ्-नाम

अभयदेव शर्मा

वेद नामक तत्त्व से वेद नामक ग्रन्थ-राशि तक और फिर वैदिक वाङ्मय तक के विकास में तीन सोपान हैं -

(1) प्रथम या आदिम स्थिति वह थी जब धर्म को साक्षात् किया गया था। ये साक्षात्कर्ता 'ऋषि' कहाए। इन्होंने धर्म को अपने अनुभवों (ऑब्जर्वेशन/विजन) में आचरण द्वारा देखा (अक्स्पीरियंस किया) था। इस 'धर्म'-दृष्टि में उनका चिन्तन (इंटैलिजंस्) और उनका विस्तृत जागतिक परिचय (इन्फॉर्मेशन), दोनों आचरण या अभ्यास (प्रैक्टिस) के बिन्दु पर एकीभूत या समन्वित थे।

(2) उन ऋषियों ने, उन लोगों के लिए जिन्हें धर्मदर्शन नहीं था, मन्त्रोपदेश द्वारा धर्म का संप्रदान किया। ***'यस्य वाक्यं स ऋषिः'*** और ***'या तेनोच्यते सा देवता'***, इन परिभाषाओं में इस द्वितीय सोपान की व्यञ्जना है। ऐसे धर्मविदों का युग वैदिक चिन्तन का द्वितीय सोपान था। वाक् और श्रुति का व्यवहार, जो कि इस गोष्ठी का विषय है, इस चरण में प्रचलित हुआ।

(3) बाद में एक ऐसा युग आया जब उपदिष्ट मन्त्र दुरूह प्रतीत होने लगे। तब उपदेश से ऊबने वाले (ग्लानियुक्त) साम्प्रदायिक कोटि के उन लोगों ने अपनी सुविधा के लिए *निघण्टु* का **समाम्नान** किया जिसमें मन्त्रों के कुछ विशिष्ट-पारिभाषिक शब्दों का सङ्कलन कर दिया गया था ताकि उनको ठीक से समझ कर वे 'थर्ड क्लास' लोग धर्म का बोध कर पाएं।

जब एक बार ग्रन्थ-रचना का श्रीगणेश हो गया तो फिर तो सङ्कलन-ग्रन्थों की परिपाटी चल पड़ी। इस क्रम में लोगों ने ***वेद*** नामक **समाम्नाय** बना डाला जिसमें वे उपदिष्ट मन्त्र रखे गऐ थे जो ऋषियों से उन्हें प्राप्त हुए थे। हो सकता है,

मन्त्रनिबद्ध धर्म* के आचरण, अर्थात् यज्ञ की दृष्टि से उपयोगी बातें (**ब्राह्मण**) भी उनमें जोड़ दी गई हों, ***'मन्त्र-ब्राह्मणयोर् वेद-नामधेयम्'***। वे याजुष संहिताओं में आज भी मिलती हैं, यद्यपि बाद में इन्हें **ब्राह्मण** नामक ग्रन्थो में पृथक् से भी सङ्कलित किया गया।

(1) ऋग्वेदीयों के कोश ***निघण्टु*** (1.11) में ***वाक्*** के **सत्तावन** पर्यायवाची शब्द दिए गए हैं।[1] इन शब्दों में स्वयं *वाक्* शब्द भी है। अर्थात्, इस शब्द का जो अभिप्राय तब की लोकभाषा में था वही अभिप्राय *वेद* में भी है। ***निघण्टु*** की सूचियां दो प्रकार की हैं। एक प्रकार की सूचियां तो वैसी हैं जैसी **वाक्** के पर्यायों की सूची है। जैसे, *यज्ञ* के पर्यायवाची शब्दों की सूची में स्वयं *यज्ञ* शब्द भी है। ऐसी अन्य भी कई सूचियां ***निघण्टु*** में हैं।

(2) पर कुछ सूचियों में वह शब्द परिगणित नहीं मिलता है जिसके पर्यायवाची शब्द सूची में दर्शाए गए हैं। जैसे, ***धन*** के पर्यायवाची शब्दों की सूची में स्वयं ***धन*** शब्द को नहीं रखा गया है। अर्थात्, इस शब्द का जो अभिप्राय तब की लोकभाषा में था वह अभिप्राय वेद में नहीं है।**

(3) **वाक्** के प्रसंग में, यह तथ्य ध्यान देने योग्य है कि *वाक्* के सत्तावन पर्यायों में से, **40** पर्यायों[2] को छोड़ कर, शेष **17** पर्यायवाची[3] शब्दों के *निघण्टु* में एक या अधिक अन्य अर्थ भी दिए गए हैं। **'वाक्'** अर्थ सहित ***गौ*** शब्द के कुल **छह** अर्थ हैं, ***इळा*** शब्द के **पांच** अर्थ हैं, ***अदिति*** और ***मही*** के **चार-चार** अर्थ हैं, ***शची*** के **तीन** अर्थ हैं और **बारह** पर्यायों***

---

* *आश्रम* और *वर्ण*

** धन का अभिप्राय वैदिक वाङ्मय में 'राष्ट्र' है। 'राष्ट्र' से अभिप्राय अंगरेजी के ***नेशन*** पद के लिए हिन्दी में प्रचलित 'राष्ट्र' शब्द से नहीं हो सकता है, यह स्पष्ट बात है।

*** पाद-टिप्पणी 4, 5, 8 में अधोरेखाङ्कित शब्द।

1. इनकी चर्चा *निरुक्त* में 2.23–24 में समेट दी गई है।

2. केवल ***वाक्*** के वाचक शब्द ये हैं : **अनुष्टुप, उपब्दिः, ऋक्, कशा, काकुत्**, [व्प्॰, पाठान्तर], **गणः**, [गणा, पाठान्तर], **गभीरा**, *गम्भीरा, गल्दा* [गलदः, गल्दः, दो पाठान्तर], **गाथा, गान्धर्वी, गीः, घोषः, जिह्वा, धमनिः, धारा, धिषणा, धेना, नना** [नग्ना, पाठान्तर], **नाळीः** [नालिः, पाठान्तर], **निवित्, नौः, बेकुरा** [वेकुः, पाठान्तर], *भारती, मन्द्रा, मन्द्राजनी, मायुः, मेळिः, वग्नुः* [गग्नुः, पाठान्तर], *वल्गुः* [वग्नुः, पाठान्तर], *वाणः, वाणी, वाणीची, वाशी, विपा, शब्दः, श्लोकः, स्वनः, स्वरः, स्वाहा*।

3. **अक्षरम्, अदितिः, इळा, गौः, गौरी, ग्नाः, धेनुः, पविः, मही** (एकवचन), **मेना, वाक्, शची, सरः, सरस्-वती, सु-पर्णी, सूर्या, होत्रा**।

के **दा-दो** अर्थ हैं।[4]

इन 17 पर्यायों में से **आठ** पर्याय मध्यस्थानी देवों या देवियों के नाम भी हैं।[5] **चार** पर्याय पृथिवीवाची[6] भी हैं। **तीन** पर्याय गो-वाची भी है।[7] **दो-दो** पर्याय उदक-वाची और 'उत्तर-पद' कोटि के भी हैं।[8]

गौ	=	वाक्,	पृथिवी,	मध्यस्थानी सत्त्व,	द्यौ,	आदित्य,	स्तोता
इळा	=	"	"	"	गौ, अन्न		
अदिति	=	"	"	"	"		
मही	=	"	"		" द्यावा-पृथिवी		
शची	=	"				कर्म,	प्रज्ञा

(4) जो **40** पर्यायवाची शब्द केवल '**वाक्**'-परक हैं उनमें से कुछ शब्दों की अर्थ-छटाओं का अनुमान करते समय, उन-उन शब्दों के लिङ्ग या वचन में परिवर्तन के साथ बने हुए रूप अध्येता का ध्यान आकर्षित करते हैं। जैसे, ***कशा*** का पुल्लिङ्ग रूप ***कशः*** उदक-पर्याय है। ***गभीरा*** का नपुंसकलिङ्ग रूप ***गभीरम्*** उदक-पर्याय है और इनका प्रथमा-द्विवचन रूप ***गभीरे*** द्यावा-पृथिवी का पर्याय है। ***गभीरा*** का नपुंसकलिङ्ग रूप ***गभीरम्*** भी उदक-पर्याय है और इनका प्रथमा-द्विवचन रूप ***गभीरे*** भी द्यावा-पृथिवी का पर्याय है। ***धिषणा*** का प्रथमा-द्विवचन रूप ***धिषणे*** भी द्यावा-पृथिवी का पर्याय है। ***सरस्-वती*** का पुल्लिङ्ग रूप ***सरस्-वान्*** भी मध्यस्थानी देव है। इसका बहुवचन रूप ***सरस्-वत्यः*** नदी-पर्याय है। ***सु-पर्णी*** का पल्लिङ्ग में

---

4. **अन्न**-वाची : इळा। **आदित्य**-वाची : गौ। **द्यौ** का पर्याय : गौ। **स्तोता**-वाची - गौ। **वज्र**-वाची : पविः। **द्यावा-पृथिवी** का पर्याय : **मही** (द्विवचन-रूप)। **कर्म**-वाची : शची। **प्रज्ञा**-वाची : शची। **द्युस्थानी** देवी : सूर्या। **यज्ञ**-वाची : होत्रा।

5. मध्यस्थानी देव/देवियां ये हैं : **अदिति, इळा, गौ, गौरी, धेनु, वाक्, सरस्**-वती, सु-**पर्णी** [सु-पर्णा, पाठान्तर]

6. पृथिवी-वाची ये हैं : **अदिति, इळा, गौ, मही**

7. गौ के वाचक ये हैं : **अदिति**, **इळा**, **मही**

8. उदक-वाची ये हैं : **अक्षरम्**, **सरः** [रसः, रासः, पाठांतर] और 'उत्तर पद' में परिगणित ये हैं : **ग्नाः**, **मेना**।

प्रथमा-बहुवचन रूप ***सु-पर्णाः*** रश्मि-वाचक और **अश्व-पर्याय** है। ***स्वाहा*** के प्रसङ्ग से, ***स्वाहा-कृतयः*** पृथ्वीस्थानी '**आप्री**' देवियां हैं।

(5) *निरुक्त* (2.23-24) ने *वाक्*-पर्यायों पर कुछ खास नहीं कहा है, सिवाय इसके कि ***वाक्*** शब्द का प्रवृत्तिनिमित्त √*वच्* धातु का अर्थ है। पर इस धातु का प्रातिस्विक वैदिक अर्थ *निघण्टु* से पता नहीं चलता है। यास्क से परवर्ती पाणिनि के 'धातु'-उपदेश के अर्थ देते हुए भीमसेन, आदि ने इस धातु का अर्थ '**व्यक्ता वाक्**' दे रखा है। इसी को भाष्यकारों ने लिया हुआ है। पर इस अर्थ की वेद में सङ्गति होना या न होना एक भिन्न बात है। इस प्रसंग में 'निघण्टु' के कुछ हस्तलेखों में √*वद्* (वदति) धातु और उसका अर्थ 'व्यक्ता वाक्' या इससे मिलता-जुलता न दे कर 'गति' अर्थ दिया गया है। यदि एक √वद् धातु गत्यर्थक हो सकती है तो 'व्यक्ता वाक्' से भिन्न गति-जैसा कोई अर्थ √वच्' धातु को भी दे कर *वाक्* के प्रयोगों का पुनरीक्षण किया जाना चाहिए। *निघण्टु* (2.14) में 122 धातुएं गति-अर्थ वाली सङ्गृहीत हैं। इसमें कुछ धातुएं 'बोलना' अर्थ की भी हो सकती हैं।

(6) वाक् के नामों के अनन्तर ***उदक*** (1.12) नाम हैं और फिर ***नदी*** (1.13) नाम हैं। वाक् नामों में '**सरस्-वती**' है तो नदी नामों में '**सरस्-वत्यः**' है। *वाक्* के पर्यायों में से *निरुक्त* ने केवल ***सरस्-वती*** पर गौर करना उपयुक्त तो समझा पर, ध्यान दें कि, 'वाक्' की दृष्टि से नहीं, बल्कि विषयान्तर हो कर उसको 'नदी' अर्थ वाला पद मानते हुए जबकि **सरस्-वत्यः** इस प्रथमान्त बहुवचन रूप में ही *निघण्टु* को 'नदी' अर्थ अभिप्रेत है, एकवचन-रूप '**सरस्-वती**' में नहीं। आगे *निघण्टु* (5.3) के पदों में मौजूद नदियों (***नद्यः***) को निरुक्त ने अपनी व्याख्या में पार्थिव सत्त्व माना है, जब कि **सरस्-वती** तो स्वयं निरुक्त के अनुसार *निघण्टु* (5.5) की व्याख्या में मध्यस्थानी देवी है न कि पृथिवीस्थानी। ***सरस्-वती*** का पु.-रूप 'सरस्-वान' भी मध्यस्थानी देव है। यहीं (5.5) में परिगणित वाक् को भी *निरुक्त* ने मध्यस्थानी माना है। *वाक्* के उन पर्यायों में से जो मध्यस्थानी देवियों के नाम हैं, *निघण्टु* ने सरस्वती के अनन्तर 'वाक्' को रखा है। यही कारण हो सकता है कि क्यों ***निरुक्त*** ने 'वाङ्'-नामों की व्याख्या के प्रसङ्ग में केवल 'सरस्वती' को विस्तृत टिप्पणी के लिए चुना। लेकिन *निरुक्त* सरस्-वती को यदि 'नदी' मान रहा है तो यह नदी वाग्-रूपिणी नदी होनी चाहिए, न कि पार्थिव सरस्-वतियां।

(7) एकवचन और बहुवचन में अर्थभेद को *निरुक्त* यदि महत्त्व नहीं देना चाहता हो तो भी एक तथ्य तो स्पष्ट है कि सरस्वती 'वाग्-उदक्' है, जैसा कि *सरः*, इस वाक्पर्याय के उदकार्थक होने से विदित होता है। *सरः* ठहरा हुआ उदक नहीं है, बल्कि प्रवाह-रूप है। प्रवाह वह होता है जो अपने स्रोत और गन्तव्य, दोनों से एक साथ जुड़ा हुआ हो। एक छोर से भी सम्बन्ध टूटा तो अपर छोर स्वतः व्यर्थ हो जाएगा और उदक एक तालाब-मात्र रह जाएगा। 'सरः' अवस्था ही 'अक्षर' कहला सकती है जो कि *निघण्टु* में वाक् और उदक दोनों का पर्याय है। दीर्घतमाः जब *'ऋचो अक्षरे परमे व्य्-ओमन'* (ऋ. 1.164.39) कहते हैं तो 'अक्षर' से उनका नैघण्टुक अभिप्राय वाग्-धारा ही होना चाहिए जो परमाकाश में प्रवाहित रहती है और जिसमें ऋग्-रूप 'वाक्' भरी हुई है जिससे कि वाङ्मयी नदी का स्वरूप बना हुआ है। ध्यान देने की बात है कि 'ऋक्' को यदि वेदचतुष्टय में से एक वेद-संहिता माना जाए तो भी उन शेष तीन वेदों का अन्तर्भाव '**ऋक्**', इस वाक्पर्याय में सङ्केतित माना जाना अभिप्रेत हो सकता है जिनको 'वाक्' कहने की पृथक् से ज़रूरत *निघण्टु* को महसूस नहीं हुई। **वाक्** के पर्यायों में *धारा* शब्द भी मौजूद है जिसे लोकभाषा में प्रवाह माना जाता है। मधुच्छंदाः (ऋ. 9.1.1 में) जब पवमान सोम की 'स्वादिष्ठा, मदिष्ठा धारा' की चर्चा करते हैं तो वे सोम के वाङ्मयीन स्वरूप की बात करते हो सकते हैं न कि मात्र लता-विशेष को निचोड़ने से टपकते हुए द्रव (***सुत***) की।

(8) वाक् के *कशा, गभीरा, गम्भीरा,* पर्यायों में भी उदक या प्रवाहमयत्व का इङ्गित निहित है क्योंकि इनके 'कश, गभीर, गम्भीर', ये शब्दरूप *उदक* के पर्याय हैं। इतना ही नहीं, ***गभीर***, *गम्भीर* के साथ अन्य भी एक वाक्-पर्याय है ***धिषणा*** जिसका धिषणे यह शब्दरूप, *गभीरे, गम्भीरे* के साथ द्यौ और पृथिवी के लिए प्रयुक्त होते हुए उन दोनों लोकों के वाङ्मय और उदकबहुल होने का सङ्केत देते प्रतीत होते हैं।

(9) परोक्षतः मौजूदगी के अलावा, *वाक्* के पर्यायों में भी **मही**, द्यावा-पृथिवी का यह पर्याय प्रत्यक्षतः मौजूद है। इन पर्यायों में द्यौ और पृथिवी, दोनों का पृथक्-पृथक् वाचक *गौ* पद भी है तो पृथिवी के वाचक *अदिति* और *इळा* पद भी हैं। *गौ* आदित्य देव का वाचक भी है जिसे परम्परा से द्युस्थानी सूर्य माना जाता है और जिसके नाम ('आदित्याः' — पदवाच्य रूपान्तर) भी द्युस्थानी सत्त्व के हैं। उधर 'वाक्' के पर्यायों में *सूर्या* देवी भी मौजूद है जो यास्क के अनुसार द्युस्थानी है।

(10) निघण्टु 5.5 में ***सरस्-वती*** देवी को यास्क ने ऋग्वेद 1.3.10-12 के प्रमाण से 'मध्यस्थानी वाक्' माना है जो **उदक** (महः अर्णः, ऋ. 1.3.12) को प्रज्ञा (*केतु*, ऋ. 1.3.12) द्वारा प्र-चेतना प्रदान करती है। स्पष्ट है कि यास्क के अनुसार मध्य या अन्तरिक्ष की **वाक्** उदकबहुल है और प्रज्ञा और कर्म से भी सम्बद्ध है। इधर वाक्-पर्यायों में ***शची*** पद मौजूद है ही जिसके कर्म और प्रज्ञा, दो अन्य अर्थ भी हैं जो कि ऋ. 1.3.10; 12 में मौजूद ***धीः*** पद के भी अर्थ हैं, पर वाक्-पर्याय *धीः* नहीं है, *शची* है। ऐसा क्यों है, यह सोचने की बात है।

(11) मन्त्र के तीन भेदों में से केवल *ऋक्* को वाक् का पर्याय माना गया है। साम का अन्तर्भाव ऋक् में हो जाता है। शेष बचा यजुः जो गद्यमय होने से छोड़ दिया गया हो, यह अनुमान किया जा सकता है। छन्दोबद्ध पद्य को ही वाक्-पर्याय मानना सम्भवतः निघण्टुकार को अभिप्रेत हो। गायत्र, आदि अन्य किसी भी छन्द को वाक्-पर्याय न मान कर, छन्दों में केवल ***अनुष्टुप्*** को **वाक्** का पर्यायवाची माना गया है। रामायण, महाभारत, पुराणों और लौकिक संस्कृत काव्य में अनुष्टुप् सर्वाधिक प्रयुक्त छन्द है, इस तथ्य से यह चयन मेल खाता है।

(12) *वाक्* के अधिकतर (44) पर्याय-पद स्त्रीलिङ्गान्त हैं, जो स्वाभाविक है। पर 11 पर्याय-पद पुलिङ्गान्त[9] और 2 नपुंसकलिङ्गान्त[10] भी हैं। ***ग्नाः***, यह बहुवचनान्त पद भी वाक्-पर्यायों में है।

(13) ***निघण्टु*** के वाक्-पर्यायों में सारे शब्द वाग्व्यवहार-परक धातुओं से व्युत्पन्न नहीं हैं। इनमें से अनेक शब्द ऐसे हैं जिनके व्युत्पत्ति-निमित्तों को जैसे-तैसे अनेक वैकल्पिक धातुओं से व्याकरण के बल पर समझा गया है। व्युत्पत्ति-निमित्तों से निरुक्तियों का कोई लेना-देना नहीं होता है। निरुक्त अर्थप्रधान विद्या है, जबकि व्याकरण शब्द प्रधान शास्त्र है। ***निघण्टु*** के प्रत्येक शब्द की अर्थप्रवृत्ति के निमित्त यदि ***निरुक्त*** ने दिए होते तो *निर्वचन* के नाम पर

---

9. पुंलिङ्गात पद : गणः, **घोषः, मायुः, वग्नुः, वल्गुः, वाणः, शब्दः, श्लोकः, स्वनः, स्वरः।**

10. नपुंसकलिङ्गात पद : **अक्षरम्, सरः।**

[*पुरुष शब्द *निघण्टु* के 'मनुष्य'-पर्यायों में सम्मिलित न होने से, *निघण्टु* के अनुसार 'मनुष्य' का वाचक नहीं है।]

व्युत्पत्तियों के अंबार न लगते। ***निघण्टु*** के वाक्पर्यायों में काफी शब्द ऐसे हैं जिनके वाग्व्यवहार-सूचक प्रवृत्तिनिमित्त बूझे जाने शेष प्रतीत होते हैं, जैसे, **अदितिः, उपब्दिः, कशा, गभीरा, गम्भीरा, गल्दा, गांधर्वी, गौरी, ग्नाः, धमनिः, धारा, धिषणा, धेना, धेनुः, नग्ना** (*न+ग्ना?*), **नाळीः, नौः, बेकुरा, भारती, मंद्रा, मंद्राजनी, मही, मेडिः, मेना, सरस्-वती, सु-पर्णी, सूर्या**।

किसी वाक्-पर्याय के एक से अधिक अर्थ होने पर, यदि उन सब अर्थों को एक साथ ले कर विचार किया जाए तो सम्भवतः वेद के अभिप्राय को बेहतर समझा जा सके। उदाहरणार्थ गौ के छह अर्थ हैं – पृथिवी, द्यौ, आदित्य, वाक्, स्तोता, मध्यस्थानी सत्त्व। इस प्रसङ्ग में सबसे पहली बात तो यह है कि गौ नामक पशु-विशेष की चर्चा इन अर्थों में नहीं है। अतः वेदों में *गौ* के प्रसङ्गों को पशु-विशेष पर घटाने के लिए ***निघण्टु*** की सहमति नहीं है। दूसरे 'गौ' कोई ऐसा मध्यस्थानी तत्त्व होना चाहिए जो त्रिलोकव्यापी है और जिसका पृथिवी, द्यौ और अदितिपुत्र (*आदित्य*) के स्वरूपनिर्धारण में योगदान हो, वाक् व स्तोता से भी जो सम्बद्ध हो। ध्यान दें कि ***गौ*** शब्द बहुवचन में *रश्मि* का पर्यायवाची है और गौएं *उषा* की आदिष्टोपयोजन (अरुणियाँ) हैं।

(14) *निघण्टु* की अर्चनार्थक धातुओं में से कई धातुएं वाग्व्यवहार-परक हैं, जो (वाग्व्यवहार) उच्चार्य और श्रव्य के अलावा मानसिक भी होता है, जैसे, गॄ, **गै, जॄ, णु, नद्, पृच्छ्, पण्, पन्, पृच्, भन्** (**भण्**), **मद्** (आत्मनेपदी), **मन्, रस्, रिभ्, रु, शंस्, स्तु, स्तुभ्, स्वृ, ह्वे**। इन धातुओं से व्युत्पन्न अनेक वैदिक शब्द हैं जो वाक्-पर्यायवत् हैं यद्यपि *निघण्टु* में ये लिए नहीं गए हैं, जैसे **गान, नव** (जैसे, **प्र-णव, अभि-प्र-णव**), **प्रश्न, मति, मनना, मन्त्र, रवः, शस्ति** (जैसे, **प्र-शस्ति**), **शस्त्रम्, स्तवः, स्तवथः, स्तुति** (जैसे, **सु-ष्टुति**), स्तोत्रम्, स्वरः, हवः, हवनम्, हवस्, हुवनम्, हूति।

वाग्व्यवहार-परक अनेक नामपद *मेधावी, स्तोता* और *ऋत्विक्* के पर्यायों में मौजूद हैं, जैसे, **आकेनिपः, कण्वः, कविः, कीस्तासः, मतयः, मतुथाः, विग्रः विप्रः, विपन्यवः** (*मेधावी* के पर्याय)। **कीरिः, जरिता, नदः, नादः, रुद्रः, रेभः, स्तुप्** (*स्तोता* के पर्याय)। *ऋत्विक्* के पर्यायों में एक पद है **भारताः**, जो वाक्-पर्यायों में गृहीत *भारती* से सम्बद्ध है।

भारती का सम्बन्ध 'भरत' या 'भारत' से है जो वेदों में अग्नि नामक देव के विशेषण हैं। अतः 'भारती' आग्नेयी वाक् हैं। दैवी वाक् का वाचक एक अन्य वाक्-पर्याय है ***वग्नु*** जो इन्द्र नामक देव की वाक् है। ऐसा ही ऐन्द्र वाक्-पर्याय गान्धर्वी है, गन्धर्वों से सम्बद्ध होने के साथ-साथ। सु-पर्णी सु-पर्ण की वाक् है।

(15) *निरुक्त* ने वाक् का पुष्प और फल अर्थ को माना है और अर्थ के तीन स्तर बनाए हैं, *याज्ञ, दैवत, अध्यात्म*। अतः वाक् के पर्यायवाची शब्दों के अभिप्रायों के भी ये तीन उच्चावच स्तर *निरुक्त* को अभीष्ट हैं। पर इस ग्रन्थ की निरुक्तियों में ये तीनों स्तर प्रायः नहीं बताए गए हैं। इनको स्पष्ट समझने की अपेक्षा बनी हुई है।

(16) इस सब चर्चा से निवेदन यह करना है कि *वाक्* का स्वरूप प्राचीन वैदिक चिन्तकों के अनुसार सम्भवतः मात्र *वैखरी* ध्वनि नहीं है बल्कि *मध्यमा* के अलावा, सूक्ष्मतर, सूक्ष्मतम स्तरों पर वाक् *पश्यन्ती* और *परा* भी हो सकती है, अर्थात्, पृथिवी से द्यौ तक वाक् के नाना पक्ष उभरने चाहिएं। ***निघण्टु*** के 57 वाक्-पर्यायों पर समूचे वैदिक साक्ष्यों की दृष्टि से गहन अनुशीलन की अपेक्षा बनी हुई है। *मेना* और *ग्नाः* देवस्त्रियां या देवशक्तियां होते हुए भी यदि वाक् हैं तो क्या वाक् के अन्य 55 भेद भी शक्ति-रूप नहीं होने चाहियें? वाक् की 'व्यक्तता' आत्मा की अभिव्यक्ति के रूप में है, अन्यथा *वैखरी* वाक् तो आत्मदृष्ट्या अव्यक्ता ध्वनि-मात्र है। वाक् पौरुषेय (पुरुष*=आत्मा की) शक्ति है, जबकि भाषा मानुषी कृति है। वेद पौरुषेय शक्ति की बात करता है, मानुषी कृति की नहीं।

14

Ramblings on Nirukta

Wagish Shukla

I

THE *Nirukta* is a lexicon, an etymological exegesis on a selected compilation of words from the Vedic corpus with an avowed purpose of 'understanding the meaning' of Vedic verses. This is merely one, not perhaps the primary, of the purposes of the work. Its major part is devoted to the 'Theogony' of the Vedic pantheon. The etymological exegesis is subservient to this objective. As far as 'understanding the meaning' is concerned, if it is interpreted narrowly as a negotiation through a dictionary, this is again subservient to this objective. However, in a wider but more concrete sense on a higher plane, 'understanding the meaning' of a Vedic verse can be regarded as identical with 'Theogony.'

This raises certain questions. What is meant by 'understanding the meaning?' The Vedic verses can hardly be regarded as 'communications' or 'messages.' They are not meant to be codes which need to be broken. They are supposed to be not the compositions of any conscious being, certainly they are not 'Words of God.' No human beings of course are supposed to have written them. They are not dated. They just exist, but not in the sense that life forms or the celestial bodies exist. Certain *ṛṣis* have just *seen* them. These *ṛṣis* are limited by finitude of space and time but their vision occasionally transcends the boundaries of this finitude. The word *ṛṣi* is itself an example of an etymological mining: apparently it is *dṛśi* which became *ṛṣi* through the razoring off of *d* and transformation of *ś* to *ṣ* by the repeated use of the word by mere human beings.

The *Nirukta* abounds in such *folk etymologies* frowned upon by modern scholars like Prof. Rajwade and enthusiastically expatiated by ancient scholars like Durgācārya. Before one starts looking at these bickerings within the arena of the modern science of linguistics, one must have a look at the primary concern of the work — the determination of 'gods' in the Vedic verses.

Such a 'determination' has been accepted as context-dependent by our thinkers, one of the most eminent and the most senior being Yāska, the author of *Nirukta*. Thus one of the properties of a 'god' is mutability: the same 'god' incarnates as *agni* (= fire) in the night but incarnates as *sūrya* (= sun) in the morning. However, these are two *different* 'gods.' By contrast, a human being remains the same during night and day. Seeing that in the illustration taken above, *agni* is 'located on earth,' i.e. is a *pṛthivī-sthānīya* 'god' and *sūrya* is 'located in the heavens,' i.e. is a *dyu-sthānīya* 'god,' not only the bodies but the dwellings also change and the three fundamentally different gods located in three different levels of the cosmic structure move freely from one level to the other by a carnation technology denied to non-gods. For this reason, a god is generated and in turn generates other gods — *agni* is both the father and the son of other gods, to give just one example. The contradictions that obtain in the linear world of human beings, if the before and after boundaries are thus broken, do not obtain in the geometry in which gods are configured. Unless this background is kept in mind, the 'folk etymology' in *Nirukta* cannot be understood. One problem with linguistics, and in general all 'humanities and social sciences' disciplines, is that they aspire to be 'science' on the model of physical sciences, more pointedly on the model of mathematics. Mathematics is developed on the basis of axioms and rules explicitly designed to play the particular game. In spite of its success in representing the physical world around us, the 'science' in it does not lie in that success, it is in the precise rule-base that has been developed *ab initio*. When mathematical entities are confused with physical entities, the consequences are sometimes drastically undesirable. As a particularly extreme illustration, the Pythagorean school had developed a principle of Harmony in the Universe based on 'Cosmic Music' and this rested on rational numbers. The fact that irrational numbers existed, when it was known, became a challenge to this Principle of Harmony so that irrational numbers remained a cult secret, and to bring them into the public sphere of mathematics was an offence punishable by death according to the legend as far as the Pythagorean school was concerned.

Linguistics believes that language is simply the system it can organize and has only those functions which are assigned to it by this 'science.' To confuse a system with actuality, to confuse sociology with society, economics with economy, political science with polity has led to various programmes in human history of chartered social engineering, economy reforms, and political 'revolutions.' They have been invariably powered by simple use of military force and, occasionally, by voluntary abdication by ruling ideas when it became clear that it was no longer profitable to cling to some 'theory' which has failed in practice.

To regard *Nirukta* (or the 'Pāṇinian Grammar') as a system which stands or falls by the judgements pronounced from the Testing Laboratory of Modern Linguistics should be unacceptable. Its questions are far more comprehensive than the question-bank of a 'science' like Linguistics can accommodate. The *Nirukta-kāra* has to confront questions such as why a piece of kitchen equipment like the grinding stone (*grāvan*) is a god and whether gods behave as humans do.

I would prefer to pause and examine the discussion on the point just mentioned. Xenophanes, a sixth century BC Greek thinker, attacked the contemporary theology based on Homer and Hesiod by saying that Ethiopians make their gods black and snub-nosed, the Thracians say theirs have blue eyes and red hair and so on, but there is one god neither in form like unto mortals nor in thought. Thus anthropo-morphism has been described as 'false' by Xenophanes. This attack was revived later by Plato and is in fact the root informing the depaganization drives of later discourses which dominate the thought and action right upto our own days. The *Nirukta*, after examining all the positions, concludes by a sentence which can be read in two ways to mean either "gods are like men" or "gods are unlike men" depending on whether *vā puruṣavidhāh* is deconstructed as *vā puruṣavidhāḥ* or as *vā a-puruṣavidhāḥ,* thus endorsing both the views through an ambivalent reading. More significantly, there is a supportive statement that this is the *ākhyāna-samaya,* i.e. this is how narrative art has described the gods. It is seen thus that (i) the very Homer and Hesiod, who are the objects of attack by Xenophanes, Plato, and the more virulent explicitly depaganization discourses which came later, are here respected as authority; (ii) the final conclusion is 'readerly' and not 'authorly' in its phraseology; and (iii) the device employed in pronouncing the conclusion is poetic in the sense that a particular figure of speech, *śleṣa* (= pun) has been employed.

This should clarify the narrative character of Indian thought in general and the *Nirukta* in particular. To treat it as a 'science,' as a mere branch of Linguistics as constructed by contemporary non-narrative thinkers invariably hostile to any holistic and inclusive line of thought, is to appoint a teetotaler as a taster.

With this in our mind, we can proceed to sample some of the discussions in *Nirukta* which have inspired and informed much of modern linguistics, mainly after the mediation by Pāṇini and Patañjali and Bhartṛhari but at the same time invite attacks from the self proclaimed 'scientific' people.

II

In 12/13, Yāska comments on *adhorāmaḥ sāvitraḥ* which is indicated to be taken from *Yajurveda* 29/58. According to Yāska, *adhorāma* means "dark in the lower part" and the sun is so called because when it rises, at that moment, the lower parts are dark because they are not illuminated by the sun. One would imagine that Yāska is talking about the part of the globe where there is night when in the other part of the globe it is day. In spite of the fact that this fits well, to my knowledge no modern scholar has speculated on such a 'science' being hinted at in this explanation.

But, of course, 'scientific examination' has taken place. Yāska has based his equation of *rāma* = dark on the basis of a command that one should not sexually approach a *rāmā* (= sexually attractive woman) after having performed a Vedic ceremony known as *agnicayana*. This simply means that after *agnicayana* sexual activity should be delinked from mere pleasure-seeking which does not respect the boundaries of a lawful wedding that confers the right of participation in religious acts automatically on the wife. Apparently, 'dark-genetic' (*kṛṣṇa-jātīya*) women were pleasure-providers. This has been read racially to mean that *anārya* women were used as sex-slaves and you have the full force of some of the most abhorrent exploits of some twentieth century armies straightaway shifted into the Vedic civilization.

This is the way sociological readings of all our texts, including *Nirukta*, reconstruct our past. However, it is worthwhile to point out that in the available text of *Śukla-Yajurveda* 29/58, the relevant reading is *adhorāmau sāvitrau* which means "two animals whose lower parts are *white*," according to the commentary by Mahīdhara. Thus, conceding that Yāska had a different reading of *adhorāmaḥ sāvitraḥ* (= one animal whose lower parts are *dark*) the same word *rāma* has been read as *dark* by Yāska and *white* by Mahīdhara. Thus in the particular animal sacrifice, the kind of animal to be sacrificed has changed its colours in the two commentaries!

To return to the commentary by Yāska, accepting that pleasure-providing woman is *dark*, one can go to the racial reading only if one completely ignores the connotation of *dark* in the context of the description of female beauty in Indian Literature. The Yakṣa in the *Meghadūtam* of Kālidāsa describes his wife as *śyāmā* (= dark); indeed all the texts use *śyāmā* as a descriptor of the most attractive and beautiful woman. The colour of the erotic mood (*śṛṅgāra rasa*) is *śyāma*. Two of our most important gods, Rāma and Kṛṣṇa are dark. This preference for *dark* being glossed over in favour of a racial interpretation is but one instance of how the sins of the European Civilization have been transfered to the Indian society in the name of scholarship.

III

By this time, we believe the 'etymological technique' of Yāska is more or less explained. However, a system with rules have been provided by him and we take a brief look. This is outlined in chapter 2 of the *Nirukta* at the beginning.

The most striking feature of this system is doubtless the statement : *na tveva na nirbrūyāt*, it should never happen that no exegesis is made. At work, this means that words are classified into three categories:

1. Those in which certain grammatical rules are more or less clearly identifiable. They should be explained accordingly.
2. Those in which grammatical rules are not clearly identifiable but basing oneself on the meaning of the word, a direction can be taken from some indication in the word which looks like a grammatical rule. One should explain accordingly.
3. Those in which no grammatical rules seem to be even remotely discernible which can provide a lead. In that case, one should not bother to find any rational argument. From the arsenal of the grammar, one should go ahead and explain on the basis of a word which resembles this word. For, *the rule-base of a grammar is an artificial construct and no arbiter of truth.*

The italicized sentence is a basic axiom of Indian linguistics. As against that, Western Linguistics, the wannabe 'science,' believes that it has a monopoly on truth and seeks to rearrange social structures accordingly. This I believe to be true not only of linguistics but a fundamental differential between Indian thinking and Western thinking.

15

प्रातिशाख्य ग्रन्थों में स्वरवर्ण

दीप्ति शर्मा त्रिपाठी

स्वर शब्द का प्रयोग अलग-अलग शास्त्रों में अलग-अलग तत्त्वों की ओर सङ्केत करने के लिए हुआ है। जैसे सङ्गीत शास्त्र में षड्ज, रिषभ, गन्धार, मध्यम, पञ्चम, धैवत और निषाद को स्वर कहते हैं तो भाषाशास्त्र में वर्णों के विशेष प्रकार को। इसके अतिरिक्त उदात्तादि, क्रुष्टादि तथा यम के लिए भी स्वर शब्द का प्रयोग मिलता है। इन सभी सन्दर्भों में जो बात समान है वह यह कि सर्वत्र स्वर शब्द के सङ्केत का सम्बन्ध किसी न किसी रूप में उसके व्युत्पत्तिलभ्य अर्थ से है। पाणिनीय शिक्षा के पञ्जिका भाष्य में स्वर की व्युत्पत्ति बताते हुए कहा गया है:–

स्वृ शब्दोपतापयोः स्वर्यते शब्द्यतेऽनेन-- करणे अच् प्रत्ययः।

उच्चारणार्थक धातु से निष्पन्न स्वर शब्द जहाँ कहीं भी प्रयुक्त हुआ है किसी न किसी प्रकार के उच्चारण को ही अभिव्यक्त करता है।

यहाँ हमारा लक्ष्य स्वर शब्द के विभिन्न आयामों की व्याख्या करना नहीं है, अपितु हम भाषा के सन्दर्भ में स्वर-विवेचन को ही लेकर चलेंगे। आधुनिक ध्वनिविज्ञान के प्रेरक-स्रोत हमारे प्राचीन शिक्षा एवं प्रातिशाख्य ग्रन्थों में वर्ण-भेद तथा उच्चारण-भेद का कितनी सूक्ष्मता से विवरण प्रस्तुत किया गया था, यह इस विवेचन से स्पष्ट हो जायेगा।

वैदिक साहित्य में संहिता, ब्राह्मण तथा आरण्यक ग्रन्थों में स्वर शब्द का प्रयोग मिलता है, लेकिन इसका प्रयोग विभिन्न अर्थों में हुआ है। ऐसा प्रतीत होता है जैसे उस काल तक पारिभाषिक रूप में यह रूढ नहीं हुआ था। ऋग्वेद में वाक् के अर्थ में सर्वप्रथम इसका प्रयोग मिलता है (8-72-7)। संहितोपनिषद् ब्राह्मण तथा गोपथ ब्राह्मण में अकारादि के लिए स्वर का प्रयोग हुआ है –

यथा स्वरेण सर्वाणि व्यञ्जनानि व्याप्तानि
एवं सर्वान् कामान् आप्नोति यश्चैवं वेद। (सं. उ. ब्रा. खण्ड २)

यहाँ स्वर एवं व्यञ्जन के परस्पर सम्बन्ध का उपमान के रूप में प्रयोग किया गया है। ताण्ड्य ब्राह्मण में स्वर प्राणवायु के लिए प्रयुक्त हुआ है – **प्राणो वै स्वरः** (24-11-9)। लेकिन इन सभी सन्दर्भों में एक बात समान है कि स्वर शब्द उच्चरित ध्वनि का वाचक है।

प्रातिशाख्य एवं शिक्षा ग्रन्थों में स्वर का लक्षण नहीं बताया गया, केवल परिगणन किया गया है। इससे ऐसा प्रतीत होता है कि उस परम्परा में यह प्रचलित संज्ञा थी और इसके लक्षण की आवश्यकता का अनुभव नहीं किया गया, लेकिन टीकाग्रन्थों में स्वर की परिभाषा एवं व्युत्पत्ति बताने का प्रयास अनेकत्र देखने को मिलता है, जैसेः-

1. ऋक् प्रातिशाख्य के उवट भाष्य में - **स्वर्यन्ते शब्द्यन्ते इति स्वराः।** (1/3)
2. याज्ञवल्क्य शिक्षा की शिक्षावल्ली विवृति में - **स्वर्यते शब्द्यते व्यञ्जनमेभिः स्वेन राजन्त इति वा।** (पृ. 76)
3. तैत्तिरीय प्रातिशाख्य की वैदिकाभरण टीका में - **स्वेन राजन्ते नान्येन व्यञ्जन्त इति स्वराः।** (1/5)
4. महाभाष्यकार ने भी स्वर का लक्षण कुछ इसी प्रकार किया है - **स्वयं राजन्त इति स्वराः अन्वग्भवति व्यञ्जनमिति।** (1/2/29)

इन समस्त लक्षणों को देखने पर आपाततः ऐसा प्रतीत होता है जैसे स्वर शब्द की व्युत्पत्तिपरक व्याख्या की जा रही हो। पर यदि हम सूक्ष्मता से देखें तो यह स्पष्ट हो जायेगा कि निर्वचनात्मक होने के साथ ये स्वर के स्वरूप को पूरी तरह बतलाने में भी समर्थ हैं। स्वर वैसी ध्वनियाँ हैं जो उच्चारण-प्रक्रिया में बिना किसी अवरोध के उत्पन्न होती हैं। इसलिए ये स्वतन्त्र रूप से उच्चरित हो सकती हैं। इतना ही नहीं इनके उच्चारण का काल भी वक्ता की इच्छा के अनुसार नियन्त्रित किया जा सकता है। व्यञ्जन के उच्चारण में मुख-विवर में न्यूनाधिक घर्षण अवश्य होता है। जब घर्षण के अनन्तर मुख-विवर खुलता है तब व्यञ्जन के बाद स्वर का उच्चारण भी सुनायी पड़ता है। इसीलिए व्यञ्जनों को स्वरों पर आश्रित माना जाता है। व्यञ्जनों का परस्पर अन्तर घर्षण के स्थान, करण और प्रयत्न (प्रक्रिया) पर निर्भर करता है जबकि स्वरों का अन्तर मुख-विवर के अन्दर उच्चारण अवयव के बननेवाले आकार पर। घर्षण का अभाव होने के कारण एवं मुख-विवर की विशिष्ट आकृति पर ही निर्भर होने के कारण स्वर स्वतन्त्र कहे जाते हैं।

प्रातिशाख्य ग्रन्थों में स्वरों की सङ्ख्या को लेकर परस्पर मत-विभेद दिखलायी पड़ता है। ऋक् प्रातिशाख्य में 12 स्वर माने गये हैं, तैत्तिरीय प्रातिशाख्य में 16, वाजसनेयी प्रातिशाख्य में 23 और ऋक्तन्त्र में 14। यह सङ्ख्या-भेद प्लुत को स्वर के अन्तर्गत गिनने और नहीं गिनने पर आधारित है। ऋक् प्रातिशाख्य में अ, आ, ऋ, ॠ, इ, ई, उ, ऊ, ए, ओ, तथा ऐ, औ की स्वर संज्ञा की गयी है। वर्णों के परिगणन में ऌ तथा ई3 (त्रिमात्रिक ई) का परिगणन तो किया गया है किन्तु उनकी स्वर संज्ञा नहीं की गयी। यहाँ यह ध्यातव्य है कि स्वरों का विभाजन वहाँ पर समानाक्षर और सन्ध्यक्षर इन दो भागों में किया गया है जो इस बात का परिचायक है कि प्रथम आठ स्वरों (अ आ ऋ ॠ इ ई उ ऊ) तथा परवर्त्ती चार स्वरों (ए ओ ऐ औ) की उच्चारण-प्रक्रिया के सूक्ष्म अन्तर से तत्कालीन आचार्य अवगत थे और उसे रेखाङ्कित करने से नहीं चूके। आधुनिक ध्वनिविज्ञान में भी इस भेद को मूल-स्वर तथा सन्धि-स्वर के रूप में स्वीकार किया गया है।

तैत्तिरीय प्रातिशाख्य में वर्णमाला के लिए वर्ण-समाम्नाय शब्द का प्रयोग किया गया है और कहा गया है कि आरम्भ के 16 वर्ण स्वर संज्ञक होते हैं, **षोडशादितः स्वराः** (1/3)। ये सोलह वर्ण हैं – अ आ आ3, इ ई ई3, उ ऊ ऊ3, ऋ ॠ, ऌ, ए, ऐ, ओ तथा औ। यहाँ, हम पाते हैं, कि चार ऐसे वर्ण-जिन्हें ऋक् प्रातिशाख्य में स्वर के अन्तर्गत परिगणित नहीं किया गया-उन्हें भी स्वर की संज्ञा दी गयी है। ये वर्ण हैं प्लुत आ3, ई3, ऊ3 तथा ऌ। वहाँ प्लुत ई3 तथा ऌ को वर्णमाला में पढ़ा तो गया है पर स्वर केवल समानाक्षर तथा सन्ध्यक्षर को कहा गया है जबकि तैत्तिरीय प्रातिशाख्य में सभी प्लुत वर्णों के साथ ऌ को भी स्वर ही माना गया है।

वाजसनेयी प्रातिशाख्य में स्वरों की गणना उपर्युक्त दोनों प्रातिशाख्यों से अलग की गयी है। वहाँ मूल-स्वर तथा सन्ध्यक्षर सभी के प्लुत रूप का परिगणन किया गया है। इस प्रकार अ आ आ3, इ ई ई3, उ ऊ ऊ3, ऋ ॠ ॠ3, ऌ ॡ ॡ3, ए ए3, ऐ ऐ3, ओ ओ3, औ औ3, इन तेईस वर्णों की स्वर संज्ञा की गयी है। पाणिनीय व्याकरण में भी सन्ध्यक्षरों के प्लुत रूप को स्वीकार किया गया है, अन्तर केवल इतना है कि वहाँ ऌ का दीर्घ रूप नहीं माना गया इसलिए ऌ के केवल बारह भेद बताये गये। अनुनासिक स्वरों को गिनने तथा उदात्तादि के भेद को ग्रहण करने के कारण वहाँ स्वरों की संख्या अधिक हो गयी है जैसे अ, इ, उ ऋ के 18 तथा ऌ, ए, ओ, ऐ, औ के 12। अन्यथा, वाजसनेयी प्रातिशाख्य में स्वर जिस प्रकार से बताये गये हैं वह पाणिनीय परम्परा के सर्वाधिक निकट है।

ऋक् तन्त्र में 14 वर्णों का परिगणन करने के बाद उनकी स्वर संज्ञा की गयी है। ये 14 वर्ण हैं अ, आ, इ, ई, उ, ऊ, ऋ, ॠ, ऌ, ॡ, ए, ऐ, ओ तथा औ। (अ इति आ इति------इति स्वराः। (ऋक् तन्त्र 1/2) ऋक् प्रातिशाख्य तथा ऋक् तन्त्र के स्वरों की तुलना करने पर हम पाते हैं कि प्रथम ग्रन्थ में ऌ को स्वरों से अलग वर्ण के रूप में लिया गया है जबकि द्वितीय ग्रन्थ में ऌ को न केवल स्वर के अन्तर्गत रखा गया अपितु उसके दीर्घ रूप को भी स्वीकार किया गया है। इसलिए ऋक् प्रातिशाख्य में स्वरों की सङ्ख्या 12 है और ऋक् तन्त्र में 14। इस प्रकार हम पाते हैं कि प्रातिशाख्यों में स्वर की सङ्ख्या को लेकर पर्याप्त मत वैभिन्य है। यह विभिन्नता उस आधारशिला पर खड़ी है जिसके कारण वेदों की शाखायें अलग हुईं और यह केवल सङ्ख्या पर आधारित नहीं है अपितु उस सूक्ष्म विश्लेषण का सङ्केत करती है जिसके कारण यह भेद उत्पन्न हुआ। आज भी इस भेद के सैद्धान्तिक आधार का अन्वेषण स्थान भेद से उच्चारण में होने वाले भेद को समझने में सहायक हो सकता है।

आधुनिक ध्वनिशास्त्र में दो प्रकार के स्वरों की बात कही गयी है – मूल-स्वर एवं सन्धि-स्वर। पाणिनीय माहेश्वर सूत्रों में परिगणित प्रथम तीन स्वर अ इ उ – इस विभाजन के अनुसार – मूल-स्वर की कोटि में आते हैं तथा ए, ऐ, ओ, औ, सन्धि-स्वर में। यह देखकर सुखद आश्चर्य होता है कि प्रातिशाख्य ग्रन्थों में इस भेद का स्पष्टतः वर्णन किया गया है। आश्चर्य इसलिए कि आधुनिक यन्त्रों का प्रयोग करने के बाद उच्चारण-प्रक्रिया के जिस सूक्ष्म भेद के आधार पर यह वर्गीकरण किया गया है उसे प्राचीन आचार्यों के विवरण में यथावत् पाया जाता है। मूल-स्वरों में वाग्यन्त्र के किसी एक अंश का ही प्रयोग होता है और सन्धि-स्वर में दो मूल-स्वरों में प्रयुक्त अंशों का। यथा अ में केवल कण्ठ एवं इ में केवल तालु का किन्तु ए में क्रमशः कण्ठ और तालु दोनों का प्रयोग होता है। यही आधार है आधुनिक भाषाशास्त्र में स्वरों के द्विभागीय वर्गीकरण का।

प्रातिशाख्य ग्रन्थों में मूल-स्वर के लिए समानाक्षर शब्द का प्रयोग किया गया है। ऋक् प्रातिशाख्य, तैत्तिरीय प्रातिशाख्य एवं चतुरध्यायिका में यह संज्ञा उपलब्ध है। वाजसनेयी प्रातिशाख्य में समानाक्षर के स्थान पर सिम् एवं ऋक्तन्त्र में केवल समान संज्ञा का प्रयोग मिलता है। तैत्तिरीय प्रातिशाख्य के वैदिकाभरण भाष्य में स्पष्टतः कहा गया है -

एकारादयस्स्वराः सन्ध्यक्षराणीत्याख्यायन्ते स्वरद्वयसन्धिरूपत्वात्।
तदभावात्तु समानरूपाः अकारादय इतरे स्वराः समानाक्षराणीति। अत

> **एव शौनकेन अष्टौ समानाक्षराण्यादितः ततश्चत्वारि सन्ध्यक्षराण्युत्तराणीति इति सन्ध्यक्षरेभ्यः प्राचां सर्वेषां समानाक्षरसंज्ञोच्यते।**
>
> (1/2)

समानाक्षरों का सम्पूर्ण रूप में एक समान उच्चारण होता है। उच्चरित ध्वनि भी एक प्रकार की ही सुनायी पड़ती है सम्भवतः इसीलिए उन्हें समानाक्षर कहा गया है। समानाक्षर संज्ञा का एक और भी कारण हो सकता है — प्रत्येक मूल-स्वर की दीर्घ के रूप में एक और भेद की उपलब्धि। दीर्घ-स्वर, उच्चारण-प्रक्रिया की दृष्टि से ह्रस्व के समान ही होता है, और दोनों में अन्तर केवल काल अर्थात् मात्रा का होता है। अतः ह्रस्व एवं दीर्घ के लिए समानाक्षर का प्रयोग सर्वथा समीचीन है।

विभिन्न प्रातिशाख्यों में जिन स्वरों का समानाक्षर के अन्तर्गत परिगणन किया गया है उसमें कुछ भेद देखने को मिलता है। ऋक् तन्त्र में अ आ, ऋ ॠ, इ ई, और उ ऊ की समानाक्षर संज्ञा की गयी है। किन्तु तैत्तिरीय प्रातिशाख्य में समानाक्षर के अन्तर्गत ऋ ॠ का ग्रहण नहीं किया गया है, इसके अतिरिक्त मूल-स्वरों के दीर्घ के साथ प्लुत रूप का भी ग्रहण किया गया है। वस्तुतः प्लुत स्वर का भेद भी काल की मात्रा पर ही आधारित है, अतः एक दृष्टि से उसे भी इस विभाजन में स्थान दिया जाना उचित है। परन्तु अन्य प्रातिशाख्यों में प्लुत का अनुल्लेख भी विचारणीय है। यदि हम प्लुत के प्रयोग की स्थिति पर दृष्टिपात करें तो हमें इस प्रश्न का समाधान मिल सकता है। प्लुत का प्रयोग हमेशा प्रयोजन अथवा सन्दर्भ पर आश्रित होता है, अतः इसे हम सन्दर्भ-सापेक्ष स्वर कह सकते हैं जबकि ह्रस्व या दीर्घ स्वरों की सत्ता वाक्य में प्रयोग के सन्दर्भ पर आश्रित नहीं होती, उनका स्वतन्त्र अस्तित्व होता है। ऐसे में यदि अधिकांश प्रातिशाख्यों ने समानाक्षर के अन्तर्गत प्लुत का परिगणन नहीं किया तो कोई आश्चर्य नहीं।

ऋ ॠ को ग्रहण नहीं करने का कारण बताते हुए कहा गया है कि उसमें रेफ का अंश होता है। वैसे तो ऋक् प्रातिशाख्य में भी ऋ ॠ में रेफांश की सत्ता की बात कही गयी है और वाजसनेयी प्रातिशाख्य तथा चतुरध्यायिका में भी, ऋ ॠ को समानाक्षर के अन्तर्गत मानते हैं। चतुरध्यायिका की दृष्टि के विषय में कुछ स्पष्ट नहीं होता क्योंकि उसमें समानाक्षर संज्ञा का विधान नहीं किया गया है। ऋक् एवं वाजसनेयी प्रातिशाख्य में रेफ की सत्ता की बात (**ॠलृवर्णें रेफलकारौ संश्लिष्टौ अवश्रुतिधरावेकवर्णौ**।) (वा॰ प्रा॰ 4/148) करते हुए भी ऋ ॠ को समानाक्षर के अन्तर्गत ग्रहण किये जाने का एक ही कारण प्रतीत होता है और वह यह कि काल के आधार पर इनके भी ह्रस्व और दीर्घ भेद होते हैं। सम्भवतः इन ग्रन्थों में समानाक्षर संज्ञा

का आधार एक अन्य समान स्वर की सत्ता है, उच्चारण-प्रक्रिया में केवल एक ही स्थान का प्रयोग या श्रवण-प्रक्रिया में केवल एक ही ध्वनि का श्रवण नहीं। ऋक् तन्त्र में तो समानाक्षर के अन्तर्गत लृ तथा लॄ का भी ग्रहण किया गया है। इस दृष्टि से तैत्तिरीय प्रातिशाख्य का वर्गीकरण अधिक वैज्ञानिक कहा जा सकता है।

समानाक्षर के स्वरूप की अवधारणा में भेद होने के कारण प्रातिशाख्यों में परिगणित स्वरों की सङ्ख्या में भी भेद हो जाता है। ऋक् प्रातिशाख्य में अ आ, ऋ ॠ, इ ई, उ ऊ, आठ और वाजसनेयी प्रातिशाख्य में भी क्रमभेद से ये ही आठ समानाक्षर माने गये हैं **अष्टौ समानाक्षराण्यादितः,** (*ऋ॰ प्रा॰* 1/1)। **सिमादितोऽष्टौ स्वराणाम्,** (*वा॰ प्रा॰* 1/44)। यहाँ ध्यातव्य है कि वा॰ प्रा॰ में समानाक्षर के स्थान पर संक्षिप्त सिम् संज्ञा का प्रयोग हुआ है। किन्तु ऋकतन्त्र में लृ तथा लॄ का भी ग्रहण होने से दस तथा तैत्तिरीय प्रातिशाख्य में मूल-स्वरों के दीर्घ तथा प्लुत दोनों भेदों का ग्रहण किये जाने के कारण नौ समानाक्षर माने गये हैं। इस सङ्ख्याभेद का आधार समानाक्षर की मूल अवधारणा में भेद है, इसकी ओर पहले ही सङ्केत किया जा चुका है।

ऋक् प्रा॰	**तै॰ प्रा॰**	**वा॰ प्रा॰**	**ऋक्तन्त्र**
अ आ, ऋ ॠ,	अ आ आ3	अ आ, इ ई,	अ आ, इ ई,
इ ई, उ ऊ,	इ ई ई3	उ ऊ, ऋ ॠ,	उ ऊ, ऋ ॠ,
=8	उ ऊ ऊ3 = 9	=8	लृ लॄ = 10

(विभिन्न प्रातिशाख्यों में समानाक्षर का स्वरूप एवं संख्या)

सन्ध्यक्षर शब्द का प्रयोग गोपथ ब्राह्मण में मिलता है जहाँ कहा गया है **द्विस्थानं सन्ध्यक्षरम्** (1/1/27)। प्रातिशाख्य ग्रन्थों में सन्ध्यक्षर के इसी लक्षण का अनुपालन किया गया है। ऋक् तथा वाजसनेयी प्रातिशाख्यों में सन्ध्यक्षरों का केवल परिगणन किया गया है और ए ओ ऐ औ को इसके अन्तर्गत रखा गया है। यहाँ यह ध्यान देने योग्य है कि ऋक् प्रा॰ में सन्ध्यक्षरों के विषय में दो प्रकार के मतों का उल्लेख है। 1/42 में ए ऐ का उच्चारण-स्थान तालु और 1/47 में ओ औ का उच्चारण-स्थान ओष्ठ बतलाया गया है किन्तु 13/38 में कहा गया है कि कुछ आचार्य सन्ध्यक्षरों को सन्धि से उत्पन्न बतलाते हैं अतः इनमें द्विस्थानता है (**सन्ध्यानि सन्ध्यक्षराण्याहुरेके द्विस्थानतैषु तथोभयेषु**।) "एके" कहकर उल्लिखित इस मत से स्पष्ट है कि ए ओ ऐ औ की उच्चारण-प्रक्रिया के विषय में आचार्यों में मतैक्य नहीं था। बाद में चलकर सन्ध्यक्षर का स्वरूप और अधिक स्पष्ट कर दिया गया क्योंकि ऋक् प्रातिशाख्य के टीकाकार उवट ने न

केवल सन्ध्यक्षरों की व्याख्या की अपितु किन वर्णों के मेल से ये स्वर बने हैं इसका भी वर्णन किया –

> **अकारस्य इकारेण उकारेण एकारेण औकारेण च सह सन्धौ यान्यक्षराणि निष्पाद्यन्ते तानि तथोच्यन्ते।** (1 / 2)

ऋक् प्रातिशाख्य में भी शाकटायन का मत उद्धृत करते हुए स्वरों के इसी प्रकार के मेल की बात कही गयी है। वहाँ यह भी स्पष्ट किया गया है कि इनमें दोनों स्वरों की मात्रा बराबर की होती है अर्थात् पूर्वार्ध अ होता है और उत्तरार्ध अन्य स्वर। वहाँ ए ओ तथा ऐ औ में उच्चारण तथा श्रवण में एकवर्णता तथा द्विवर्णता का प्रश्न भी उठाया गया है। इसके उत्तर में स्पष्ट करते हुए कहा गया है कि ए और ओ जहाँ समानाक्षरों के समान एक ही सुनायी पड़ते हैं वहाँ ऐ और औ में स्पष्टतः द्विस्वरता है। वस्तुतः उच्चारण.प्रक्रिया में तो ए और ओ में भी दो स्थानों का स्पष्ट उपयोग होता है, किन्तु श्रवण में वह भेद उतना स्पष्ट नहीं होता। उच्चारण.प्रक्रिया और श्रवण के इस अन्तर के कारण ही यह शंका उठी होगी, ऐसा प्रतीत होता है। यह भी सम्भव है कि कालक्रम में ए और ओ के उच्चारण में थोड़ा भेद भी आया हो वैसे ही जैसे आज हम ऐ तथा औ का उच्चारण अइ और अउ नहीं करके ऐ औ ही करते हैं।

ऋक् प्रातिशाख्य में इस विशेषता की व्याख्या एक और प्रकार से की गयी है। वहाँ कहा गया है कि ए तथा ओ में प्रयुक्त दोनों स्वर समानमात्रिक होते हैं इसलिए उनमें श्रवण-भेद स्पष्ट नहीं होता, किन्तु ऐ तथा औ में अ तथा इवर्ण और उवर्ण समान मात्रा में विद्यमान नहीं होते इसलिए उनका पृथक् श्रवण होता है। तैत्तिरीय प्रातिशाख्य में तो दोनों स्वरों की मात्रा भी शब्दशः वर्णित है। वहाँ ऐ तथा औ में प्रथम तत्त्व अ की आधी मात्रा तथा द्वितीय तत्त्व इ तथा उ की डेढ़ मात्रा बतायी गयी है।

चतुरध्यायिका में दो स्थानों से उच्चरित किन्तु श्रवण में एक प्रतीत होनेवाले वर्ण की प्रवृत्ति की बात कितनी स्पष्टता से कही गयी है, यह द्रष्टव्य है – **सन्ध्यक्षराणि संस्पृष्टवर्णान्येकवर्णवद्वृत्ति** (1/40)। उच्चारण-प्रक्रिया तथा श्रवण-प्रक्रिया का यह सूक्ष्म भेद प्राचीन आचार्यों की दृष्टि से छूटा नहीं था। आधुनिक ध्वनिविज्ञान में विभिन्न यन्त्रों की सहायता से इस भेद को उद्भासित किया गया है किन्तु वर्ण-विभाग की बात करते हुए प्राचीन परम्परा में जिन पाँच आधारों को गिनाया गया है उनके अतिरिक्त नवीन आधार नहीं बनाये जा सके हैं – **तेषां विभागः पञ्चधा स्मृतः स्वरतः कालतः स्थानात् प्रयत्नानुप्रदानतः** (पा॰ शि॰ 10)। आज आवश्यकता है इन अवधारणाओं के पुनर्व्याख्यान की एवं उनके वास्तविक स्वरूप को उद्घाटित कर आधुनिक सन्दर्भों में उनके सार्थक प्रयोग की।

16

विकृतिसम्मर्शः

रमेशचन्द्र दाश शर्मा

भारतीयदर्शने वेदानांस्थानं सर्वोपरिवर्तते। समाङ्पसर्गपूर्वकं म्नाते-रभ्यसार्थकस्य धातोः समभ्यस्यते मर्यादयायमितिव्युत्पत्त्या समाम्नायः शब्दो निष्पद्यते। अतोऽस्याभ्यासोऽध्येतृभिः शिक्षोक्ताध्ययनधर्मानुसारं क्रियते[1]। वेदाध्ययनविधिर्वहुभिर्नियमविशेषैरूप-निबद्धत्वादस्याध्ययनं गुरुपूर्वकमेव[2] क्रियते। अनादि-सिद्धगुरुपरम्परयाप्रचलितस्यास्य-वेदपाठस्याविकृतपरम्परासंरक्षणाय तन्नियमाः प्रातिशाख्यशिक्षाप्रतिज्ञासूत्रादिषु ग्रन्थेषु ऋषयःग्रन्थयामासुः। यतो हि ते विवुधिरे यदग्रे येऽधिकारिणोभविष्यन्ति तेषु तादृशी प्रतिभा न भविता यया ते - वेदाध्ययनप्रयुक्तसमस्तविधिनिषेधान् सम्यग्गृह्णीयुः। वैदिक-सम्प्रदायेषु तादृशनियमानां परिपालनादेवाद्यावधि गुरुपरम्पराधीतवेदानां वैदिकानां वेदपाठसमये न कस्यापि हस्तस्वरे कण्ठस्वरे वा वैषम्यमवलोक्यते। प्रथमन्तावदगुरुकुले शिष्यः संहितापाठस्याभ्यासमकरोत्। ततः पदपाठस्य ततश्च क्रमपाठस्य [3]। सर्वेष्वेतेषुपाठेषु निपुणेषु जायमानेषु जटादिविकृतिपाठाः[4] प्रारभन्त।

---

१. (क) शुचिर्नां — *शु० य० प्रा० ८।२७*

(ख) शुचौदेशे — *शु० य० प्रा० ८।२८*

(ग) हस्तौ सुसंयुक्तौ धार्यौ जानुनोरुपरिस्थितौ।
गुरोरनुमतिं कुर्यात्पठन्नाऽन्यमतिर्भवेत्॥ — *या० व० शि० २०*

२. वेदाध्ययनं नित्यं गुर्वध्ययनपूर्वकम्।
वेदाध्ययनसामान्यादधुनाध्ययनं यथा॥ — कुमारिलभट्ट

३. संहितानयते सूर्यं पदन्तु शशिनः पदम्।
क्रमश्च नयते सूक्ष्मं यत् तत् पदमनामयम्॥ — *या० व० शि० ३२*

४. जटामालाशिखारेखाध्वजोदण्डोरथोघनः।
अष्टौविकृतयः प्रोक्ताः क्रमपूर्वा महर्षिभिः॥

विकृतीनां प्रवर्तकः प्रयोजनञ्च

वैदिकवाङ्मये विकृतीनामुत्तुङ्गाधिष्ठानं वर्तते । महर्षिव्याडिः[5] आसां प्रवर्तको वर्तते। मन्त्राणामविकृतरूपरक्षायै ऋषयः जटादिविकृतीनांप्रवर्तनं चक्रुः। आसां पाठेन प्रत्यक्षरपदमन्त्रादीनां नैकवारं सन्ध्यवग्रहादिविघट्टनेन स्वरसमासादीनां लिङ्गानि पुरस्फुरन्तीव विराजन्ते। येनाम्नायविदूषकाणां पदशब्दवर्णमात्रार्धमात्रोपचयापचय-कृतप्रयासो न सेत्स्यति। अत एवाद्यापि वेदमन्त्रेषु न किमपि मिश्रणमवलोक्यते[•]। आसामभ्यासो मन्त्राणां साकल्येन सस्वरं ग्रहणाय भवति। अत एव महर्षिकात्यायनेन लिखितं क्रमः - स्मृतिप्रयोजन[6] इति।

---

५. शैशिरीये समाम्नाये व्याडिनैव महर्षिणा।
जटाद्याविकृतिरष्टौलक्ष्यन्तेनातिविस्तरम्॥

मधुशिक्षायां मधुसूदनमुनिमते तु —
भगवान् संहितां प्राह पदपाठन्तुरावणः।
वाभण्यर्षिः क्रमंप्राह जटां व्याडीरवोचत॥

मालापाठं वसिष्ठश्च शिखापाठं भृगुर्व्यधात्।
अष्टाबक्रोऽकरोद्रेखां विश्वामित्रोऽपठद्ध्वजम्॥

दण्डंपराशरोऽवोचत्कश्यपो रथमब्रवीत्।
घनमत्रिर्मुनिः प्राह विकृतीनामयं क्रमः॥

• स्वशारणागतानिवाक्यानि पदानि वर्णात् तत्स्वरान् तद्गतदेवताकरण- स्थानकालमात्रादींश्च विशेषतः परिपालयन्तोऽधुनापिदृश्यन्ते वैदिकाः। तथाहि—अग्निपदस्य रक्षणप्रकारः॥ वैदिकाः वेदाध्यापका-अध्यापनात्पूर्वं शुद्धंवर्ण-स्वरवर्ण- मात्रावर्ण-अङ्गवर्ण-वर्णसारक्रमैः पञ्चविधैः क्रमैः प्रतिपदं संरक्षन्ति। तत्र (अग्निः) — इति पदस्य तान् प्रदर्शयामः — (१)अकारगकारद्वित्व-तृतीययमनकारेकारविसर्जनीया इतिशुद्धंवर्णक्रमः। (२) अनुदात्ताकारगकारद्वित्व-तृतीययमन-कारोदात्तेकारविसर्जनीया इति स्वरक्रमः। (३) एकमात्रिकानु-दात्ताकारार्धमात्रिकविरामद्वयणुमात्रिकगकार-द्वित्वाणुमात्रिक-तृतीययमार्धमात्रिकनकारैकमात्रिकोदात्तेकाराणुमात्रिकवि-रामाधमात्रिकविसर्जनीय-द्विमात्रिकविरामा इति मात्रा-वर्णक्रमः। (४) एकमात्रिकानुदात्ता-कारार्धमात्रिकविराम-द्वयणुमात्रिकपूर्वाङ्ग भूतगकारद्वित्वाणुमात्रिक पूर्वाङ्गभूत-तृतीययमार्धमात्रिकपराङ्ग भूतनकारैकमात्रिकोदात्तेकाराणुमात्रिकविरामार्ध-मात्रिकपूर्वाङ्गभू-तविसर्जनीय द्विमात्रिकविरामा इत्यङ्गवर्णक्रमः। (पञ्चमो वर्णसारक्रमोऽत्र विस्तारभिया न लिख्यते)

६. *शु० य० प्रा० ४।१८२.*

यद्यपि विकृतिपाठजन्यापूर्वमेवशास्त्रेषु गीयते[7] कर्मकाण्डविधौ विकृतिपाठानां किमपि प्रयोजनं नास्ति, एवञ्च संहितापाठापेक्षया विकृतिपाठः वहुक्लिष्टतरः श्रमसाध्यश्च वर्तते, तथापि ऋषयस्तादृशमपि कठिनपरिश्रमं कृत्वा वेदाक्षरसंरक्षणाय कीदृशं प्रयत्नं चक्रुरिति तेषां वेदविषयिणीनिष्ठैव तत्सर्वमभिव्यञ्जयति।

अथाष्टविकृतीनां लक्षणविवेचनपूर्वकमुदाहरणान्यपि प्रस्तोष्यन्ते। तत्रादौ विकृति-पाठेषु संहितापाठस्याधाररूपेण स्वीकृतत्वात् तदेव विविच्यते। संहितापदक्रमेतिपाठत्रयानन्तरं ततोऽन्याः विकृतयः पठ्यन्ते। तत्र "परः सन्निकर्षः संहिता,"[8] "पूर्वेणोत्तरः[9] संहिताः," "वर्णानामेकप्राणयोगः *संहिता,*"[10] "संहितापदप्रकृतिरिति",[11] संहितापदं विमृश्यते विभिन्न शास्त्रकृद्भिः। समेषां सङ्कलितसूत्राणामाशयानुसारं संहिताशब्दः- स्वरैः-स्वराधिरूढव्यञ्जनैर्वा सङ्घटितानां पदानां पदाद्यन्तयोः सन्धिजन्यार्धमात्राधिककालव्यवधानाभावपरः सन्निकर्षरूपेऽर्थे पर्यवतिष्ठते।

---

७. जटादिविकृतीनां ये पारायणपरा नराः॥
महात्मानो द्विजा श्रेष्ठास्ते ज्ञेयाः पङ्क्तिपावनाः॥ — *वाराहपुराणे*

मार्कण्डेये यथा —

क्रमाध्ययनसम्पन्नो मन्त्रब्राह्मणपारगः॥
जटापारायणपरोविष्णुलोकेमहीयते॥

वृद्धमनुः — वेदवेदार्थतत्त्वज्ञाः जटाक्रमविशारदाः॥
श्रोत्रियाः ब्राह्मणाः श्राद्ध ये-नराः पंक्तिपावनाः॥

पराशरः — संहितावित्स्वर्गगामी पदवेदीमहर्गतिः॥
क्रमीजनतपः सप्तगामी वैकुण्ठभुग्जटी॥

८. वर्णानामतिशयितः सन्निधिः संहितासंज्ञःस्यात्॥ वालमनोरमायाम् — परः अतिशयितः सन्निकर्षः सामीप्यम् — अर्धमात्राधिककालव्यवधानाभावः, अर्धमात्रा — कालव्यवधानस्य अवर्जनीयत्वात्। — *पा०अ० १.४.१०९. सिद्धान्तकौमुदी संज्ञाप्रकरणम्*

९. पूर्वेणपदान्तेन उत्तरः पदादिः संहिता यदाक्रियते स्वरतो वर्णतश्च तदा द्विपदसंहितोच्यते॥ — *शु०य०प्रा०* १-१५५ उ०भा०

१०. एवतावत् पादसंहिता ऋक्षुकर्तव्या, यजुष्षुत्वयं विधिः। वर्णाना मेकोच्छवासोच्चारणयोगः, पदे वा वाक्ये विश्रामः सा च प्राण संहिता। यत्र भूयांसि पदान्यतिक्रम्यावसानं भवति नत्वेकेन प्राणेन तान्व्याप्तुं शक्यन्ते तत्रायं विधिः। — *शु०य०प्रा०* १५८ उ०भा०

११. पदानि प्रकृतिभूतानि यस्याः संहितायाः सा पदप्रकृतिः संहितात्र विकारः। — *ऋ० प्रा०* २.१ उ० भा०

तथाहिषत्वणत्वादयो विकाराः संहिताया एव भवन्ति। प्रकृतिभूतत्वाच्च पदानां सिद्धत्वम्॥

ननु पदविच्छेदोऽसंहितेतिकात्यायनः,[12] संहिताप्रकृतिरिति शौनकः[13]। तर्ह्यत्र पदानां प्रकृतिरिति तत्पुरुषसमासः। पदान्येव प्रकृतिभूतानि यस्याः सेयं पदप्रकृतिरित्युभयथा समासः सम्पद्यते। आद्यविग्रहस्वीकारेण प्रकृतित्वं संहितायाः, विकारत्वं पदानाम्। द्वितीयविग्रहस्वीकारेण प्रकृतित्वं पदानां विकृतित्वं च संहितायाः। तर्हि कतरो गरीयानितिचेदुच्यते। संहितायाः प्रकृतित्वमित्येवपक्षः गरीयान्। यतोहि-मन्त्रदृशः ऋषेस्तपसाभिव्यज्यमानो मन्त्रः संहितारूपेणैवभवति, तथैव ऋषिभिः स्वशिष्येभ्य उपदिश्यते, वेदारम्भश्चापि संहितात एव क्रियते। एवञ्च कर्मकाण्डादौ संहितामन्त्राणामेवप्रयोगोभवति न पदानाम्। एवमेभिः हेतुविशेषैः प्रकृतित्वमेव संहितायाः सिद्धयति। एवं सति पदविच्छेदोऽ- संहितेतिकात्यायनवचनमपिस्वाभिहितेऽर्थेऽनुगृह्यते। तर्हि पदप्रकृतीनिसर्वचरणानां पार्षदानीति[14] वचनस्य का गतिरिति चेदुच्यते-पदं येषु शास्त्रेषु (प्रातिशाख्यग्रन्थेषु) संहितायाः प्रकृतित्वेन चिन्त्यते तानि पदप्रकृतीनि सर्वचरणानां पार्षदानि तेष्वेवग्रन्थेषु व्याख्यायमानेषु पदानां प्रकृतित्वं भवति न सर्वत्र। अयमर्थः-सर्वत्र-प्रातिशाख्य-ग्रन्थेषु पदानां प्रकृतित्वं स्वीकृत्य व्याख्या क्रियते। यतो हि स्वरसंस्कारयोर्विधायकोऽयं[15] प्रातिशाख्यग्रन्थः। अतोऽत्र पदयोः पदानां वा सङ्घातेन संहिता स्वरश्चिन्त्यते। उक्तञ्च-ऋते न च द्वैपदसंहितास्वराविति। तस्मात् संहितायाः एव प्रकृतित्वं सुसम्पन्नम्।

---

१२. *यु० य० प्रा० शा० १.१५६।*

१३. *ऋ० प्रा० शा० २.१॥*

१४. "पदप्रकृतीनि सर्वचरणानां पार्षदानि"। सर्वेषां चरणानां सर्वशाखान्तराणामित्यर्थः। किम्। "पार्षदानि" स्वचरणपर्षद्येव यैः प्रतिशाखानियतमेव पदावग्रहप्रगृह्य-क्रम संहितास्वरलक्षणमुच्यते। तानीमानि "पार्षदानि" प्रातिशाख्यानीत्यर्थः। आह — किं तेषाम्? इति॥ उच्यते — तानि पदप्रकृतीनि। पदं येषु संहितायाः प्रकृतित्वेन चिन्त्यते, तानीमानि पदप्रकृतीनि तेषामपि स एव समय इत्यभिप्रायः। *निरुक्ते दुर्भाष्यम्*

१५. स्वरसंस्कारयोश्छन्दसि नियमः — *शु० य० प्रा० १.१*

स्वर उदात्तानुदात्तस्वरितप्रचितलक्षणः, संस्कारो लोपागमवर्णविकारप्रकृतिभा- वलक्षणः, तयोः स्वरसंस्कारयोः छन्दसिविषये नियमोऽधिकृतो वेदितव्यः। प्रतिज्ञासूत्रमेतत्। प्रतिज्ञा च शिष्यबुद्धिसमाधानार्था॥ (उवट भाष्यम्)

विकृतिपाठे पौर्वापर्यम्

अष्टविकृतिषु जटादण्डयोः प्रामुख्यं प्रथितमस्ति। यतो ह्यन्याः विकृतयः आभ्यामेव निःसरन्ति। जटापाठमनुशिखापाठो भवति। मानदण्डभूतायाः दण्डविकृतेरनुसरणं मालारेखाध्वजरथविकृतयः[16] कुर्वन्ति। घनपाठस्तु जटादण्डावनुसरति। मालारेखाघनपाठेषु योऽवान्तरभेदोऽस्ति तद्यथास्थानं प्रतिपादयिष्ये।

संहितापाठः

ओषधयः सम्वदन्ते सोमेन सह राज्ञा।
यस्मै कृणोतिब्राह्मणस्तं राजन्पारयामसि॥

---

१६. अष्टविकृतिषु मालापाठ तथा रथपाठ विषये च मतभेदाः दृश्यन्ते। ते चेत्थम्—

अवसानाच्चावसानातं क्रमादुत्क्रमणं पठेत्।
मालाख्यां विकृतिं धीमान् संहितायाः सदापठेत्।
पंचविशत् प्रभेदांहि मालाख्यां विकृतिं विदुः।
पंचबिशतिभेदाश्च मालायाः सम्भवन्तिहि॥

१. पद, २. पदव्युत्क्रम, ३. क्रम, ४. जटा, ५. शिखा, ६. संहितापद, ७. संहिताक्रम, संहिताजटा, ९. संहिताशिखा, १०. पदक्रम, ११. पदजटा, १२. पदशिखा, १३. क्रमजटा, १४. क्रमशिखा, १५. जटाशिखा, १६. संहितापदक्रम, १७. संहिताक्रमजटा, १९.. संहिताजटाशिखा, १९. संहिता पदक्रमजटा, २०. पदजटाशिखा, २१. क्रमजटाशिखा, २२. संहिता पदक्रमजटा, २३. संहिता क्रमजटाशिखा, २४. संहितापदक्रमजटाशिखा, २५. माला॥ इतिमालाभेदाः।

रथभेदाः
वल्ल्याः क्रमसमाख्यातो जटाख्यातं पदद्वयम्।
क्रमवत्क्रमणं कुर्यात् व्युत्क्रमञ्च पदे पदे॥

अनुलोमं जटातन्तुं विलोमन्तु पृथक् पृथक्।
रथाख्यंविकृतिंब्रूयात् रथभेदाः प्रकथ्यन्ते॥

अनुलोमं जटातन्तुं प्रपठेद्वै पृथक् पृथक्
रथाख्यां विकृतिं धीमान् विलोमन्तु पृथक् पृथक्॥

रथस्यैकादशभेदाभवन्ति ते तु विलोमेनैव जायन्ते।

इमेश्लोकाः श्रीपद सातवलेकरलिखितवैदिव्याख्यानमालायाः षोडशतमेव्याख्यानभागेसंगृहीताः वर्तन्ते। तेऽपि महोदयाः कुत्रचित् जीर्णपाण्डुलिपिग्रन्थात् संग्रहं कृतवन्तः। "वल्ली" ति ग्रन्थे इमेश्लोकाः सन्तीति तैरनुमीयते। परन्तु एतावन्तः पाठभेदाः सम्प्रति वैदिकमण्डले नोपलभ्यन्ते। याःखलु प्रसिद्धाः सन्ति ता अत्र मया सलक्षणं सोदाहरणञ्च प्रतिपाद्यन्ते।

अतःपरं पदपाठः

विकृतिपाठस्य सौविध्यार्थं पदपाठावसरे पदानां गणना संख्यानिर्देशपूर्वकं कार्या। येनाग्रिमासु विकृतिषु पदानामनुलोमकरणे सौविध्यं-स्यात्। यथा —

१	२	३	४	५	६
ओषधयः।	सं।	वदन्ते।	सोमेन।	सह।	राज्ञा।
७	८	९	१०	११	१२
यस्मै।	कृणोति।	ब्राह्मणः।	तं।	राजन्।	पारयामसि॥

अत्र प्रसङ्गाद् विकृतिपाठेषु प्रयुक्तपारिभाषिकशब्दाःसोदाहरणं प्रस्तूयन्ते —

१. क्रमः ओषधयः सम्। (१२) सङ्क्रमोऽप्येवमेव।
२. व्युत्क्रमः समोषधयः (२१)
१. उत्क्रमाभिक्रमे सदृशे स्तः- सं सं (२२)।*

√क्रमपाठः

क्रमपाठे द्वे द्वे पदे पठ्येते। जलौकासङ्क्रमणवदयमपि पाठरादानविसर्गाभ्यां पठ्यते। अस्य पाठस्य योगरूढासंहितेतिनाम प्रसिद्धमस्ति। अस्योदाहरणं यथा —

१	२	२ ३	३	४	
ओषधयः।	सं।	सम्वदन्ते ।	वदन्ते	सोमेन।	
४	५	५	६	६	
सोमेन	सह।	सह	राज्ञा।	राज्ञेति	राज्ञा।
७	८	८	९	९ १०	
यस्मै	कृणोति।	कृणोति	ब्राह्मणः।	ब्राह्मणस्तं।	
१०	११	११	१२		
तं	राजन्।	राजन्पारयामसि।	पारयामसीतिपारयामसि॥		

अत्र पठ्यमानपदानि - १२.२३-३४.४५.५६. इत्यादि। द्वं द्वं पदानिसहैव पठ्यन्ते।

---

* पञ्चसन्धियुक्तघनपाठप्रकरणे एतेषां विस्तृतं वर्णनं वर्तते।

√ (पद्भ्यां) द्वाभ्यामभिक्रम्य प्रत्यादायोत्तरं तयोः।
उत्तरेणोपसंदध्यात्तथार्धर्चं समापयेत्॥ *ऋ० प्रा०* १०.२

1. जटापाठः[x]

जटापाठेऽनुलोमविलोमाभ्यां त्रिवारं क्रमपाठं पठेत्। विलोमसमये पदवत् सन्धिं कृत्वाऽनुलोमपाठे च संहितावतं पठेत् यथा —

१ २ २ १ १ २

ओषधयः सं समोषधयः ओषधयः सम्॥

२ ३ ३ २ २ ३

सम्वदन्ते वदन्ते संसं वदन्ते।

३ ४ ४ ३ ३ ४

वदन्ते सोमेन सोमेन वदन्ते वदन्ते सोमेन॥

४ ५ ५ ४ ४ ५

सोमेन सह सह सोमेन सोमेन सह॥

५ ६ ६ ५ ५ ६

सह राज्ञा राज्ञा सह सह राज्ञा॥ राज्ञेति राज्ञा॥

७ ८ ८ ७ ७ ८

यस्मै कृणोति कृणोति यस्मै यस्मै कृणोति॥

८ ९ ९ ८ ८ ९

कृणोति ब्राह्मणो ब्राह्मणः कृणोति कृणोति ब्राह्मणः॥

९ १० १० १९ १९ १०

ब्राह्मणस्तं तं ब्राह्मणो ब्राह्मणस्तम्॥

१० ११ १० १० ११

तं राजन्राजंस्तं तं राजन्॥

११ १२ १२ ११ ११ १२

राजन्पारयामसि पारयामसि राजन् राजन्पारयामसि॥

पारयामसीति पारयामसि॥

---

x अनुलोमविलोमाभ्यां त्रिवारं हि पठेत् क्रमम्।
विलोमे पदवत्सन्धिरनुलोमे यथाक्रमम्॥

क्रमेयथोक्ते पदजातमेव द्विरभ्यसेदुत्तरमेवपूर्वम्।
अभ्यस्य पूर्वं च तथोत्तरे पदेऽवसानमेवं जटाभिधीयते॥

2. माला*

माला द्विविधा। क्रममाला पुष्पमाला च। अर्धर्च आदितोऽन्तपर्यन्तमन्ततश्चादिपर्यन्तं युगपदेव पठेत्। एतेन क्रममाला सिद्ध्यति। यथा —

१ २ ६
ओषधयः सम्। राज्ञेति राज्ञा।

२ ३ ६ ५
सम्वदन्ते। राज्ञा सह।

३ ४ ५ ४
वदन्ते सोमेन। सह सोमेन।

४ ५ ४ ३
सोमेन सह। सोमेन वदन्ते।

५ ६ ३ २
सह राज्ञा। वदन्ते सं।

६ २ १
राज्ञेति राज्ञा। समोषधयः।

•पुष्पमाला

पुष्पमाला जटावदेव भवति। परन्त्वत्रायं विशेषो यदत्रपाठसमये प्रतिपदद्वयान्तरं विरामो भवति। यथा —

१ २ २ १ १ २
ओषधयः सं। समोषधयः। ओषधयःसम्॥

२ ३ ३ २ २ ३
सम्वदन्ते। वदन्ते सम्। सम्वदन्ते॥

---

* ब्रूयात्क्रमं विपर्यासावर्धर्चस्यादितोऽन्ततः।
अन्तं चादिं नयेदेवं क्रममालेति गीयते॥

• माला मालेवपुष्पाणां पदानां ग्रन्थिनी हि सा।
आवर्तन्ते त्रयस्तस्यां क्रमव्युत्क्रम सङ्क्रमाः॥

अस्यार्थः — उवटभाष्यम्-द्वाभ्यां पदाभ्यां अभिक्रम्य आरभ्य तयो, द्वयोरभिक्रान्तयोः उत्तरं पदं प्रत्यादाय गृहीत्वा ताभ्यामुत्तरेण पदेन सन्दध्यात्। एतेन कल्पेन अर्धर्चं समापयेत्॥

३	४	४	३	३	४
वदन्ते	सोमेन।	सोमेन	वदन्ते।	वदन्ते	सोमेन।
४	५	५	४	४	५
सोमेन	सह।	सह	सोमेन।	सोमेन	सह।
५	६	६	५	५	६
सह	राज्ञा।	राज्ञा	सह।	सह	राज्ञा॥ राज्ञेति राज्ञा॥.....

3. शिखा*

जटामुक्त्वा तदग्रेऽग्रिमपदस्यैकस्य संयोजने सति शिखापाठो भवति। यथा —

ओषधयः सं समोषधय ओषधयः सं वदन्ते।
सम्वदन्ते वदन्ते संसं वदन्ते सोमेन ॥

4. रेखा·

संहिताक्रमेण पदद्वयं त्रयं चतुष्टयं पञ्च वा पदान् पठित्वा तेषां पुनः विलोम-पाठं कुर्यात्। अथ तत्पङ्क्तौ पठितपदेष्वाद्ययोः द्वयोः पदयोः क्रमपाठं कृत्वा विरमेत्। यथा —

क. पदद्वयं गृहीत्वा यथा — ओषधयः सं। समोषधयः। ओषधयः सम्॥

ख. पदत्रयं गृहीत्वा यथा — सम्वदन्ते सोमेन। सोमेन वदन्ते सं। सम्वदन्ते ॥

ग. पदचतुष्टयं गृहीत्वा यथा — वदन्ते सोमेन सह राज्ञा। राज्ञा सह सोमेन वदन्ते। वदन्ते सोमेन॥ सोमेन सह। सह राज्ञा। राज्ञेतिराज्ञा॥.....

5. ध्वजः+

मन्त्रादितोऽन्तपर्यन्तमन्ततश्चादिपर्यन्तं यदा क्रमपाठः क्रियते तदा ध्वजपाठो भवति। अयं पाठः एकस्याः ऋचः वर्गस्य वा भवति। यथा —

---

* पदोत्तरां जटामेव शिखामार्याः प्रचक्षते॥

· क्रमाद्वित्रिचतुष्पञ्चपदक्रममुदाहरेत्।
पृथक्-पृथक् विपर्यस्य लेखामाहुः पुनः क्रमात्।

\+ ब्रूयादादेः क्रमं सम्यगन्तादुत्तारयेद्यदि।
वर्गे वा ऋचि वा यत्र पठनं स ध्वजः स्मृतः॥

आदितः पाठः	*अन्ततः पाठः*
ओषधयः सम्।	पारयामसीति पारयामसि।
सम्वदन्ते।	राजन्पारयामसि।
वदन्ते सोमेन।	तंराजन्।
सोमेनसह।	ब्राह्मणस्तम्।
सहराज्ञा।	कृणोति ब्राह्मणः।
राज्ञेति राज्ञा।	यस्मै कृणोति।
यस्मै कृणोति।	राज्ञेति राज्ञा।
कृणोति ब्राह्मणः।	सह राज्ञा।
ब्राह्मणस्तम्।	सोमेन सह।
तं राजन्।	वदन्ते सोमेन।
राजन्पारयामसि।	सम्वदन्ते।
पारयामसीति पारयामसि।	ओषधयः सम्।

6. दण्डः•

आदौ मन्त्रादितः पदद्वयं गृहीत्वा क्रमपाठं कृत्वा तस्य विलोमपाठं कुर्यात्। पुनस्तयोरेव पदयोः क्रमपाठावसरेऽग्रिमं पदमेकं संयोज्य पाठं कुर्यत्। पुनः विलोमपाठं कुर्यात्। अनेनैवप्रकारेणैकैकं पदं गृहीत्वा पुनः समेषां क्रमपाठमनुलोमविलोमाभ्यां कुर्वन् मन्त्रार्धपर्यन्तमानयेत्। एतेन दण्डपाठो भवति। यथा (मन्त्रपूर्वार्धस्य) —

ओषधयः सम्। समोषधयः॥
ओषधयः सम्। सम्वदन्ते॥ वदन्ते समोषधयः।
ओषधयः सम्। संवदन्ते। वदन्ते सोमेन॥ सोमेन वदन्ते समोषधयः।
ओषधयः सम्। सम्वदन्ते। वदन्ते सोमेन। सोमेन सह॥
सह सोमेन वदन्ते समोषधयः॥
ओषधयः सम्। सम्वदन्ते। वदन्ते सोमेन। सोमेन सह। सह राज्ञा॥
राज्ञा सह सोमेन वदन्ते समोषधयः।
ओषधयः सम्। सम्वदन्ते। वदन्ते सोमेन। सोमेन सह। सह राज्ञा॥
राज्ञेति*राज्ञा॥

• क्रममुक्त्वा विपर्यस्य पुनश्चक्रममुत्तमम्।
अर्धर्चादेवमुक्तोऽयंक्रमदण्डोभिधीयते॥

* (इति करणमवग्रहः वेष्टनमितिनार्थान्तरम्) अवग्रहः कुत्र भवतीत्यत्र प्रातिशाख्यग्रन्थेषु बहुचर्चा - वर्तते। अत्र कानिचित् सूत्राणि प्रस्तूयन्ते। समासेऽवग्रहो ह्रस्वसमकालः *शु०य०प्रा०शा०* ५/१ अगृह्याण्यतिक्रम्य सहेति करणानिच। धक्षि धुक्षिप्रवादौ च विकृतादी प्लुतादिच॥ अन्तः पदञ्च येषां स्याद्विकारोऽनन्यकारितः, एतनि परिगृह्णीयात्॥ (*ऋ० प्रा०* १०-७ वहुमध्यगतानि च॥८॥ अर्धर्चान्त्यं च॥ — *ऋ० प्रा०* १० पटल

7. रथः[x]

एकस्य पदोऽर्धर्चौ वा पदद्वयं यत्र दण्डपाठविधिनोचार्यते स रथ उच्यते। रथस्त्रिविधः। द्विचक्रत्रिचक्रश्चतुश्चक्रभेदात्। तत्र द्विचक्ररथः चऽर्धर्चशः पठयते। (यथा — अर्धर्चशः)

मन्त्रपूर्वार्धः	*उत्तरार्धः*
ओषधयः सम्।	यस्मै कृणोति।
समोषधयः।	कृणोति यस्मै।
ओषधयः सम्।	यस्मै कृणोति।
सम्वदन्ते।	कृणोति ब्राह्मणः।
वदन्ते समोषधयः।	ब्राह्मणः कृणोति यस्मै।
ओषधयः सम्।	यस्मै कृणोति।
सम्वदन्ते।	कृणोति ब्राह्मणः।
वदन्ते सोमेन।	ब्राह्मणस्तम्।
सोमेन वदन्ते समोषधयः।	तं ब्राह्मणः कृणोति यस्मै।‴

मन्त्रद्वयं सहोक्त्यापि द्विचक्ररथो भवति। अस्मिन्पक्षेऽपि द्विविधः पाठभेदः। प्रथमस्तावदाद्यमन्त्रस्य (पदद्वयं गृहीत्वा क्रमेण पादान्तं यावत्) दण्डपाठविधिना पठित्वा ततो-द्वितीयमन्त्रस्यापि तेनैवप्रकारेण पाठं कुर्यात् यथा —

•अग्निमीडे अयं देवाय॥*

ईडेऽग्निम्। देवायायम्॥ अग्निमीडे। ईडे पुरोहितम्। अयं देवाय। देवाय जन्मने॥ पुरोहितमीडेऽग्निम्। जन्मने देवायायम्॥

अग्निमीडे। ईडे पुरोहितम्। पुरोहितं यज्ञस्य॥ अयं देवाय। देवाय जन्मने। जन्मने स्तोमः॥ यज्ञस्य पुरोहितमीडेऽग्निम्। स्तोमो जन्मने देवायायम्॥

---

x पादशोऽर्धर्चशोवापि सहोक्त्यादण्डवद्रथः॥

• अग्निमीडे पुरोहितं यज्ञस्य देवमृत्विजम्। होतारं रत्नधातमम्॥ — *ऋ० वे० सं०* १.१.१

पदपाठः — अग्निम्। ईडे। पुरःऽहितम्। यज्ञस्य। देवम्। ऋत्विजम्। होताराम रत्नधातमम्॥

* अयं देवाय जन्मने स्तोमो विप्रेभिरासया। अकारि रत्नधातमः॥ (*ऋ० वे० सं०* १.२०. १)

पदपाठः — अयम्। देवाय। जन्मने। स्तोमः। विप्रेभिः। आसया। अकारि। रत्नऽधातमः॥

• विष्णोः कर्माणि पश्यत यतो व्रतानि पस्पशे। इन्द्रस्य पुज्यः सखा॥ — *ऋ० वे० सं०* १।२२।१९

पदपाठः — विष्णोः। कर्माणि। पश्यत। यतः। व्रतानि। पस्पशे। इन्द्रस्य। युज्यः। सखा॥

अग्निमीडे। ईडे पुरोहितम्। पुरोहितं यज्ञस्य। पुरोहितमितिपुरःऽहितम्। यज्ञस्य देवम्॥ अयं देवाय। देवायजन्मने। जन्मनेस्तोमः। स्तोमोविप्रेभिः॥

देवं यज्ञस्यय पुरोहितमीडेऽग्निम्॥ विप्रेभिः स्तोमो जन्मने देवायायम्॥

द्वितीयप्रकारस्तु पर्यायेण पठ्यते। प्रथममन्त्रस्य क्रमपाठं विधाय द्वितीयस्यापि क्रमपाठं कुर्यात्। अथ विलोमपाठमपि प्रथमस्यादौ विधाय ततो द्वितीयस्य कुर्यात्। यथा —

अग्निमीडे।	अयं देवाय॥
ईडेऽग्निम्।	देवायायम्॥
अग्निमीडे।	अयंदेवाय॥
ईडेपुरोहितम्।	देवायजन्मने॥
पुरोहितमीडेऽग्निम्।	जन्मनेदेवायायम्॥···

त्रिचक्ररथः

यस्य मन्त्रस्य त्रिषु पादेषु समानपदानि भवन्ति तादृशस्यैव मन्त्रस्य त्रिचक्ररथपाठः सम्भवति। पूर्वं प्रतिपादादितः पदद्वयं गृहीत्वा समेषां क्रमपाठं कृत्वा ततस्तेषां विलोमपाठमपि कुर्यात्। पुनस्त्रयाणां पादानामादितः पदद्वयं गृहीत्वैव क्रमपाठं कृत्वा तत्पश्चात् संक्रमपाठं कुर्यात्। अथ क्रमशः विलोमपाठं कुर्यात्। तद्यथा —

प्रथमपादः	*द्वितीयः पादः*	*तृतीयः पाद*
विष्णोः कर्माणि।	यतो व्रतानि।	इन्द्रस्य युज्यः।
कर्माणि विष्णोः।	व्रतानि यतः।	युज्य इन्द्रस्य।
विष्णोः कर्माणि।	यतो व्रतानि।	इन्द्रस्य युज्यः।
कर्माणि पश्यत।	व्रतानि पस्पशे।	युज्यः सखा।
पश्यतकर्माणि विष्णोः।	पस्पशे व्रतानि यतः।	खायुज्य इन्द्रस्य।

चतुश्चक्ररथः

अयं पाठश्चतुर्षु पादेषु समानपदयुक्तस्य मन्त्रस्य भवति। त्रिचक्ररथपाठस्य यो विधिरुक्तः स एवात्राप्यनुगृह्यते। यथा —

प्रथमः पादः	*द्वितीयः पादः*	*तृतीयः पादः*	*चतुर्थः पादः*
ओषधयः सम्।	सोमेन सह।	यस्मैकृणोति।	तं राजन्।
समोषधयः।	सह सोमेन।	कृणोति यस्मै।	राजंस्तम्।
ओषधयः सम्।	सोमेन सह।	यस्मैकृणोति।	तं राजन्।
सं वदन्ते।	सह राज्ञा।	कृणोति ब्राह्मणः।	राजन्पारयामसि।
वदन्ते समोषधयः।	राज्ञा सह सोमेन।	ब्राह्मणः कृणोति-	पारयामसि- यस्मै। राजस्तम्।

8. घनः

घनो द्विविधः। घनः, घनवल्लभश्चेति। तत्र घनवल्लभोऽपि द्विविधः। तत्राद्यस्तावत् घनः क्रमपाठरीत्या मन्त्रान्तादादिपर्यन्तमानयेत्। आदितश्च तथैवक्रमेणान्तं नयेदेवायमेकः घनपाठः। यथा —□

राज्ञेतिराज्ञा। सह राज्ञा। सोमेन सह। वदन्ते सोमेन। सम्वदन्ते। ओषधयः सं सम्वदन्ते। वदन्ते सोमेन। सोमेन सह। सह राज्ञा। राज्ञेति राज्ञा॥

पारयामसीति पारयामसि। राजन्पारयामसि। तं राजन्। ब्राह्मणस्तम्। कृणोति ब्राह्मणः। यस्मै कृणोति कृणोति ब्राह्मणः। ब्राह्मणस्तम्। तं राजन्। राजन्पारयामसि। पारयामसीति पारयामसि॥

द्वितीयघनस्तु[17]-शिखां पठित्वा तस्य विलोमं कृत्वा तत्रोक्तानि पदानि पुनः पठेत्। यथा —

ओषधयः सं समोषधयः ओषधयः सम्वदन्ते वदन्ते समोषधय ओषधयः सम्वदन्ते॥ सम्वदन्ते वदन्ते सं सं वदन्ते सोमेन सोमेन वदन्ते सं सं वदन्ते सोमेन॥

घनवल्लभोऽपि द्विविधः। क्रमोत्क्रमव्युत्क्रमाभिक्रमसंक्रमैः पञ्चसन्धियुक्तो घनपाठः प्रथमः। स एव यदा अन्तादादिपर्यन्तमादितश्चान्तपर्यन्तं तदा द्वितीयघनवल्लभ इत्युच्यते।

अत्र क्रमोत्क्रमव्युत्क्रमाभिक्रम सङ्क्रमाणां साम्प्रदायिकस्वरूपं व्युत्पाद्यते। तत्र क्रमो नाम पदपाठपठितानां शब्दानामादानविसर्गाभ्यां क्रमणम्। यथा — परा[18] मे। मे यन्ति॥ इत्यादि।

उत्क्रमः — क्रमपाठस्योत्तरमेवपदं यत्र द्विरभ्यस्यते तदुत्क्रमः। यथा परा मे (क्रमः) मे मे (उत्क्रमः)।

□ अन्तात्क्रमं नयेत्पूर्वमादिपर्यन्तमानयेत्। आदिक्रमनयेदन्तं घनमाहुर्मनीषिणः॥

१७. शिखामुक्त्वा विपर्यस्य तत्पदानिपुनः पठेत्।
अयंघनइति प्रोक्तः इत्यष्टौ बिकृतीः पठेत्॥

१८. परा मे यन्ति धीतयो गावो न गव्यूतीरनु।
इच्छन्तीरुरुचक्षसम्॥ — *ऋ०वे०सं०* १२५.१६

पदपाठः— परो। मे। यन्ति। धीतयः। गावः। न। गव्यूतीः। अनु। इच्छन्तीः। उरुऽचक्षसम्॥

"व्युत्क्रमः"— व्युदासेनक्रमःव्युत्क्रमः। यथा — परामे (इति क्रमः) मे परा इति — व्युत्क्रमः।

अभिक्रमः क्रमस्थपूर्वपदस्याभिमुख्येन द्विरभ्यसनमभिक्रमः। यथा — परा मे (इतिक्रमः) तत्पूर्वस्थपदं परा तस्य द्विरभ्यासः — "परा परा" इत्यभिक्रमः।

सङ्क्रमः— अभिक्रमपाठस्थपदेन सहोत्तरपद-पठनं *सङ्क्रमः*। यथा — "परा परा" इत्यभिक्रमः। परेति पदोतरवर्त्तमानं मे पदेन सह "परा मे" इति रूपेणपठनं सङ्क्रमः।*

क्रमोत्क्रमव्युत्क्रमाभिक्रमसङ्क्रमैः सम्वलितः पञ्चसन्धीत्यपरनामको घनपाठः सम्प्रदायविद्भिः प्रवर्तितः। सोऽयं पञ्चसन्धियुक्तो घनपाठः[19] शाब्दिकलोपागमविकारवर्णव्यापत्तिप्रकृतिभावादिसन्धिनियमैरसम्वद्धः पठ्यते। सन्धिसामान्यनियमैरेवसुवद्धः वैदिकसम्प्रदायप्रवर्तितक्रमोत्क्रमव्युत्क्रमाभिक्रम-सङ्क्रमाख्यपञ्च-सन्धानसमयबद्धत्वादेवास्य पञ्चसन्धियुक्त-घनपाठेतिनामप्रसिद्धः। अस्मिन्नेवपाठे पदद्वयस्यादौ पञ्चसन्धि-युक्तपाठस्तयोरेव जटादण्डाभ्यां पाठेन घनपाठः सिद्ध्यति। यथा —

परो मे। मे मे। मे परा। परा परा। परामे॥

परा मे मे परा परा मे यन्ति यन्ति मे परा परामे यन्ति॥

एवं सम्पूर्णमन्त्रस्य घनपाठं कृत्वा ततो यदा मन्त्रान्तात्पञ्चसन्धियुक्तघनपाठं विधाय पुनरादेस्तेनैव प्रकारेणान्तपर्यन्तमानयेत्तदा द्वितीयोघनवल्लभो जायते। अनेन प्रकारेणाष्टौ विकृतयः पठ्यन्ते।

---

* यद्यपि क्रमसङ्क्रमयोरुत्क्रमाभिक्रमयोश्च न कश्चन विशिष्टो भेदः सारूप्यात् तथापि सम्प्रदायकृद्भिर्यत्पृथक् लक्षणोपादानं पाठसिद्ध्यर्थम्। अनेन पञ्चसन्ध्याख्य लक्षणविशिष्टेन वेदपाठेन पदानामनुलोम विलोमपाठेऽपि पौर्वापर्यं निश्चीयते। एतेन वेदाक्षराणां रक्षासुदृढा जायते। यदिकश्चित् कुत्रचिद्वेदमन्त्रेषु कमपिशब्दं प्रक्षिपति तर्हि तादृशप्रक्षिप्तशब्दस्य निष्कासनमासां विकृति-पाठेन तथैव भवति यथा तितउना पिष्टेभ्योऽपद्रव्यम्।

१९. अनुक्रमश्चोत्क्रमश्च व्युत्क्रमोऽभिक्रमस्तथा।
सङ्क्रमश्चेतिपञ्चैते जटायां कथिताः क्रमाः॥

इमे पञ्चसन्धयोऽत्रवर्णिताः सन्ति। एतैः साकं घनपाठोऽपि भवति। जटापाठोऽपि।

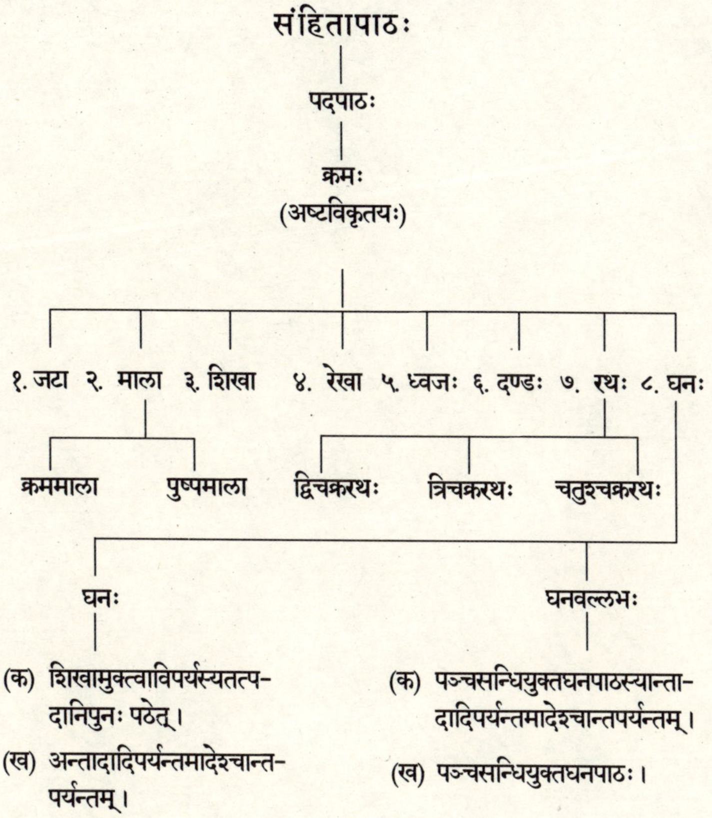
संहितापाठः
पदपाठः
क्रमः
(अष्टविकृतयः)
१. जटा
२. माला
३. शिखा
४. रेखा
५. ध्वजः
६. दण्डः
७. रथः
८. घनः
क्रममाला
पुष्पमाला
द्विचक्ररथः
त्रिचक्ररथः
चतुश्चक्ररथः
घनः
घनवल्लभः
(क) शिखामुक्त्वाविपर्यस्यतत्प-
दानिपुनः पठेत्।
(ख) अन्तादादिपर्यन्तमादेश्चान्त-
पर्यन्तम्।
(क) पञ्चसन्धियुक्तघनपाठस्यान्ता-
दादिपर्यन्तमादेश्चान्तपर्यन्तम्।
(ख) पञ्चसन्धियुक्तघनपाठः।

17

ऋग्वेद में वाणी की अवधारणा

सत्यदेव चौधरी

[1]

प्रकृति की सुरम्य गोद में पले हुए वैदिक ऋषि ने जब सूर्योदय अथवा सूर्यास्त की लालिमा को देखा और रात्रि होने पर कभी चन्द्रमा की छिटकती और कभी मद्धम पड़ती चाँदनी में अथवा नक्षत्रों की टिमटिमाती रोशनी में आकाश के भव्य सौन्दर्य को निहारा तो आश्चर्य-चकित होकर वह ठगा-सा रह गया कि यह सब क्या है? वर्षा ऋतु में उमड़ते-घुमड़ते बादलों को देख उसका मन-मयूर नाच उठा। वर्षा होते ही जब नदी-नाले फूट पड़े तो इनकी कलकल-ध्वनि से वह आनन्द-विभोर हो गया।

इधर उसे अग्नि से प्रकाश मिला, साथ ही उसकी ऊष्मा से उष्णता भी मिली तो वह इसके देदीप्यमान रूप से चमत्कृत हो गया। उसे वनों में बहुविध जड़ी-बूटियाँ मिलीं, उनके खट्टे, मीठे, कसैले, कड़वे और तीखे स्वाद को उसने चखा, और न जाने फिर उसे ऐसी कौन-सी जड़ी-बूटी मिल गयी कि जिसके रस से उसे अभूतपूर्व तृप्ति मिली और वह प्रमत्त हो उठा। इस रस को उसने 'सोम रस' नाम दिया।

इन सब आश्चर्य और आह्लाद-मिश्रित अनुभूतियों को वह वाणी द्वारा अभिव्यक्त किये बिना रह न सका — अभिव्यक्ति प्राणी का सहज और अनिवार्य धर्म भी तो है। किन्तु क्या हर प्रकार की अभिव्यक्ति काव्य कहाती है? नहीं, केवल वही अभिव्यक्ति, जो ललित होती है, मधुर होती है, कल्पना-प्रसूत होती है, जिसका प्रभाव शाश्वत रहता है, सार्वकालिक और सार्वदेशिक होता है — सृष्टि के अन्त तक बना रहता है। ऋग्वेद के ऋषि की अभिव्यक्ति में लालित्य के बहुविध रूप आज भी पाठक के मन को आकृष्ट करते हैं। अब केवल दो कुछ मनोरम स्थल लीजिए, जिन्हें हम सृष्टि के आदिम सरस एवं आह्लादक काव्य की संज्ञा तो देते ही हैं, साथ ही, परवर्ती काव्य, विशेषतः भारतीय काव्य, का उद्गम स्रोत भी मानते हैं।

रात्रि का शान्त अन्धकार धीरे-धीरे मिटता चला जा रहा है, सूर्य उगने में बस अभी थोड़ी ही देर है, उस समय **उषा** का सौन्दर्य देखते ही बनता है —

उषा-रूपी कुमारी प्रकाश के वस्त्र पहनकर पूर्व दिशा में प्रकट होती है और अपनी आकर्षक छवि को अनावृत करती है —

एषा दिवो दुहिता प्रत्यदर्शि ज्योतिर्वसाना समना परस्तात्। — ***ऋग्.*** 1.124.3

तरुणी उषा का मन अपने वल्लभ सूर्य को देखकर नाच उठा। वह स्मितवदना अपने प्रिय को उसका अभीष्ट [सुख] प्रदान करने के लिए उसके सम्मुख खड़ी हो गयी और उसने अपना वक्षःस्थल खोल दिया —

कन्येव तन्वा शाशदानाँ एषि देवि देवमियक्षमाणम्।
संस्मयमाना युवतिः पुरस्तादाविर्वक्षांसि कृणुषे विभाती॥ — ***ऋग्.*** 1.123.10

[2]

ऋग्वेदीय ऋषि ने वाणी की महत्ता को अनेक रूपों में दर्शाया है। वाक् सूक्त (10.125) में ऋषि ने वाणी की महिमा स्वयं उसके मुख से मुखरित करायी है—

मैं वाणी, सारे जग का कारण बनकर
निज इच्छा से ऐसे बहती जैसे पवन हिलोरें लेता,
जा पहुँचे – परे क्षिति से, परे गगन से,
शक्ति मेरी प्रबला ऐसी।[1]

और ऋग्वेद का यह भाव आगे चलकर 'जहाँ न पहुँचे रवि, वहाँ पहुँचे कवि' इस रूप में कहा जाने लगा —

अभिव्यंजन की क्षमता देती मैं वाणी, देवों अरु, सामान्य जनों को,
जिसको मैंने नेह से सींचा, क्षमता उसने अर्जित कर ली –
बनता कोई स्रष्टा जग का,
कोई द्रष्टा, मेधावी।[2]

---

1. अहमेव वात इव प्र वाम्यारभमाणा भुवनानि विश्वा।
परो दिवा पर एना पृथिव्यैतावती महिना सं बभूव।। — ऋग्. 10.125.8.

2. अहमेव स्वयमिदं वदामि जुष्टं देवेभिरुत मानुषेभिः।
यं कामये तं तमुग्रं कृणोमि तं ब्रह्माणं तमृषिं तं सुमेधाम्।। — ऋग्. 10.125.5.

अब ध्वनि (वाणी)-विषयक यह मन्त्र लीजिए –

> **गौरीर्मिमाय सलिलानि तक्षत्येकपदी द्विपदी सा चतुष्पदी।**
> **अष्टापदी नवपदी बभूवुषी सहस्राक्षरा परमे व्योमन्॥** — ***ऋग्.*** 1.164.41

> अति विस्तीर्ण आकाश में बादलों की, घनी ध्वनि, सहस्रों (असंख्य) नाद करती हुई गूँज उठी और उसने वृष्टिजल को व्यवस्थित कर दिया। यह ध्वनि एकपदी, द्विपदी, चतुष्पदी, अष्टापदी और नवपदी थी।

वर्षा से पूर्व यह प्रतीत होता है कि यह ध्वनि केवल बादलों से आयी है, फिर थोड़ी देर में ऐसा लगता है कि नहीं, यह बादलों और आकाश, दोनों से आयी है। और फिर ऐसा आभासित होता है कि यह चारों दिशाओं, साथ ही, चार दिक्कोणों अर्थात् आठ दिशाओं से आयी है, फिर ऐसा लगता है कि यह उधर सुदूर क्षितिज से, कुल नौ दिशाओं से, भागी चली आ रही है। यह तो हुआ मन्त्र का एक अर्थ जिस में वृष्टि से पूर्व सुनायी देती हुई ध्वनियों की चर्चा है। अब इस मन्त्र से अभिप्रेत **एक अन्य अर्थ** लीजिए –

> यह गौरी (हमारे मुख से निकलती वाणी) आकाश के समान व्यापक हमारे हृदय में अवस्थित है। यह सलिल आदि अनेक पदार्थों को अपने-अपने नामों से सङ्केतित कर व्यवस्थित किये हुए है।

यह वाणी एकपदी है – मौखिक रूप से बोलने पर यह एक ही प्रतीत होती है, अर्थात् व्याकरण की दृष्टि से यह वर्गीकृत (विभाजित) नहीं होती।

यह द्विपदी है – इसमें सुबन्त (संज्ञा, सर्वनाम और विशेषण) भी हैं तथा तिङन्त (क्रियाएं) भी।

यह चतुष्पदी है – इसमें नाम (संज्ञा और सर्वनाम), आख्यात (सिद्ध और असिद्ध क्रियाएं, यथा पाक और पचति), उपसर्ग और निपात (अव्यय) हैं।

यह अष्टापदी है – इसमें सम्बोधन-सहित आठ कारक हैं।

यह नवपदी है – इसमें उक्त आठ कारक तथा अव्यय हैं। इसके अतिरिक्त नवपदी से अभिप्रेत है कि ये वाणी देह के निम्नोक्त नौ द्वारों (छिद्रों) में से निकलती है – मुख, दो कान, दो आँखें, दो नथुने, गुदा और जननेन्द्रिय।

उल्लेख्य है कि के॰ एफ॰ गैल्डनर महोदय ने इस मन्त्र का अर्थ किया है –

> The buffalo has bellowed, bringing forth water-flood, becoming one-footed, two-footed, four-footed, eight-footed, nine-footed, thousand syllabled in the highest heaven.

[गैल्डनर ने 'गौरी' का अर्थ buffalo (भैंस) किया है और अक्षर का अर्थ syllable (सॅइलेबल)। पर भैंस का संबन्ध अक्षर से जुड़ता नहीं है।]

और इधर इसी अनुवाद के आधार पर एक विद्वान् ने निष्कर्ष निकाला है –

> The twelve moons of Jupiter have been born in two series of bursts, four in the first series and eight in the second.
>
> — *Astrophysics in the Vedas* by M.L. Gupta, p. 13.

अर्थात् 'बृहस्पति नामक ग्रह के 12 चन्द्रमा दो विस्फोट-क्रमों में उत्पन्न हुए – 4 पहले क्रम में और 8 दूसरे क्रम में।' पर इस मन्त्र में 12 की संख्या तो किसी रूप में सिद्ध नहीं हो रही। यों, श्री गुप्त महोदय का यह निष्कर्ष चिन्त्य तो है ही।

अब एक ख्यात मन्त्र –

चत्वारि वाक्परिमिता पदानि तानि विदुर्ब्राह्मणा ये मनीषिणः।
गुहा त्रीणि निहिता नेङ्गयन्ति तुरीयं वाचो मनुष्या वदन्ति ॥ — *ऋग्.* 1.164.45

(यह मन्त्र *अथर्ववेद* 9.10.27 में भी उपलब्ध है।)

वाणी के चार सुनिश्चित स्तर हैं। इन्हें मनीषी ब्राह्मण (वेदज्ञ) जन जानते हैं। इनमें से तीन तो गुहा में (रहस्य-रूप में) स्थित हैं [और ये कुछ भी अर्थ] सङ्केतित नहीं करते। सभी मानव वाणी के चौथे स्तर को ही बोलते हैं – इसी में अपने वक्तव्य का आदान-प्रदान करते हैं।

पद के ये चार प्रकार कौन से हैं? यास्क के उद्धरणानुसार – (1) आर्ष पद्धति के अनुसार ये चार प्रकार हैं – ओम् तथा तीन महाव्याहृतियाँ – भूः, भुवः, स्वः। (2) वैयाकरणों के अनुसार – नाम, आख्यात, उपसर्ग और निपात। (3) याज्ञिकों के अनुसार – मन्त्र, कल्प, ब्राह्मण और व्यावहारिक वाक् (वाणी)। नैरुक्तों के अनुसार – ऋग्, यजु आदि चार वेद। महाभाष्य के अनुसार उपर्युक्त नाम, आख्यात, उपसर्ग और निपात, किन्तु (5) महाभाष्य के टीकाकार नागेश भट्ट के अनुसार परा, पश्यन्ती, मध्यमा और वैखरी।

यहाँ हमारा अभीष्ट विषय है – वाणी के निम्नोक्त परा आदि चार रूप।[3] इस विषय में सर्वप्रथम उल्लेख्य है कि एक ही शब्द मूलाधार, नाभि, हृदय तथा कण्ठ के संयोग से क्रमशः परा, पश्यन्ती, मध्यमा तथा वैखरी कहाता है।

---

3. इस सम्बन्ध में पठनीय *'वाक्यपदीय'* (1.144)।

(1) परा से अभिप्रेत है – मूलाधार[4] में स्थित नाद-रूपिणी वाणी। परा वाणी के विषय में कहा गया है कि यह आत्मा की मुख्य शक्ति रूप है। इसका कोई स्वरूप निश्चित नहीं किया जा सकता।

(2) पश्यन्ती – वह शब्द, जो उक्त मूलाधार में उत्पन्न होने वाले सूक्ष्म शब्द की उत्पत्ति के अनन्तर, वायु के संयोग से, नाभि देश में उत्पन्न होता है। पश्यन्ती की स्थिति में माना गया है कि शब्द और अर्थ एक-रूप में रहते हैं। दोनों का विभाग नहीं होता।

(3) मध्यमा – परा और पश्यन्ती की उपर्युक्त स्थिति के अनन्तर, वायु के संयोग से, हृदय में उत्पन्न शब्द। मध्यमा में शब्द् और अर्थ का विभाग तो हो जाता है, किन्तु शब्द मन-ही-मन मंडराते रहते हैं। इस स्तर पर कण्ठ-तालु आदि का कोई व्यापार नहीं होता, और न ही, इन शब्दों को कोई सुन सकता है। लोक में इसे ही सम्भवतः मन-ही-मन बात करना कहते हैं।

(4) वैखरी – उपर्युक्त तीनों स्थितियों के अनन्तर कण्ठ, तालु आदि उच्चारण-स्थानों की सहायता से, धीमे या तेज़ स्वर में, उच्चारित शब्द। मानवों द्वारा बोली जाने वाली वाणी वैखरी कहाती है।[5] इस तरह परा का सम्बन्ध आत्मा से है, पश्यन्ती का बुद्धि से, मध्यमा का मन से और वैखरी का वाग्यन्त्र से। इसी तथ्य को निम्नोक्त रूप में प्रस्तुत किया गया है –

> **आत्मा बुद्ध्या समेत्यार्थान् मनो युङ्क्ते विवक्षया,**
> **मनः कायाग्निमाहन्ति, स च प्रेरयति मारुतम्,**
> **सोदीर्णो मूर्धन्यभिहतो वक्त्रमापाद्य मारुतः।**
> **वर्णान् जनयते.......... ॥** — ***पाणिनीयशिक्षा***

इस प्रकार वाणी के उपर्युक्त पहले तीन स्तरों को चिन्तन-मनन का रूप मान सकते हैं, और चौथे स्तर को बोलने का, परस्पर आदान-प्रदान करने का, साधन। किन्तु प्रश्न है कि क्या चिन्तन-मनन की भी कोई भाषा होती है? प्रायः विद्वान् इसकी कोई भाषा नहीं मानते, पर मेरा मन कहता है कि इसकी कोई अव्यक्त भाषा है अवश्य। यह भाषा प्रत्येक व्यक्ति के अन्तर्मन में, परा आदि तीनों स्थितियों में, किञ्चित् भिन्न-भिन्न

---

4. मूलाधार कहते हैं नाभि और शिश्न के बीच स्थित एक चक्र को। यह चक्र निःसन्देह काल्पनिक ही है।

5. स्थानेषु विवृते वायौ कृतवर्णपरिग्रहा,
वैखरी वाक-प्रयोक्तॄणां प्राणवृत्तिनिबन्धिनी। — पुण्यराज, *वाक्यपदीय* 1.144.

रूप में अथवा न्यूनाधिक पृथक्-पृथक् रूप में, सदा क्रियाशील रहती है – उमड़-घुमड़ कर रही होती है। तो कौन-सी होती होगी वह भाषा? सम्भवतः यह उस व्यक्ति की ठेठ मातृभाषा होती होगी, अथवा वह भाषा जिसे वह सामान्य व्यवहार में सर्वाधिक रूप में सुविधापूर्वक बोल सकता है।

[3]

ऋग्वेद एक अद्भुत काव्य भी तो है। अतः इसमें सिद्धान्तों को भी काव्य के रूप में प्रस्तुत किया गया है। वाणी-विषयक यह एक श्लेष-परक मन्त्र लीजिए –

यस्ते स्तनः शशयो यो मयोभूर्येन विश्वा पुष्यसि वार्याणि।
यो रत्नधा वसुविद्यः सुदत्रः सरस्वति तमिह धातवे कः॥ — ***ऋग्.*** 1.164.49

मन्त्र का सरलार्थ जानने से पूर्व ज्ञातव्य है कि इस मन्त्र में विद्या को सरस्वती देवी के मूर्त रूप में प्रस्तुत किया गया है। 'सरस्वती' विद्या की अधिष्ठात्री देवी है। सरस्वती देवी के स्तन (स्तन-द्वय) की विशेषताएं बताते हुए कामना की गयी है कि हम इसका पान करें। यहाँ 'स्तन' पद का वाच्यार्थ तो 'पयोधर' है, पर इसमे स्तनन-ध्वनन अर्थात् 'शब्द' (नाद्, ध्वनि) अर्थ भी व्यञ्जित होता है – 'पयोधर' अर्थ सरस्वती नामक शरीरधारी देवी के पक्ष में, और 'शब्द' अर्थ वाणी (विद्या) के पक्ष में।

> हे सरस्वति देवी! तुम्हारे देह से संलग्न तुम्हारा स्तन (स्तन–द्वय) मानवों के लिए ऐसा सुखकारी है जैसे कि दुधमुँहे शिशुओं के लिए माता का स्तन सुखकारी होता है, यह तो मानो रत्नों को धारण करने वाला और विविध सम्पदाओं को देने वाला है। शिशु को यह जो कुछ भी (शक्ति एवं ऊर्जा) प्रदान करता है, वह अति शोभन तथा कल्याणकारी (स्वास्थ्य-वर्धक) है। हे देवि! तुम इसके माध्यम से अनेकानेक वरणीय पदार्थों द्वारा शिशु की पुष्टि करती हो। आप ऐसी व्यवस्था कीजिए कि जिससे इस प्रकार की अनेक ईश्वरीय देनों (नेअमतों) का पान (सेवन) हम भी कर सकें। यह हमारी कामना है।

उक्त मन्त्र का **अप्रकृत (प्रतीकात्मक)** अर्थ लीजिए –

> हे श्रीवाणि! तुम्हारा देह शब्दों से निर्मित है। तुम्हारा प्रत्येक शब्द अत्यन्त सुखकारी है, इससे जगत् का व्यवहार चलता है। जब यह [शब्द] काव्य का रूप ग्रहण कर लेता है तो रसास्वाद प्रदान करता है। इसका अध्येता एवं प्रयोक्ता इससे रत्न और धन (जागतिक ऋद्धि-सिद्धि) प्राप्त करता है। इससे मानव को विचार-विनिमय-क्षमता, स्फूर्ति एवं प्रेरणा प्राप्त होती है। हे वाणि! तुम शब्द के माध्यम से

मानव को अनेकानेक वरेण्य फल प्राप्त कराती हो। हमें शब्द जैसे उपादेय तत्त्व सदा उपलब्ध रहें – यह हमारी कामना है।

[4]

आधुनिक भाषा-विज्ञान 'भाषा की उत्पत्ति' के विषय में अनेक सिद्धान्त प्रस्तुत करने के बाद कह उठता है कि भाषावैज्ञानिक यदि किसी एक मत पर सहमत हैं तो वह यह है कि भाषा की उत्पत्ति के सम्बन्ध में किसी निर्णय पर नहीं पहुँच सकते। ऋग्वेद के निम्नोक्त मन्त्र में भाषा की उत्पत्ति के विषय में एक सङ्केत प्राप्त होता है –

बृहस्पते प्रथमं वाचो अग्रं यत्प्रैरत नामधेयं दधानाः।
यदेषां श्रेष्ठं यदरिप्रमासीत्प्रेणा तदेषां निहितं गुहाविः॥ — ***ऋग्.*** 10.71.1

हे बृहस्पति! वाणी का [वह अंश] अग्रगण्य है जिसे उन लोगों ने सबसे पहले उच्चारित किया जो [पदार्थों के] नाम रखेंगे। इन [वाणियों] में जो वाणी सर्वोत्तम है और निर्दोष (निर्मल) है, वह इन्हें स्नेहवश प्रकट हुई है – [यद्यपि यह] गुहा में रखी हुई थी (रहस्यमय थी)।

[बृहस्पति अपने आप से विस्मयपूर्वक कहता है–] हे बृहस्पति (हे मेरी अन्तरात्मा)! वाणी का [वह अंश] अग्रगण्य (सर्वश्रेष्ठ) है जो [बालकों] ने ['त त' आदि वर्णों के रूप में] सबसे पहले उच्चारित किया, और ये बालक आगे चलकर विभिन्न पदार्थों के नाम रखते हुए सार्थक वाणी बोलेंगे। उन [सार्थक वाणियों] में जो सर्वोत्तम और निर्दोष (निर्मल) वेद-ज्ञान है उसे [सरस्वती ने] स्नेहवश इन्हें प्रकट किया, यद्यपि यह ज्ञान गुहा में स्थित था – अति रहस्यमय था।

इस मन्त्र के भाष्य में सायण को यह कहना अभीष्ट है कि बालक उत्पन्न होने के बाद 'त त' आदि निरर्थक वर्ण (ध्वनियाँ) उच्चारित करने लगते हैं (देखिए, *ऐतरेय अरण्यक* 1-14)।[6] इन्हीं आरम्भिक वर्णों (ध्वनियों) को ही वाणियों में पहला स्थान मिलना चाहिए। वे बालक कुछ बड़े होकर विभिन्न पदार्थों को अलग-अलग नाम देते हुए पूर्ण वाक्य बोलने लगते हैं। सम्भवतः वे, पदार्थों की आकृति अथवा उनके विशिष्ट गुणों के आधार पर, उन्हें अलग-अलग नामों से पुकारते रहते हैं। फिर इसके बाद, एक स्थिति ऐसी आती है कि उनकी [अन्तश्चेतना रूपी] गुफा में जो निर्दोष (निर्मल) कथ्य अथवा वेदार्थ छिपा रहता है, सरस्वती उन्हें स्नेहवश प्रकट कर देती है (देखिए, *ऐतरेय आरण्यक* 1.3.6)।

---

6. *ऋग्वेदसंहिता* (एच० एच० विल्सन द्वारा अनुवाद तथा टिप्पणी)।
— *ऋग्.* X.71.1.

सायण सम्भवतः यह कहना चाहते हैं कि ऋषियों की अन्तश्चेतना में जो वेदज्ञान निहित था, सरस्वती ने निर्मल वाणी (निर्दोष शब्दों) के द्वारा इन्हें प्रकट कर दिया। 'सरस्वती' शब्द का उल्लेख यद्यपि उक्त मन्त्र में नहीं है, पर अभीष्ट यह हो सकता है कि ऋषियों को वेदों का ज्ञान तो उनकी अपनी पुनीत अन्तश्चेतना में पहले से विद्यमान था, पर इसे शब्दों के रूप में प्रकट करने के लिए सरस्वती ने (परमेश्वर की विद्या-प्रदात्री शक्ति ने) इन्हें सहायता प्रदान की।

स्वामी दयानन्द के अनुयायी भाष्यकार कुछ इस प्रकार का आशय इस मन्त्र से लेते हैं – "आदि सृष्टि में निष्पाप (पवित्र) ऋषियों की बुद्धि में ईश्वर ने वेद-शब्द प्रेरित किये अर्थात् वेद-वाणी प्रेरित की। वेद-शब्दों में ऋषियों ने जगत् के पदार्थों के नाम रखे और फिर प्रेम से (श्रद्धा एवं निष्ठापूर्वक) उस वाणी का प्रचार किया।" (*ऋग्वेद-भाष्य*, पं॰ जयदेव विद्यालंकार)

इधर आधुनिक भाषा-विज्ञान सम्बन्धी ग्रन्थों में भाषा की उत्पत्ति के विषय में जो अनेक मन्तव्य प्रचलित हैं उनमें से एक 'अनुरणन-सिद्धान्त' है। हम इस मन्त्र को इस सिद्धान्त का स्रोत एक सीमा तक स्वीकार कर सकते हैं। 'अनुरणन' से अभिप्रेत है किसी वस्तु से, स्वतःनिःसृत ध्वनि के आधार पर, उस वस्तु का नाम पड़ जाना। यथा – पत्र (पत्ता), नदी, जल आदि शब्द। पत्ता पेड़ से गिरा, उसके गिरने से 'पत्' ध्वनि हुई तो इसका नाम पत्र (पत्ता) पड़ गया। इसी प्रकार प्रबल वेग से बहते जल-प्रवाह की नद्-नद् ध्वनि से इस जल-प्रवाह को नदी कहा जाने लगा, आदि, आदि।

इस मन्त्र में '**यद् एषां निहितं गुहाविः** (गुहायाम्)' (जो अर्थ इन ऋषियों की अन्तश्चेतना में छिपा था) वाक्य अति महत्त्वपूर्ण है। इसी के आधार पर निम्नोक्त धारणाएं स्वीकृत हुई प्रतीत होती हैं —

(1) *ऋषिर्दर्शनात्* (निरुक्त 2.11), अर्थात् ऋषि (मन्त्रद्रष्टा) उसे कहते हैं जिसे वेदों के अर्थ का (न कि पाठ का) दर्शन (ज्ञान) हुआ था।

यास्क को ऋषि शब्द से 'मन्त्र का अर्थद्रष्टा' अभीष्ट है, न कि वेद के पाठ का रचयिता – **साक्षात्कृतधर्माण ऋषयो बभूवुः**.............. (निरुक्त 1.20.1), अर्थात् पुरातन काल में [ऐसे] ऋषि थे, जिन्हें वेदों का धर्म (अर्थ) साक्षात् (प्रत्यक्ष, स्पष्ट) था। इस कथन से प्रतीत होता है कि उन्होंने वेदों का अर्थ छह वेदाङ्गों की सहायता के बिना प्राप्त किया था, और परवर्ती सामान्य जनों ने वेदार्थ के ज्ञान के लिए वेदाङ्गों की सहायता ग्रहण की।

हमें तो इस मन्त्र से ऐसा प्रतीत होता है कि पुरातन जनों की अन्तश्चेतना में ज्ञान विद्यमान था और वह भगवत्कृपा से शब्दों के रूप में प्रकट हुआ। इस पाठ (टैक्स्ट) को हम वेद (ऋग्वेद आदि) कहते हैं, और उन पुरातन जनों को ऋषि। इस प्रकार उन ऋषियों के मन में वेद का ज्ञान पहले विद्यमान था जो कि स्वतः ही पाठ का रूप धारण करता चला गया। यों भी, कोई भी कथन जो हम बोलते हैं उसका ज्ञान (आशय) हमारे मन में पहले से विद्यमान रहता है। यही स्थिति आदिकाल से ही प्रत्येक वक्ता की रही है जिसमें कवि भी सम्मिलित हैं, चाहे वे पद्यकार हों अथवा गद्यकार। इसी अभिप्राय को कालिदास ने निम्नोक्त रूप में प्रकट किया है –

चित्रे निवेश्य परिकल्पितसत्त्वयोगाद्,
रूपोच्चयेन मनसा विधिना कृता नु।
स्त्रीरत्नसृष्टिरपरा प्रतिभाति सा मे,
धातुर्विभुत्वमनुचिन्त्य वपुश्च तस्याः॥ (*अभिज्ञान.* 2.9)

उस विधना की 'रचना-शक्ति', अरु इसकी यह 'सुन्दर-काया',
कि विधि ने जैसे –
इन दोनों को देख के लगता ऐसे
पहले कल्पित आकार को इसके, अपने मन में सिञ्चित कर,
फिर सब सुन्दर साधन लेके, कुछ और ही मानो
अद्भुत ही यह नारी-रत्न बना डाला।

इस प्रकार वाणी की महिमा के विषय में न जाने कितने वचन विद्यमान होंगे वेदों में, और उसकी महिमा परवर्ती काल में आधुनिक युग तक निरन्तर गायी जाती रही है। काव्यादर्शकार दण्डी (सातवीं शती ई॰) पुकार उठता है –

इदमन्धन्तमः कृत्स्नं जायेत भुवनत्रयम्।
यदि शब्दाह्वयं ज्योतिरासंसारं न दीप्यते॥ — *काव्यादर्श* 1.4.

सरस्वती के विषय में नाना प्रकार के स्तोत्र प्रचलित हुए। इसे एक मानवी के रूप में प्रस्तुत करते हुए इसे शुक्लवर्णा, 'वीणा-पुस्तक-धारिणी' जगद्व्यापिनी, बुद्धिप्रदा आदि विशेषणों से सुशोभित किया गया और कहा गया जो कि हमें यह अभय प्रदान करती है तथा हमारे अज्ञान-रूपी अन्धकार को दूर करती है। और इधर आधुनिक युग में सरस्वती के उपासक हिन्दी-कवि सूर्यकान्त त्रिपाठी 'निराला' पुकार उठे –

वर दे, वीणा वादिनी! वरदे,
नवगति नव लय ताल छन्द नव,
नवयुग के नव विहग-वृन्द को
नव पर, नव स्वर दे।

इसी प्रकार वाणी की प्रशस्ति, वेद-वाणी के अनुरूप, विश्व की हर भाषा में युगों-युगों तक निरन्तर उच्चरित होती जाएगी।

18

वैदिक शब्द

श्रौत याग के सन्दर्भ में

उमेश प्रसाद दाश

वेद मन्त्रों में ऐसे अनेक शब्द आये हैं, जो पारिभाषिक हैं। प्रस्तुत निबन्ध में हम वाजसनेयी संहिता के ऐसे मन्त्र को लेंगे जिनमें तीन छन्दों का नाम आया है – गायत्री, त्रैष्टुप् और जगती –

> **गायत्रेण त्वा छन्दसा परिगृह्णामि त्रैष्टुभेनत्वा छन्दसा परिगृह्णामि जागतेन त्वारछन्दसा परिगृह्णामि ॥ — वाजसनेयी संहिता ॥१.२५॥**

छन्दः-शास्त्र की दृष्टि से सामान्यतया यह कहा जा सकता है कि क्योंकि छन्द अक्षरों का परिमाण गिनाते हैं –

> **यदक्षरपरिमाणं तच्छन्दः। — कात्यायनसर्वानुक्रमणी ।१२.६॥**

इसलिए गायत्री छन्द में प्रत्येक पाद में आठ अक्षर होते हैं, त्रैष्टुप् में 11 और जगती में 12 अक्षर होते हैं। इतना कह देने मात्र से इन तीन छन्दों का स्वरूप स्पष्ट हो जाता है, किन्तु श्रौत यागों के प्रकृतभूत दर्शपौर्णमास याग के सन्दर्भ में इन तीन छन्दों का स्वरूप यदि हम देखें तो बहुत ही व्यापक पटल हमारे सामने आ जाता है जिसमें तीन लोक, तीन देव, तीन द्विज, तीन सवन और तीनों अग्नियों का सम्बन्ध इन तीन छन्दों से जुड़ता है।

श्रौत सूत्र कहते हैं कि दर्शपौर्णमास याग में वेदि का निर्माण करते समय वाजसनेयी संहिता के "**गायत्रेण त्वा छन्दसा परिगृह्णामि**" इत्यादि मन्त्र का विनियोग करना चाहिए। इस प्रसङ्ग में हम इन तीन छन्दों में से एक-एक छन्द को लें तो पता चलेगा कि किस प्रकार इन तीन छन्दों के माध्यम से ब्राह्मण ग्रन्थ एक व्यापक पटल हमारे सामने ले आते हैं। सर्वप्रथम गायत्री छन्द को देखें –

गायत्री छन्द

शतपथ ब्राह्मण ने गायत्री का सम्बन्ध अग्नि से जोड़ा "**अग्नि वै गायत्री**" (*शतपथ ब्राह्मण* 3.4.1.19) साथ ही गायत्री को पृथ्वी भी बताया "**सा वै गायत्रीयं पृथ्वी**" (*श॰ ब्रा॰* 1.7.2.15) क्योंकि पृथ्वी अग्निगर्भा है। इसलिए *शतपथ ब्राह्मण* का गायत्री को अग्नि और पृथ्वी बताना उचित है। कथा कहती है कि देव और असुरों में भूमि के विभाजन को लेकर परस्पर विवाद हुआ तो देवताओं ने कहा कि हमें उतनी भूमि दे दी जाए जितने में यज्ञ होता है। उन्होंने यह भी कहा कि क्योंकि विष्णु यज्ञ हैं "**यज्ञो वै विष्णुः**," अतः विष्णु परिमाण के बराबर उन्हें पृथ्वी दी जाए। "**यज्ञमेव विष्णुं पुरस्कृत्येयुः**" (*श॰ ब्रा॰* 1.7.2.15)

विष्णु उस समय वामन रूप में थे "**वामनो ह विष्णुरास**" (*श॰ ब्रा॰* 1.2.5.5) इसलिए असुरों को यह सोचकर कि हमें थोड़ी सी ही पृथ्वी देनी होगी इस प्रस्ताव पर कोई आपत्ति नहीं हुई। पृथ्वी को नापने कि लिए पूर्व की ओर सिर करके जब विष्णु को भूमि पर लिटाया गया तो "**ते प्राञ्चं विष्णुं निपाध**" (*श॰ ब्रा॰* 1.2.5.6) विष्णु ने विराट रूप धारण कर लिया और देवताओं ने तीन छन्दों से पृथ्वी को घेरा और पूर्व की ओर विष्णु का विराट रूप इतना विस्तृत हो गया कि उस तरफ कोई रेखा खींचना संभव नहीं रहा। इस प्रकार वेदि का स्वरूप इतना विस्तृत हो गया कि असुरों के लिए कोई भूमि बची ही नहीं, क्योंकि तीन छन्दों से पृथ्वी को आच्छादित किया था। इस प्रक्रिया में शत्रु असुरों को देवताओं ने नष्ट कर दिया।

गायत्रेण छन्दसा ततो निर्भक्तो योऽस्मान्द्वेष्टि यञ्च वयं द्विष्मः। — *वा. स.* ॥१.२५॥

अतः सर्वप्रथम दक्षिण में खींची गई रेखा गायत्री कहलाई क्योंकि उसने गान करने वाले देवताओं की रक्षा की – "**गातारं त्रायते इति गायत्री**" और असुररूपी शत्रुओं को नष्ट कर दिया। इसलिए गायत्री को वीर्य्य और प्राण कहा गया "**वीर्य्यं गायत्री**" (*श॰ ब्रा॰* 1.3.3.5) "**प्राणो वै गायत्री**" (*श॰ ब्रा॰* 6.4.25)।

क्योंकि प्राण एवं वीर्य्य से ही अपनी रक्षा होती है और असुरों का नाश होता है। प्रशंसा के रूप में गायत्री को ब्रह्म भी कहा गया है "**ब्रह्म गायत्री**" (*श॰ ब्रा॰* 1.3.5.5)। यह तो दैशिक विजय की बात हुई, इस प्रक्रिया के द्वारा देवों ने कालिक विजय भी प्राप्त की। इसकी प्रक्रिया इस प्रकार है – दर्शपौर्णमास याग के अन्तर्गत सामधेनी ऋचाओं का पाठ होता है – **समिन्धेते तस्मात्सामधेनीभिर्होता तस्मात् सामधेन्यो** (*श॰ ब्रा॰* 1.3.5.1)। ये सामधेनी मूलतः 11 हैं – "**समिन्धते तस्मादेकादशान्वाह**" (*श॰ ब्रा॰* 1.3.5.5) किन्तु प्रथम एवं अन्तिम मन्त्र क्योंकि तीन बार पढ़े जाते हैं, अतः इन ऋचाओं की संख्या 15 हो जाती है।

तां पञ्चदश सामधेन्यः सम्पद्यन्ते। — *श. ब्रा.* 1.3.5.9.

एक और गायत्री वीर्य्य थी – **वज्रो वीर्य्यं वज्रो वीर्य्यमेवैतत्** (*श. ब्रा.* 1.3.5.9) जिसके 24 अक्षर होते हैं। दूसरी पञ्चदश सामधेनी भी वज्र अथवा वीर्य्य मानी गई। गायत्री के 24 अक्षरों का ***चतुर्विंशत्यक्षरा गायत्री*** (*ऐ. ब्रा.* 3.39) 15 सामधेनी ऋचाओं से गुणा करने पर 360 का अंक आता है, जो वर्ष-दिनों की संख्या है। इस प्रकार दर्शपौर्णमास यज्ञ में सामधेनी ऋचाओं नें गायत्री के पदों के अक्षरों की सहायता से सम्पूर्ण संवत्सर को प्राप्त कर लिया। यह देवों की कालिक (काल की, काल पर) विजय थी।

पञ्चदशानामु वै गायत्रीणाम्। त्रीणि च शतानि षष्टिश्चाक्षराणि त्रीणि च वै शतानि षष्टिश्च संवत्सरस्याहानि तदाहान्याप्नोति तद्देव संवत्सरमाप्नोति। — *श. ब्रा.* 1.3.5.9.

इस प्रकार देवों ने गायत्री छन्द की सहायता से देश और काल के ऊपर विजय प्राप्त करके गायत्री के गान वाले देवों को त्राण देकर अपने गायत्री नाम को सार्थक बनवाया।

त्रिष्टुप्

गायत्री के द्वारा दक्षिण में रेखा खींची गई जबकि त्रिष्टुप् छन्द से पश्चिम की ओर रेखा खींची गई। हमने ऊपर में कहा कि सामधेनी ऋचाओं की संख्या मूलतः 11 होती है। त्रिष्टुप् छन्द भी 11 अक्षर के होते हैं —

एकादशाक्षरा वै त्रिष्टुप् ब्रह्म गायत्री। — *श. ब्रा.* 1.3.5.5.

यह ग्यारह संख्या भी अति महत्त्वपूर्ण हैं। जहाँ गायत्री में आठ अक्षर होते हैं, जो आठ वसुओं का प्रतीक है, जो वसु अग्नि रूप होने के कारण पृथ्वी से जुड़े हैं जबकि त्रिष्टुप् के ग्यारह अक्षर ग्यारह रुद्रों के प्रतीक हैं जो अन्तरिक्ष देवता हैं –

रुद्रास्त्रिष्टुभं समभरन्। — *जै. उ. ब्रा.* 1.18.5.

त्रैष्टुभोऽन्तरिक्षलोकः। — *कौषीतकी ब्राह्मण* 8.9.

इसलिए जहाँ गायत्री को पृथ्वी से जोड़ी गई, त्रिष्टुप् को अन्तरिक्ष से जोड़ा गया। वस्तुतः गायत्री के आठ और त्रिष्टुप् के ग्यारह अक्षरों का एक और भी महत्त्व है। गायत्री ब्रह्म है, इसलिए ब्राह्मण बालक के यज्ञोपवीत की अवस्था आठ वर्ष है किन्तु त्रैष्टुप् इन्द्र है जो कि क्षात्रत्व का प्रतीक है ***त्रैष्टुभो इन्द्रः*** (*कौषीतकी ब्राह्मण* 3.2.22.7) इसलिए क्षत्रिय बालक के यज्ञोपवीत की अवस्था ग्यारह वर्ष है।

जगती छन्द

हम कह चुके हैं कि जगती छन्द के एक पाद में 12 अक्षर होते हैं। वैश्य के बालक की यज्ञोपवीत अवस्था भी 12 वर्ष मानी गई है। अतः जगती का सम्बन्ध वैश्य से है। **"जगतो वै वैश्य"** (*तै. ब्रा.* 1.1.9.7) **ता वा एता जगत्यो यद् द्वादशा क्षराणि पदानि** (*ताण्ड्य महाब्राह्मण* 16.11.10)।

जगती छन्द के द्वारा वेदी के उत्तर में रेखा खींची जाती है, पूर्व से देवता आते हैं। अतः उत्तर दिशा को आच्छादित नहीं किया जाता। इस प्रकार गायत्री, त्रिष्टुप् और जगती छन्द मिलकर सारी पृथ्वी को घेर लेते हैं इसलिए इसे जगती कहा जाता है –

सर्वं जगदस्यां तेन जगती। — *श. ब्रा.* 1.8.2.11

गायत्री के आठ अक्षर जहाँ आठ वसुओं का प्रतीक है, त्रिष्टुप् के ग्यारह अक्षर 11 रुद्रों के प्रतीक हैं, वहीं जगती के 12 अक्षर 12 आदित्य के प्रतीक हैं – **"द्वादशाक्षरा वै जगती"** (*ऐ. ब्रा.* 3.12)। गायत्री प्रातः सवन का छन्द है, त्रिष्टुप् मध्याह्न सवन का, वहीं जगती छन्द तृतीय सवन का प्रतीक है – **"जागतमु वै तृतीयसवनम्"** (*गोपथ ब्राह्मण* 2.22)।

उपसंहार

इस प्रकार हम देखते हैं कि वाजसनेयी संहिता में आये गायत्री, त्रिष्टुप और जगती छन्द का विस्तार दर्शपौर्णमास याग के वेदि-निर्माण की प्रक्रिया में इतना विस्तृत हो जाता है कि उसमें समस्त अस्तित्व अन्तगर्भित हो जाता है। यदि हम श्रौतयाग की इन प्रक्रिया के सहारे वेद में आये शब्दों का स्वरूप न समझेंगे तो वैदिक शब्द अत्यन्त संकुचित अर्थ ही दे पायेंगे। इसलिए शब्दराशि वेद का उपवृहंण करने के लिए व्यक्ति को बहुश्रुत होना होगा क्योंकि **बिभेत्यल्पश्रुताद् वेदो मामयं प्रहरिष्यति**। यह सत्य है – वेद शब्द राशि है किन्तु यह भी सत्य है कि उस शब्द का उपवृहंण करनेवाले ब्राह्मण साहित्य ही उस शब्द को 'शब्द-ब्रह्म' बना देते हैं। हमने ऊपर एक उदाहरण के द्वारा गायत्री, त्रिष्टुप् और जगती वेद मन्त्र में आये इन तीन छन्दोवाचक शब्दों का ब्राह्मण ग्रन्थों में प्रतिपादित दर्शपौर्णमास नामक श्रौतयज्ञ के द्वारा किस प्रकार उपवृहंण हुआ है – यह स्थालीपुलाकन्याय से प्रतिपादित करने का एक विनम्र प्रयास किया कि वैदिक शब्दों को समझने का यह भी एक महत्त्वपूर्ण आयाम है।

इतिशम्

19

Vidhivākyas

Their Significance in Human life

P. Shashi Rekha

VEDO 'khilo dharmamūlam — says Manu at the outset of his work *Manusmṛti*. The commentator Medhātithi explains the statement *"Vidanti ananya pramāṇa-vedyam dharmalakṣanamasmāditi vedaḥ* । *Tachcha vedanāmekaikasmāt vākyāt-bhavati* ॥." He further goes on commenting on the word "Veda" which is as follows: — Veda is a special collective form of words which is *apauruṣeya* and manifold with the branches of *Mantra, Brāhmaṇa* etc. It is the means and source to know what is *dharma*. "One who does not respect such Veda and abuses it should be banished," says Manu. What is that *dharma* which is so important in human life?

The general meaning of *dharma* is that which sustains or supports mankind *dharṇāt dharmamityāhuḥ*. All the Indian philosophical systems focus one way or the other on the aspect of *dharma*. There are many schools of philosophy. But three *nāstikadarśanas* and six *āstikadarśanas* are considered as important ones because of their distinct nature. Of the six *āstikadarśanas:* Sāṁkhya, Yoga, Nyāya, Vaiśeṣika, Mīmāṁsā and Vedānta, the Mīmaṁsā which is also known as *Pūrvamīmāṁsā* deals with *Karmakāṇḍa* and has much to its credit for its contribution to the society.

The author of *Pūrvamimāṁsā* is Maharṣi Jaiminī. Āpadeva at the outset of his work *Mimāṁsā-Nyāya-Prakāṣa* states that revered Jaimini has discussed the *dharma* in twelve chapters with the compassion towards human beings. Laugākṣī Bhāskara too expresses the same view in his *Arthasaṁgraha*. Defining *dharma*, Jaiminī says *Codanalakṣno'rtho dharmaḥ*, "That which directs or inspires is *dharma*". Āpadeva explains that it is *dharma* which is ordained by Vedas keeping some *prayojana* in view. Laugākṣi Bhāskara agrees with the same. He has explained each word of this statement. Medhātithi, while commenting on Manu, says, "that which makes the man understand his duty and the means of prosperity is *dharma*."

Thus it is needless to say that Veda has laid a path for the people to reach their goals. But Vedas are beyond the understanding capacity of a common man. Hence, *Brāhmaṇa*s were composed by the seers which help to understand the Vedic injunctions. The Mīmāṁsā *dharma* is totally devoted for *vākyavichāra*, the discussion about Vedic sentences. A question may arise here "how Mīmāṁsā helps the society in general when it talks of *karmakāṇḍa*, i.e. *yajñas*, which are no more in practice." No doubt *dharma* according to Mīmāṁsakas is — *'Yāgādireva.'* This *yāga* is a performance. Any assignment or undertaking should have a perfect plan without which there is no good result and the effort would be futile. Hence, the Mīmāṁsā instructs the doer *puruṣa* how best to understand the Vedic words. Veda which is regarded as *prabhusammita* by *ālaṁkārika*s is on the highest seat like a king, the order of which should be obeyed by one and all. But to obey also one should be able to understand what it means. Hence, the Mīmāṁsakas took the lead to teach what Veda intends.

In this light the Vedic *vākya*s, their intention, their utility in human life etc. are very well explained by the scholars like

Kumārila Bhaṭṭa, Prabhākara, Maṇḍana Miśra etc. Hence, an attempt is made to focus on the role of *vidhivākyas* in human life and the discussion is mainly based on *Arthasaṁgraha* of Laugākṣī Bhāskara. The main paper deals with all such details.

Śrī Sukthaṅkar in the introduction to *Arthasaṁgraha* edited by him says "The *Pūrvamīmāṁsā* is essentially a system aiming at an interpretation of doubtful sacrificial texts and an elucidation of obscure sacrificial details." He feels that at the earlier stage of the *Pūrvamīmāṁsā*, sages must have assembled to discuss doubtful sacrificial points. The word *mīmāṁsante* occurring very often in Vedic literature signifies such attempt to take the problems faced by the persons in understanding Vedic injunctions. In course of time after the composition of the Brāhmaṇas and ritualistic Saṁhitās, the sacrificial system became typed. Then there came a change in the intellectual activity of the Mīmāṁsaka. He is engaged in bringing the harmony between the apparently discrepant and doubtful sacrificial texts. Thus it is a later development of the *Pūrvamīmāṁsā* that is embodied in the *sūtras* of Jaiminī. There appeared many commentaries on the *sūtras* of Jaiminī but the credit of systematising the principles for the first time goes to Prabhākara and Kumārila Bhaṭṭa (700 CE).

The *Pūrvamīmāṁsā* and *Uttaramīmāṁsā* are the organic parts of one system. Both share the common features of being Mīmāṁsās, i.e., investigating sciences. When the former one investigates into the sphere of rituals comprised in the Saṁhitās, Brāhmaṇas and the Śrauta-sūtras, the latter concerns itself with the philosophical speculation of the Upaniṣads. The *Pūrvamīmāṁsā* deals with *karmakāṇḍa* which is translated into actions of a person in the second stage of life, i.e, *gṛhastha*. The *Uttaramīmāṁsā* deals with Upaniṣads which is concerned with the life of a *vāṇaprastha*.

Sukthāṅkar draws a common line between *Purvamīmāṁsā* and *Dharmasāśtra* which is as follows:- "the Mīmāṁsakas were ignorant of the immense potentialities of the instrument when they were evolving their maxims." Though originally intended for sacrificial purpose, their doctrines entered into the field of law. The presence of a Mīmāṁsaka was considered essential in the assembly *(pariṣad)* of the justices. The commentators Medhatithī and Vijñaneshvara on Manu and Yājñavalkya respectively discussed the issues in their works based on the principles of Mīmāṁsā.

Coming to the principles of Mīmāṁsā about *dharma,* the view of Āpadeva and Laugakṣī are already quoted. The *dharma* as stated by the Mīmāṁsaka is *'Yāgādireva dharmaḥ.'* A doubt arises then what about the statement *'Codanalakṣanortho dharmaḥ.'* The answer is — the word *codana* or "impulsion" does not mean a portion of the Veda but it signifies Veda in its entirety (*mātrā*). Because, the entire Veda teaches *dharma* that constitutes its purpose (*tātparya*). This *dharma* is understood through the Brāhmaṇas by the words in potential mood.

This *yāgādi* etc. is enjoined by the sentence like *yajeta svargakāmaḥ* with reference to a man, who wishes to go to heaven. In the word *yajeta* there are two elements. The root *√yaj* and the suffix. The suffix again has twofold role, i.e. *ākhyātattva* and *liṅgtva*. This *ākhyātattva* is common in all the *lakara*s whereas *liṅgtva* is confined only to *liṅg*. Both the elements express creativity (= *bhāvanā*) only. "*Bhāvanā* is the activity of the agency favourable to the production of the thing about to take place."

This *bhāvanā* is twofold — 1. *śābdī,* 2. *ārthī*. The *śābdībhāvanā* is a verbal creativity, consists in the peculiar activity tending to make a person out, on the part of an agency bringing it about. This particular activity again, as far as Veda is concerned, abides in the word itself as there is no person but are only Vedic words, that too the potential suffix in particular."

Ārthībhāvanā is easy to understand because it is *puruṣānisṭha,* i.e, abides in an agent person. It is clear that Vedic sentences should be understood as per the above *bhāvanā.* But what is Veda? The answer is: *Apauruṣeyam Vākyām Vedaḥ.* Veda is not the product of a person. It is stated in *Ślokavārtika* that the study of the Veda is preceded by the study under a preceptor like the study under *guru* in present-day study. The scholars had much debate on the *apauruṣeyatva* of Veda. After establishing the *apauruṣeyatva* of Veda the discussion turned towards the body of the Veda. The Veda is of five types. It means to say that the sentences of Veda are of five kinds which are as follows:- 1. *Vidhi*, 2. *Mantra*, 3. *Nāmadheya*, 4. *Niṣedha* and 5. *Arthavāda*. Now the focus is to be centred on *vidhi*. The definitions of *vidhi* differ according to the scholars of different schools. Only a few are illustrated here

The grammarians who follow the *sūtra* of Pāṇini: *"Vidhi-nimaṅtraṇa-āmantraṇa-adhīṣta-sampraśna-prārthaneṣu liṅ lot ca"*; according to which these six meanings are denoted or implied. They take the meaning of *vidhi* as *iṣtasādhanatva*. Persons do proceed to take up the assignment which gives favourable remarks to them.

Tārkikas say that *Balavadaniṣṭānubandhitvam, iṣtasādha-natvaṁ 'kṛtisādhyatvaṁ ca vidhyārtham.* All these views are very extensively discussed in *Vidhiviveka* of Maṇḍana Miśra and *Prakaraṇa-Pañcika* of Salikanātha and other works on Mīmāṁsā.

Now let us see the scope of *vidhivākya*s in the light of *Arthasaṁgraha* which is a precise and systematic work explaining the *artha*s (topics) treated in the *sūtra*s of Jaimini. *Vidhi,* the injunction is that which conveys a matter not known by any other means.

The statement *"Agnihotram juhuyāt svargakāmāḥ"* is an injunction which enjoins a sacrifice with heaven as a goal to a person.

The sense to be understood here is that heaven should be realised by means of the *agnihotra* sacrifice. When the action is established by a separate authority (sentence only), then only the subservient is established. For example one should sacrifice with curds (*Dadhnā juhuyāt*). At times the sacrifice and its subservient are established together in a possessive suffix *matup* such as *'Somena Yajeta.'* Hence the sacrifice is qualified by *soma* as its material. Here there is no *vākyabheda* (diversity) of two sentences because both are not individually enjoined, but one only as qualified by the other.

This *vidhi* is fourfold; of these four the *viniyogavidhi* and *prayogavidhi* are nothing but organising an activity in a systematic manner. The *viniyogavidhi* is also known as *guṇavidhi* because it deals with the *aṅgas* that are associated with the performance.

How to understand and apply the *vidhivākyas*? The Mīmāṁsaka explains in the following way. Take the sentence *"Agnihotraṁ juhoti."* This is a *vidhivākya*. Though there is no *liṅ* it is to be understood in the sense of potential only. Otherwise no person would take initiative to perform certain activity. Medhātithi commenting on *'Pitā rakṣati kaumāre'*. . . etc. says that the suffix *ti* is to be taken as potential suffix. Hence, the meaning of *"rakṣatī"* is 'should protect' not 'protects'. Similarly, in the above sentence *'Agnihotram juhoti'* the meaning is *'Agnihotrahomena iṣṭam bhavayet,'* one should realise the desired object by offering the *agnihotra* sacrifice. There are arguments throghout, which are well answered by the Mīmāṁsakas. All the arguments are not going to be presented here because the intention here is only to present the interpretations of Mīmāṁsakas on Vedic *vākyas* which elevate the person to a higher level in understanding the sentences which are burdened with complexity.

The *viniyogavidhi* deals with the explanation of the relation between *aṅga* (subservient) and *pradhāna* (the principal). This plays an important role in human life. All undertakings have their subservients. One who enters into an activity or takes up an assignment, should have the perfect knowledge about the subservients of that particular work. This is what is explained in *bhāvanā;* whether it is *śābdī* or *ārthī*, it has three *ākāṅkṣā*s or expectancies to plan for the work. This is nothing but perfect planning of a work. The three *ākāṅkṣā*s are — 1. *sādhyākāṅkṣā* — what is to be done? 2. *sādhanākāṅkṣā* — with which it is to be done? 3. *itikartavyatākāṅkṣā* — how it should be done?

For example — 'A tree should be cut' is *sādhyākāṅkṣā;* with which it should be cut, with an axe, and how it should be cut, by raising and lovering the axe. Similarly *'Iṣṭam bhāvayet'* — a sacrifice should be perfomed. But with what? *'Dadhnā juhoti'* is an answer. The curd is an *aṅga* of a particular sacrifice. This *viniyogavidhi* focuses on all the things required for a particular sacrifice. These subservients vary in accordance with the sacrifices. Hence, the knowledge of *pradhāna* and *aṅga* is a must for the performer. For example, in *laukika vyavahāra*, Vināyaka is offered *modaka*s (*laḍḍu*s). The same is not offered to all the deities. What more to say, there is a beautiful *śloka* in this regard.

'Alaṁkārapriyo Viṣṇuḥ Jaladhārāpriyassivaḥ'. . . The devotees offer ornaments to Lord Viṣṇu, i.e. to please Tirupati Veṅkaṭeśvara and water to Lord Śiva whether it is Śrī Śaila or Kālahasti elsewhere. Thus *viniyogavidhi* talks about subservient when *prayogavidhi* lays a procedure for action. To cite an example *Vedaṁ kritvā vedīṁ karoti* — "one should prepare the sacrificial altar after preparing the Veda." Here Veda is *Darbhamuṣṭitviśeṣa,* i.e. tufts of *darbha*s used for sweeping the altar etc. *Vedi* is a pit, four inches in depth where the oblations are placed. The *prayogavidhi* has another special feature of explaining procedures. The Veda *vākya*s should be understood

as per the context. There are six *pramāṇas* to know the procedure. They are 1. *Śruti* — statement, 2. *Artha* — purpose, 3. *Pāṭha* — text, 4. *Sthāna* — Juxtaposition, 5. *Mukhya* — The principals, 6. *Pravṛtti* — continual performance.

In fact *prayogavidhi* is a teacher of the order to be maintained in doing or arranging the subsidiaries of the above said six *pramāṇas*; the *śruti* directly instructs the duty of a person. It does not depend on or expect any other *pramāṇa*. The second one *arthakrama* is so important in daily life that the order is to be decided according to purpose. The example given in the *Arthasaṁgraha* is 'one should offer Agnihotra and one should cook the barley gruel.' Here, the barley gruel is intended for the sacrifice and as such, the purpose of it is to serve. Hence, it should be prepared before the sacrifice is performed. One may question how this *arthakrama* is relevant today. It is very interesting to know the idea behind these *vidhivākyas*. In modern times a devotee offers *pūjā* but if the food for *nivedana* is not ready, the modern priest or the devotees themselves utter a *mantra* of their own '*Sadyāskāla śarkarānaivedyam samarpayāmi*.' God may keep quiet. But if a guest is invited for lunch and the food is yet to come from caterers, the householder offers the guest a bread toast or a cup of tea, will it be alright? Hence, any performance should have a proper planning without which the purpose cannot be served.

Another instance of *prayogavidhi* which falls under the category of *pāṭhakrama* is also well explained where the *mantra pāṭha*, and *Brāhmaṇa pāṭha* come into conflict; *mantra pāṭha* is given importance here. An important injunction is *sthānakrama*. Probably this is the need of the hour which may be incorporated in administrative procedures.

Present day system, i.e., *vartamāna* is becoming sandwitched between the past and future. Take for instance the competitive examination system. The students who had already appeared before but could not secure a seat are *bhūtakālikas*. The students eligible at present are *vartamānas*, those who do not fulfil the conditions and still appear for the examination are — *bhaviṣyat*. Thus all the categories are brought on to a common dais. On such occasion what is the way to deal with the things? Mīmāṁsakas show a way out.

There is a sacrifice *Jyotiṣṭoma* which is a *prakṛtiyāga*. *Sādyaska* is one day sacrifice which is a *vikṛtiyāga* of *Jyotiṣṭoma*. Here, the three animals which are to be immolated on three different days are to be immolated on the same day.

	Jyotiṣṭoma	
Aupavāsathya Day	*Sutya* day	*Avabhṛtha day*
Agnīṣomiya	*Savanīya*	*Anubandhya*
	Sadyaska	

The day chosen for their immolation is the *sutyaday* which originally belongs to *savanīyapaśu* in *prakṛtiyāga*. Hence, the reason for this choice is due to the connection of *savanīya* with *sutya*, because *soma* is pressed on that day. As *sādyaska* is a *somayāga*, it is but natural that the *sutya* day would be appropriate. Therefore, the *savaniya* is first, then followed by *Agnīṣomīya* and *Anubandhya*.

A	B		C
1	2		3
	B	A	C
	1	2	3

The order is not much violated. The delay is in the case of A, that too a little. B is on right time. C remains as it is. Like this all the Vedic injunctions have potency to decide the matters on the occasions.

20

वैदिक आख्यानों के व्यावहारिक सन्दर्भ

रूपकिशोर शास्त्री

वेदों की व्याख्या शैली में आख्यानों का अप्रतिम योगदान माना गया है, जिनका प्रचुर प्रयोग ऐतरेय, कौषीतकी, शतपथ, तैत्तिरीय, जैमिनीय, जैमिनीयोपनिषद्, जैमिनीयार्षेय, आर्षेय, वंश, संहितोपनिषद्, दैवताध्याय, ताण्ड्य, षड्विंश, सामविधान, छान्दोग्य एवं गोपथ इत्यादि ब्राह्मणों एवं पुराणों में पदे पदे दृष्टव्य है। इस परम्परा एवं आख्यानों के समुचित सन्दर्भ वैदिक साहित्य में यथावत् अथवा कहीं-कहीं किञ्चित् परिवर्तित स्वरूप में अवलोकित हैं। उक्त ग्रन्थों में जहाँ कहीं भी कतिपय प्रचलित ऐतिहासिक पदों का प्रयोग होता है, उनके उल्लेख में प्रत्यक्षतः सम्बन्ध नाराशंस्य से जोड़ दिया जाता है, इन्हें ही आख्यान संज्ञा से उपहित माना गया है, यथा च्यवन-सुकन्या आख्यान, बलि-वामनावतार आख्यान, इन्द्र-दधीचि आख्यान, पुरुरवा-उर्वशी आख्यान, सरमा-पणि आख्यान, अगस्त्य-लोपामुद्रा आख्यान, यम-यमी आख्यान, इन्द्र-अहल्या आख्यान, मनु-मत्स्य आख्यान, सूर्य-चन्द्र और राहु-केतु आदि आख्यान। इन सभी आख्यानों एवं पदों का उल्लेख यथाप्रसङ्ग समान रूप से प्राप्त होता है। इन आख्यानों का मानव जीवन के विभिन्न पहलुओं में व्यवहार्य एवं औचित्य निहित है, यद्यपि आख्यानों का मनभावन व ऐतिहासिक स्वरूप अवश्य प्रतीत होता है, परन्तु उनमें आध्यात्मिक तथा दार्शनिक रहस्यों की गुत्थियाँ ग्रथित रहती हैं। उनके प्रतीकों की व्याख्याएं जब वैदिक और व्याकरणगत यौगिक पद्धति की निकष पर कसी जाती हैं तो उन रहस्यों की निगूढ गुत्थियाँ उद्घाटित होकर मानव कल्याणकर बन जाती हैं।

यहाँ एक बात अवश्य ही स्पष्ट करने योग्य है कि इतिहास नित्यानित्य दो रूपों में विभक्त हुआ करता है। अनित्य इतिहास निश्चित कालखण्ड के ऐतिह्य पक्ष को प्रस्तुत करता है, वहीं नित्य इतिहास सार्वकालिक है, अजर है। संहिताओं एवं ब्राह्मणग्रन्थों में ऐसे स्थल पर्याप्त हैं, जहाँ वचनों व संवादों के कारण मानवीय इतिवृत्त

का भ्रम होने लगता है और उस स्वतः प्रमाणस्वरूप वेद में धातुजार्थ-अज्ञानता के फलस्वरूप अनर्थ हो जाते हैं। लोकप्रसिद्ध एवं बहुश्रुत नामों के कारण वैदिक साहित्य में अनित्येतिहास आरोपित हो गया है, जबकि ये रूपक तथा आलङ्कारिक वर्णन हैं। आख्यान, उपाख्यानों में निहित सन्दर्भित प्रतीक वेदविहित ज्ञान-विज्ञान के रहस्यों, पारमार्थिक व व्यावहारिक पहलुओं को उद्घाटित करने की गहन सामर्थ्य रखते हैं। वैदिक ग्रन्थों में जिन आख्यानों के आधार पर ऐतिह्य की कल्पना कर ली गई है, वस्तुतः वे ऐतिहासिक व्यक्तित्व अथवा उनकी गाथाएं नहीं हैं। वेद संहिताओं, ब्राह्मणग्रन्थों, पुराणों में अनेक आख्यानों का वर्णन पर्याप्त कालखण्ड व्यतीत हो जाने पर भी अनवरत चर्चित हैं। ये नितान्ततः गहन शोध की अपेक्षा रखते हैं। यह बिन्दु ध्यातव्य है कि आख्यान सम्बन्धी जितने नामपद मिलते हैं, वे वेदों से गृहीत हैं, यहीं से उनका नामकरण हुआ है जो उपाधि भेद से सम्यक् ज्ञेय हैं। महर्षि मनु ने स्पष्ट सङ्केत दिया है कि इस अखिल ब्रह्माण्ड के पदार्थों के नाम, पृथक्-पृथक् कर्म और पृथक्-पृथक् संस्थाएं वेदों के पदों से ही निर्मित एवं नामाभिहित हैं[1]। इसी तथ्य को पुष्ट करते हुए महाभारतकार ने संसार की समस्त प्रवृत्तियों, क्रिया-कलापों का आदि ज्ञानस्रोत वेदों को ही माना है।[2]

विष्णु-वामनावतार आख्यान के प्रसङ्ग में विष्णु के वामनावतार की कल्पना की गई है और वामनावतार की घटना को असुरमात्र से पृथक् कर केवल राजा बलि से सन्नद्ध कर दिया गया है। सिद्धाश्रम में विष्णु तपस्यारत थे तो विरोचनकुमार राजा बलि ने इन्द्र और मरुद्गणों सहित समस्त देवताओं को पराजित करके उनका राज्य अपने अधिकार में कर लिया। त्रिलोकराज्येच्छु बलि ने एक यज्ञ का आयोजन किया। अग्नि आदि देवता विष्णु के पास जाकर बोले कि यज्ञ में याचकों को अभीष्ट वस्तुओं का दान करेंगे। अतः आप योगमाया का आश्रय ले, वामनरूप धारण कर उस यज्ञ में जाइये और देवताओं का हित किजिए। इसी बीच कश्यप ने वहाँ आकर विष्णु से अपने पुत्र के रूप में उत्पन्न होने की प्रार्थना की। फलतः विष्णु ने अदिति के उदर से जन्म लिया और राजा बलि के यज्ञ में पहुँचे। उन्होंने तीन पग भूमि माँगी और उन तीन पगों में तीन लोकों को नाप डाला। त्रिलोकी का राज्य प्राप्त कर उसे पुनः इन्द्र को सौंप दिया।

---

1. सर्वेषां तु स नामानि कर्माणि च पृथक्-पृथक्।
   वेदशब्देभ्य एवादौ पृथक् संस्थाश्च निर्ममे।। — *मनुस्मृति* 1/21
2. अनादिनिधना नित्या वागुत्सृष्टा स्वयम्भुवा।
   आदौ वेदमयी दिव्या यतः सर्वाः प्रवृत्तयः।। — *महा॰ भा॰* शा॰ पर्व॰ 232/24

वेदभाष्यों से लेकर रामायण-महाभारत परम्परा और आधुनिक साहित्यपर्यन्त अतिप्रसिद्ध एवं अतिप्रचलित बलि-वामनावतार आख्यान का वर्णन वेदों में कहीं नहीं है। यहाँ तक कि विष्णु के लिए '**वामन**' संज्ञा या विशेषण का प्रयोग भी वेदों में नहीं हुआ है, इसके उपरान्त भी कुछ भाष्यकार और विचारक इस आख्यान की सङ्गति विष्णु देवता के मन्त्रों से लगाते हैं और उन मन्त्रों को आख्यान का स्रोत मानते हैं। इसका कारण है—वेदों में विष्णु द्वारा और परवर्ती साहित्य में वामन द्वारा देवों या पीड़ितों के कल्याण के लिए तीन पगों में तीन लोक का अतिक्रमण करना। इस बिन्दु को इस आख्यान का मुख्यांश माना जाता है। यहाँ यह तथ्य विशेषतः उल्लेखनीय है कि अवान्तर साहित्य में विष्णु के लिए सर्वत्र व्यवहृत "**वामन**" विशेषण और संज्ञा के सर्वथा विपरीत ऋग्वेद में उसे "**बृहत्शरीरी और युवाकुमार कहा गया है।**"[3]

ऋग्वेद में विष्णु एक गौण देवता है। वहाँ इसके केवल 5 सूक्त और कतिपय सूक्तांश ही इसको सम्बोधित हैं, और कुल मिलाकर 100 बार इसका नाम तथा 12 बार '**उरुगाय**' व '**उरुक्रम**' विशेषण आये हैं। इन विशेषणों का सङ्केत भी इनके तीन पदों की ओर है। यहाँ विष्णु सम्बन्धी उन मुख्य मन्त्रों को उद्धृत किया जा रहा है जो परवर्ती वामनावतार के प्रेरक माने जाते हैं—

१. अतो देवा अवन्तु नो यतो विष्णुर्विचक्रमे। पृथिव्या सप्तधामभिः॥

२. इदं विष्णुर्विचक्रमे त्रेधा निदधे पदम्। समूळ्हमस्य पांसुरे॥

३. त्रीणि पदा विचक्रमे विष्णुर्गोपा अदाभ्यः। अतो धर्माणि धारयन्॥

४. तद्विष्णोः परमं पदं सदा पश्यन्ति सूरयः। दिवीव चक्षुराततम्॥

***ऋग्*॰ 1/22/16-20**

आचार्य सायण, वेङ्कटमाधव, उद्गीथादि ने इस स्थल पर विष्णु के वामन-अवतार का आख्यान दिया है और वे तीन पदों का विक्रमण बलिबन्धन के अवसर पर वामनावतार के समय मानते हैं। यजुर्वेद भाष्यकार उव्वट और महीधर ने यजुर्वेद 5/15 में वामनावतार का आख्यान माना है। ऋग्वेद भाष्यकार स्कन्दस्वामी ने मुख्यतः इतिहासपरक और गौणतः सूर्यपरक अर्थ किया है। इनके अनुसार अध्यात्म अर्थ में विष्णु का परम पद यज्ञ है, सप्तछन्द सातधाम हैं, मनुष्यों के कर्मों को बाँधना कर्म है। सूर्यपरक अर्थ में विष्णु, इन्द्र का नियोज्य सखा है और आकाश में फैला तेज '**परमपद**' है।[4] वेङ्कटमाधव ने इन मन्त्रों का अध्यात्म और सूर्यपरक अर्थ किया है और मुद्गल

---

3. बृहच्छरीरो विभिमान ऋक्वभिर्युवाकुमारः प्रत्येत्याहवम्। — *ऋग्*॰ 1/155/6

4. *ऋग्भाष्य* स्कन्दस्वामी — 1/22/17–21

ने अध्यात्मपरक अर्थ करते हुए ईश्वर को जगत् का पालक, रक्षक कहा है। त्रेधा से उनका अभिप्राय ईश्वर के कर्त्ता, धर्त्ता और संहर्त्ता रूप से है। गायत्र्यादि सात छन्द '**सप्तधाम**' हैं।[5] महर्षि दयानन्द ने उक्त समस्त मन्त्रों का आध्यात्मिक अर्थ किया है और विष्णु को संसार में व्याप्त होने से निराकार परमेश्वर का पर्यायवाची माना है। विष्णु पद पर महर्षि दयानन्द ने अपने वेदभाष्यों में दशाधिक निरुक्तियाँ दी हैं। √विष्लृ-व्याप्तौ धातु में "**विषेः किच्च**" – (*उणादि कोष* 3/39) सूत्र से 'णुः' प्रत्यय करके सम्पन्न विष्णु पद की निरुक्तियों में "**वेवेष्टि व्याप्नोति चराचरं जगत् स परमात्मा**" (*ऋग्॰ भा॰* 3.55.10, 1.154.1, 6.49.13) इत्यादि स्थलों पर जो चराचर जगत् को अपनी शक्ति से व्याप्त करके विराजमान रहता है वही विष्णु है। ऐसी ही निरुक्तियाँ यजुर्वेद, उणादिकोषवृत्ति तथा सत्यार्थप्रकाश में भी की हैं।[6]

शतपथ ब्राह्मण में सर्वप्रथम उक्त आख्यान विस्तार से दिया गया है, जहाँ विष्णु को 'वामन' विशेषण से रेखाङ्कित किया है।[7] ब्राह्मण ग्रन्थों में विष्णु यज्ञ का अर्थद्योतक है तथा यज्ञीय देवता है।[8] *बृहद्देवता* नामक ग्रन्थ में विष्णु के विभिन्न पक्षों पर विचार हुआ है। उसके अनुसार विष्णु एक देव हैं।[9] यह अग्नि एवं ऊर्जा के साथ सम्बद्ध है और इन्द्र इसके साथ स्तुति ग्रहण करता है।[10] यह सूर्यास्त के समय (वृषाकपायी) आश्रम में स्थित है।[11] यह प्रजापति के वंश में कश्यप-अदिति युगल में उत्पन्न बारह पुत्रों में से अन्तिम पुत्र है।[12] इसी कारण इसे आदित्य कहा जाता है। बृहद्देवताकार ने सूर्य के नामों के अन्तर्गत विष्णु की निरुक्ति इस प्रकार मानी है –

---

5. वही, मुद्गल भाष्य
6. (i) यो वेवेष्टि व्याप्नोत्यन्तरिक्षस्थलवाय्वादिपदार्थान् स यज्ञः।
   — *यजु॰* 1/4, 2/25, 5/15, 19/59, 34/43
   (ii) वेवेष्टि व्याप्नोति चराचरं जगदिति विष्णुः जगदीश्वरः।
   — *उणा॰ को॰ वृ॰* 3/39, (3)
   (iii) *सत्यार्थ प्रकाश* प्रथम समुल्लास
7. वामनो ह विष्णुरास। — *शत॰ ब्रा॰* 1/1/5/5
8. (i) यज्ञो वै विष्णुः स यज्ञः। — *शत॰ ब्रा॰* 5/2/3/6,
   (ii) विष्णुर्वै यज्ञः– *ऐत॰ ब्रा॰* 1/15, *तां॰ ब्रा॰* 9/7/10, *कौ॰ ब्रा॰* 4/3, *तैत्ति॰ ब्रा॰* 1/6/1/5
9. बृहद्देवता, 1/82
10. वही, 1/117, 2/2
11. वही, 2/10–12
12. वही, 5/143–48

विष्णातेर्विशतेर्वा स्याद् वेवेष्टेर्व्याप्तिकर्मणः।
विष्णुर्निरुच्यते सूर्यः सर्वं सर्वान्तरश्च यः॥ (*बृह. दे.* 2.69)

अर्थात् व्याप्ति को व्यक्त करते हुए विष्णु नाम √विष्लृ व्याप्तौ (विष्णाति) अथवा √विश्-प्रवेशने (विशति) अथवा √वेविष् (वेवेष्टि) धातु से व्युत्पन्न है, अतः विष्णु की उस सूर्य के रूप में व्याख्या की गई है, जो सब कुछ है और सब में व्याप्त है। विष्णु को तीन पाद प्रक्षेप करने वाला कहते हैं, क्योंकि तीनों क्षेत्र उन्हीं के पादों के रूप में प्रकाशमान होते हैं अर्थात् तीनों लोकों में पादप्रक्षेप करने वाला विष्णु वस्तुतः सूर्य ही है।[13]

इन्द्र-अहल्या आख्यान भी अत्यन्त प्रसिद्ध आख्यान रहा है। आख्यान का कथानक बहुचर्चित व प्रसिद्ध है, जिसमें इन्द्र और अहल्या को गौतम ऋषि का शाप मिला। पत्नी अहल्या के स्पष्टीकरण एवं अनुनय-विनय करने पर ऋषि गौतम पुरुषोत्तम राम के आतिथ्य करने व उनके आशीर्वाद से कृतार्थ होने सम्बन्धी सन्देश देकर उस आश्रम को छोड़कर तपस्या करने चले गये।

वैदिक साहित्य के अन्तर्गत यजुर्वेदीय ब्राह्मणग्रन्थ शतपथ में सोमयागनिरूपण प्रसङ्ग में इन्द्र सम्बन्धी एक सम्बोधनात्मक संक्षिप्त उल्लेख है,[14] जिसमें उक्त आख्यान के स्रोत मिलते हैं। षड्विंश ब्राह्मण में उक्त शतपथीय व्याख्या ने एक लघुकरण का रूप ग्रहण कर लिया[15]। जैमिनीय ब्राह्मण में भी इस आख्यान का सङ्केत प्राप्त है।[16] यद्यपि वेदों में उक्त आख्यान का स्पष्ट उल्लेख कहीं नहीं है, जबकि इन्द्र सम्बन्धी सूक्त एवं मन्त्र सर्वाधिक हैं। फिर भी वैदिक साहित्य से लेकर आधुनिक साहित्य तक इन्द्र-अहल्या आख्यान का अस्तित्व न्यूनाधिक्य उपलब्ध होता है। वस्तुतः इस आख्यान का स्वरुप रामायण में भी विकसित रूप ले चुका था, उसी का प्रभाव परवर्ती साहित्य पर प्रचुर रूप से दिखाई देता है।

---

13. वही, 2/64
14. इन्द्रो वै यज्ञस्य देवता, तस्मादाह इन्द्रागच्छेति। हरिव आगच्छ मेधातिथेर्मेषवृषणश्वस्यमेने, गौरावस्कन्दिन्, अहल्यायै जारेति। तद् यान्येवास्य चरणानि, तैरेवैनमेतत् प्रमुमोदयिष्यति। — *शत. ब्रा.* 3/3/4/18
15. अहल्यायै जारेति, अहल्याया ह मैत्रेय्या जार आस। कौशिक ब्राह्मणेति कौशिको ह स्मैनां ब्राह्मण उपन्येति, गोतमब्रुबाणेति, देवासुरा ह संयुत्ता आसंस्तानन्तरेण गोतमः शश्राम, इन्द्र उवाच अहं भवतः रूपेण चराणीति यथा मन्यस इति स यत्तद्गोतमो वा ब्रुवाणश्चचार, गोतमरूपेण वा तदेतदाह।। — *षड्विंश ब्रा.* 1/1
16. *जै. ब्रा.* 2/79

अतः उक्त आख्यान परम्परा द्वारा समस्त शास्त्रों में वैदिक एवं व्यावहारिक पहलुओं तथा प्रतीकों का चिन्तन अवश्य ही विवेचनीय है जो वस्तुनिष्ठ तत्वों की ओर सङ्केत करते हैं। वाल्मीकि रामायण, पुराणों तथा परवर्ती संस्कृत साहित्य में इन्द्र-अहल्या का वर्णन ऐतिहासिक घटना सदृश मिलता है, परन्तु वैदिक साहित्य में इसका प्राकृतिक स्वरूप भी व्यक्त किया गया है। वस्तुतः प्राकृतिक पदार्थों और दृश्यों को आधार बनाकर इस आख्यान को कल्पित किया गया है, इसके समस्त पात्र प्रतीकात्मक हैं। इन्द्र कोई व्यक्ति न होकर यज्ञ का देवता है।[17] सूर्य और विद्युत् ये दो इन्द्र के सुप्रसिद्ध अर्थ हैं। निरुक्तानुसार यह मध्यस्थानीय देवता है। *निरुक्ति* के अनुसार यह **"इरां ददाति"** – वर्षा द्वारा अन्न प्रदान करता है, **"इन्धे भूतानि"** – प्राणियों और भौतिक पदार्थों को जलाता है, **"इदं दर्शनाय"** – यह प्रत्येक वस्तु को देखने-दिखाने, ऐश्वर्यशाली मेघरूपी शत्रु को विदीर्ण करने वाला तथा याज्ञिकों का आदरयिता होने के कारण इन्द्र कहलाता है।[18] बृहद्देवताकार ने भी इसे मध्यस्थानीय देवता मानते हुए सूर्य घोषित किया है, जो अपनी रश्मियों से जलों को ग्रहण कर वायु के साथ इस लोक पर वर्षा करता है, अतः यही इन्द्र है।[19] आख्यान के अन्तःसाक्ष्यों में भी इसे सूर्य कहा गया है, दिन के पूर्वपक्ष और उत्तरपक्ष इसके अश्व हैं, इनके द्वारा ही सूर्य रसों का आहरण अथवा जारण करता है।[20] ब्राह्मण ग्रन्थों में प्रचुर मात्रा-संख्या में ऐसे प्रमाण मिलते हैं, जिनमें स्पष्ट शब्दों में सूर्य को इन्द्र कहा गया है, यथा– **"इन्द्र एतत् आचक्षते य एष सूर्य तपति"**[21], **"इन्द्रो असौ आदित्यः"**[22] इत्यादि। महर्षि दयानन्द भी इन्द्र को सूर्य का वाचक मानते हैं, ऐसा उन्होंने अपने ऋग्भाष्य में सङ्केतित किया है[23]। इन प्रमाणों से अनुमान लगाया जा सकता है कि यह आख्यान मानवीय घटना को अभिव्यक्त नहीं करता।

दूसरा पात्र अहल्या है। अहल्या के **'रात्रि'** और **'उषा'** दोनों ही अर्थ प्रचलित एवं व्याकरण सम्मत हैं। √अह्-व्याप्तौ धातु से औणादिक यक् प्रत्यय तथा अलुगागम होकर

17. इन्द्रो वै यज्ञस्य देवता। — *शत॰ ब्रा॰* 3/3/4/18
18 *निरुक्त* 10/8
19. रसान् रश्मिभिरादाय वायुनायं गतः सह।
 वर्षात्येष च यल्लोके तेनेन्द्र इति स स्मृतः।। — *बृहद्देवता* 1/68– 69
20. *शत॰ ब्रा॰* 3/3/4/18, *षड्॰ ब्रा॰* 1/1/1, *जै॰ ब्रा॰* 2/79
21. *शत॰ ब्रा॰* 4/5/5 - 7, 4/5 - 9/4, 4/6/7/11 तथा *जैमि॰ उ॰ ब्रा॰* 1/28/2
22. *शत॰ ब्रा॰* 8/5/3/2
23. दारयिता सूर्यः। — *ऋग्॰ भा॰* 2/12/1

निष्पत्ति होगी **"अहति व्याप्नोतीति अहल्या रात्रिः उषा वा"** अर्थात् जो व्याप्त करती वा होती है, फैलती है, उसका नाम अहल्या है। यह सङ्केत रात्रि और उषा दोनों के लिए है। अथवा **"अहः लीयते अस्यामहनि लीयमाना वा"** अर्थात् जिसमें दिन लीन होता है वह रात्रि अथवा वह जो दिन में लीन होती है, वह उषा है। महर्षि दयानन्द ने भी इसी प्रकार के अर्थ के पक्ष में उणादिकोष के भाष्य में निर्वचन करके पुष्टि प्रदान की है।[24] तैत्तिरीय ब्राह्मण ने रात्रि और उषा में विरोधात्मक अन्तर न मानकर कहीं-कहीं इनको सम्बद्ध रूप में निरूपित किया है।[25] इसी दृष्टिकोण से यास्क ने भी उषा को रात्रि का ही एक भाग मानकर उसे रात्रि का अपरकाल कहा है।[26] दोनों ही अवस्थायें सूर्य के द्वारा जीर्ण होती हैं, अतः सूर्य (इन्द्र) दोनों का समान रूप से **"जार"** है। इन वेदों में कुछ ऐसे प्रमाणस्वरूप मन्त्र हैं, जिनमें रात्रि और उषा के वर्णन के साथ सूर्य को जार रूप में वर्णित किया गया है।[27] निरुक्त 3/16 तथा 10/21 में सूर्य को रात्रि और नक्षत्रों का जार कहा गया है। इस प्रकार सूर्य के जारकर्म से सम्बद्ध रात्रि और उषा हैं, अतः प्रकृतिपक्ष में अहल्या का अर्थ रात्रि और उषा ही सङ्गत है, और व्यवहार पक्ष में इस प्रतीक से सुन्दर नारी की कल्पना की गई है।

कुछ चिन्तक अहल्या शब्द की निरुक्ति **"हल्यते कृष्यते इति हल्या, न हल्या अहल्या"** – करते हुए जोताई या कृषि योग्य भूमि को **'हल्या'** तथा जिस भूमि को पथरीली होने के कारण न हल चलाने योग्य माना उसे अहल्या कहा गया है। यही कारण है कि ऐसी भूमि को अहल्या-शिलामयी कहते हैं।

गोतम चन्द्रमा का प्रतीक माना गया है, आप्टे के अनुसार **"गोभिः ध्वस्तं तमो यस्य सः गोतमः"**[28] अर्थात् गो नाम सूर्य किरणों का है, ऐसा निघण्टुकार ने उल्लेख किया है, उनके द्वारा जिसका तमस् नष्ट हो जाता है, वही चन्द्रमा है। वस्तुतः आलङ्कारिक शैली में रात्रि या उषा रूपी अहल्या चन्द्रमा की आभावती पत्नी है। संस्कृत साहित्य में चन्द्र के साथ ही रात्रि का पति-पत्नी भाव कल्पित किया गया है, अतः प्रायः चन्द्रमा को निशापति, निशानाथ, निशाधीश, रजनीपति, क्षपाकर और उषाकर

---

24. अहति व्याप्नोतीति अहल्या रात्रिर्वा। अहर्लीयतेऽस्यामिति। — *उणा॰ को॰* 4/112
25. रात्रिर्वा उषाः — *तैत्ति॰ ब्रा॰* 3/8/16/4
26. रात्रेपरः कालः — *निरु॰* 2/18
27. (i) उषो न जारः — *ऋग्* 1/69/1, (ii) उषो न जारो विभावः — *ऋग्॰* 1/69/5, (iii) जार उषसां — पावकः – *ऋग्॰* 7/9/1, (iv) उषो न जारः पृथुपाजः — *ऋग्॰ 7/10/1*
28. *संस्कृत हिन्दीकोश*, वामन शिवराम आप्टे, गोतम शब्द

आदि नामों से व्यवहृत किया गया है। प्रकृतिगत अवधारणा में रात्रि या उषा चूँकि चन्द्रमा की पत्नी है। प्रातः काल के समय चन्द्रमा जब अस्त होने के कारण मानो दिनचर्या के लिए अथवा प्रातःकालीन तपस्या में लीन होने के लिए दूर निकल जाता है तो उसके पीछे सूर्य उदित होकर उसको जीर्ण कर देता है, उसकी अवस्था को परिवर्तित कर देता है। चन्द्रमा रूपी गौतम जब सायंकाल लौटता है, तब उसे उस घटना का ज्ञान होता है, तथा सन्ध्याकाल में दोनों का सामना होता है। वह सूर्य रूपी इन्द्र को वृषणरहित अर्थात् प्रजननसामर्थ्य रहित होने का शाप देता है। सूर्य का रात्रि में आभाहीन और प्रकाशोत्पादनविहीन हो जाना ही मानो शाप स्वरूप है। महर्षि दयानन्द ने अपने ऋग्भाष्य में निरन्तर क्रियाशील, गतिशील रहने वाले स्तोता या तपस्वी को गोतम कहा है।[29]

अब रही अन्तिम स्थिति जारकर्म की। इस सम्बन्ध में लोगों की विकट भ्रान्तियाँ है। यह भ्रम लौकिक संस्कृत साहित्य में जार पद का अर्थापकर्ष होकर मात्र 'व्यभिचार' में रूढ़ हो जाने के कारण है। वहाँ धातुजार्थ अथवा यौगिक प्रक्रियानुसार अर्थ न लेना ही मूल में रहा है। व्याकरणानुसार जार पद दो धातुओं से सिद्ध होता है (1) √जॄ-वयोहानौ अर्थात् – आयु या अवस्था का विनाश (2) √जॄ-स्तुतौ (स्तुति करना)। प्रथम धातु के अर्थ में किसी भी प्राणी या पदार्थ की आयु की अवस्था को जीर्ण करना है वहाँ भी व्यभिचार अर्थ प्रत्यक्षतः ग्राह्य नहीं है। ऋग्वेद (1/46/4) में जलों को जीर्ण करने वाला,[30] **"पूर्भित् जारः"**[31] – शत्रुदुर्गों को ध्वस्त करने वाला, उषाओं को जीर्ण या विकृतदशा करने वाला[32] आदि ऐसे प्रयोग हैं, जिनमें जार पद का अर्थ सूर्य है क्योंकि वह अपनी ज्योति या रश्मियों से जलों को सुखा देता है या उषा का स्वरूप ही विदीर्ण कर देता है। यही मौलिक अर्थ महर्षि यास्क ने निरुक्त में किया है जिसमें उन्होंने आदित्य को जार संज्ञा से उपहित किया तथा वह रात्रि को जीर्ण करने वाला है।[33] स्तुत्यर्थक √जॄ–धातु का स्पष्ट उल्लेख स्वयं ऋग्वेद एवं अथर्ववेद में विद्यमान हैं जहाँ स्तुतियोग्य इन्द्र को प्रबोधित करना बताया है।[34] ब्राह्मणग्रन्थों में यज्ञस्थल पर

---

29. गच्छतीति गोः स्तोता सोऽतिशयितः सः। — *ऋग्. भाष्य* 1/62/13/, 1/85/22
30. जारो अपाम् — *ऋग्.* 1/46/4
31. *ऋग्.* 10/111/10
32. उषसां जारः — *ऋग्.* 1/69/1/, 1/69/5, 7/9/1, 7/10/1
33. आदित्योऽत्र जार उच्यते। रात्रेर्जरयिता। — *निरु.* 3/16
34. सखायं प्रबोधय जरितं जारमिन्द्रम्। — *ऋग्.* 10/42/2, *अथर्व.* 20/89/2

सामूहिक रूप में इन्द्र को **"अहिल्यायै जार"**[35] कहा गया है यह इन्द्र-सूर्य का विशेष चरित्र है। इस प्रशंसात्मक सम्बोधन के कारण इन्द्र प्रसन्न होता है। इन्द्र अर्थात् सूर्य रात्रि और उषा के लिए स्तुत्य है। वैदिक साहित्य में भूयांस रूप में रात्रि और उषा का सूर्य के साथ पति-पत्नी भाव ही वर्णित किया गया है।[36]

कुमारिल भट्ट ने इस आख्यान के निहितार्थ को स्पष्ट करते हुए *तन्त्रवार्तिक* (1/3/7) में कहा है कि "सम्पूर्ण तेजस्वी पदार्थों में ऐश्वर्य है, इस कारण तेजपुञ्ज को इन्द्र कहा गया है। दिन में लीन होने के कारण 'अहल्या' का शाब्दिक अर्थ रात्रि है। सूर्य ही रात्रि के क्षयस्वरूप जरण का कारण है। अहल्या (रात्रि) जिसमें जीर्ण हुई अथवा जिसके उदय होने से अहल्या जीर्ण है उसी को अहल्या-जार कहते हैं '**अहल्या-जार**' शब्द का अर्थ सूर्य है। अहल्या रात्रि है और इन्द्र सूर्य। रात्रि के पीछे सूर्य का दौड़ना तो एक प्राकृतिक सत्य है।

निष्कर्षतः यहाँ रात्रि, सूर्य और चन्द्रमा का अलङ्कारिक वर्णन है। रात्रि का जार आदित्य है, जिसके उदय होने से रात्रि का वर्तमान रूप-श्रृंगार बिगड़ जाता है। स्त्री-पुरुष की तरह रात्रि और चन्द्रमा साथ-साथ रहते हैं। चन्द्रमा का नाम गोतम है।

इस प्रकार विस्तार भय से कुछ आख्यानों पर ही विचार हुआ है। वैदिक साहित्य में ऐसे अनेक आख्यान है, जो रहस्यों एवं गुत्थियों का आलङ्कारिक वर्णन करते हैं, जिन पर उसी दृष्टि से शोध अपेक्षित है।

---

35. *शत॰ ब्रा॰* 3/3/4/18
36. सूर्य-उषा सूक्त *ऋ॰* 1/115, 7/76/3; *ऋ॰* 6/55/5 *निरुक्त* 3/16

21

Śaṅkara on Śruti as Verbal Testimony

Ram Nath Jha

Definition of Vāk and Verbal Testimony

Vāk is the organ which, clinging to the eight localities, viz. chest, throat, head, root of tongue, teeth, nose, lips and palate, and being presided over by the fire, expresses the letters.[1] The letters too as limited in their number and as subject to a certain sequence, in conformity with the meaning intended to be conveyed, are also called *vāk*.[2] Also *śabda* or *pada* expressible through letters is called *vāk*.[3] *Akāro vai sarvā vāk saiṣā sparśāntasthoṣmabhirvyajamānā bahvī nānārūpā bhavati* (*Ai.Ā.* II.III. VII.13) *iti śruteḥ*.[4] The *akāra* is all speech being manifested as *sparśa*, *antaḥstha*, *uṣman* etc. and becomes many and multifarious. The *Ṛk* (*mita*), the *Yajus* (*amita*) and the *Sāman* (*svara*) are the manifestations of the same *vāk* (*Ken.U.* I.4). In

1. *Vāgiti jihvāmūlādiṣvaṣṭasu sthāneṣu viṣaktam-āgneyaṁ varṇānām abhivyñjakaṁ karaṇam.* — KenUSB, I.4
2. *Varṇāścārtha-saṅketa-paricchinnā etāvanta evaṁ karma-prayuktā iti.* — Ibid.
3. *Evaṁ tadabhivyaṅgyaḥ śabdaḥ padaṁ vāgiti ucyate, akāro vai sarvā vāk saiṣā.* — Ibid.
4. Ibid.

the *Sambandhabhāṣya* of *Kaṭhopaniṣad*, Śaṅkara says that the word *Upaniṣad* is used in its primary sense as *vidyā* and in secondary sense as verbal testimony.[5]

Verbal Testimony is accepted as a distinct and independent source of knowledge in non-dualistic thought of Indian philosophical traditions. Verbal testimony is that which causes knowledge through words (*vāk*).[6] When the purport (*tātparya*) of a sentence is not contradicted by other means of knowledge as well as unknown through other means of knowledge such as perception, inference etc. then that sentence is known as verbal testimony or *śabda pramāṇa*.[7]

Nature of Word

According to Śaṅkara, the letters which are eternal,[8] are the word.[9] Letters are eternal, because they are recognized as the same whenever pronounced.[10] If each time a man utters a new letter, nobody would be able to recognize it. When a man says "go" and "go"; we do not say that he has uttered two "go"s; but pronounced "go" twice,[11] since we have such a cognition. Differences in pronunciation and tone cannot prove that letters are different, for recognition of letters as the same

---

5. *Tasmād-avidyāyāṁ mukhyatayā vṛttyopaniṣac-chabdo vartate granthe tu bhaktyeti. Sambandhabhāṣya.* — *KUSB*
6. *Śrauta-śabda-janitārtha-pratipattau śreyaḥ.* — *BṛUSB,* I.III.20.
7. *Na ca pramāṇaṁ pramāṇāntareṇa virudhyate, pramāṇāntarāviṣayam-eva hi pramāṇāntaraṁ jñāpayati.* — *BṛUSB,* II.I.20
8. *Tasya ca pratyuccāraṇaṁ pratyabhijñāya-mānatvān-nitytvam.* — *BSSB,* I.III.28.
9. *Varṇā eva tu śabdaḥ iti Bhagavān-upavarṣaḥ.* — Ibid.
10. *Nata eveti-pratyabhijñānāt.* — Ibid.
11. *Dvir-gośabda uccārita iti hi pratipattirna tu dvau gośabdāviti.* — Ibid.

is a fact. The apparent difference is due to the difference in the communication medium.[12] When one utters a word, what happens is the manifestation of an already existing letter. Letters, though eternal, are heard different due to differences in the audible sounds (*dhvani*) made by men while pronouncing.[13] The "softness" or "loudness" is due to the voice or tone associated with them.[14] So, however, much the difference in voice or tone, it is the same letter which is uttered again and again.

These eternal letters in a word conjointly signify the referent. Each letter after being heard leaves a "residual impression" (*saṁskāra*) in the mind,[15] and after the last letter of a word is heard, this together with those impressions becomes a combined unit (*samudāya*) and this, which is called a "word," produces the idea of the referent.[16] By "residual impression" is meant modification (*bhāvanā*) capable of evoking memory. As soon as the preceding and succeeding letters, being recollected, stand unified as a word, because of its relation to the referent, the meaning becomes evident. Though made up of the same letters "*jā*" and "*rā*" or "*ka*" and "*pi*" there can be two words "*jārā*" and "*rājā*" or "*kapi*" and "*pika*" depending upon the order in which they are uttered, and since they will be recollected in the same order, there would be no confusion. Just as the ants entering into a hole as a line in a definite order, the letters enter into the notion of a word in

---

12. *Tāsu ca paropādhiko bheda-pratyaya ityabhyupa-gantavyam.* — Ibid.
13. *Dhvanikṛto 'yaṁ pratyayabhedo na varṇakṛta ityadoṣaḥ.* — Ibid.
14. *Pratyāsīdataśca paṭu-mṛdu-tvādi-bhedaṁ varṇeṣvāsañjayati.* — Ibid.
15. *Varṇānāṁ pratyuccāraṇaṁ pratyābhijñāyamānatvāt.* — Ibid.
16. *Pūrva-pūrva-varṇānubhava-janita-saṁskāra-sahito 'ntyo varṇo 'rthaṁ pratyāyayiṣyati.* — Ibid.

their definite sequence.[17] That being the case there is nothing illogical in understanding a particular word arising from a particular arrangement, even though the letter may be the same.[18] At the time of apprehending the meaning of words used by older people, these letters, as uttered in a certain sequence, were understood by a child to be related to certain meaning; so at the time of his own dealings with them by the child, the letters apprehended individually, appear in that very sequence in the intellect which groups them together, and in this way they invariably convey those particular senses.[19] So, Śaṅkara concludes that since letters are recognized as the same every time, they are heard, they are eternal, and as the letters are words, words are also eternal.[20]

Śaṅkara maintains that a word denotes a universal (*ākṛti*) and not individuals; for the individuals are infinite in number and it is impossible to comprehend the relation of a word with all of them.[21] Again, individuals may have an origin, but

---

17. *Yadi varṇā eva sāmastyenaika-buddhi-viṣayatām-āpadyamānāḥ padaṁ syustato jārā-rājā kapiḥ pika ityādiṣu pada-viśeṣa-pratipattirna syāt. Ta eva hi varṇā itaratra cetaratra ca pratyavabhāsanta iti. Atra vadāmaḥ satyapi samasta-varṇa-pratyavamarśe yathā kramārodhinya eva pipī likāḥ paṅkti-budddhim-ārohanti, evaṁ kramānurodhina eva varṇāḥ padabuddhim-ārokṣyanti.* — Ibid.

18. *Tatra varṇānām-aviśeṣe 'pi karma-viśeṣa-kṛtā pada-viśeṣa-patipatirna virudhyate.* — Ibid.

19. *Vṛddha-vyavahāre ceme varnāḥ kramādyanugṛhitārthāviśeṣa-sambandhāḥ santaḥ svavyavahāre 'pye-kaika-varṇa-grahaṇānantaraṁ samasta-pratyava-marśinyaṁ buddhau tadṛśā eva pratyavabhāsamānās-taṁ tam-artham-avyabhicāreṇa-pratyāyayiṣyanīti.* — Ibid.

20. *Tataśca nityebhyaḥ śabdebhyo devādi-vyktīnāṁ prabhava ityaviruddham.* — Ibid.

21. *Akṛtibhiśca śabdānāṁ sambandhe, na vyaktibhiḥ, vyaktīnām-ānantyāt-sambandha-grahaṇānupapatteḥ.* — Ibid.

their universals don't have origins[22] since they are eternal. So, word is also eternal. Thus, the eternal words are eternally related to their eternal meanings[23] and established as a means of valid knowledge.

These words used for expressing objects, when heard by listeners, make them understand their meanings through their association with universal, action, quality and their dependence on a comprehension of a certain mode of relation.[24] To illustrate this: a cow or a horse etc. is comprehended through universal: cooking or reading through action; white or black through quality; and a rich person or an owner of cows through relation.[25]

Types of Verbal Testimony

There are two types of verbal testimony (1) *śruti* and (2) *smṛti.*

DEFINITION OF ŚRUTI

The *mantras* and *Brāhmaṇas* are the *śruti*[26]

(a) The *Mantras*[27] :-

---

22. *Na hi gavādi-vyaktīnām-utpattimattve tadākṛtīnām-apyutpatti-mattvaṁ syāt.* — Ibid.

23. a. *Nityasya śabdasya nityenārthena nitye sambandhe pratīyamāne.* — Ibid.

 b. *Gavādi-śabdārtha-sambandha-nityatva-darśanāt.* — Ibid.

24. *Sarvo hi śabda artha-prakaśanāya prayuktaḥ śrūyamāṇaśca śrotṛbhiḥ jāti-kriyā-guṇa-sambandha-dvāreṇa-saṅketa-grahaṇa-savya-pekṣaḥ arthaṁ pratyāyayati.* — *GSB*, XIII.12.

25. *Tad yathā gauḥ aśvah iti vā jātitaḥ pacati paṭhati iti vā kriyātaḥ śuklaḥ kṛṣṇaḥ iti vā guṇataḥ dhanī gomān iti vā sambandhataḥ.* — Ibid.

26. *Evaṁ mantra-brāhmaṇayoreva grahaṇam.* — *BṛUSB*, II.IV.10.

27. *Yadṛgvedo yajurvedaḥ sāmavedo 'tharvāṅgirasaḥ caturvidhaṁ mantrajātam.* — Ibid.

There are four types of *mantras*:-

(i) The *ṛgveda*,

(ii) The *yajurveda*,

(iii) The *sāmaveda*, and

(iv) The *atharvāṅgirasa*.

(b) The *Brāhmaṇas*:-

There are eight types of *Brāhmaṇas*:-

(i) *Itihāsa* (History):- such as the dialogue between Urvaśī and Pururavas[28]— "The nymph Urvaśī and so on"[29] (*SB*, XI.IV.IV.1).

(ii) *Purāṇa* (Mythology):- such as "This universe was in the beginning unmanifested"[30] etc. (*TU*. II.VII.1).

(iii) *Vidyā* (Arts):- which treats of music, dancing etc. "This is also *Veda*"[31] etc. (*S*. XIII. IV. III. 10-14).

(iv) *Upaniṣads*:- such as "It should be meditated upon as dear,"[32] etc. (*Br.U*. IV.1-3).

(v) *Ślokas* (pithy verses):- The *mantras* occurring in the *Brāhmaṇas*, such as "Regarding this, are the following pithy verses,"[33] (*Bṛ.U*. IV.III.2,IV.IV.8).

---

28. *Evam-aṣṭa-vidhaṁ brāhmaṇam*. — Ibid.
29. *Itihāsa ityurvaśī-purūravasoḥ saṁvādādiḥ "urvaśī hāpsarāḥ" ityādi brāhmaṇam-eva*. — Ibid.
30. *Purāṇam "asad-vā idam-agra āsīt"* (*TU* II.VII.1) *ityādi*. — Ibid.
31. *Vidyā deva-janavidyā "vedaḥ so 'yamityādyā."* — Ibid.
32. *Upaniṣadaḥ "priyam-ityetad-upāsita" ityādyāḥ*. — Ibid.
33. *Ślokā brāhmaṇa-prabhavā mantrāḥ "tadeva ślokāḥ"* (*BṛU* I.IV.II) *ityādayaḥ*. — Ibid.

(vi) *Sūtras* (Aphorisms):- Those passages of the *Vedas* that present the truth in a nutshell, for example "The Self alone is to be meditated upon"[34] (*Bṛ.U.* I.IV.7).

(vii) *Anuvyākhyānas* (Elucidations):- Explanations of the *Mantras* or explanation of the "Aphorisms." As the passage, "The Self alone is to be meditated upon," or the passage; "He (who worships, another god) — "He is one, and I am another," does not know. He is like an animal" (*Bṛ.U.* I.IV.10), has this concluding portion of the present chapter as its elucidation.[35]

(viii) *Arthavādaḥ* (Eulogistic passages):- The laudatory explanation of the *Mantras*.[36]

ŚRUTI: THE MEANS OF SUPRA-SENSUOUS KNOWLEDGE

Śruti is the only source of knowledge of the truth regarding the supersensible.[37] Neither sense-perception, nor any of the other means of knowledge dependent on it, can impart knowledge of supersensible fact i.e. *Brahman*, *ātman*, their

---

34. *Sūtrāṇi vastu-saṅgraha-vākyāni vede yathā "ātmetyevopāsīt" ityadīni.* — Ibid.

35. *Anu-vyākhyānāni mantra-vivaraṇāni athavā vastu-saṅgraha-vākya vivaraṇānyanuvyākhyānāni yathā caturthādhyāye "ātmetyevopāsīta" ityasya, yathā vā "anyo" sāvanyo 'ham-asmīti na sa vede yathā paśu revam'* (*BṛU* I.IV.10) *ityasyāyam-evādhyāyaśeṣaḥ.* — Ibid.

36. *Vyākhyānānyartha-vādāḥ, mantra-vivaraṇāni vyākhyānāni.* — Ibid.

37. (a) *Etad-alaukikaṁ vastu pratyakṣādyaviṣayaṁ tathābhūtaṁ ca veda-vākyair-eva jñāpyate.* — *BṛUSB*, I.III.1.

(b) *Śrutiśca naḥ pramānam-atindriyārtha-vijñānotpatau.* — *BSSB*, II.III.1

(c) *Tasmāc-chabda-mūla evātindriyārtha-yāthātmyādhigamaḥ.* — *BSSB*, II.I.27.

relation, *ātman*'s journey after death, heaven, hell, the origin of the universe, merit and demerit accruing from righteous and unrighteous deeds, their fructification, man's highest destiny and its fulfilment.[38] It is so because it has no form and colour. So, it cannot be perceived by the senses.[39] For example we see the divergence of opinion among different schools. Were the existence of the *ātman* in a future body a matter of perception, the materialists and Buddhists would not stand opposed to the Advaita Vedānta, saying that there is no *ātman*, since nobody disputes regarding an object of perception such as a jar, saying it does not exist. Again, the Buddhists, in spite of the fact that there is the ego-consciousness, persistently deny the existence of *ātman* other than the subtle body. Therefore, being different from object of perception, the existence of the *ātman* cannot be proved by this means[40] (perception). It can't be inferred too, since it is unconnected with any invariable concomittance.[41] For example, *ātman* cannot be known by any other means of knowledge, except the *śruti*, as having any relation to another life. But when its existence has been known from the *śruti* and from certain empirical grounds of inference cited by it, the Mīmāṁsakas and Naiyāyikas, who follow its footsteps, fancy that those Vedic grounds of inference such as the ego-consciousness are the products of their own minds and declare that the *ātman* is knowable through perception and inference.[42]

---

38. *Tathā, paramātmeśvara-devatādi-vastu asthūlādi-dharmakam-aśanāyādyatītaṁ cetyevam-ādiviśiṣṭam-iti veda-vākyair-eva jñāpyate.* — *BṛUSB*, I.III.1.
39. *Rūpādyabhāvāddhi nāyam-arthaḥ pratyakṣa-gocaraḥ.* — *BṛUSB*, II.1.11
40. *BṛUSB*, I.I. *Sambandha Bhāṣyam.*
41. *Liṅgādyabhāvācca nānumānādīnām-iti.* — Ibid.
42. Ibid.

To illustrate, the *brahman* is revealed only by the *Upaniṣad* and by no other means of knowledge. So says the sage Yājñavalkya, *Tvaupaniṣadam puruṣam pṛcchāmi.*[43] Again the *śruti* by these sentences *Satyam jñānamanantaṁ brahma,*[44] *Vijñānamānandam brahma*[45] gives us the intrinsic characteristics of the Supreme Consciousness.

The most significant teaching of the *śruti* is the declaration of the identity of the individual *ātman* with *Brahman*. While disclosing the oneness of the individual consciousness and the universal consciousness, the *śruti* points to the sole reality of non-dual pure consciousness that *brahman* is. There are four such pithy sentences in the four *śruti*s and each is called a *Mahāvākya* — (1) *Prajñānam brahma*[46] (Consciousness is *brahman*), (2) *Aham brahmāsmi*[47] (I am *brahman*) (3) *Tattvamasi*[48] (Thou art That) and (4) *Ayamātmā brahma*[49] (This Ātman is *brahman*). These great teachings become the cause of *akhaṇḍārthabodha*.

Not only *Brahman* but also *dharma* (the law of *karma*) is beyond the scope of normal experience and reason, being rooted in supra-sensuous truth.[50] This is evident from Kṛṣṇa's instruction to Arjuna: "He who, disregarding the directions of the *śāstra*, acts under the impulse of desire, attains no ability, nor happiness, nor the supreme goal. Therefore, let the *śāstra* be your authority in determining what ought to be done and

---

43. *BṛU*, III.IX.26.
44. *TU*, II.I.3.
45. *BṛU*, III.IX.28.
46. *AU*, III.I.3.
47. *BṛU*, I.IV.10.
48. *ChU*, I.VI.VIII.7.
49. *ManU*, 2.
50. *Ayaṁ dharmo 'yam-adharma iti śāstram-eva vijñāne kāraṇam, atīndriyatvāt-tyoḥ.* — *BSSB*, III.I.25.

what ought not to be done. Having ascertained what is prescribed or prohibited by the *śāstra*, you should act here.[51]

The basis of this opinion is the inability of human beings to establish the invariable relation between *karma* and its result, since it is beyond the sense-contact. Again, *dharma* and *adharma* are supra-sensuous realities and they are not invariable for all space, time and environment.[52] So, any duty that is performed as virtuous in relation to certain place, time and circumstances,[53] becomes non-virtuous to other places, times and circumstances. So nobody can have any knowledge about *dharma* and *vice*, unless it be from scripture."[54]

Even the things of this world like gems, incantations, herbs and so on, are seen to possess many powers capable of producing incompatible effects under the influence of a variety of space (environment), time and cause. And even those powers can be known not from mere reasoning but from such instruction through the scripture as: "Such a thing has such kind of potency with the aid of such things, or such things are for such purposes."[55] Therefore, the cognition of what is supra-

---

51. *Yaḥ śāstra-vidhi-mutsṛjya vartate kāma-kārataḥ* ı
Na sa siddhim-avāpnoti na sukhaṁ na parāṁ gatim ıı
Tasmāc-chāstraṁ pramāṇaṁ te kāryākāryavyavasthitau ı
Jñātva śāstra-vidhānoktaṁ karma-kartum-ihārhasi ıı — G, XVI.23-24.

52. *Atīndriyatvāt-tayoḥ aniyata-deśa-kāla-nimittatvācca.* — *BSSB*, III.I.25

53. *Yasmin-deśe kāle nimitte ca yo dharmo 'nusthiyate sa eva deśa-kāla-nimittāntaresvadharmo bhavati.* — Ibid.

54. *Tena śāstrādṛte dharmādharma-viśayaṁ vijñānaṁ na kasyacid-asti.* — Ibid.

55. *Laukikānām-api maṇi-mantrauṣadhi-prabhṛtīnāṁ deśa-kāla-nimitta-vaicitrya-vaśāc-chaktayor-viruddhānekakārya-viṣayā dṛśyante. Tā api tāvan-nopadeśam-antareṇa kevalena tarkeṇāvagantuṁ śakynte 'sya vastuna etāvatya etatsahāyā etad-viṣayā etat-prayojanāśca śaktaya iti.* — *BSSB*, II.I.27.

sensuous is based on the *śruti* or *śāstra* only.[56]

SELF-VALIDITY OF THE ŚRUTI

In the view of Śaṅkara, *śruti* means the direct revelation, since it doesn't depend on any other means of knowledge for its validity.[57] It means that the *śruti* is as valid for the knowledge of supra-sensuous as perception is valid for the knowledge of sensuous. Again the *śruti*, which is eternally composed and already existent, is manifested from the *Brahman* like a man's breath — without any thought or effort on his part. Hence the *śruti* is independent as well as valid in itself[58] and does not derive its authority from any other source.[59] Hence it is perfectly valid.

ETERNITY OF THE ŚRUTI

Śaṅkara holds that, the *śruti* is eternal, but renewed at the beginning of each world cycle.[60] Proofs for the eternity of the *śruti* are underneath:-

(a) The *śruti* is eternal, because it is the cause of the generation of the world.[61] This theory does not conflict

---

56. *Tasmāc-chabda-mūla evātīndriyārtha-yāthātmyadhigamaḥ.* — Ibid.

57. *Pratykṣaṁ śrutiḥ, prāmāṇyaṁ pratyanapekṣatvāt.* — *BSSB*, II.III.28.

58. (a) *Niyata-racanāvato vidyamānasyaiva vedasyābhivyaktiḥ puruṣa-niḥśvāsa-vat, na ca puruṣa-buddhi-prayatna pūrvakaḥ ataḥ pramāṇaṁ nirapekṣa eva svārthe.* — *BṛUSB*, II.IV.10.

    (b) *Yasmāt sākṣāt paramātmākhyāt akṣarāt puruṣa niḥśvāsavat samudbhūtam.* — *GSB*, III.15.

    (c) *Ṛgvedādyākhyasya sarva-jñānākarasyāprayatnenaiva līlānyāyena puruṣa-niḥśvāsa-vadyasmānmahato bhūtādyoneḥ sambhavaḥ.* — *BSSB*, I.I.3

59. *Nirapekṣatvād-vedasya prāmāṇyaṁ prati.* — *BṛUSB*, II.III.6.

60. *Samāna-nāmarūpatvāc-cāvṛttāvapyavirodho darśanāt-smṛteśca.* — *BSSB*, I.III.30.

61. *Ataeva hi vaidikāc-chabdād-devādikaṁ jagat-prabhavati.* — *BSSB*, I.III.28

with the doctrine that *Brahman* is the cause of the world; because, here this theory means that when an eternal word stands as the sign (*vācaka*) eternally related to its referent (which is always a universal), from that issue forth individuals capable of being denoted by the word.[62] Generally, when anyone wants to make a thing he first recollects the word signifying it and then makes it. This is evident to us in experience and the creation of the world was also similar.[63] For instance, from the word *"bhur"* (earth) which occurred in the mind of *Prajāpati*, he created the terrestrial world.[64]

(b) The *śruti* is eternal, because its words signify forms (*ākṛti*) and universal (*jāti*), not individuals.[65] The forms and universal are eternal,[66] so the *śruti* is eternal. For example words such as *"vasu"*[67] signify universal,

---

62. *Na cedaṁ śabda-prabhavatvaṁ brahma-prabhavatvavad-upādāna-kāraṇābhi-prāyeṇocyate. Kathaṁ tarhi? sthite vācakātmanā nitye śabde nityārtha-sambandhini śabda-vyavahāra-yogyārtha vykti-niṣpattiḥ.* — Ibid.

63. *Api ca cikīrṣitam-artham-anutisṭhaṁstasya vācakaṁ śabdaṁ pūrvaṁ smṛtvā paścāt tam-artham-anutiṣṭhatīti sarveṣāṁ naḥ pratyakṣam-etat. Tathā prajāpater-api sraṣṭuḥ sṛṣṭeḥ pūrvaṁ vaidikāḥ śabdā manasi prādur-babhūvuḥ, paścāt-tadanugatān-arthān-sasrjeti gamyate.* — Ibid.

64. *Tatha ca sṛutiḥ sa bhūriti vyāharat sa bhūmim-asṛjat.* (*TB*, II.II.IV.2). *ityevam-ādikā bhūrādi-śabdebhya eva manasi prādur-bhūtebhyo bhūrādi-lokān-sṛṣṭān-darśayati.* — Ibid.

65. *Akṛtibhiśca śabdānaṁ sambandhaḥ na vyaktibhiḥ.* — *BSSB*, I.III.28.

66. *Vyaktiṣūtpadyamānāsvapyākṛtinaṁ nityatvān-na gavādi-śabdeṣu kaścid-virodho dṛśyate.* — Ibid.

67. *Tatha devādi-vyakti-prabhāvābhyupagame 'syākṛti-nityatvān-na kaścid-vasvādi-śabdeṣu virodha iti drasṭavyam.* — Ibid.

words such as "*indra*" are titles,[68] i.e. they signify a certain status.[69] Again, when a man says "go" and "go" and "go" we do not say that he has uttered three "go"s but he has pronounced "go" thrice, so forms and universal never change.[70]

(c) The *śruti* is eternal because it is as it was in the past world cycle. Śaṅkara, quoting the *smṛti*, says that as all world cycles are similar, at the beginning of each creation *Brahman* gives to the newly generated sages the *Veda* with the names and power which they respectively had in the previous aeon.[71]

(d) The *śruti* is eternal, because it has no independent author.[72] Generally, other books have authors mentioned with in those books themselves. But the *śruti* nowhere speaks anyone as its author. The sentence in the *śruti* which says that "He created all this, the *Ṛk*s, the *Yaju*s and the *Sāmans*," speaks only of the ancestor of all people (*Prajāpati*) who, having come to know the *Veda*, uttered it in sequence. The word "creation" here refers only to the manifestation of the *śruti* in *Prajāpati*'s intellect at the beginning of

---

68. *Sthāna-viśeṣa-sambandha-nimittaścendrādi-śabdāḥ senāpatyādi śabdavat. Tataśca yo yastat-tat-sthānam-adhirohati sa ca indrādi-śabdair-abhīdhiyata.* — Ibid.

69. *Ākṛti-viśeṣastu devādīnāṁ mantrādi-vādādibhyo vigraha-vatvādyavagamādavagantavyaḥ.* — Ibid.

70. *Dvir-go śabda uccārita iti hi pratipattirna tu dvau gośabdāviti.* — Ibid.

71. *Smṛtirapi-Ṛṣīṇāṁ nāmadheyāni yāśca vedeṣu dṛṣṭayaḥ.*
Śarvaryante prasūtānaṁ tānyevaibhyo dadātyajaḥ.
Ityevaṁ jātiyakā draṣṭavyā. — *BSSB*, I.III.30.

72. *Svatantrasya kartur-asmaraṇādibhiḥ sthite vedasya nityatve.* — *BSSB*, I.III.29.

the world-cycle,[73] since it is eternally composed and existent.[74]

Though the *śruti* is eternal, its eternity can't be conceived as *kūṭastha nityatā*, because after self-realisation only the *ātman* or *Brahman* is existent, nothing else. In fact, two types of eternity are distinguished in Advaita Vedānta:-

(a) *Kūṭastha nityatā*, and

(b) *Pravāharūpa nityatā*[75] or *pariṇāminityatā.*

A thing is *kūṭastha nitya* if it is unchanged for ever, while a thing has *pravāharūpanityatā* if though incessantly changing it does not alter its pattern.[76] *Brahman* has the former kind of reality[77] and a river or the earth the latter kind.[78] Śaṅkara seems to conceive the eternity of the *śruti* as *pravāharūpa nityatā* and says that all the three worlds and creatures are a flux, but have a pattern.[79]

ŚRUTI AND SENSE-PERCEPTION

In Śaṅkara's view, *śruti* means perception, since it does not

---

73. *PPV, ṣaṣṭhavarṇakam.*

74. *Niyata-racanāvato vidyamānasyaiva vedasyābhivyaktiḥ.*
— *BṛUSB,* II.IV.10

75. *Tatra kiñcit-pariṇāminityaṁ . . . idaṁ tu pārmārthikaṁ, kuṭastha-nityam.*
— *BSSB,* I.I.4.

76. *Tatra kiñcit-pariṇāminityaṁ yasmin-vikriyamāṇe 'pi tadevedam iti buddhirna vihanyate.* — Ibid.

77. *Idam tu pārmārthikaṁ, kūṭastha-nityaṁ, vyomavat-sarvavyāpi, sarva-vikriyā-rahitaṁ, nitya-tṛptaṁ, niravayavaṁ. svayañjyotiḥ svabhāvām.*
— Ibid.

78. *Yathā pṛthivyādi-jagan-nityatva-vādinām.* — Ibid.

79. *Tataśca vicchidya vicchidyāpyudbhavatāṁ bhūrādi-loka-pravāhāṇāṁ, deva-tiryaṅ-manuṣya-lakṣaṇānāṁ ca prāṇi-nikāya-pravāhāṇāṁ, varṇāśrama-dharma-phala-vyavasthānāṁ cānādau saṁsāre niyatatvam-indriya-viṣaya-sambandha-niyatatvavat pratyetavyam.* — *BSSB,* I.III.30.

depend on any other means of knowledge for its validity.[80] By this definition it seems that there must be contradiction between *śruti* and sensual-perception. But it is not right, since the former deals with the super-sensible, the latter with sensible.[81] They both are valid in their spheres. It is so because empirical experiences are valid until the identity of the *ātman* with *Brahman* is realized, as are dream-experiences until awakening.[82]

So far as the world of experience is concerned the *śruti* does not question the validity of perceptual knowledge but denies its authoritativeness in the supra-sensuous reality. Empirical facts can be known by sense-perception and by all other means of knowledge that are based on it. As regards transcendental truths, the *śruti* is the sole valid source of knowledge.[83]

According to Śaṅkara, things in the world are known to possess certain fixed characteristics such as grossness or fineness.[84] By citing them as examples the scriptures seek to

---

80. *Pratyakṣaṁ śrutih, prāmāṇyaṁ pratyanapekṣatvāt.* — *BSSB*, I.III.28.
81. (a) *Tasmāc-chabda-mūla evātindriyārtha-yāthātmyādhigamaḥ.* — *BSSB*, II.I.27.

    (b) *Sarvo 'pyayaṁ vedaḥ pratyakṣānumānābhyām-anavagaṭeṣtāniṣṭa-prāpti-parihāropāya-prakāśana-paraḥ.* — *BNSB*, I.I.I, *Sambandha-Bhāṣya.*

    (c) *Tatprāmāṇyasya adṛṣṭa-viṣayatvāt.* — *GSB*, XVIII.66.
82. *Tasmāt-prāg-brahmātā-pratibodhād-upapannaḥ sarvo laukiko vaidikaśca vyavahāraḥ. Prāk-prabodhāt, na ca pratyakṣābhāsābhiprāyas-tatkāle bhavati, tadvat.* — *BSSB*, II.I.14.
83. *Tasmāc-chabda-mūla evātindriyārtha-yāthātmyādhigamaḥ.* — *BSSB*, II.IX.27.
84. *Bhūtā mūrtāmūrtādi-padārtha-dharmā loke prasiddhāḥ.* — *BṛUSB*, II.I.20.

tell us about some other thing which does not contradict them.[85] They would not cite an example from life if they wanted to convey an idea of something contradictory to it.[86] Even if they did, it would be to no purpose, for the example would be different from the thing to be explained.[87] We cannot prove that fire is cold, or that the sun does not give heat, even by citing hundreds of examples, for the facts would already be known to be otherwise through another source of knowledge.[88] And one source of knowledge does not contradict another, for it only tells us about those things that cannot be known by any other means.[89] Nor can the scriptures speak about an unknown thing without having source to conventional words and their meanings.[90]

Though the *śruti* cannot controvert facts of experience, nevertheless, any statement that is obviously contradictory to them (facts) should not be taken literally. Here, one should assume that the intended meaning of the *śruti* is different, for its validity can't be maintained[91] otherwise. And at this stage other means of knowledge must be held to be

---

85. *Tad-dṛṣṭāntopādānena tadavirodhyeva vastvantaraṁ jñāpayituṁ pravṛttaṁ śāstram.* — *BṛUSB*, II.I.20.

86. *Na laukika-vastu-virodha-jñāpanāya laukikam-eva dṛṣṭāntam-upādatte.* — Ibid.

87. *Upādīyamāno 'pi dṛṣṭānto 'narthakaḥ syād-dārṣṭāntikāsaṅgateḥ.* — Ibid.

88. *Na hyagniḥ śītaḥ āditya na tapatīti vā dṛṣṭānta-śatenāpi pratipādayituṁ śakyam, prāmāṇāntareṇānyathādhigatatvād-vastunaḥ.* — Ibid.

89. *Na ca pramānaṁ pramāṇātareṇa virudhyate, pramāṇāntarāviṣayam-eva hi pramāṇāntaraṁ jñāpayati.* — Ibid.

90. *Na ca laukika-pada-padārthāśrayaṇa-vyatirekeṇāgamena śakyam-ajnātaṁ vastvanataram-avagamayitum.* — Ibid.

91. *Yadi brūyāt śītaḥ agniḥ aprakāśo vā iti athāpi arthāntaraṁ śruteḥ vivakṣitaṁ kalpyaṁ prāmānyānyathānupapatteḥ.* — *GSB*, XVIII.16.

fallacious.[92] For instance, the ignorant thinks of fire-fly as fire, or of the sky as a blue surface. These are perceptions, no doubt, but when the evidence of the other means of knowledge about them has been definitely known to be true, the perceptions of the ignorant, though they are definite experiences, prove to be fallacious.[93] So, the scriptural passage must be taken exactly in the sense it is tested to bear, and not according to the ingenuity of the human mind;[94] but, one should not assume its meaning in a way that might contradict some other valid means of knowledge or contradicts its own statement.[95] Regarding *ātman*, the *śruti* and the sense-perception seem to be contradicted, but, in fact, do not contradict each other, they represent only two different viewpoints.[96] Let us see:-

It is a normal human experience that *ātman* is variable; it suffers from hunger and thirst; it grows and decays; it becomes happy and unhappy etc. But *śruti* declares that *ātman* is birthless, changeless, eternal;[97] that is "sinless, decayless, deathless, sorrowless, free from hunger and thirst."[98] Evidently, the *śruti* contradicts the common human knowledge

92. *Śrute tu tādarthye vākyasya prāmāṇāntarasya ābhāsatvam.*
— *BṛUSB*, III.3.

93. *Yathā khadyoto 'gniriti, tala-malinam-antarikṣam-iti bālānāṁ yat pratyakṣam-api tad-viṣaya-pramāṇāntarasya yathārthatve niścite, niścitārtham-api bāla-pratyakṣam ābhāsībhavati.* — Ibid.

94. *Tasmāt veda prāmāṇyasyāvyabhicārāttādarthye sati vākyasya tathātvaṁ syāt. Na tu puruṣam-ati kauśalam.* — Ibid.

95. *Na tu prāmāṇāntara-viruddhaṁ sva-vacana-viruddhaṁ vā.*
— *GSB*, XVIII.16.

96. *NŚ*, III.44-45.

97. *Na jāyate mṛyate vā vipaścinnāya kutaścinna babhūva kaścit.*
Ajo nityaḥ śāśvato 'yaṁ purāṇo na hanyate hanyamāne śarīre.
— *KU*, I.II.18.

98. *Ya ātmāpahata-pāpmā vijaro vimṛtyur-viśoko vijighatso 'pipāsaḥ . . .*
— *BṛU*, III.VII.1.

regarding *ātman*. Yet there is no conflict between the two. The referent of common experience is *ātman* conjoined with the limiting adjuncts of the body, the senses and the mind; whereas the *Upaniṣads* point to the innermost *ātman* differentiated from all the adjuncts. The former is empirically valid, the latter is fundamentally true. The former endures as long as *jīva* (the individual) continues to be in the migratory state under the spell of ignorance. But when he is awakened to the real nature of *ātman* as declared by the *śruti*, then all contrary notions regarding this, from whatever source, prove to be fallacious. So, it may be concluded that the empirical validity of perception and other allied means of knowledge is a proven fact; this is not contradicted by the *śruti*. What is contradicted is its ultimateness, which is by no means a proven fact. Therefore, there is no conflict between the *śruti* and sense-perception.[99]

THE CONCEPT OF APAURUṢEYA

Śaṅkara explains that the *śruti*, which is eternally composed and already existent, is manifested like man's breath from *Brahman* without any thought or effort on his part.[100] Again he says that *Brahman* is the cause of the *śruti*, which is supplemented by other scriptures that are themselves sources

---

99. *Viruddhyośca dvayorahaṁ manuṣya ityādi-pratyakṣa 'ākāśavat-sarvagataśca nityaḥ 'ityādi śrutyoriva tāttvika-prāmāṇyānupattyā kasyacid vyāvahārikaṁ kasyacit-tāttvikaṁ prāmāṇyam-abhyupeyam.* — AS, I.18.

100. (a) *Asya paramātmanaḥ prakṛtasya mahato bhūtasya niśvasitam-etat . . .* — BṛUSB, II.IV.10.

(b) *Niyata-racanāvato vidyamānasyaiva vedasyābhivyaktiḥ puruṣa-niḥśvāsavat.* — Ibid.

(c) *Ṛgvedādyākhyasya sarva-jñānākarasyāprayatnenaiva līlānyāyena puruṣa-niḥśvāsavadyasmānmahato bhūtādyoneḥ sambhavaḥ.* — BSSB, I.1.3.

of knowledge, which reveals all things like a lamp and which is almost omniscient;[101] for scripture like the *śruti* possessed of all good qualities, cannot possibly emerge from any source other than an all-knowing one, *Brahman.*[102] It is so because of the well-recognized fact that the person from whom the scriptures, dealing with multifarious subjects, emerge in the world, for example, grammar etc. emanating from Pāṇini and others,[103] represent merely a part of the subject known to them. So *Brahman*, the cause of the *śruti*, is unsurpassed, omniscient and omnipresent.

By these statements, it seems that the *śruti* is *paurṣeya*. But this is not true, since Śaṅkara himself denies it.[104] According to him,[105] the *śruti* though came out of *puruṣa*, is not created by an ordinary *puruṣa.*[106] So it cannot be called *pauruṣeya*. In fact, the sages and *hiraṇyagarbhādi* gods who excel in knowledge and action by virtue of their actions in the past aeon, are able to recollect the *śruti* by supreme God's grace as it was in the past aeon, just as a man waking from sleep is able to recollect and continue his previous waking

---

101. *Mahata ṛgvedādeḥ śāstrasyāneka-vidyāsthānopabṛṁhitasya pradipavat-sarvārthāvadyotinaḥ sarjña-kalpasya yoniḥ kāraṇaṁ brahma.* — Ibid.

102. *Na hīdṛśasya śāstrasyargvedādi-lakṣaṇasya sarvajña-guṇānvitasya sarvajñādanyataḥ sambhavo 'sti.* — Ibid.

103. *Yad-yad-vistarārthaṁ śāstraṁ yasmāt-puruṣa-viśeṣāt sambhavati, yathā vyākarṇādi pāṇinyāder-jñeyaika-deśārtham-api, sa tato 'pyadhikatara-vijñāna iti prasiddhaṁ loke.* — *BSSB*, I.I.3.

104. *Svatantrasya kartur-asmaraṇādibhiḥ sthite vedasya nityatve.* — *BSSB*, I.III.29.

105. *Yasmāt sākṣāt paramātmākhyāt akṣarāt puruṣaniḥśvāsvat samūdbhūtaṁ brahma.* — *GSB*, II.15.

106. *Na ca puruṣa-buddhi-prayatna-pūrvakaḥ.* — *BṛUSB*, II.IV.10.

experience.[107] For example, Madhucchandas and other *ṛṣi*s were the seers of the *mantra*s of the *Ṛgveda*.[108] *Śruti* also supports this theory.[109] So, the supreme God makes the Vedic propositions flash in the minds of the sages in the same linguistic form in which they are now available.

The Concept of Smṛti and its Position as Verbal Testimony

According to Śaṅkara, *śruti* is the ultimate means of knowledge.[110] But all people cannot understand the *śruti*. So they have to rely on the *smṛti*s in order to understand the purport of the *śruti*.[111] But in doing so they must rely only on those *smṛti*s which are in conformity with the *śruti*.[112] *Smṛti*s which are clearly in conflict with the *śruti* must be rejected,[113] because the author of *smṛti*s being but men, cannot know anything about supra-sensuous matter.[114] So, the *smṛti*s are

---

107. *Tataścātīta-kalpānuṣṭhita-prakṛṣṭa-jñāna-karmaṇām-īśvarāṇāṁ hiraṇya-garbhādīnāṁ vartamāna-kalpādau prādur-bhavatāṁ parameśvarānugṛhitānāṁ supta-prati-buddhavat-kalpāntara-vyavahārānusandhānopapattiḥ.* — *BSSB*, I.II.30.

108. *Smaranti ca 'śaunakādayaḥ madhucchandaḥ-prabhṛtibhir-ṛṣibhir-dāśatayyo dṛṣṭāḥ.* — Ibid.

109. *Yajñena vācaḥ padavīyamāyantām-anvavindan-nṛṣu praviṣṭām.* (*ṚS*, X.71.3). — *BSSB*, I.III.29.

110. *Sāstraṁ tu antyaṁ pramāṇam.* — *GSB*, II.18.

111. *Para-tantra-prajñāstu prāyeṇa janāḥ svātantryeṇa śrutyartham-avadhārayitum-aśaknuvantaḥ prakhyāta-pranetṛ-kāsu smṛti-śvavalamberan. Tad-balena ca śrutyarthaṁ pratipitseran.* — *BSSB* II.I.1.

112. *Vipratipattau ca smṛtīnām-avaśya-kartavye 'nyatara-parigrahe 'nyatara-parityāge ca śrutyanusāriṇyaḥ smṛtayaḥ pramāṇam.* — *BSSB*, II.I.

113. *Anapekṣyā itarāḥ.* — Ibid.

114. *Na cātindriyān-arthān-śrutim-antareṇa kścid-upalabhata iti śakyaṁ sambhāvayitum, nimittābhāvāt.* — Ibid.

authoritative only when they are in agreement with the *śruti*.[115] For instance, the *Bhagvad-Gītā*, *Manusmṛti* etc. are said to be authoritative means of knowledge since they totally depend upon the *śruti* as inference depends upon perception,[116] whereas Kapila's *Sāṅkhyasmṛti* is not authoritative, since it does not follow the *śruti*.[117]

This does not, however, mean that the whole of Kapila's system has to be rejected. Even in the *smṛti*s, which are in conflict with the *śruti*, if there are any doctrines which are in conformity with the *śruti*, Śaṅkara holds, they should be accepted.[118] Kapila, for example, says that *puruṣa* has no attributes, and Patañjali lays down certain rules which are to be followed by the monks. These are in conformity with what the *śruti* says, and Śaṅkara concedes that they may be accepted.[119] Other schools of Hindu thought such as *Vaiśeṣika*, *Pāśupata* and *Pañcarātra* also are not entirely in accordance with the Vedic revelation, and so, according to Śaṅkara, they also ought to be rejected.

At last, if a passage in the *smṛti*s does not contradict anything in the *Veda*s, we may infer that it is based on some Vedic texts, even though we ourselves may not know those

---

115. *Śrutyanusāriṇī ca smṛtiḥ pramāṇam-iti sthitiḥ.* — *BSSB*, II.II.42.

116. *Anumānaṁ smṛtiḥ; prāmāṇyaṁ prati sāpekṣtvāt.* — *BSSB*, I.III.28.

117. *Na tayā śruti-viruddham-api kāpilam mataṁ śraddhātuṁ śakyam.* — *BSSB*, II.I.1

118. *Yena tvaṁśena virudhyete teneṣṭam-eva sāṁkhya-yoga-smṛtyoḥ śāvakāśatvam.* — *BSSB*, II.I.3.

119. *Tadyathā 'asaṅgo hyayaṁ puruṣaḥ'*(*BṛU*, IV.III.16) *ityevam-ādi-śruti-prasiddham-eva puruṣasya viśuddhatvaṁ nirguṇa-puruṣa-nirūpaṇena sāṁkyair-abhyupa-gamyate. Tathā ca yogair-api 'atha parivrād vivarṇa-vāsā muṇḍo 'parigraḥ'* (*JU*, 5) *ityevam-ādi śruti-prasiddham-eva nivṛtti-niṣṭtvaṁ pravrajyādyupadeśenānugamyate.* — *BSSB*, II.I.3.

texts.[120] For instance, the mind is not clearly stated as an *indriya* in the *śruti*, but in *smṛtis* eleven sense organs are mentioned and on that account the mind, like the ear and so on, is known as an *indriya*.[121]

The Essential Cause of Self-realization: Śruti or Antaḥkaraṇa

It is the burning question of the Advaita Vedānta that which of the two — *śruti vākya* or *antaḥkaraṇa* is the essential cause of the self-realization. According to Śaṅkara, the knowledge arising from the dictums such as "thou art that,"[122] "not this, not this,"[123] "only one without a second,"[124] etc. immediately leads to the realization of *ātman* or *Brahman*.[125] As soon as the knowledge of *ātman* arises as a result of hearing the *māhāvākyas*, it necessarily destroys all the previous false notions.[126] When the false notions about *ātman* i.e. that it is the body, that it is other than the *Brahman* etc. are gone, memories and habits based upon them cannot continue;[127] and things other than *ātman* are realized as evils, being full of defects

120. *Etat-smaryamāṇaṁ rūpaṁ mūlabhūtāṁ śrutim-anumāpayad-asya vaiśvānara-śabdasya parameśvara-paratve 'numānaṁ liṅgaṁ gamakaṁ syād-ityarthaḥ*. — *BSSB*, I.II.25.

121. *Smṛtau tvekādaśendriyāṇīti mano 'pīndriyatvena śrotrādivat-saṅgṛhyate*. — *BSSB*, II.IV.17.

122. *ChU*, VI.VIII.7.

123. *BṛU*, II.III.6.

124. *ChU*, VI.II.1.

125. *Ātma-vastu-svarūpa-samarpakaireva vākyaiḥ 'tattvamasi' ityādibhiḥ śravaṇa-kāla eva tad-darśanasya kṛtatvāt* . . . — *BṛUSB*, I.IV.7.

126. *Yadaivātma-pratipādaka-vākya-śravaṇād ātma-viṣayaṁ vijñānam-utpadyate, tadaiva tad-utpadyamānaṁ tad-viṣayaṁ mithyājñānaṁ nivartayad-evopadyate*. — Ibid.

127. *Ātma-viṣya-mithyā-jñāna-nivṛttau ca tat-prabhavāḥ smṛtayo na bhavanti*. — Ibid.

such as transitoriness, painfulness and impurity, while *ātman* is contrary to them.[128] So the memories of notions about the non-self die out and the train of recollection of the knowledge of non-dual nature of *ātman* is firmly implanted.[129] Besides this, the memory of *ātman* removes the painful defects such as grief, fear and effort,[130] for these defects spring from the opposite kind of knowledge.[131] So, the knowledge of *Brahman* is the essential cause of the liberation.[132]

If someone says that the control of the mind may be the ultimate means of self-realization or liberation;[133] that is not true, since the *Upaniṣads* do not speak of anything other than the knowledge of the identity of *ātman* as a means to the attainment of liberation.[134]

Again, Śaṅkara says that *Brahman* which is homogeneous is to be attained through the mind only.[135] The scriptures also repeat this again and again.[136] Śaṅkara further says that

---

128. *Ātmāvagatau hi styām-anyad-vastvanarthatvenāvagamyate, anitya-duḥkhāśuddhyādi-bahu-doṣavattvā-ātma-vastunaśca tad-vilakṣaṇatvāt.* — Ibid.

129. *Pāriśeṣyād-ātmaikatva-vijñāna-smṛti-santater-arthata eva bhāvānna vidheyatvam.* — *BṛUSB*, I.IV.7.

130. *Śoka-moha-bhayāyāsādi-duḥkha-doṣa-nivartakatvācca tatsmṛteḥ.* — Ibid.

131. *Viparīta-jñāna-prabhavo hi śoka-mohādi-doṣaḥ.* — Ibid.

132. *Na tu brahma-vijñāna-vyatirekeṇa anyanmokṣa-sādhanam-avagamyate.* — Ibid.

133. *Nirodhas-tarhyarthāntaram-iti cet.* — Ibid.

134. *Na; mokṣa-sādhanatvenāvagamāt. Na hi vetānteṣu brahmātma-vijñānād anyat-parama-puruṣārtha-sādhnatvenāvagamyate.* — Ibid.

135. *Manasedaṁ brahmaika-rasamāptavyam ātmaiva nānyadastīti.* — *KSB*, II.I.I.

136. a. *Manasaivedam-avāptavyam.* — *KU*, II.I.II.
b. *Manasaivānudraṣṭavyam* . . . — *BṛU*, IV.IV.19.

Brahman is clearly seen in the purified internal-organ as the reflected one is clearly seen by himself in a clear mirror or water.[137] And at last, Śaṅkara says that the mind which is purified by the instructions of the scriptures and the teacher, and control of the sense-organs etc. become the essential cause of self-realization.[138]

Thus, we have both types of proofs for finalizing the essential cause of the realization of *ātman*. But what side should be adopted, is a major problem for unrealized persons like us. In this regard, Śaṅkara says: "Where the meaning of a word is doubtful, it can be ascertained by a reference to a definite use of the word elsewhere or from a supplementary statement; or else on the strength of irrefutable logic.[139] So, though the knowledge arising from the *mahāvākya* is intrinsically able to make *ātman* known; still it is not useful for one who has not desisted from bad conduct, whose senses are not under control, whose mind is not concentrated and free from anxiety about the result of concentration, and finally who is not fully equipped with purified internal-organ.[140] So the role of the pure internal-organ cannot be avoided. Again, we find that even though the Upaniṣads have been heard and understood, the delusion of *Brahman* being a remote thing sometimes

137. (a) *Yathādarśe pratibimba-bhūtam ātmānaṁ paśyati loko 'tyantviviktaṁ tathehātmani svabuddhau ādarśavannirmalī-bhūtāyāṁ viviktam ātmano darśanaṁ bhavatītyarthaḥ.* — *KSB*, II.III.5.

(b) *ChUSB*, VIII.I.2.

138. (a) *Manasaiva paramārtha-jñāna-saṁskṛtena ācāryopadeśa-pūrvakaṁ cānudraṣṭavyam.* — *ChUSB*, IV.IV.19.

(b) *Śāstrācāryopadeśa-śama-damādi-samskṛtaṁ mana ātma-darśane karaṇam.* — *GSB*, II.21.

139. *Sandigdhaśca padārtho 'nyatra niścita-prayoga-darśanānnirdhārayituṁ śakyaḥ, vākyaśeṣāt niścit-nyāyabalāt vā.* — *BṛUSB*, IV.III.7.

140. *Na duścaritāt . . . brahma-vijñānenainaṁ prakṛtam-ātmānam-āpnuyāt.* — *KSB*, I.II.24.

persists. Hence, scriptural testimony cannot directly produce the immediate cognition until the mind becomes purified. It means the purified mind is as important for *ātma-jñāna* as the scriptural sentences. But the pure mind has its own limitation. It can reveal *ātman*, but there still persists the mental mode which has *ātman* for its content. *Ātman* as such is self-luminous and eternal. This pure consciousness, though devoid of all adjuncts, seems to be intuited, it is really consciousness, conditioned by the mental mode, which is intuited. At this stage the knowledge, arising from the sentences such as "thou art that" etc. which only delineate the nature of *ātman*, removes the mental mode, and immediately leads to self-realization.[141]

Thus, we can conclude that though the mind, purified by the instructions of the scriptures and the teacher, is the essential cause for the realization of *ātman* conditioned by its own mode,[142] still the knowledge arising from the *śrutivākya* is the essential cause for the realization of *ātman*,[143] which is direct and immediate. Hence, the scriptural means of knowledge is said to be the *antyaṁ pramāṇam* (final authority).

Falsity of the Śruti

Śaṅkara unhesitatingly states that when the final truth of non-dualism is realized, there will be no perception; for then the

141. (a) *"yo 'yaṁ vijñānamayaḥ"* (*BṛU.* IV.III.7) *ityevam-ādyātma-pratipādana-parābhiḥ śrutibhir-ātma-viṣayaṁ vijñānam-utpāditam. Tatrātma-svarūpa-vijnānenaiva tad-viṣayānātmābhimāna-buddhiḥ kārakādi-kriyā phalādhyāropaṇātmikā avidyā nivartitā.* — *BṛUSB*, I.IV.7.

(b) *Ātma-vastu-svarūpa-samarpakaireva vākyaiḥ "tattvamasi" ityādibhiḥ śravaṇa-kāla eva tad-darśanasya kṛtatvāt.* — Ibid.

142. *Śāstrācāryaopadeśa-śama-damādi-saṁskṛtaṁ mana ātma-darśane karaṇam.* — *GSB*, II.21.

143. *Brahmātma-bhāvasya śāstram-antareṇānavagamyamānatvāt.* — *BSSB*, I.1.4.

śruti also becomes non-existent.[144] As *śāstra* is intended only for the unenlightened, it is meaningful only in the state of bondage; and not in the liberated state.[145]

But, how can false *śruti* (false scripture) produce valid knowledge? How can the valid and the real experience of non-duality result from the *śruti* sentences, which are false themselves? The answer is that the *śruti*, though not absolutely real, can, nevertheless, make the absolutely real known to us; just as woman or a cobra seen in a dream though false, has physical as well as psychical effects which extend into waking experience.[146] For example, a man who dreams that he has been bitten by a cobra may die of shock;[147] and dreams can also be portentous of future "bad" and "good" in waking life.[148] Again, the written symbol "A" is read as "A" whenever it occurs; but in fact it is only a false representation of the letter "A" which is eternal and all pervasive.[149]

Actually, so long as the oneness of true *ātman* is not

---

144. (a) *Yatra tvasya sarvam-ātmaivābhūt-tat-kena kaṁ paśyet* (*Bṛ*, II.4.14) *ityādinā hi prabodhe pratyakṣādyabhāvaṁ darśayati. Pratyakṣādyabhāve śruterapyabhāva-prasaṅga iti cet, na iṣṭatvāt. 'Atra pitā 'pitā bhavati'* (*Br*, IV.III.22) *itypakramya 'vedā avedāḥ' iti* (*Br.*, IV.III.22) *vacanādiṣyata evāsmābhih śrutairapyabhāvah prabodhe.* — *BSSB*, IV.I.3.

(b) *Tatkarmātikramaṇād-etasmin-kāle vedā apyavedāh sampadyante.* — *BrSB*, IV.III.

145. *Yathā dvaitināṁ bandhāvasthāyām eva śāstrādyartha-vattvam na muktāvastāhyām.* — *GSB*, XIII.2.

146. *Yadyapi svapna-daṅśanāvasthasya sarpa-daṁsanodaka-snānadi-kāryam-anṛtam, tathāpi tadavagatiḥ satyameva phalam, prati-buddhasyāpyabādhymānatvāt.* — *BSSB*, II.I.14.

147. *Saṅkā-viṣādi-nimittamādi-karaṇāryaopalbdheh.* — Ibid.

148. *Prasiddhaṁ cedaṁ loke 'nvaya-vyatireka-kuśalānām-īdṛśena svapna-darśanena sadhvavagamaḥ sucyata idrsenasadhvagama iti.* — Ibid.

149. *Tathakārādi-satyākṣara-pratipattir-dṛṣṭā rekhanṛtākṣara-pratipatteh.* — Ibid.

realized, nobody entertains the idea of unreality when dealing with the means of knowledge, objects of knowledge and the results;[150] rather, all creatures discard their nature i.e. oneness with *Brahman* and to accept through ignorance as "I and mine" as oneself and belonging to oneself.[151] Hence, all common human dealings or Vedic observances are logical prior to the realization of *ātman*.[152] But at the intuitive state — "where everything has become *ātman*, then what should one see through what"?[153] All the old ideas of multiplicity become uprooted[154] and nothing is desired.[155] Hence, the *śruti* becomes false in relation to absolute reality or *ātman/Brahman* for a realized person and it is not illogical.

Abbreviations

Au	: *Aaitareyopaniṣad*	*KUSB*	: *Kaṭhopaniṣadcchāṅkara-bhāṣyam*
AiA	: *Aaitareyāraṇyakam*	*KenU*	: *Kenopaniṣad*
BṛU	: *Bṛhadāraṇyakopaniṣad*	*KenUSB*	: *Kenopaniṣadcchāṅkara-bhāṣyam*
BṛUSB	: *Bṛhadāraṇyakopaniṣac-chāṅkarabhāṣyam*	*ManU*	: *Māṇdukyopaniṣad*
BSSB	: *Brahmasūtraśāṅkarabhāṣyam*	*NS*	: *Naiṣkarmyasiddhi*
ChU	: *Chāndogyopaniṣad*	*PPU*	: *Pañcapādikāvivaraṇam*
GSB	: *Gītā Śāṅkarabhāṣyam*	*SB*	: *Satapathabrāhmaṇam*
KU	: *Kaṭhopaniṣad*	*TU*	: *Taittirīyopaniṣad*

150. *Yāvaddhi na satyātmaikatva-pratipattis-tāvat-pramāṇa prameya-phala-lakṣaṇeṣu vikāreṣvanṛtatva-buddhir-na kasyacid-utpadyate.* — Ibid.

151. *Vikārāneva tvahaṁ mametyavidyayātmātmīyena bhāvena sarvo jantuḥ pratipadyate svābhāvikīṁ brahmātmatāṁ hitvā.* — Ibid.

152. *Tasmāt-prāg-brmātmatāpratibodhād-upapannah sarvo laukiko vaidikasca vyavahārah.* — Ibid.

153. *Yatra tvasya sarvam -ātmaivābhūt-tat-kena kaṁ paśyet.* — *Br*, IV.5.15.

154. *Tasmād-antyena-pramāṇena pratipādita ātmaikatvae samastasya prācīnasya bheda-vyavahārasya bādhitatāt.* — *BSSB*, II.I.14.

155. *Apicāntyam-idaṁ pramāṇam-ātmaikatvasya pratipādakaṁ nātaḥ paraṁ kiñcid-ākaṅkṣyam-asti.* — Ibid.

The Contributors

Dr. Dayanand Bhargava (born 1937), did M.A. and Ph.D. from Delhi University, where he served as Lecturer and Reader from 1958 to 1979, when he joined Jodhpur University as Professor & Head of the Department of Sanskrit. Has eighteen research books to his credit. Five more are under publication. At present engaged in a UGC project on Veda-Vijñāna. Awarded certificate of honour by President of India for scholarship in Sanskrit. Holding eight different honorary academic posts. Honoured with prizes by many institutions all over India. Has also served as Principal and Dean, Faculty of Arts, education and social sciences. Has visited America and European countries several times. [**Address**: G - 1, Paradise Appartment, D - 148 Durga Marg, Bani Park, Jaipur - 302 011 (Rajasthan)]

Prof. S.R. Bhatt, an eminent philosopher and thinker of India, was President of Indian Philosophical Congress and retired as Professor and Chair, Department of Philosophy, University of Delhi. He has been a member/chairman of several Governmental and Non-Governmental academic committees, and lectured at many universities in India and abroad. Prof. Bhatt has authored and edited 16 books and has more than 100 research papers to his credit. He has organized above 50 national and international seminars, workshops and conferences. [**Address**: MP-23, Maurya Enclave, Pitampura, New Delhi - 110 034, E-mail : <srb_indiaphil@yahoo.co.in>]

Prof. B.B. Chaubey, born 1940, in a village in Uttar Pradesh, rose to great heights through his own efforts, having a master and Ph.D.

from Banares Hindu University and Sahitya Ratna degree from Prayag. Professor Chaubey served as Professor-Director and Visiting Professor at various institutions, and is the recipient of several awards and honours. He has authored many books and research papers on Vedic literature and culture. [**Address**: Chaturveda Niketan, Jodhamal Road, Hoshiarpur - 146 001 (Punjab)]

Dr Satya Dev Choudhary, born 1921, *in Jatoi* (now in Pakistan) received Shastri Degree from Panjab University, Lahore (1939),3 Double MA (Sanskrit and Hindi) and Ph.D (Hindi) from University of Delhi. He taught Hindi at Delhi University for 35 years and Hindi and Sanskrit for a year in University of Tübingen (Germany). His special interest is in Indian Poetics, Philology, Vedas, Medieval Hindi and Urdu Literature. Dr Choudhary has about 25 books to his credit, and has been honoured with several prizes and awards. [**Address**: F - 11/12, Model Town, Delhi -110 009]

Prof. Usha Choudhuri is former Professor, Deptt. of Sanskrit, University of Delhi. First-class-first (gold medalist) M.A. (Sanskrit) and Ph.D. from Delhi University and Vedavācaspati from Gurukul Kangari University. Has taught in Sofia University, Bulgaria and University of Bucharest, Romania and delivered lectures at many Indian and foreign Universities and institutions. Published books and papers on mythology, religion, Vedic poetry and aesthetics. Awarded the 'Sanskrit-sāhitya-sevā-sammāna' by the Delhi Sanskrit Academy and 'Vedāṅga' Award by Maharshi Sandipani Rashtriya Veda Vidya Pratishthana, Ujjain. [**Address**: 183, Tagore Park, Delhi-110009; E-mail : indraushac1@rediffmail.com]

Dr. (Mrs.) Sindhu S. Dange, a Sanskrit scholar, and former Head of the Department of Sanskrit, University of Mumbai, has authored 15 books and has presented 129 research papers, mainly in the fields of Vedic Literature and Vedic Rituals, Dharmaśāstra and Purāṇas. A recipient of several prestigious awards, Dr. Dange was given the certificate of honour by the President of India (2005). [**Address**: 603, Manisha Tower (Above MTNL Office), Navghar Cross Road, Tata Colony, Mulund East, Mumbai - 400 081]

DR. UMESH CHANDRA DASH, after obtaining first division in Acharya examination got Vidyāvāridhi (Ph.D) and Vidyāvācaspati (D. Litt.) degrees in Śrautayajñas, all his publications deal with Brāhmaṇa literature, particularly Darśpaurṇamāsayāga. Presently he is a Professor at the Government Maharaj Acharya Sanskrit College, Jaipur, and teaches Yajurveda. [**Address**: C/o Prof. Dayanand Bhargava, G - 1, Paradise Apartment, D - 148 Durga Marg, Bani Park, Jaipur - 302 011 (Rajasthan)]

DR. RAM NATH JHA was born at Sakhwar, Darbhanga, Bihar in 1966. He received his early education at his native place and subsequent, i.e. B.A. IIIrd year (Bridge course) and M.A. in Sanskrit from Hansraj College, Delhi. After getting selected for JRF and SRF by UGC, he completed his M.Phil. and Ph.D. on Śaṅkara's Epistemology under the supervision of Prof. Baldev Raj Sharma from Sanskrit Department, Delhi University. Currently he is teaching in Special Centre for Sanskrit Studies as Assistant Professor and working on a UGC Major Research Project to prepare **A Reader in Indian Philosophy**. He has also been associated with different Sanskrit projects of NCERT. [**address**: Special Centre for Sanskrit Studies, Jawaharlal Nehru University, New Delhi - 110 067, **E-mail**: <rnj12@hotmail.com>]

KAPIL KAPOOR is Professor of English, Centre for Linguistics and English, and Concurrent Professor, Centre for Sanskrit Studies, Jawaharlal Nehru University, New Delhi. He was Dean of the School of Language, Literature and Culture Studies, JNU, from 1996-1999 and Rector of the University from 1999-2002. His teaching and research interests include literary and linguistic theories — both Indian and Western, philosophy of language, nineteenth century

out, BSK I Stage, Bangalore - 560 050, E-mail: <dprahladachar@yahoo.co.in>]

Prof. P. Shashi Rekha, born in a teacher's family, joined the Osmania University, first to study in and then to serve the same institution, rising to the positon of Head of the Department of Sanskrit. A holder of double masters and Ph.D. in Sanskrit, Shashi Rekha has written six books in English and Telugu, and has contributed educative articles to some sixty Indian and international publications. She has also brought out guide books for M.Phil. and Ph.D. scholars. She is also the recipient of the international award "Ramakrishna Sanskrit 2000" from Canada for her contribution to Sanskrit literature and research. [**Address**: 'Sudharma,' Flat - 106, Indra Estates, Lane Beside Soumya Nursing Home, Street 18, Ramnagar, Hyderabad - 500 048, E-mail: <ps_rekha@yahoo.com>]

Dr. Abhaya Dev Sharma, Ph.D. in Sanskrit, born 1933, is the son of Late Swami Vidyanand "Videh," the founder-president of Ved-Sansthan, a premier institution for propagation of Sanskrit and Vedic Culture and Way of Living. Dr. Sharma, the current President of Ved-Sansthan, is well-known as a scholar and writer in the cultural world. He has been the editor of the monthly journal "Ved Savita" for fifty years, and alongwith his father, has written more than 100 literary works on Indian traditions and culture. [**Address**: Veda Sansthan, C-22, Rajouri Garden, New Delhi - 110 027, E-mail: vedic_science@yahoo.co.in]

Dr. Ram Karan Sharma, is a holder of M.A. degrees in Sanskrit and Hindi from Patna university, and a Ph.D. from University of California, USA. He is a Fulbright Scholar and had held important positions in several institutions engaged in promotion of Sanskrit studies in India and abroad. Dr. Sharma has authored twenty-five volumes, including a dozen books of Sanskrit poems and two Sanskrit novels and more than a hundred research articles. He is the recipient of many prestigious awards. [**Address**: 63, Vigyan Vihar, Delhi]

PROF. RAMESH CHANDRA DASH SHARMA, holder of Vedacharya and Ph.D. degrees from Sampurnananda University, Varanasi, is a Sanskrit scholar of repute. He heads the Department of Veda at Lal Bahadur Shastri Rashtriya Sanskrit Vidyapeeth (a Deemed University) in Delhi. He is the recipient of several awards, and has published five well-known books in Sanskrit, and has written some 28 articles for various publications. [**Address**: Acharya Niwas, 266, P-2B, Ward no. 2, Mahrauli, New Delhi - 110 030]

DR. ROOP KISHOR SHASTRI, born 1957, is the Head of the Department of Veda at the Gurukul Kāngri University in Haridwar. A teacher of 16 years experience, Dr. Shastri specializes in Veda, Vedic Literature, Linguistics and Nirukta. He has published fifteen books, mostly in Hindi, and has to his credit several research papers and articles. Dr. Shastri has participated in many conferences and seminars in India and abroad. He is the recipient of numerous awards including "Sahitya Mahopādhyāya," "Vyas Puraskar," "Sāyan Puraskar" from Indian institutions and the "Director General Award" from Government of Indonesia. [**Address**: Gurukul Kangri University, Haridwar - 249 401 (Uttaranchal)]

WAGISH SHUKLA teaches mathematics at the Indian Institute of Technology, Delhi. He has a Ph.D. in mathematics from IIT Kanpur and has been a Visiting Fellow at the School of Mathematics at the Tata Institute of Fundamental Research, Mumbai and the Laboratoire d'informateur, Ecole Normale Superieure, Paris. His interests are pure mathematics and theoretical computer science.

He is a student of Sanskrit and Persian Literature and has published articles on literary theory and culture studies in English and Hindi. [**address**: House No. 4, Street No. M-1, IIT Campus, Hauz Khas, New Delhi - 110 016, **E-mail**: <wagishs@yahoo.com>]

Dr. Karan Singh was born heir-apparent to the Maharaja of Jammu and Kashmir. In 1949, at the age of eighteen, he was appointed Regent and was Head of State thereafter for eighteen years as Regent, elected Sardar-e-Riyāsat and as Governor. In 1967, he was inducted into the Union Cabinet by Mrs. Indira Gandhi. He held important Cabinet portfolios of Tourism & Civil Aviation, Health & Family Planning and Education & Culture. His appointment as India's Ambassador to the United States was warmly welcomed by both countries. He was awarded a Ph.D. by the University of Delhi for his thesis on the Political Thought of Sri Aurobindo. He has been Chancellor of Jammu & Kashmir University and Benaras Hindu University, Chancellor of Jawaharlal Nehru University, and President of the Indian Council for Cultural Relations, having rank equal to Central Cabinet Minister. Karan Singh has written many books and has lectured on political science, philosophy, education, religion and culture, in India and abroad. He is recognized as one of India's outstanding thinkers and leaders.

Satya Prakash Singh, has been Professor and Chairman of the Department of Sanskrit and Dean, faculty of Arts, Aligarh Muslim University as also Director of the Centre of Vedic Research, New Delhi. His publications include *Sri Aurobindo and Whitehead on the Nature of God; Sri Aurobindo; Jung and Vedic Yoga; Upaniṣadic Symbolism; Vedic Symbolism; Life and Vision of the Vedic Seer vol. I. Viśvāmitra, vol. II Dīrghatamas;* and *Vedic Vision of Consciousness and Reality*. [**Address**: N - 594, Sector - 25, Noida (UP)]

Prof. Dipti S. Tripathi is Professor & Head of the Department of Sanskrit, University of Delhi. She has contributed extensively in the field of grammar, linguistics, and poetics. She has four books and more than two dozen papers to her credit. A widely travelled scholar, she has visited the U.K., U.S.A., Germany, Australia and New Zealand for academic work and lecture tour.

Prof. Vachaspati Upadhyaya, born on 1st July 1943 at Sultanpur (U.P.), is presently Vice-Chancellor, Sri Lal Bahadur Shastri Rashtriya Sanskrit Vidyapeeth (Deemed University), New Delhi. Prof. Upadhyaya earlier worked as Head of the Sanskrit Department, University of Delhi. He has held many academic as well as administrative positions including President, Association of Indian Universities, New Delhi; Member Secretary, M.S. Rashtriya Vedavidya Pratishthan, Ujjain; Director, Rashtriya Sanskrit Sansthan, New Delhi; Pro Vice-Chancellor, Gurukul Kangri Vishwavidyalaya, Haridwar; and Registrar and Controller of Examinations, Sampurnanand Sanskrit University, Varanasi.

Recipient of President's Certificate of Honour and several other prestigious titles and awards, Professor Upadhyaya is a member of various academic bodies across the country. He has authored four books and presented more than twenty-five papers in national and international seminars besides lecturing extensively in India and abroad. He has supervised research work of about sixty Ph.D and seventy M.Phil students. His specialization is in Indian Philosophy, Veda, Dharmaśastra and Sāhitya. (E.mail: vu_vidyapeetha@hotmail.com)

Index